Fruits Basket™

Volume 16

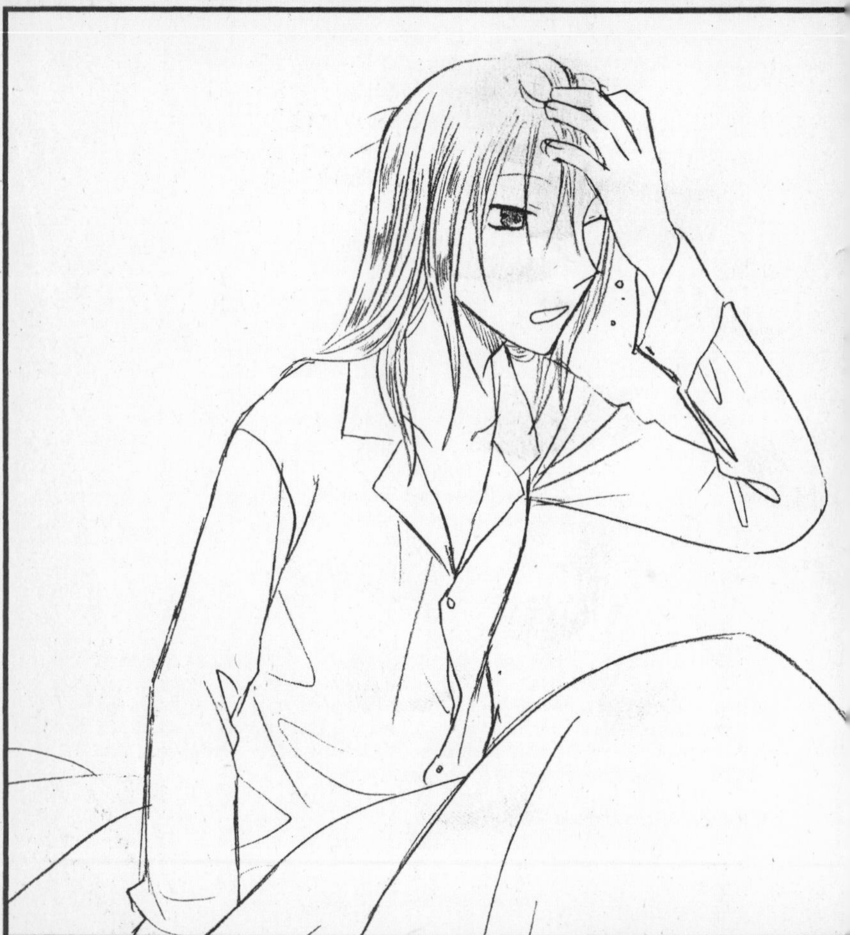

Natsuki Takaya

Fruits Basket Volume 16
Created by Natsuki Takaya

Translation - Alethea Nibley and Athena Nibley
English Adaptation - Lianne Sentar
Copy Editor - Stephanie Duchin
Retouch and Lettering - Star Print Brokers
Cover Design - Christian Lowds

Editor - Paul Morrissey
Digital Imaging Manager - Chris Buford
Pre-Production Supervisor - Erika Terriquez
Art Director - Anne Marie Horne
Production Manager - Elisabeth Brizzi
Managing Editor - Vy Nguyen
VP of Production - Ron Klamert
Editor-in-Chief - Rob Tokar
Publisher - Mike Kiley
President and C.O.O. - John Parker
C.E.O. and Chief Creative Officer - Stuart Levy

A 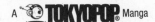 Manga

TOKYOPOP and 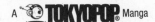 are trademarks or registered trademarks of TOKYOPOP Inc.

TOKYOPOP Inc.
5900 Wilshire Blvd. Suite 2000
Los Angeles, CA 90036

E-mail: info@TOKYOPOP.com
Come visit us online at www.TOKYOPOP.com

FRUITS BASKET Vol. 16 by Natsuki Takaya
© 2004 Natsuki Takaya All rights reserved.
First published in Japan in 2005 by HAKUSENSHA, INC.,
Tokyo. English language translation rights in the United
States of America, Canada and the United Kingdom arranged
with HAKUSENSHA, INC., Tokyo through Tuttle-Mori Agency
Inc., Tokyo.
English text copyright © 2007 TOKYOPOP Inc.

All rights reserved. No portion of this book may be
reproduced or transmitted in any form or by any means
without written permission from the copyright holders.
This manga is a work of fiction. Any resemblance to
actual events or locales or persons, living or dead, is
entirely coincidental.

ISBN: 978-1-59816-024-6

First TOKYOPOP printing: April 2007
10 9 8 7 6 5 4 3 2 1
Printed in the USA

Fruits Basket

Volume 16

By
Natsuki Takaya

Jefferson Twp. Public Library
1031 Weldon Road
Oak Ridge, NJ 07438
(973) 208-6115

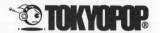

HAMBURG // LONDON // LOS ANGELES // TOKYO

Fruits Basket

Table of Contents

STORY SO FAR...

Hello, I'm Tohru Honda and I have come to know a terrible secret. After the death of my mother, I was living by myself in a tent, when the Sohma family took me in. I soon learned that the Sohma family lives with a curse! Each family member is possessed by the vengeful spirit of an animal from the Chinese Zodiac. Whenever one of them becomes weak or is hugged by a member of the opposite sex, they change into their Zodiac animal!

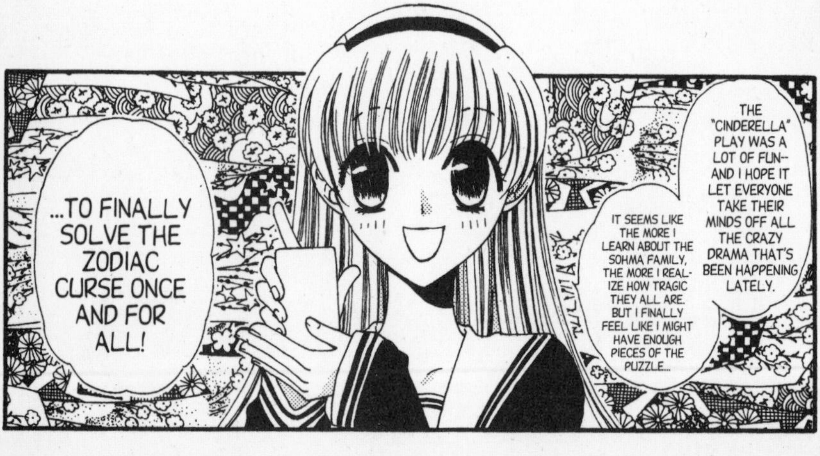
THE "CINDERELLA" PLAY WAS A LOT OF FUN--AND I HOPE IT LET EVERYONE TAKE THEIR MINDS OFF ALL THE CRAZY DRAMA THAT'S BEEN HAPPENING LATELY.
IT SEEMS LIKE THE MORE I LEARN ABOUT THE SOHMA FAMILY, THE MORE I REAL-IZE HOW TRAGIC THEY ALL ARE. BUT I FINALLY FEEL LIKE I MIGHT HAVE ENOUGH PIECES OF THE PUZZLE...
...TO FINALLY SOLVE THE ZODIAC CURSE ONCE AND FOR ALL!

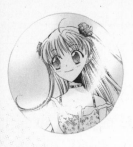

Tohru Honda

The ever-optimistic hero of our story. An orphan, she now lives in Shigure's house, along with Yuki and Kyo, and is the only person outside of the family who knows the Sohma family's curse.

Yuki Sohma, the Rat

Soft-spoken. Self-esteem issues. At school he's called "Prince Yuki."

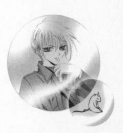

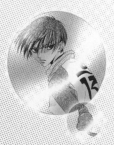

Kyo Sohma, the Cat

The Cat who was left out of the Zodiac. Hates Yuki, leeks and miso. But mostly Yuki.

Kagura Sohma, the Boar

Bashful, yet headstrong. Determined to marry Kyo, even if it kills him.

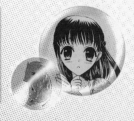

Fruits Basket Characters

Mabudachi Trio

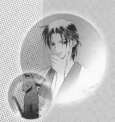

Shigure Sohma, the Dog

Enigmatic, mischievous and a little perverted. A popular novelist.

Hatori Sohma, the Dragon

Family doctor to the Sohmas. Only thing he can't cure is his broken heart.

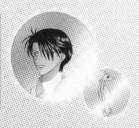

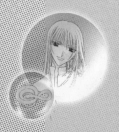

Ayame Sohma, the Snake

Yuki's older brother. A proud and playful drama queen…er, king. Runs a costume shop.

Saki Hanajima

"Hana-chan." Can sense people's "waves." Goth demeanor scares her classmates.

Arisa Uotani

"Uo-chan." A tough-talking "Yankee" who looks out for her friends.

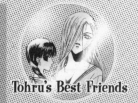

Tohru's Best Friends

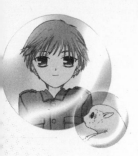

Hiro Sohma, the Ram (or sheep)

This caustic tyke is skilled at throwing verbal barbs, but he has a soft spot for Kisa.

Momiji Sohma, the Rabbit

Half-German. He's older than he looks. His mother rejected him because of the Sohma curse. His little sister, Momo, has been kept from him most of her life.

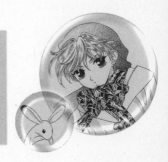

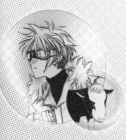

Hatsuharu Sohma, the Ox

The nicest of guys, except when he goes "Black." Then you'd better watch out. He was once in a relationship with Rin.

Kisa Sohma, the Tiger

Kisa became shy and self-conscious due to constant teasing by her classmates. Yuki, who has similar insecurities, feels particularly close to Kisa.

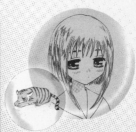

Fruits Basket Characters

Isuzu "Rin" Sohma, the Horse

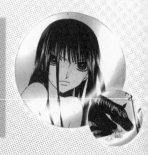

She was once in a relationship with Hatsuharu (Haru)...and Tohru leaves her rather cold. Rin is full of pride, and she can't stand the amount of deference the other Sohma family members give Akito.

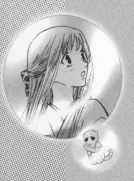

Ritsu Sohma, the Monkey

This shy kimono-wearing member of the Sohma family is gorgeous. But this "she" is really a he!! Crossdressing calms his nerves.

Akito Sohma

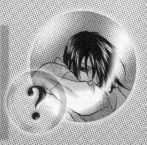

The head of the Sohma clan. A dark figure of many secrets. Treated with fear and reverence.

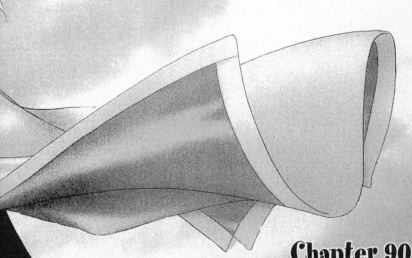

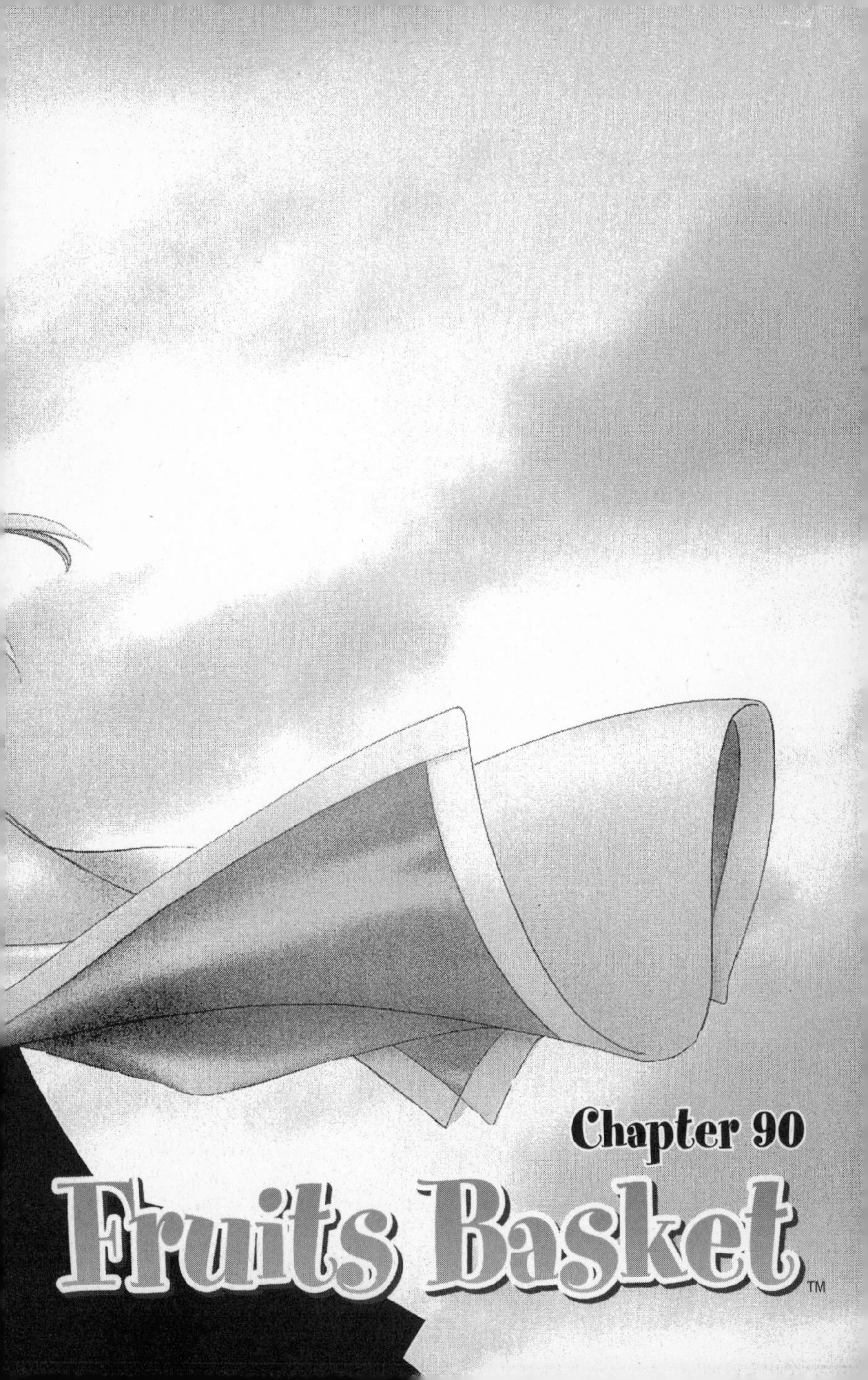

Chapter 90

Fruits Basket™

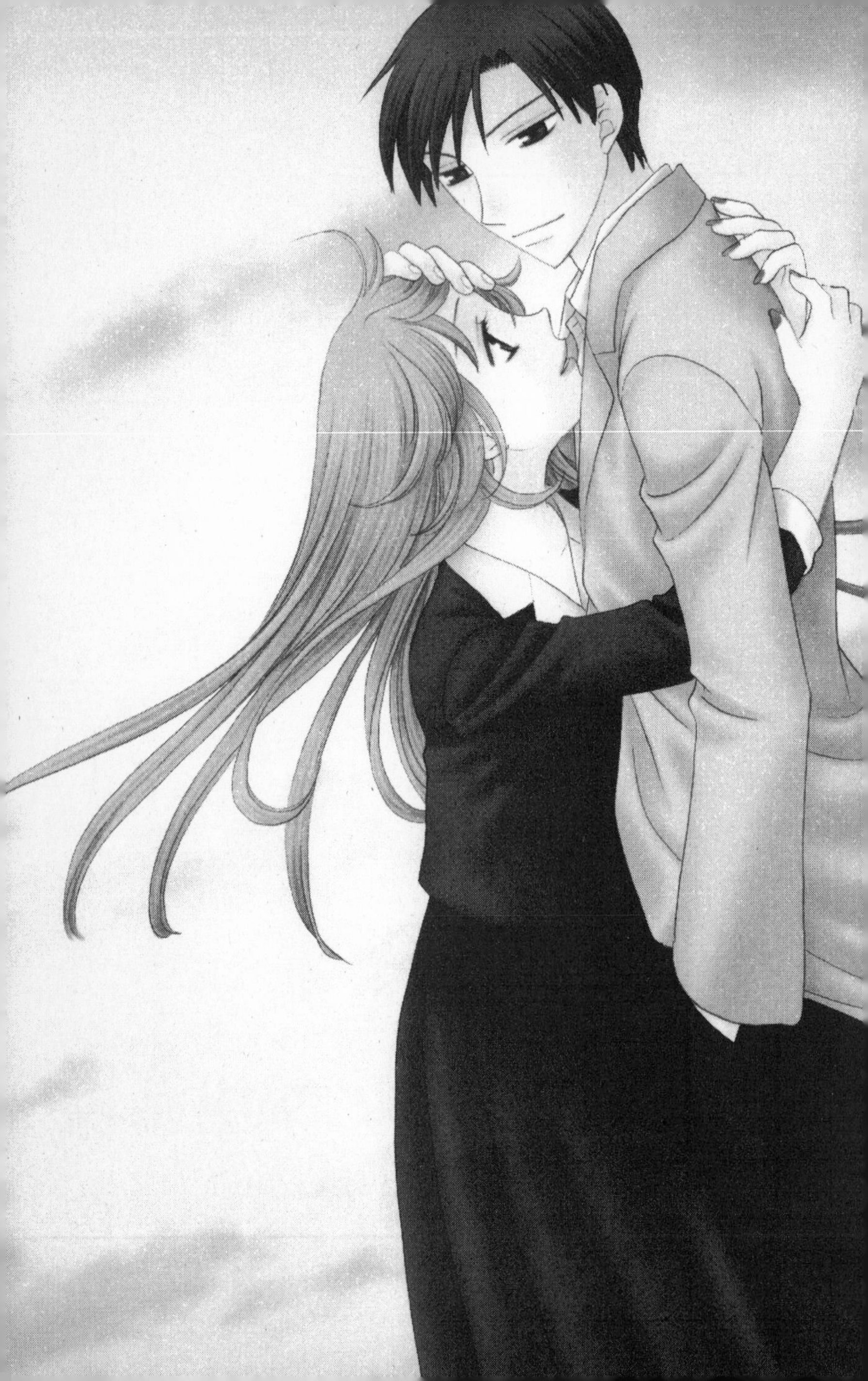

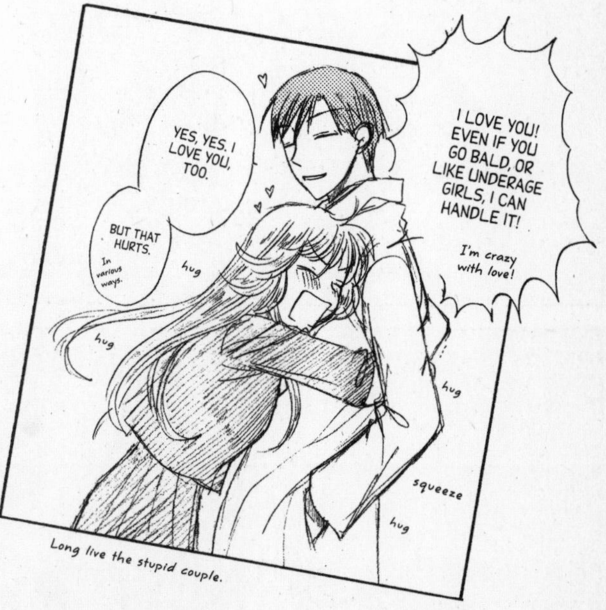
I LOVE YOU! EVEN IF YOU GO BALD, OR LIKE UNDERAGE GIRLS, I CAN HANDLE IT!
I'm crazy with love!
YES, YES. I LOVE YOU, TOO.
BUT THAT HURTS.
In various ways.
hug
hug
hug
squeeze
hug

Long live the stupid couple.

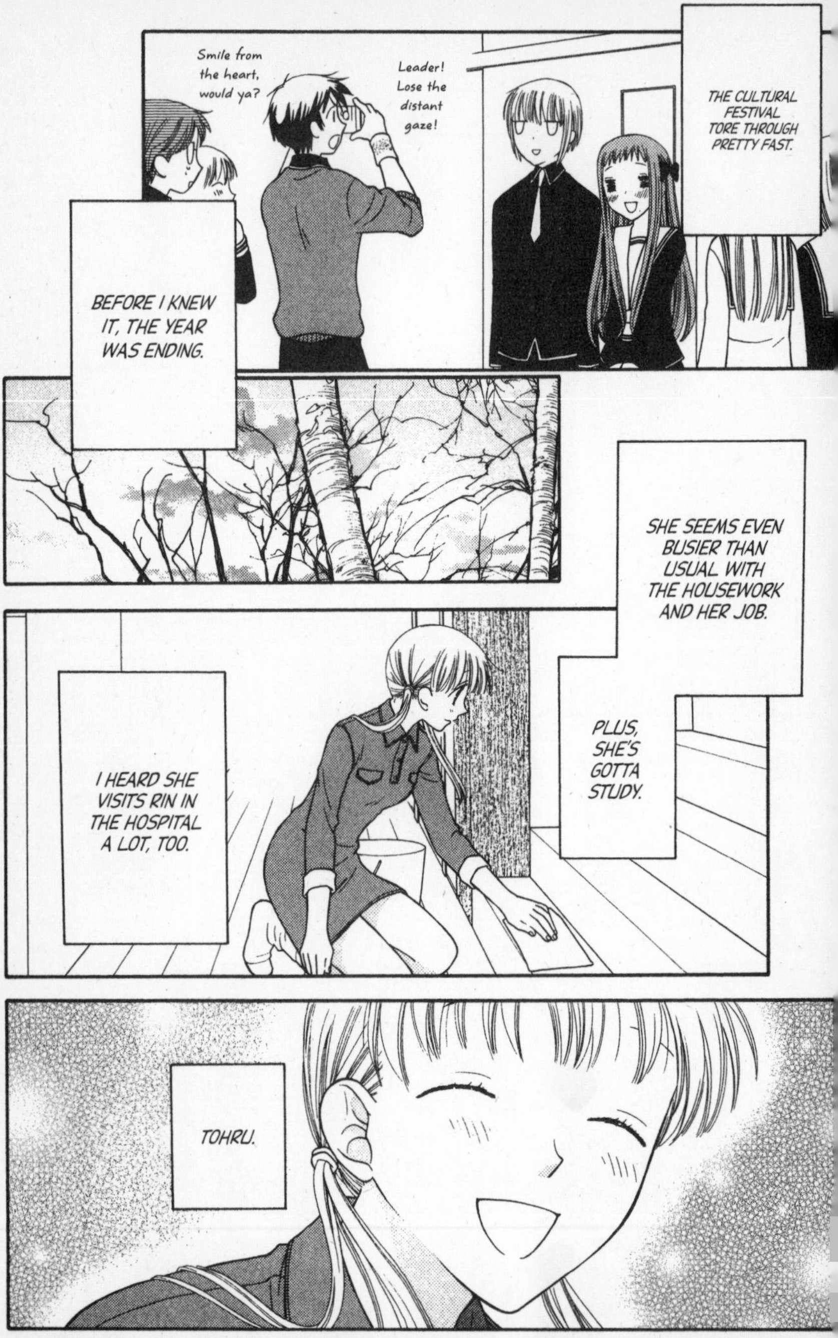
THE CULTURAL FESTIVAL TORE THROUGH PRETTY FAST.
Leader! Lose the distant gaze!
Smile from the heart, would ya?
BEFORE I KNEW IT, THE YEAR WAS ENDING.
SHE SEEMS EVEN BUSIER THAN USUAL WITH THE HOUSEWORK AND HER JOB.
PLUS, SHE'S GOTTA STUDY.
I HEARD SHE VISITS RIN IN THE HOSPITAL A LOT, TOO.
TOHRU.

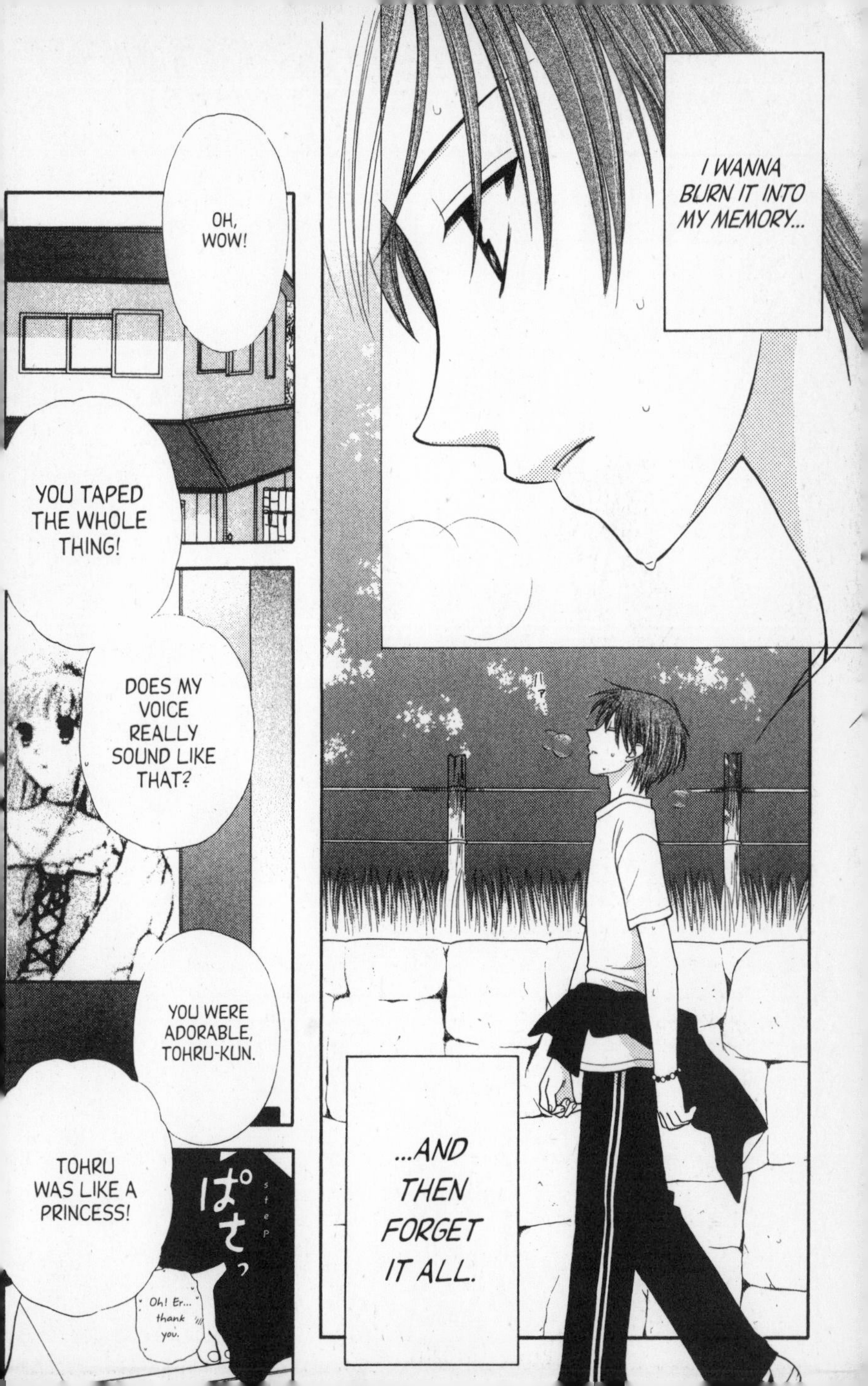

I WANNA BURN IT INTO MY MEMORY...
...AND THEN FORGET IT ALL.
OH, WOW!
YOU TAPED THE WHOLE THING!
DOES MY VOICE REALLY SOUND LIKE THAT?
YOU WERE ADORABLE, TOHRU-KUN.
TOHRU WAS LIKE A PRINCESS!
ぱさっ
step
Oh! Er... thank you.

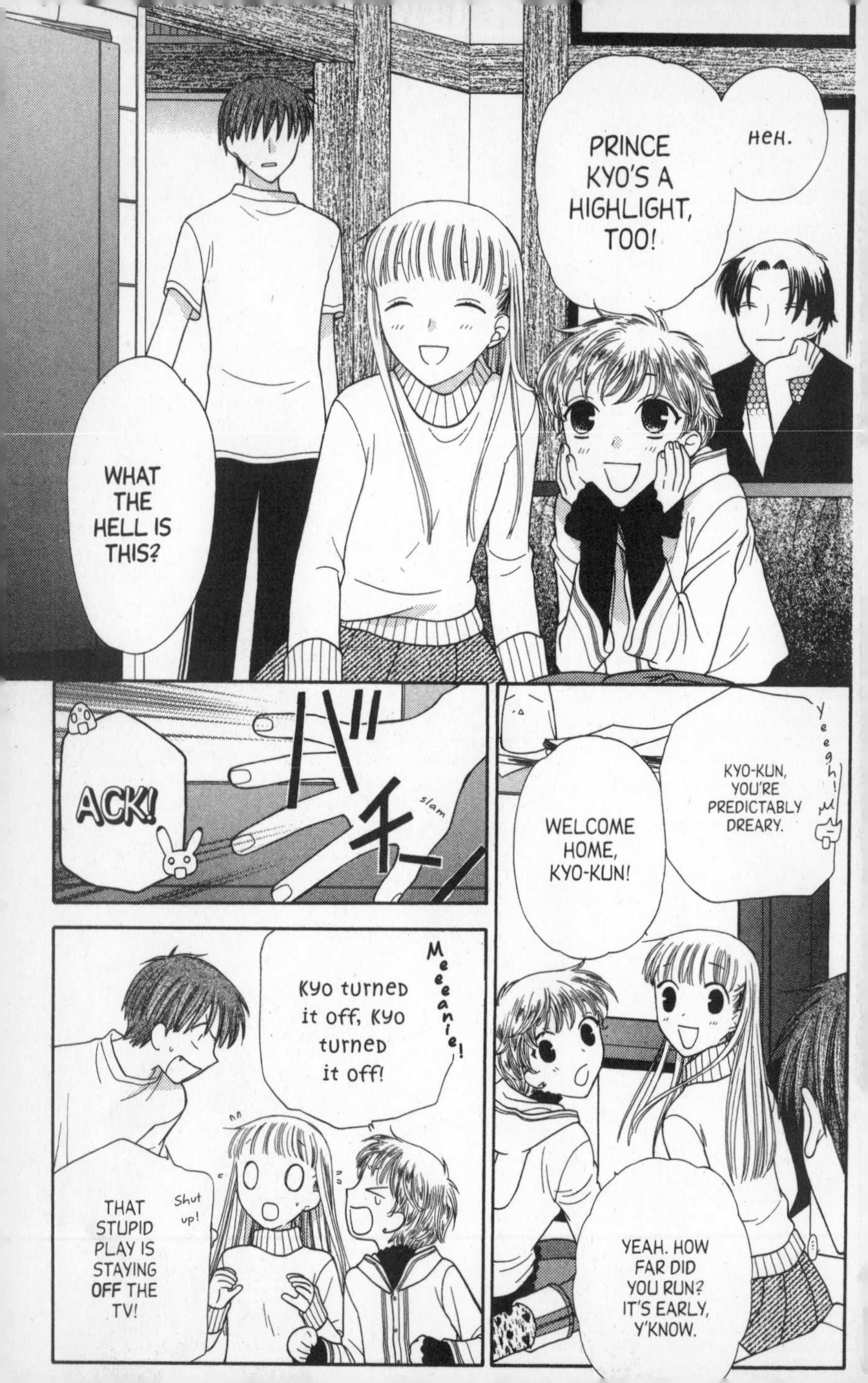
PRINCE KYO'S A HIGHLIGHT, TOO!
Heh.
WHAT THE HELL IS THIS?
KYO-KUN, YOU'RE PREDICTABLY DREARY.
Yeegh!
WELCOME HOME, KYO-KUN!
YEAH. HOW FAR DID YOU RUN? IT'S EARLY, Y'KNOW.
バチー
slam
ACK!
Meeeanie!
Kyo turned it off, Kyo turned it off!
Shut up!
THAT STUPID PLAY IS STAYING OFF THE TV!

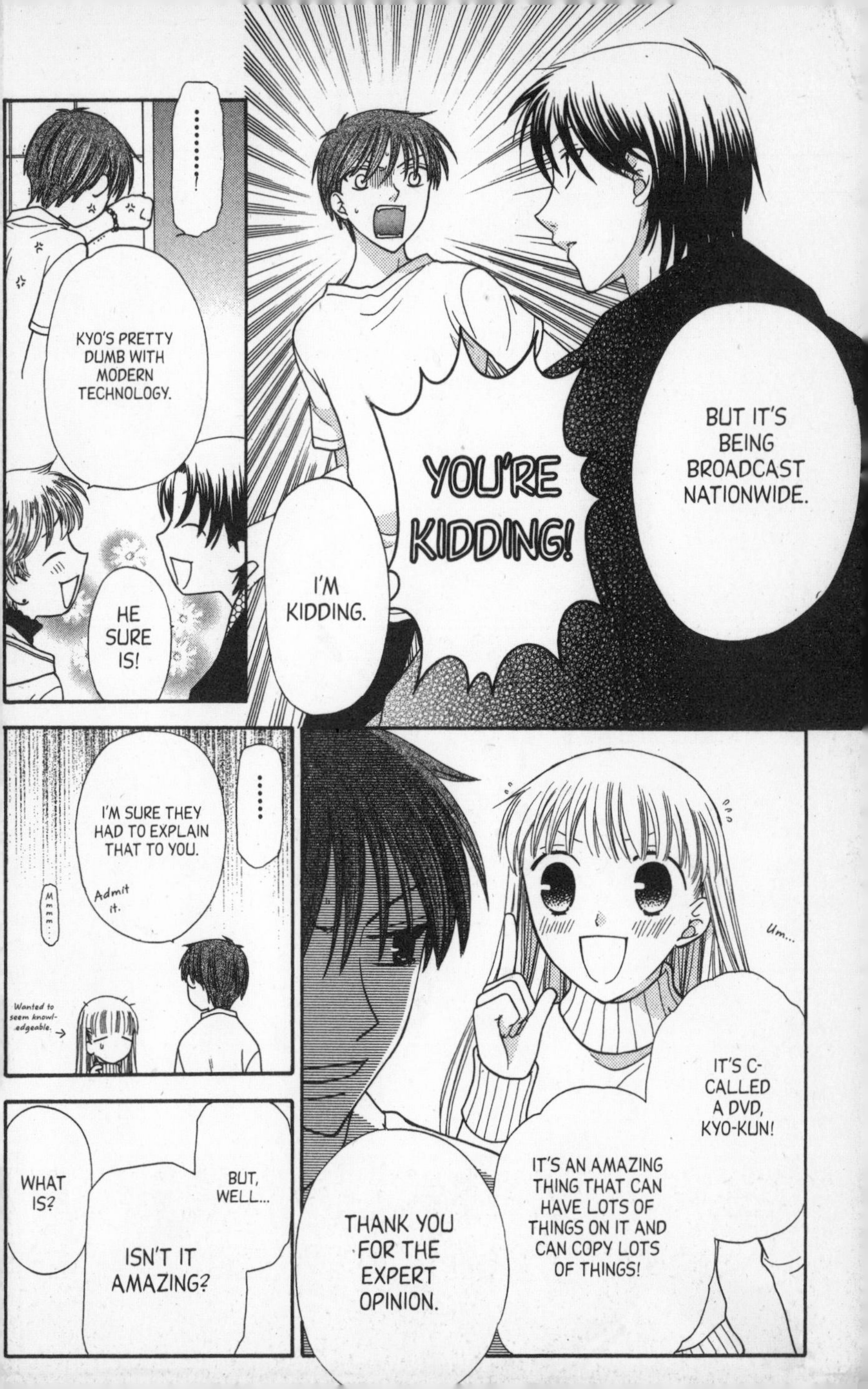
BUT IT'S BEING BROADCAST NATIONWIDE.
YOU'RE KIDDING!
I'M KIDDING.
......?
KYO'S PRETTY DUMB WITH MODERN TECHNOLOGY.
HE SURE IS!
Um...
IT'S C-CALLED A DVD, KYO-KUN!
IT'S AN AMAZING THING THAT CAN HAVE LOTS OF THINGS ON IT AND CAN COPY LOTS OF THINGS!
THANK YOU FOR THE EXPERT OPINION.
......
I'M SURE THEY HAD TO EXPLAIN THAT TO YOU.
Admit it.
Meeee...
Wanted to seem knowl-edgeable.
BUT, WELL...
WHAT IS?
ISN'T IT AMAZING?

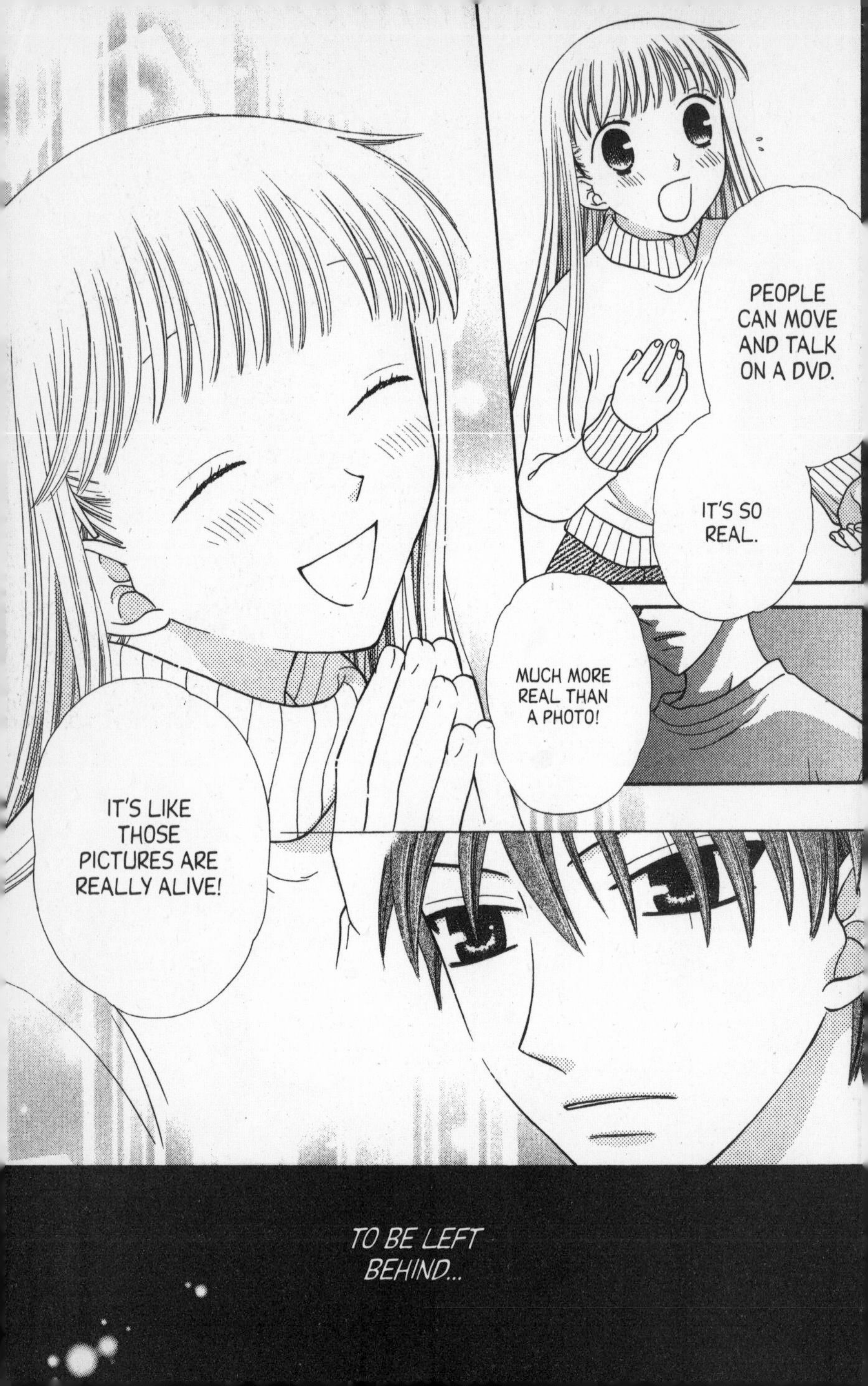
PEOPLE CAN MOVE AND TALK ON A DVD.
IT'S SO REAL.
MUCH MORE REAL THAN A PHOTO!
IT'S LIKE THOSE PICTURES ARE REALLY ALIVE!
TO BE LEFT BEHIND...

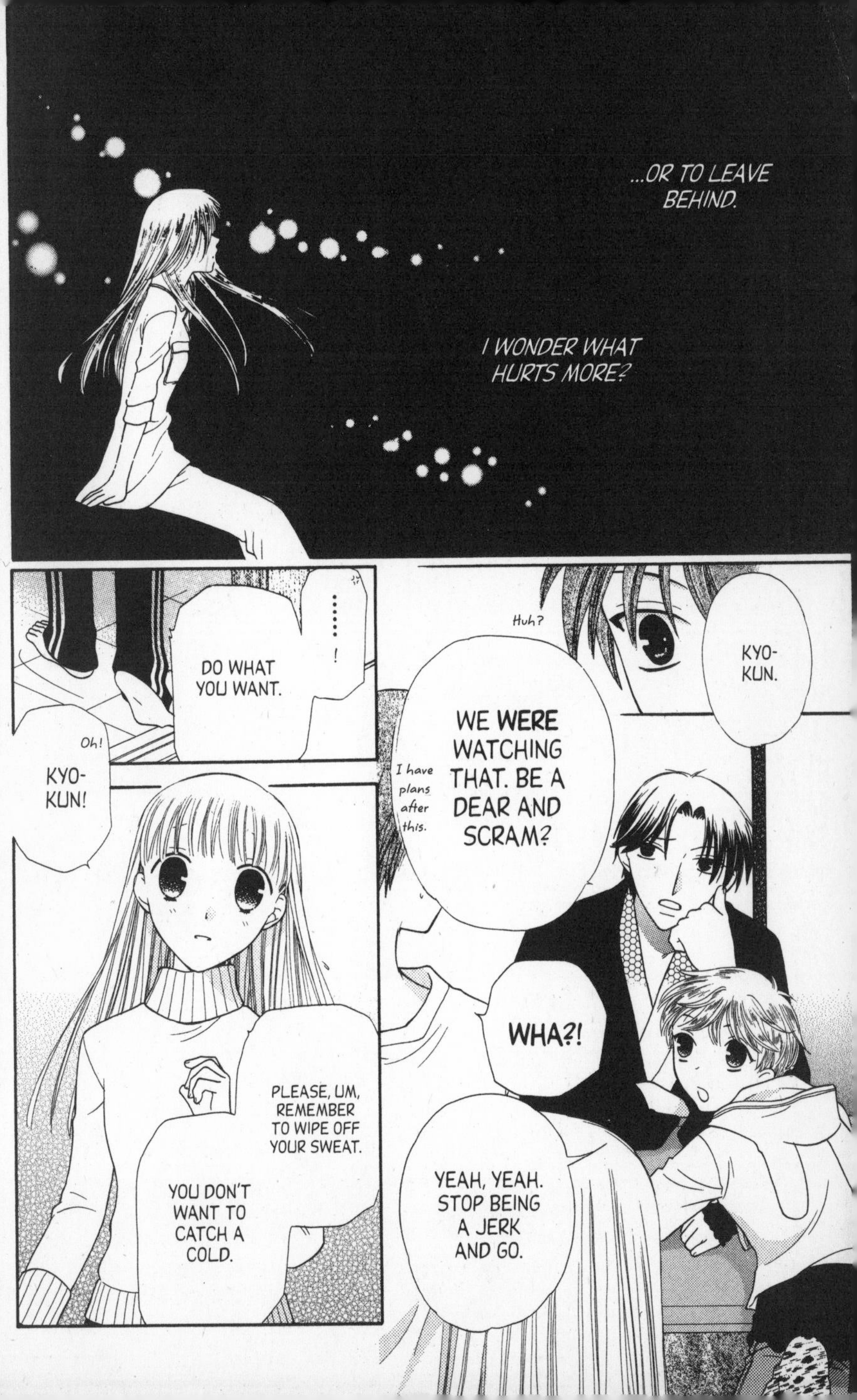
...OR TO LEAVE BEHIND.
I WONDER WHAT HURTS MORE?
Huh?
KYO-KUN.
WE WERE WATCHING THAT. BE A DEAR AND SCRAM?
I have plans after this.
WHA?!
YEAH, YEAH. STOP BEING A JERK AND GO.
......!
DO WHAT YOU WANT.
Oh!
KYO-KUN!
PLEASE, UM, REMEMBER TO WIPE OFF YOUR SWEAT.
YOU DON'T WANT TO CATCH A COLD.

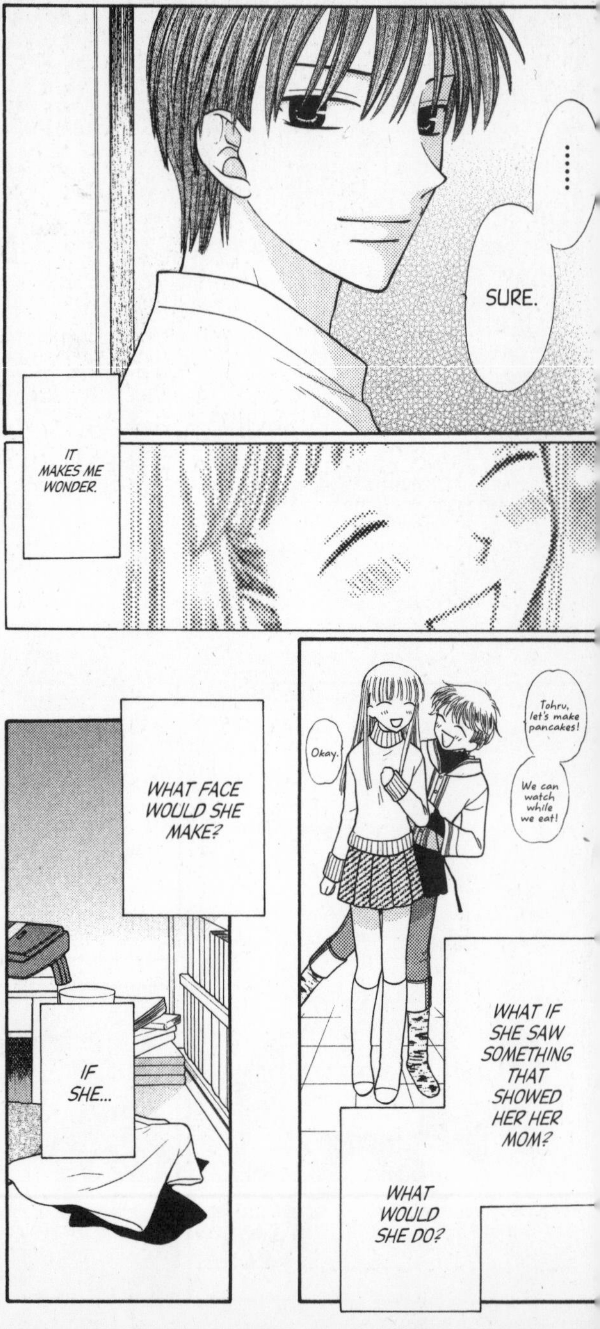
......
SURE.
IT MAKES ME WONDER.
Tohru, let's make pancakes!
We can watch while we eat!
Okay.
WHAT IF SHE SAW SOMETHING THAT SHOWED HER HER MOM?
WHAT WOULD SHE DO?
WHAT FACE WOULD SHE MAKE?
IF SHE...

Fruits Basket 16

Nice to meet you and hello! This is Takaya speaking. *Fruits Basket* is breaking into Volume 16 with Anego--"elder sister." That's Arisa!

Finally, I guess, the number of characters adorning the cover has broken through to 16. Which makes sense, since it's Volume 16.

There may be some people out there who are worried. "What will she do about characters after this?" they'll think. There may not be any. But don't worry--I've thought it through!

I may not worry about things that don't warrant worry, but I still think when I have to. (laughs)

...To be honest, I didn't have the confidence to assume that I would be allowed to draw this far. It looks like I'll be able to tell this story to its end, and for that I'm truly grateful. With that in mind, please enjoy Volume 16.

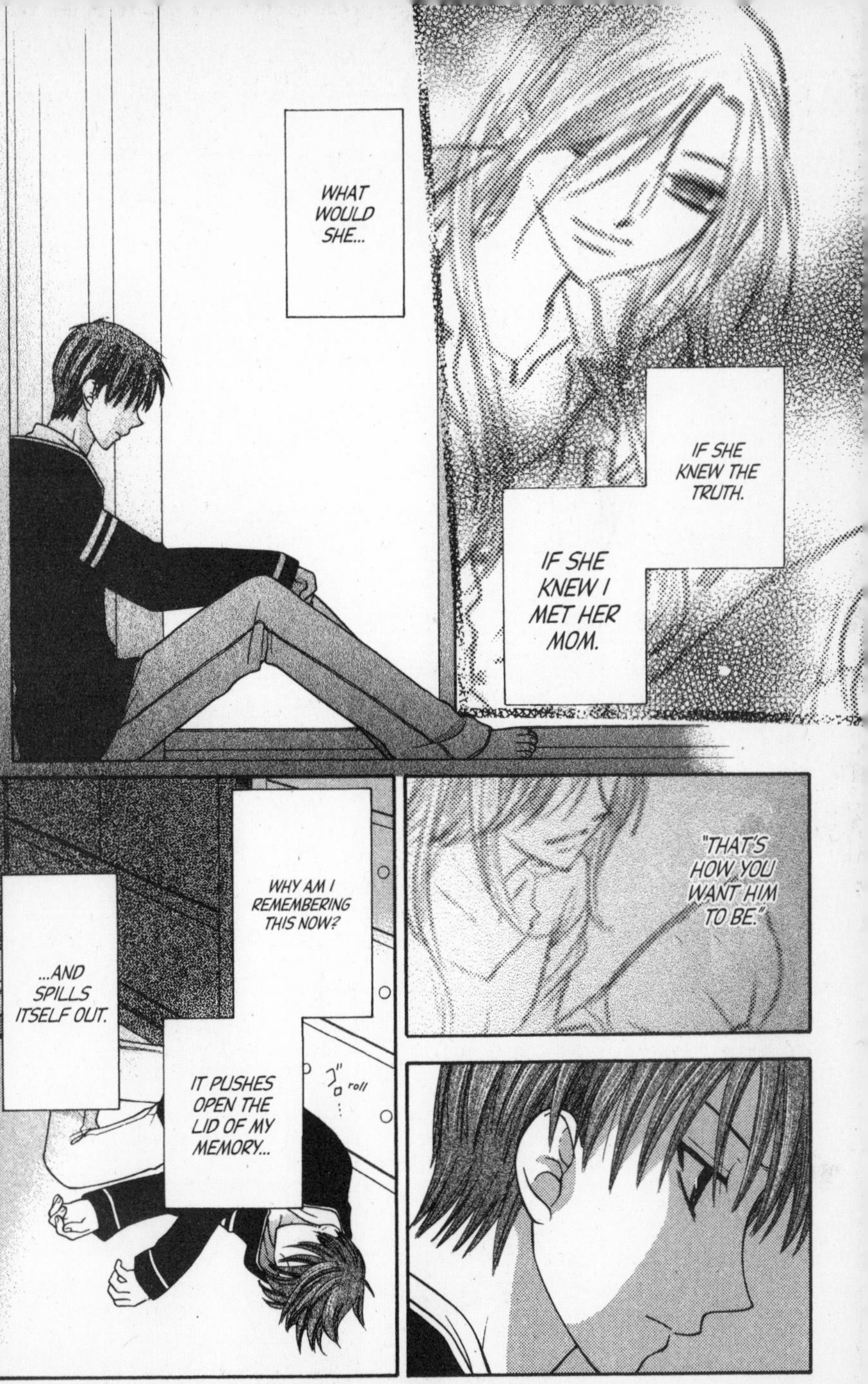

WHAT WOULD SHE...
IF SHE KNEW THE TRUTH.
IF SHE KNEW I MET HER MOM.
"THAT'S HOW YOU WANT HIM TO BE."
WHY AM I REMEMBERING THIS NOW?
IT PUSHES OPEN THE LID OF MY MEMORY...
...AND SPILLS ITSELF OUT.
roll

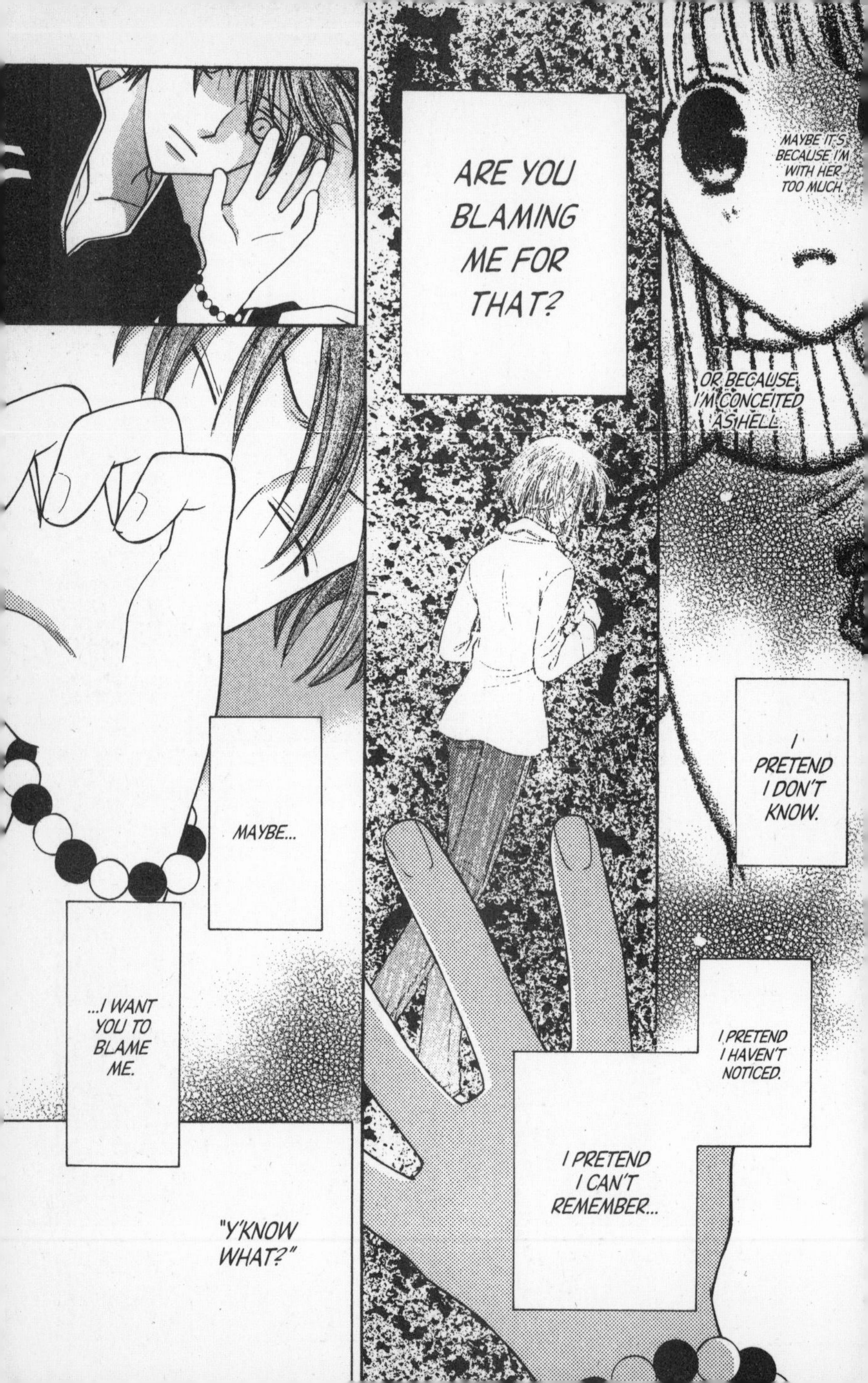
MAYBE IT'S BECAUSE I'M WITH HER TOO MUCH.
ARE YOU BLAMING ME FOR THAT?
OR BECAUSE I'M CONCEITED AS HELL.
I PRETEND I DON'T KNOW.
I PRETEND I HAVEN'T NOTICED.
I PRETEND I CAN'T REMEMBER...
MAYBE...
...I WANT YOU TO BLAME ME.
"Y'KNOW WHAT?"

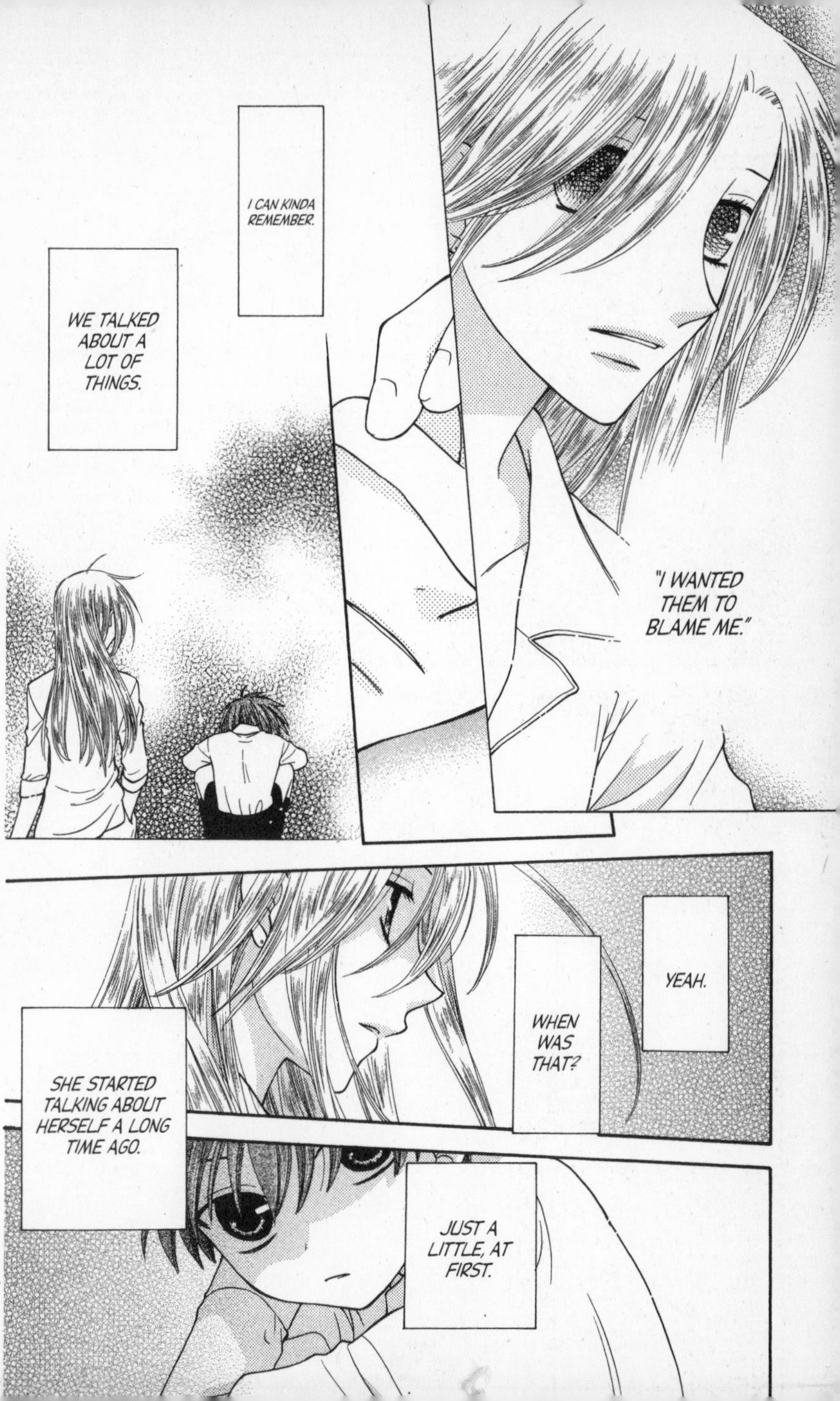
"I WANTED THEM TO BLAME ME."
I CAN KINDA REMEMBER.
WE TALKED ABOUT A LOT OF THINGS.
YEAH.
WHEN WAS THAT?
SHE STARTED TALKING ABOUT HERSELF A LONG TIME AGO.
JUST A LITTLE, AT FIRST.

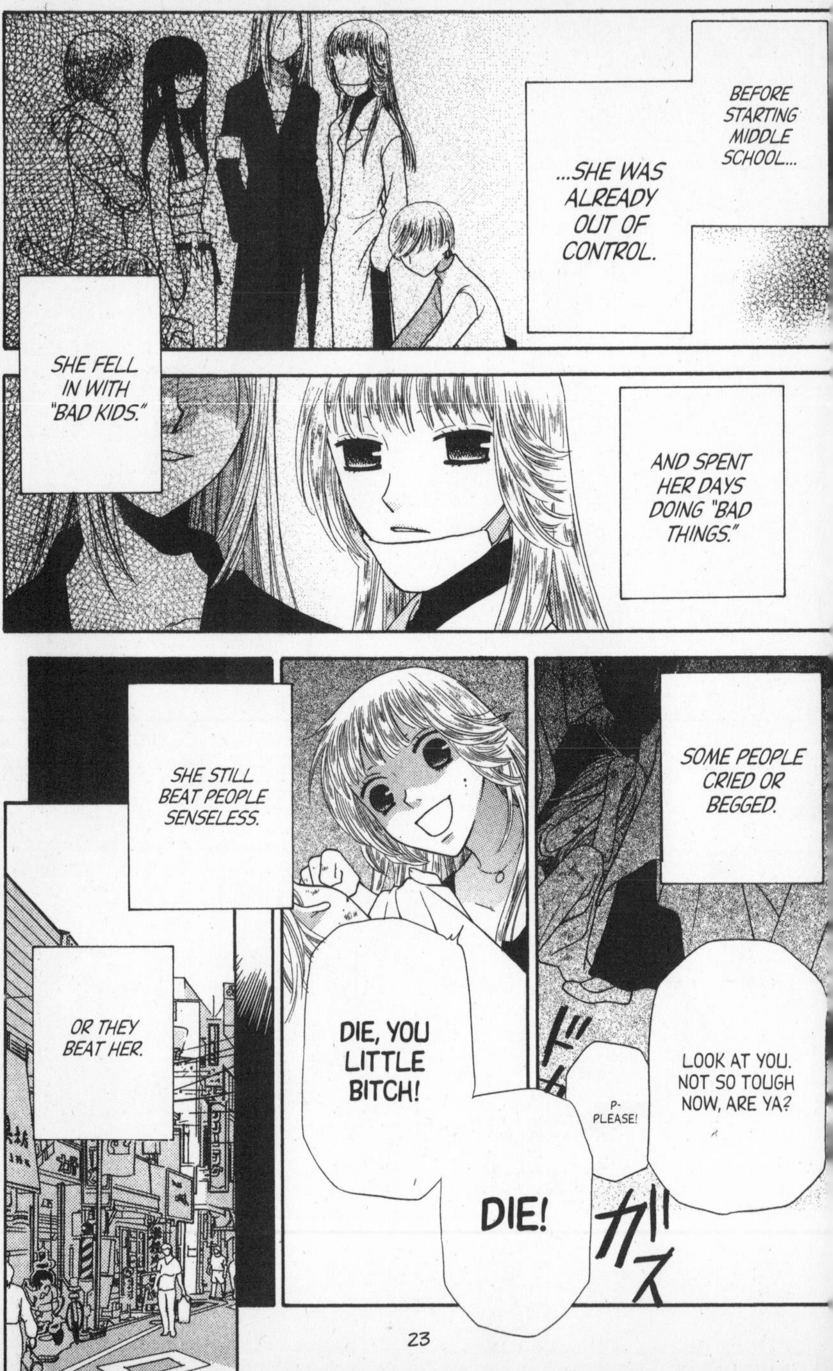
BEFORE STARTING MIDDLE SCHOOL...
...SHE WAS ALREADY OUT OF CONTROL.
SHE FELL IN WITH "BAD KIDS."
AND SPENT HER DAYS DOING "BAD THINGS."
SOME PEOPLE CRIED OR BEGGED.
LOOK AT YOU. NOT SO TOUGH NOW, ARE YA?
P- PLEASE!
ガス
SHE STILL BEAT PEOPLE SENSELESS.
DIE, YOU LITTLE BITCH!
DIE!
OR THEY BEAT HER.

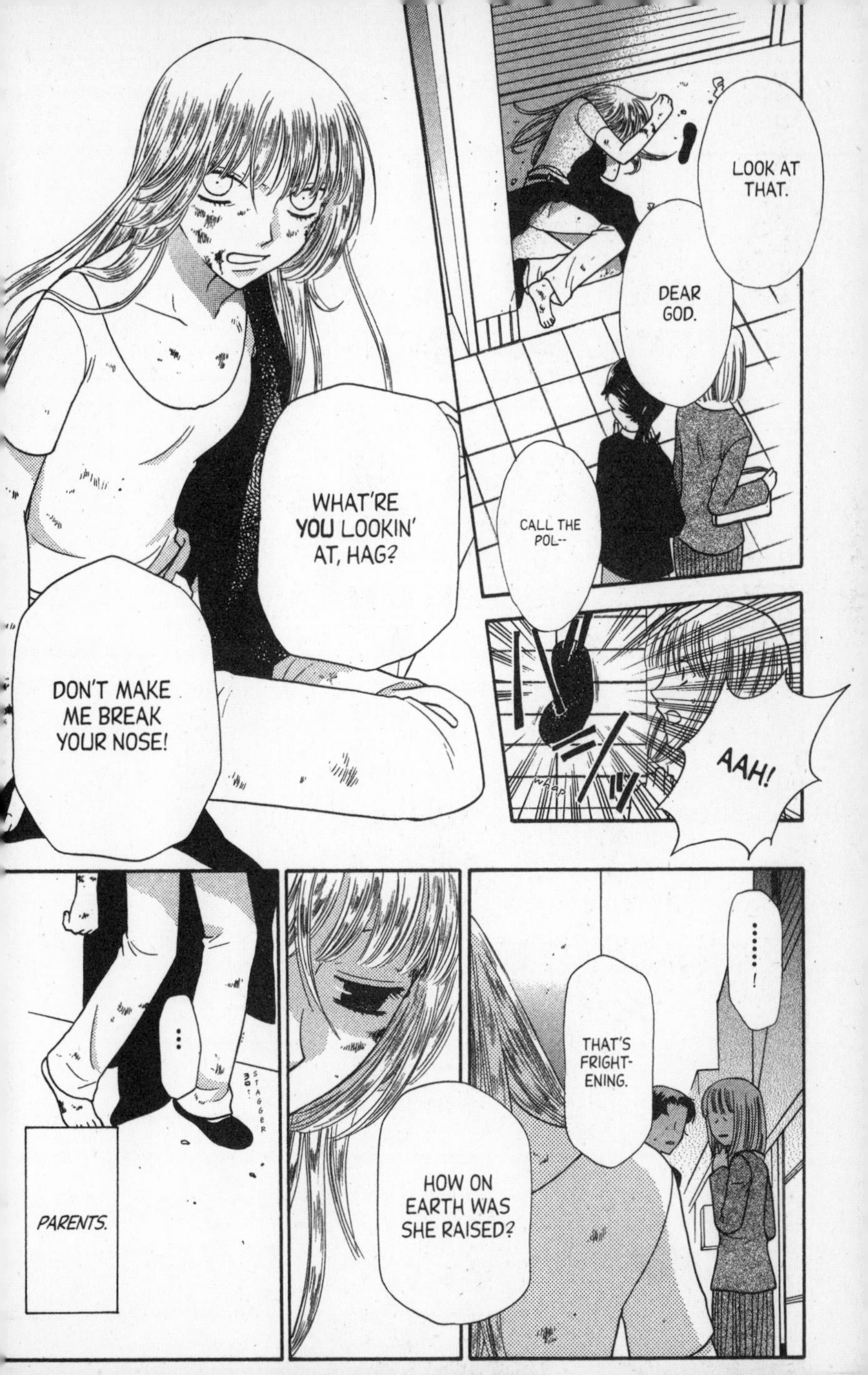
LOOK AT THAT.
DEAR GOD.
CALL THE POL--
whap
AAH!
WHAT'RE YOU LOOKIN' AT, HAG?
DON'T MAKE ME BREAK YOUR NOSE!
......!
THAT'S FRIGHTENING.
HOW ON EARTH WAS SHE RAISED?
...
STAGGER
PARENTS.

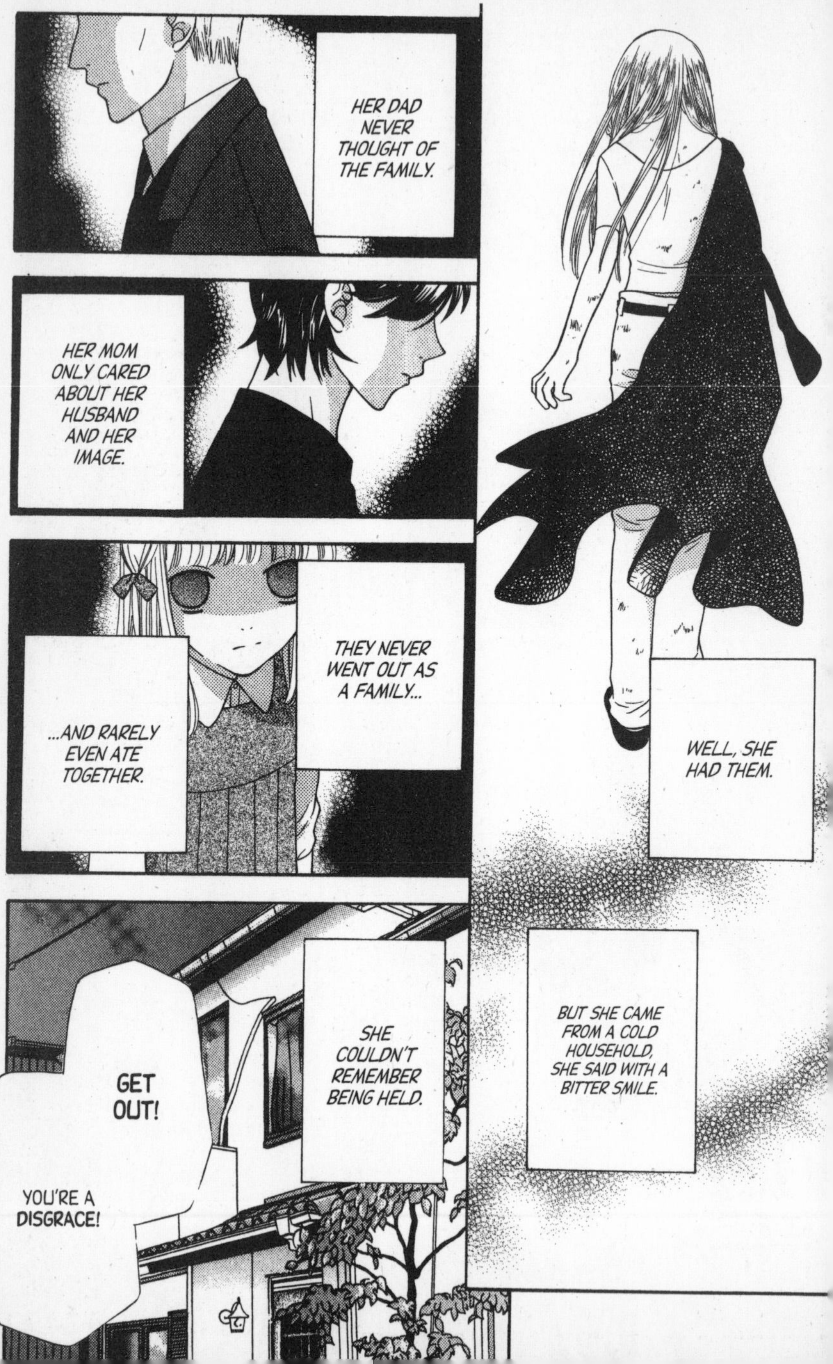
WELL, SHE HAD THEM.
BUT SHE CAME FROM A COLD HOUSEHOLD, SHE SAID WITH A BITTER SMILE.
HER DAD NEVER THOUGHT OF THE FAMILY.
HER MOM ONLY CARED ABOUT HER HUSBAND AND HER IMAGE.
THEY NEVER WENT OUT AS A FAMILY...
...AND RARELY EVEN ATE TOGETHER.
SHE COULDN'T REMEMBER BEING HELD.
GET OUT!
YOU'RE A DISGRACE!

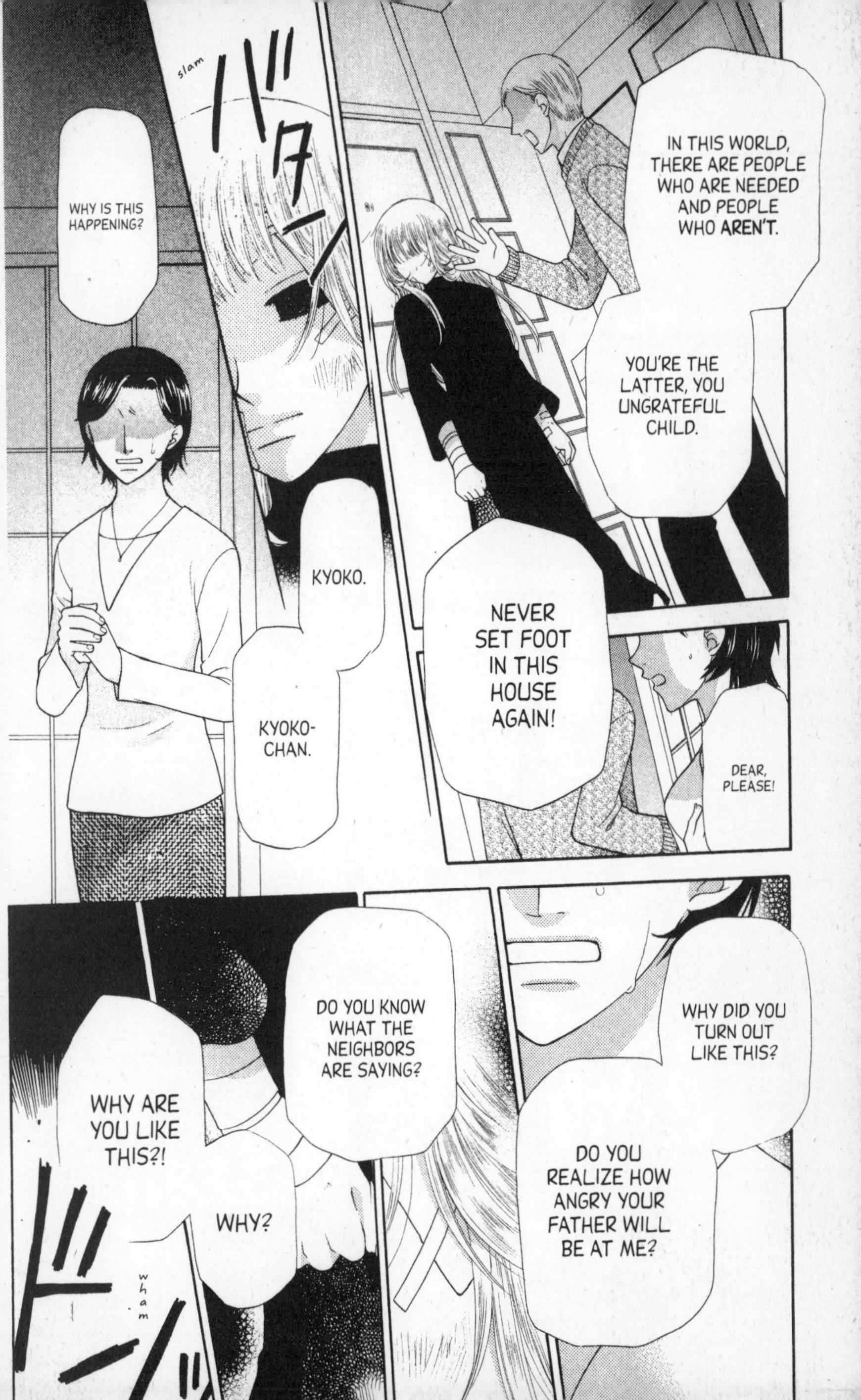
IN THIS WORLD, THERE ARE PEOPLE WHO ARE NEEDED AND PEOPLE WHO **AREN'T**.
YOU'RE THE LATTER, YOU UNGRATEFUL CHILD.
NEVER SET FOOT IN THIS HOUSE AGAIN!
DEAR, PLEASE!
slam
WHY IS THIS HAPPENING?
KYOKO.
KYOKO-CHAN.
WHY DID YOU TURN OUT LIKE THIS?
DO YOU REALIZE HOW ANGRY YOUR FATHER WILL BE AT ME?
DO YOU KNOW WHAT THE NEIGHBORS ARE SAYING?
WHY ARE YOU LIKE THIS?!
WHY?
wham

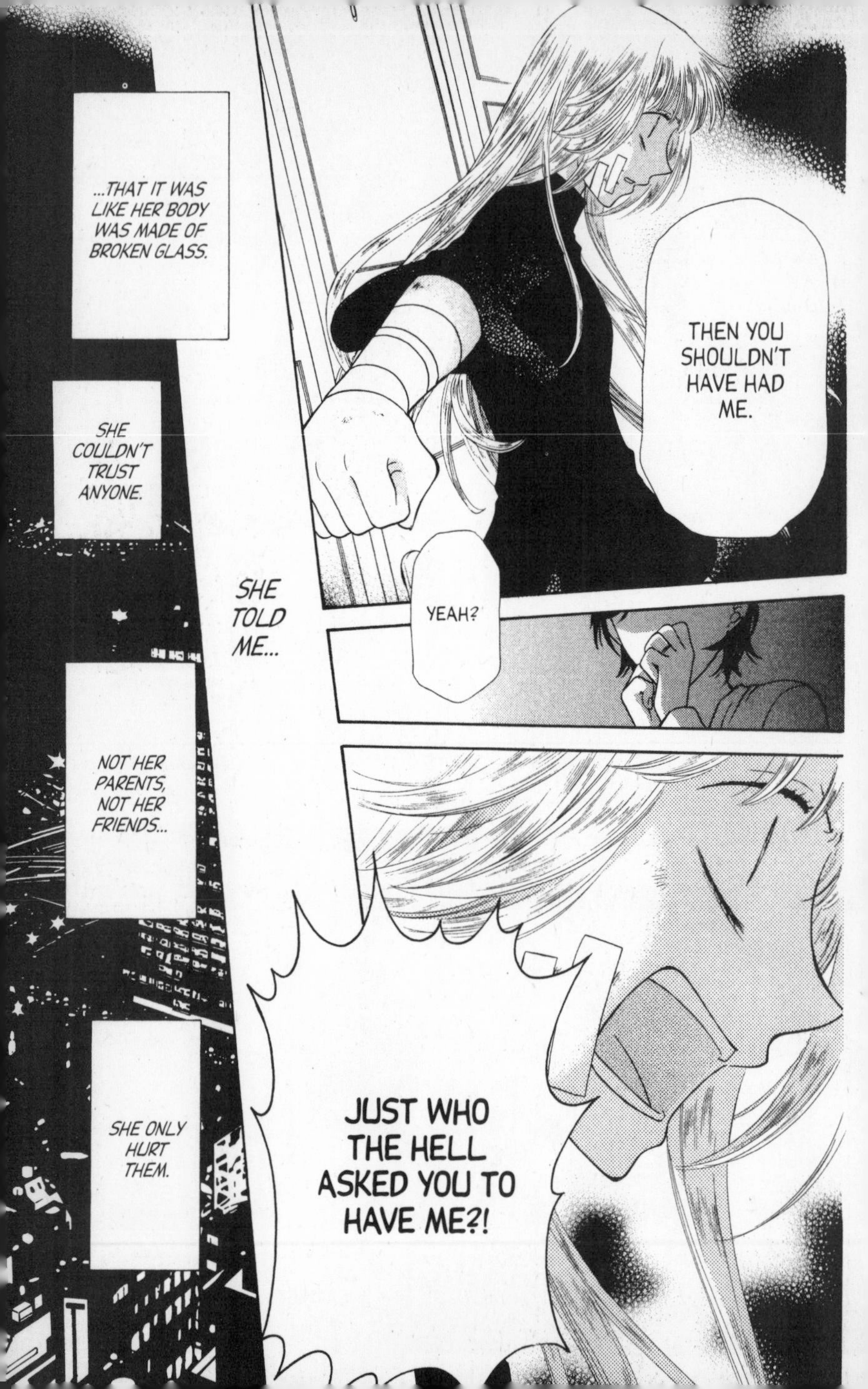
THEN YOU SHOULDN'T HAVE HAD ME.
YEAH?
JUST WHO THE HELL ASKED YOU TO HAVE ME?!
SHE TOLD ME...
...THAT IT WAS LIKE HER BODY WAS MADE OF BROKEN GLASS.
SHE COULDN'T TRUST ANYONE.
NOT HER PARENTS, NOT HER FRIENDS...
SHE ONLY HURT THEM.

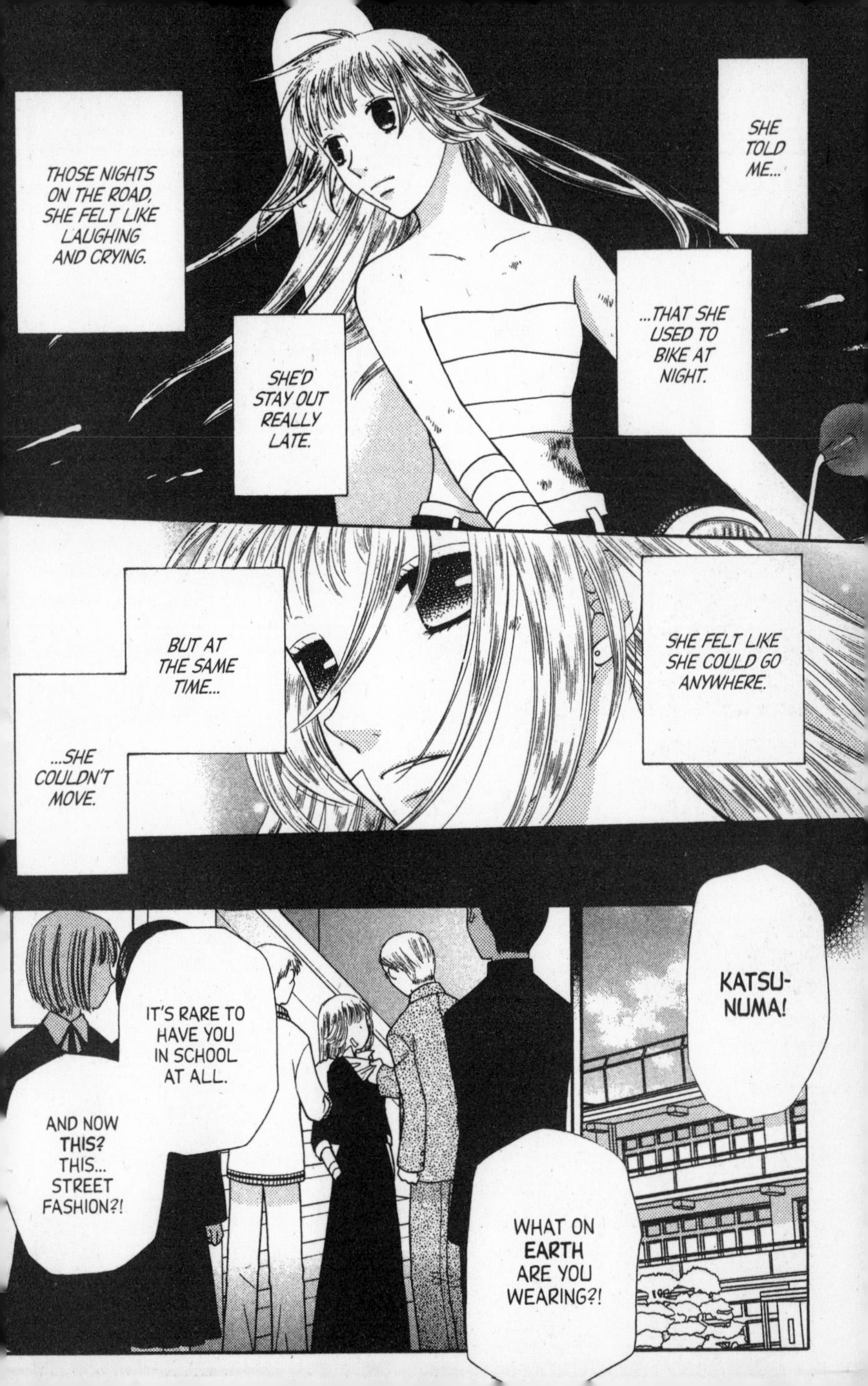
SHE TOLD ME...
...THAT SHE USED TO BIKE AT NIGHT.
SHE'D STAY OUT REALLY LATE.
THOSE NIGHTS ON THE ROAD, SHE FELT LIKE LAUGHING AND CRYING.
SHE FELT LIKE SHE COULD GO ANYWHERE.
BUT AT THE SAME TIME...
...SHE COULDN'T MOVE.
KATSU-NUMA!
WHAT ON EARTH ARE YOU WEARING?!
IT'S RARE TO HAVE YOU IN SCHOOL AT ALL.
AND NOW THIS? THIS... STREET FASHION?!

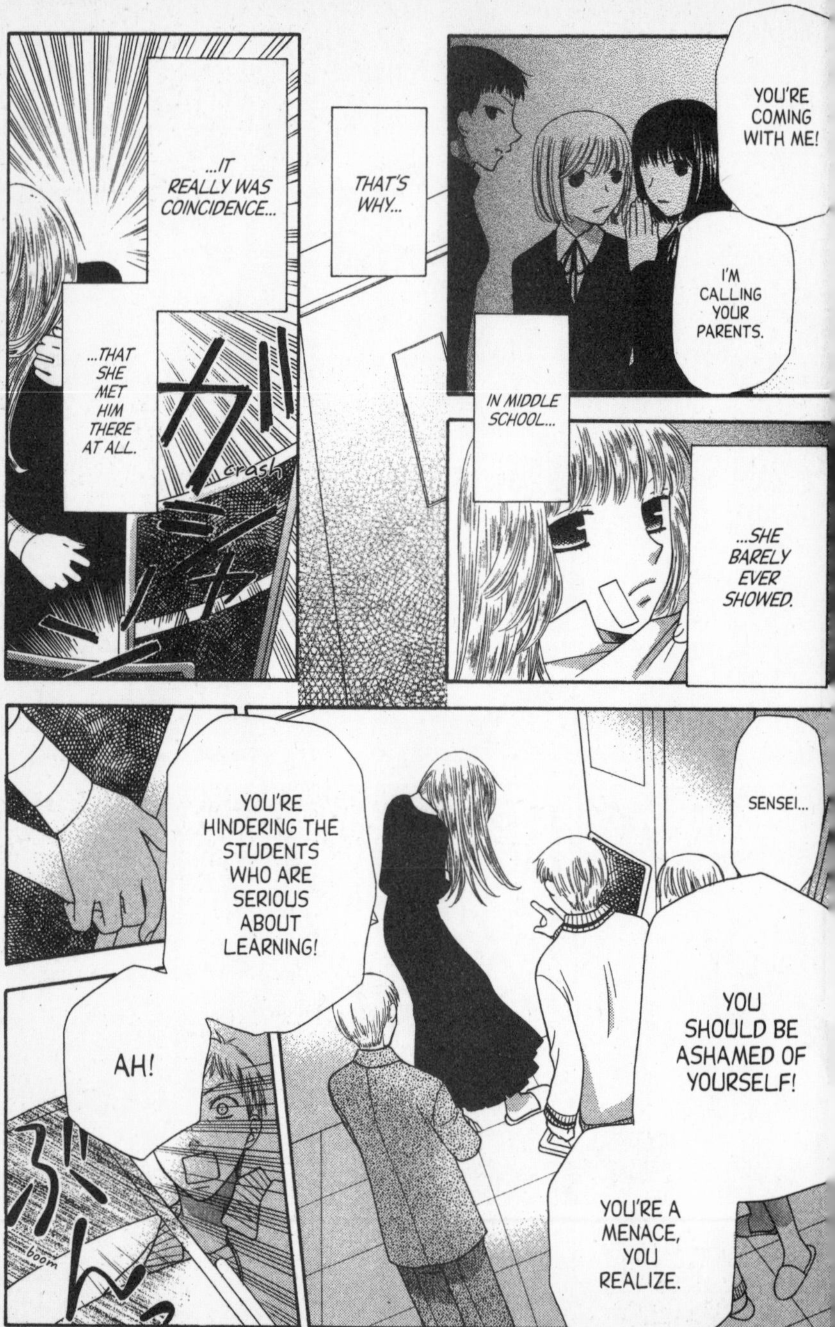
YOU'RE COMING WITH ME!
I'M CALLING YOUR PARENTS.
IN MIDDLE SCHOOL...
...SHE BARELY EVER SHOWED.
THAT'S WHY...
...IT REALLY WAS COINCIDENCE...
...THAT SHE MET HIM THERE AT ALL.
crash
SENSEI...
YOU'RE HINDERING THE STUDENTS WHO ARE SERIOUS ABOUT LEARNING!
YOU SHOULD BE ASHAMED OF YOURSELF!
YOU'RE A MENACE, YOU REALIZE.
AH!
boom

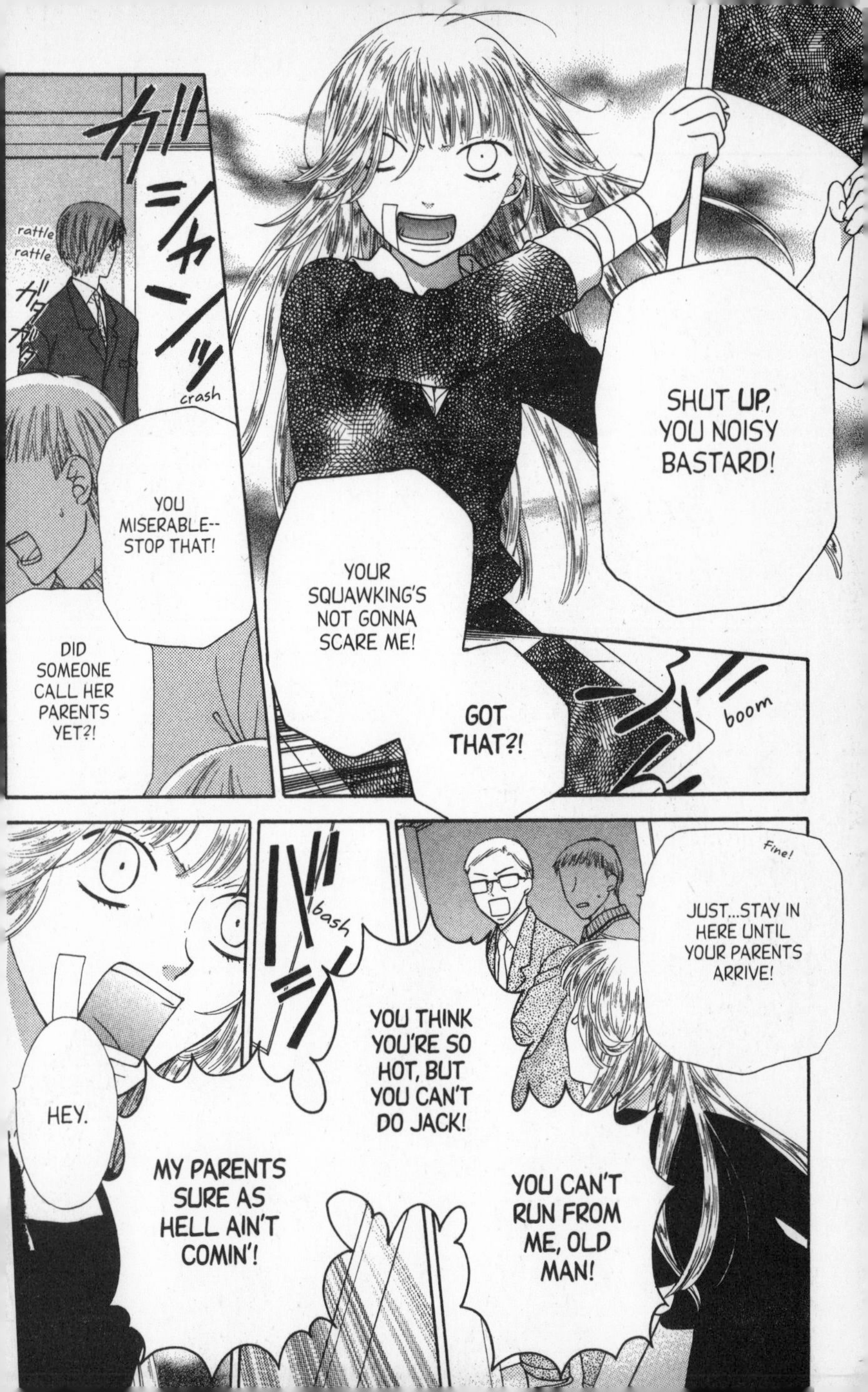

SHUT UP, YOU NOISY BASTARD!
YOUR SQUAWKING'S NOT GONNA SCARE ME!
GOT THAT?!
boom
crash
rattle
rattle
YOU MISERABLE-- STOP THAT!
DID SOMEONE CALL HER PARENTS YET?!
Fine!
JUST...STAY IN HERE UNTIL YOUR PARENTS ARRIVE!
bash
YOU THINK YOU'RE SO HOT, BUT YOU CAN'T DO JACK!
YOU CAN'T RUN FROM ME, OLD MAN!
MY PARENTS SURE AS HELL AIN'T COMIN'!
HEY.

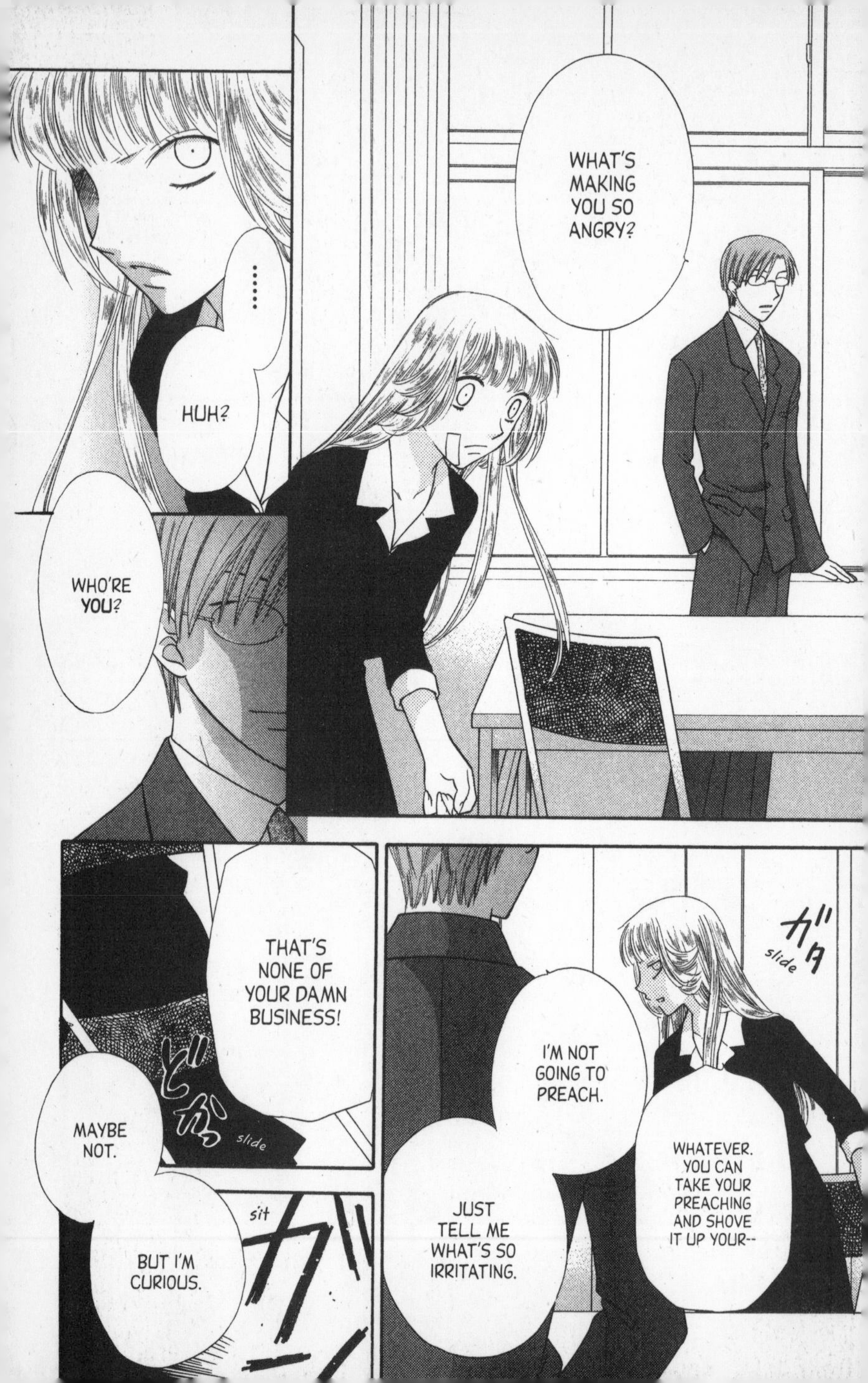
WHAT'S MAKING YOU SO ANGRY?
......
HUH?
WHO'RE YOU?
ガタ
slide
WHATEVER. YOU CAN TAKE YOUR PREACHING AND SHOVE IT UP YOUR--
I'M NOT GOING TO PREACH.
JUST TELL ME WHAT'S SO IRRITATING.
THAT'S NONE OF YOUR DAMN BUSINESS!
slide
MAYBE NOT.
sit
BUT I'M CURIOUS.

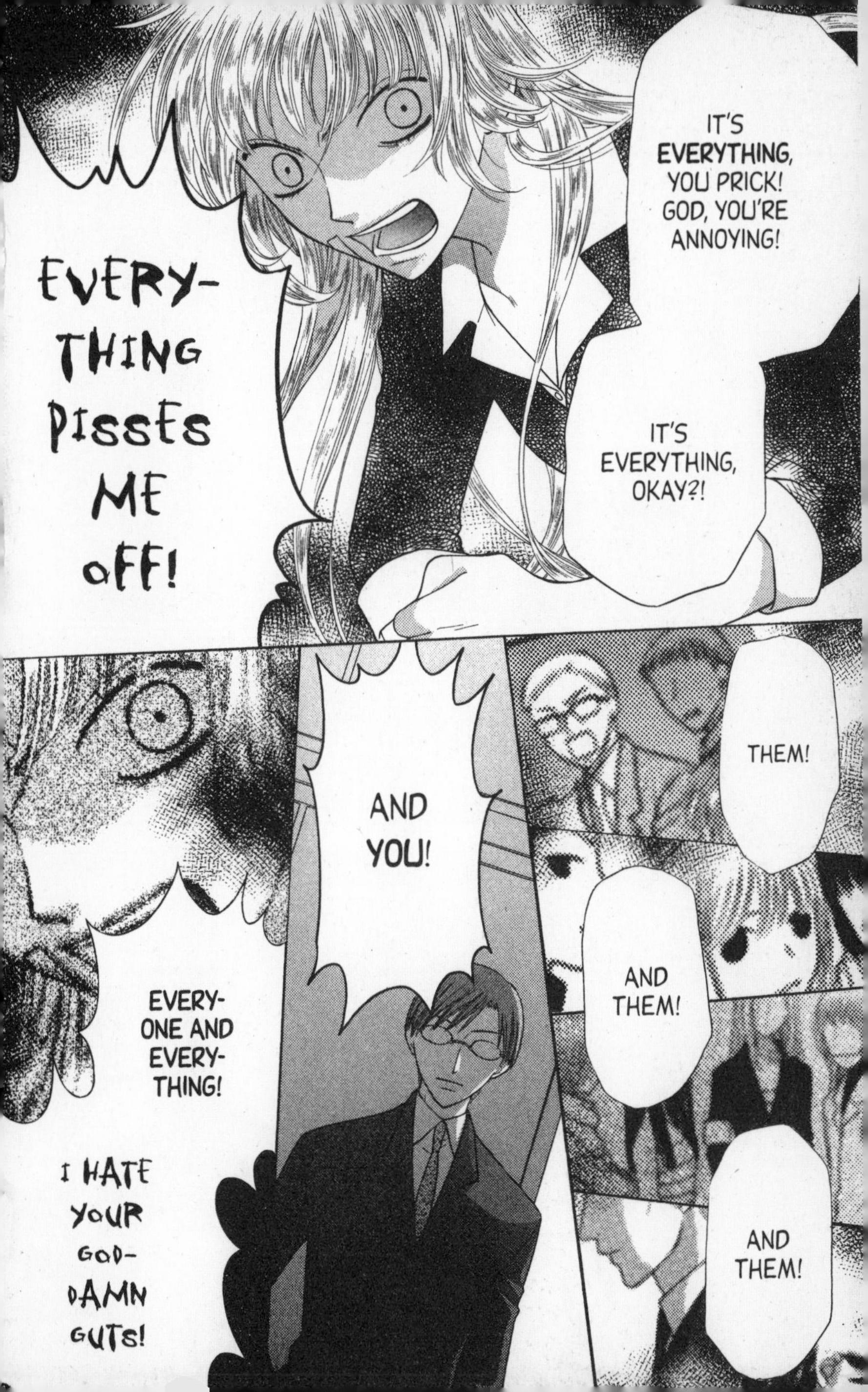
IT'S EVERYTHING, YOU PRICK! GOD, YOU'RE ANNOYING!
IT'S EVERYTHING, OKAY?!
EVERYTHING PISSES ME OFF!
THEM!
AND THEM!
AND THEM!
AND YOU!
EVERYONE AND EVERYTHING!
I HATE YOUR GODDAMN GUTS!

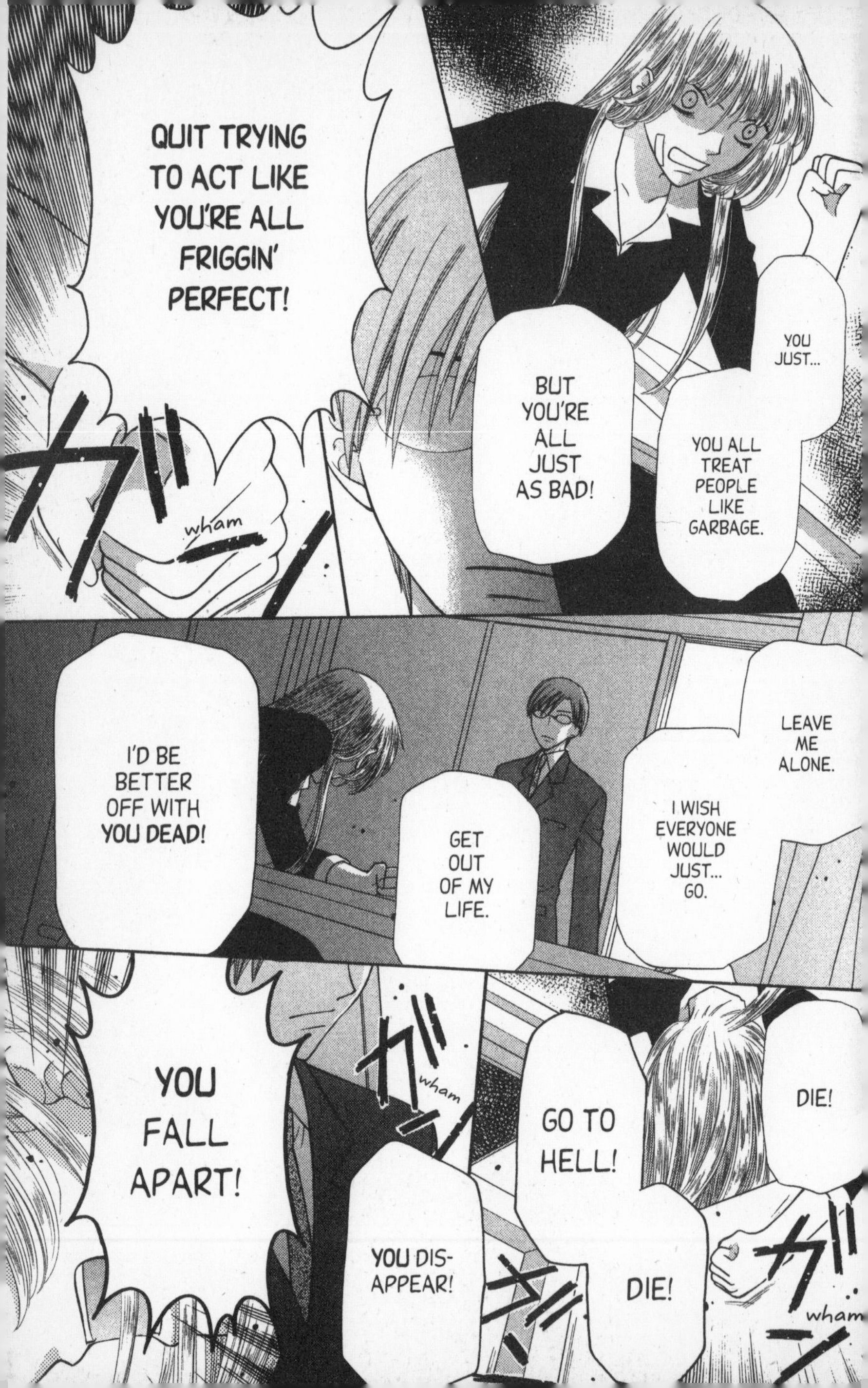
YOU JUST...
YOU ALL TREAT PEOPLE LIKE GARBAGE.
BUT YOU'RE ALL JUST AS BAD!
QUIT TRYING TO ACT LIKE YOU'RE ALL FRIGGIN' PERFECT!
wham
LEAVE ME ALONE.
I WISH EVERYONE WOULD JUST... GO.
GET OUT OF MY LIFE.
I'D BE BETTER OFF WITH YOU DEAD!
DIE!
GO TO HELL!
wham
DIE!
YOU DIS-APPEAR!
wham
YOU FALL APART!

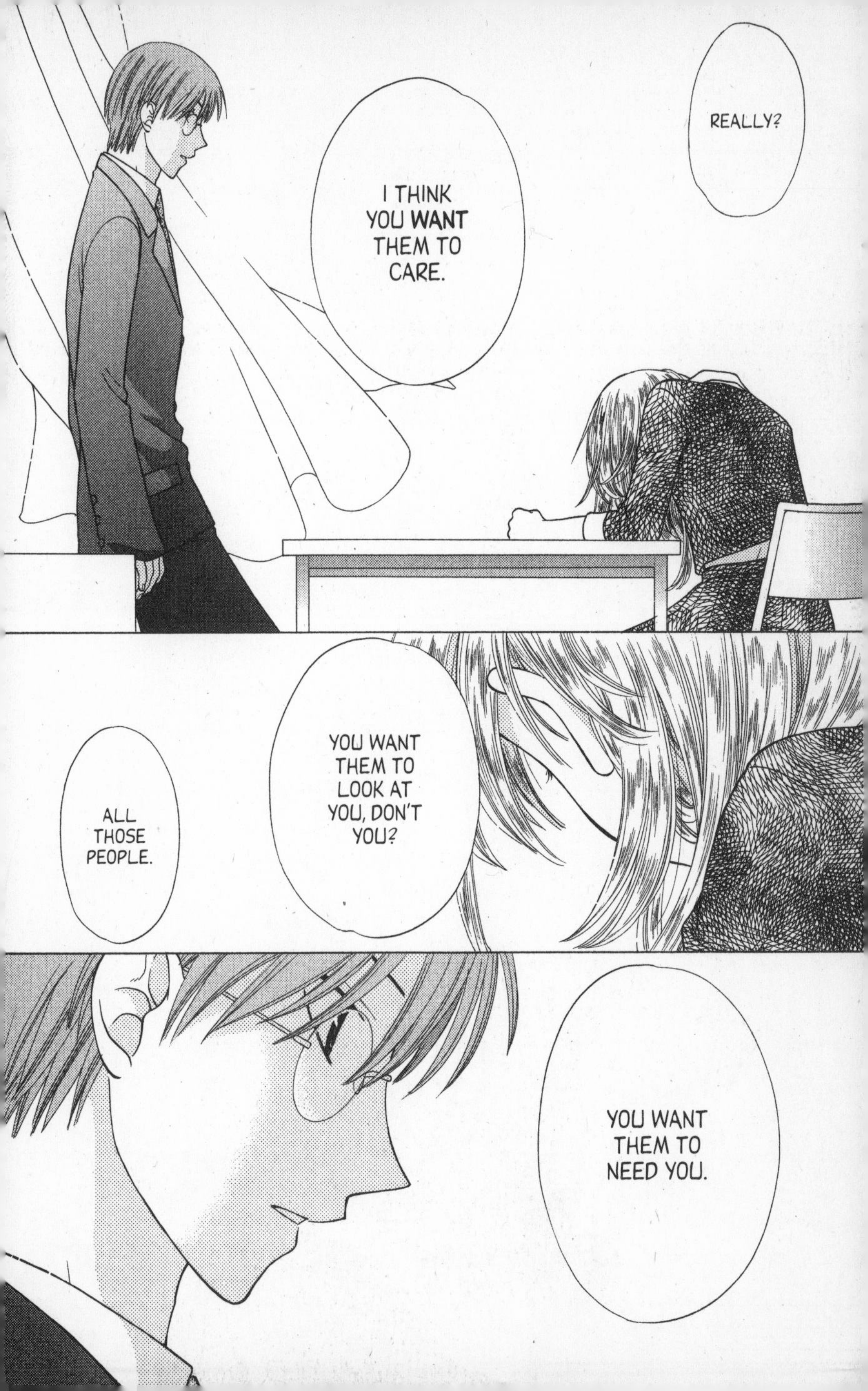
REALLY?
I THINK YOU WANT THEM TO CARE.
YOU WANT THEM TO LOOK AT YOU, DON'T YOU?
ALL THOSE PEOPLE.
YOU WANT THEM TO NEED YOU.

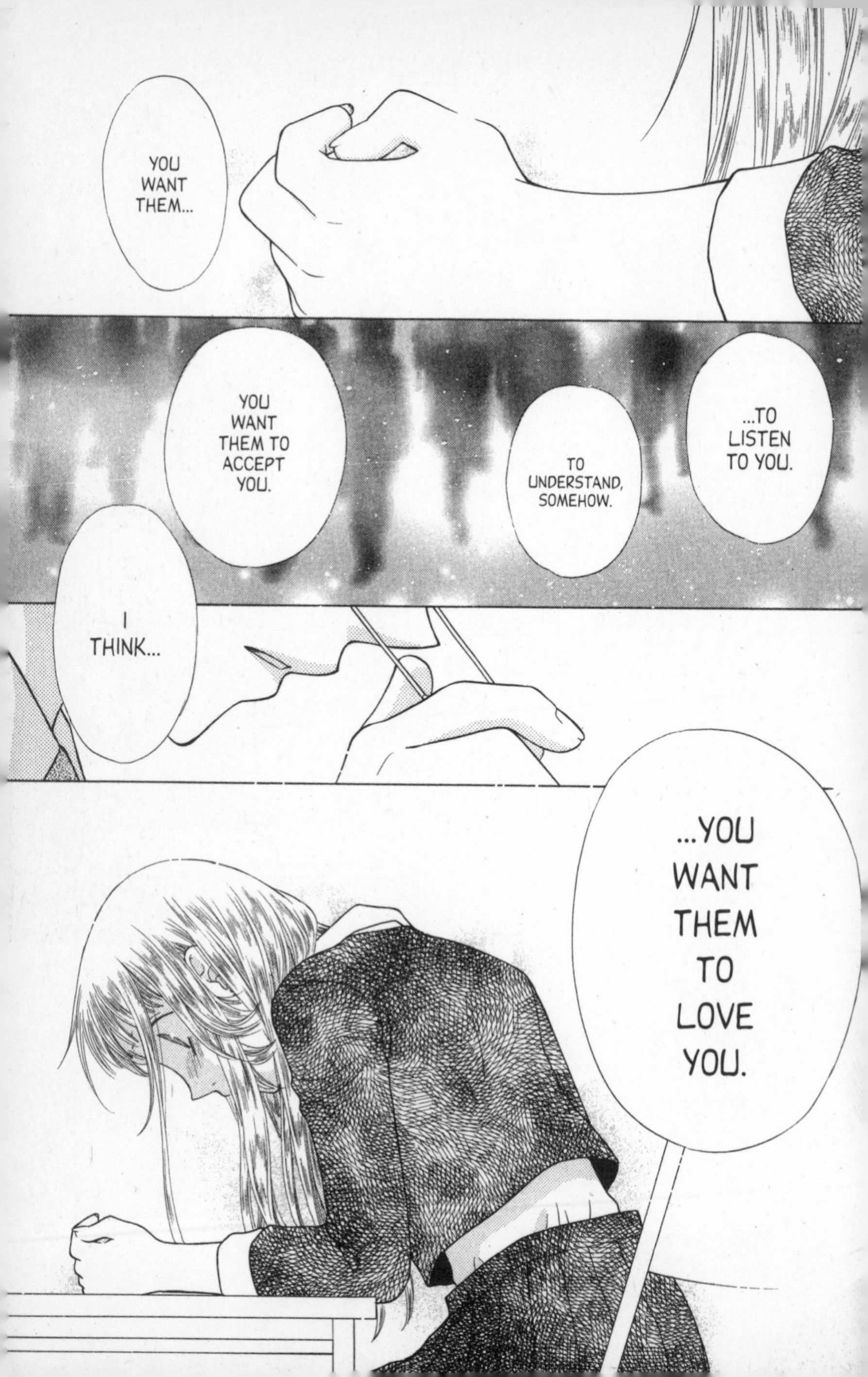
YOU WANT THEM...
...TO LISTEN TO YOU.
TO UNDERSTAND, SOMEHOW.
YOU WANT THEM TO ACCEPT YOU.
I THINK...
...YOU WANT THEM TO LOVE YOU.

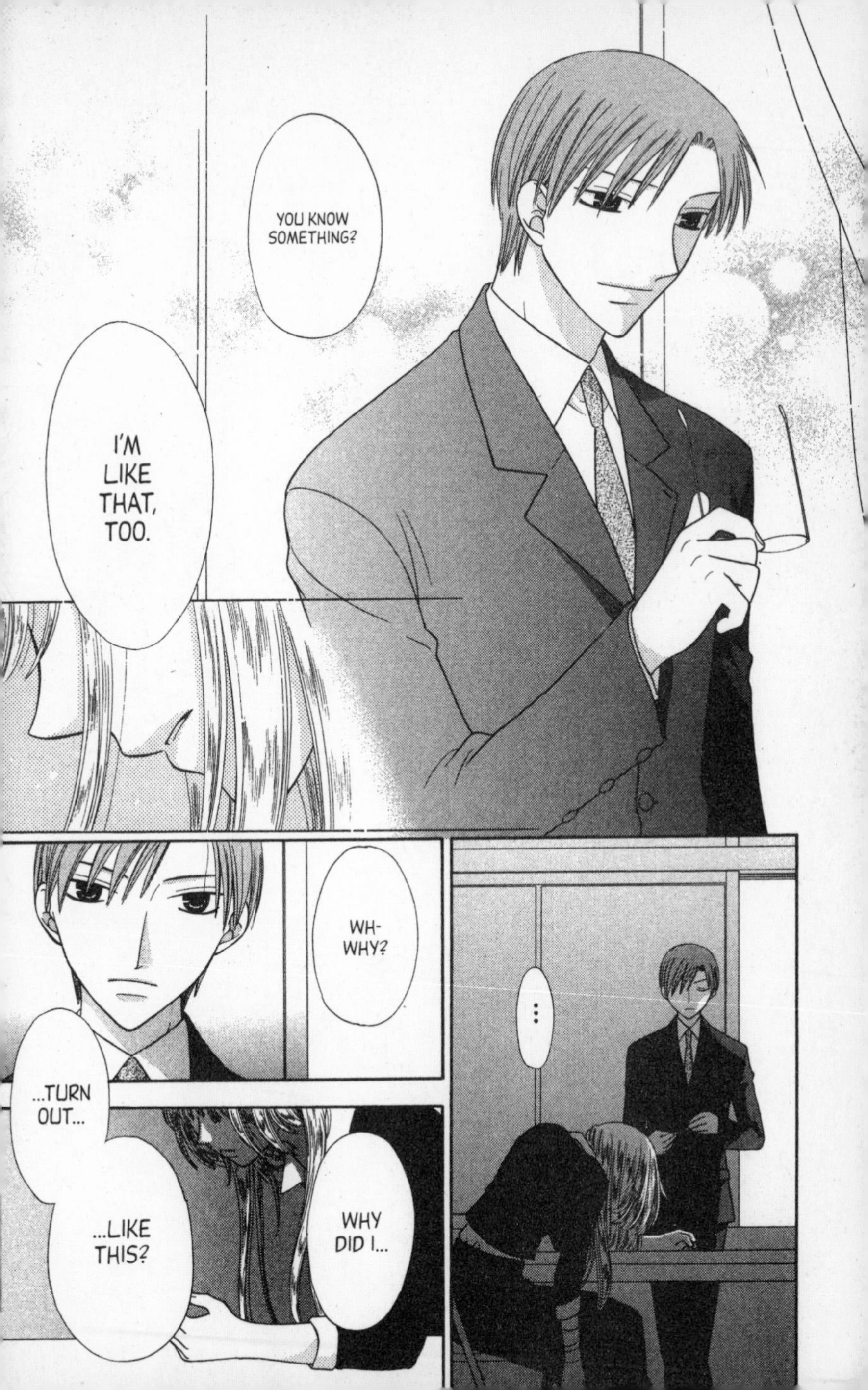
YOU KNOW SOMETHING?
I'M LIKE THAT, TOO.
...
WH- WHY?
WHY DID I...
...TURN OUT...
...LIKE THIS?

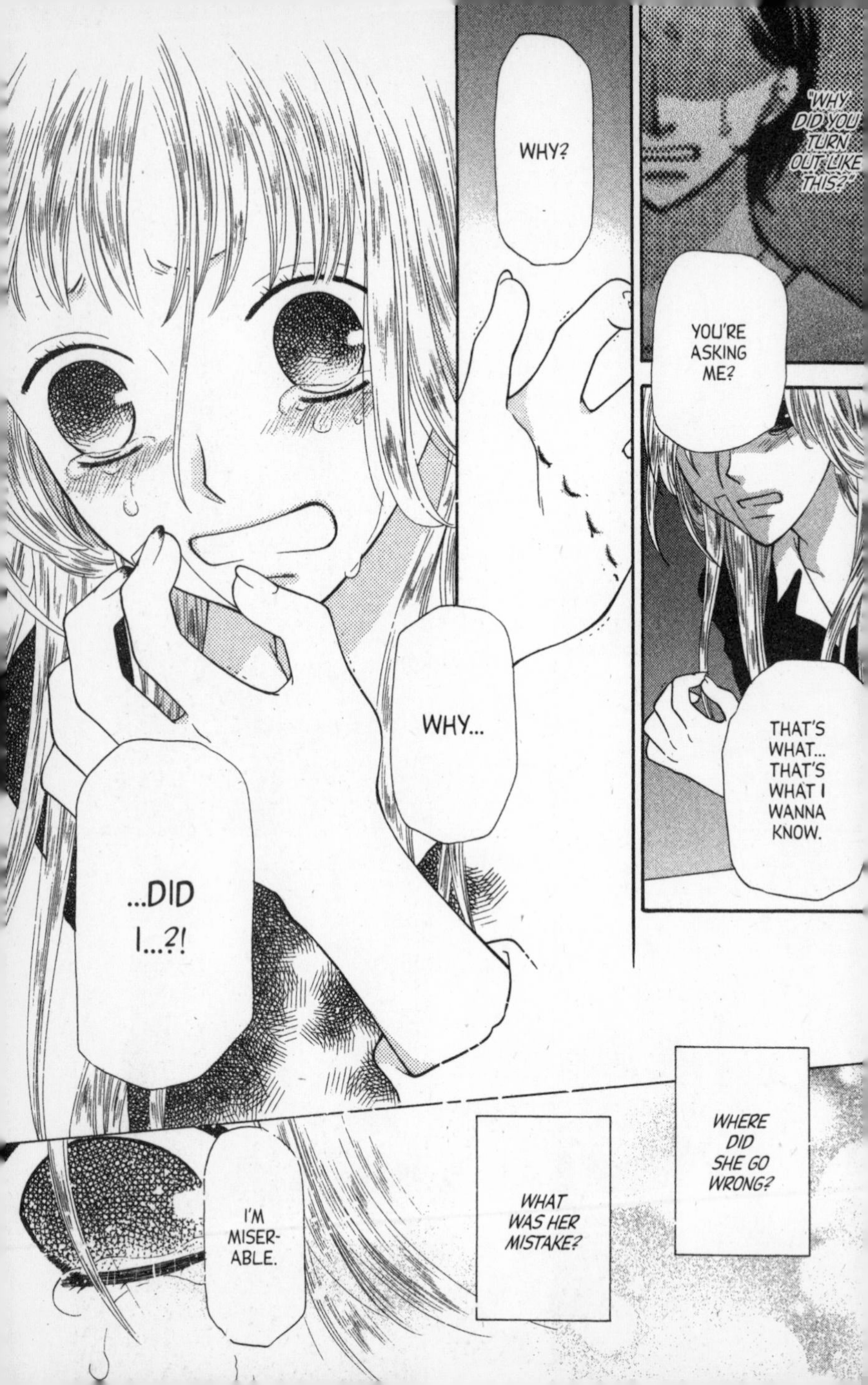
"WHY DID YOU TURN OUT LIKE THIS?"
YOU'RE ASKING ME?
THAT'S WHAT... THAT'S WHAT I WANNA KNOW.
WHY?
WHY...
...DID I...?!
WHERE DID SHE GO WRONG?
WHAT WAS HER MISTAKE?
I'M MISER-ABLE.

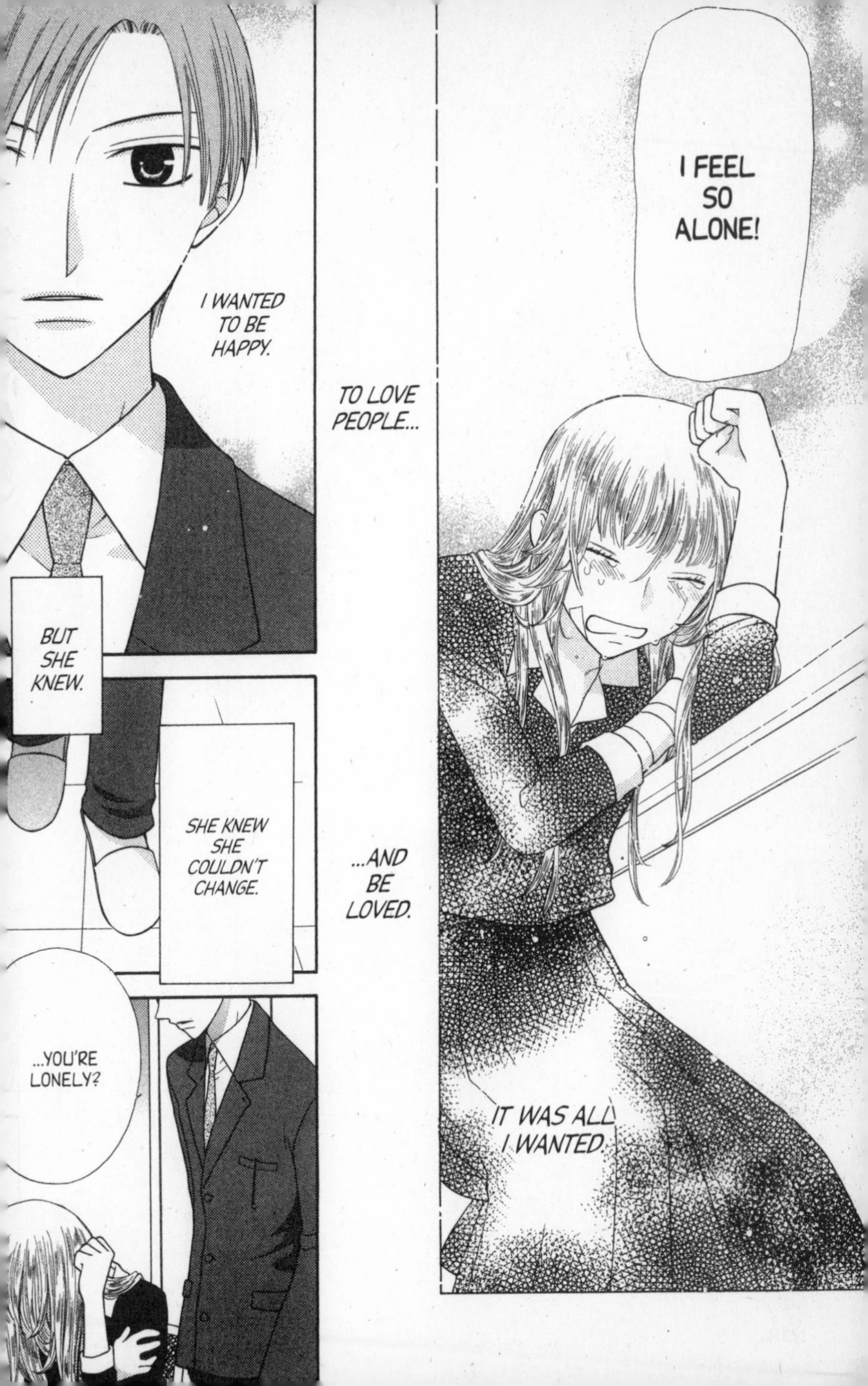
I FEEL SO ALONE!
IT WAS ALL I WANTED.
TO LOVE PEOPLE...
...AND BE LOVED.
I WANTED TO BE HAPPY.
BUT SHE KNEW.
SHE KNEW SHE COULDN'T CHANGE.
...YOU'RE LONELY?

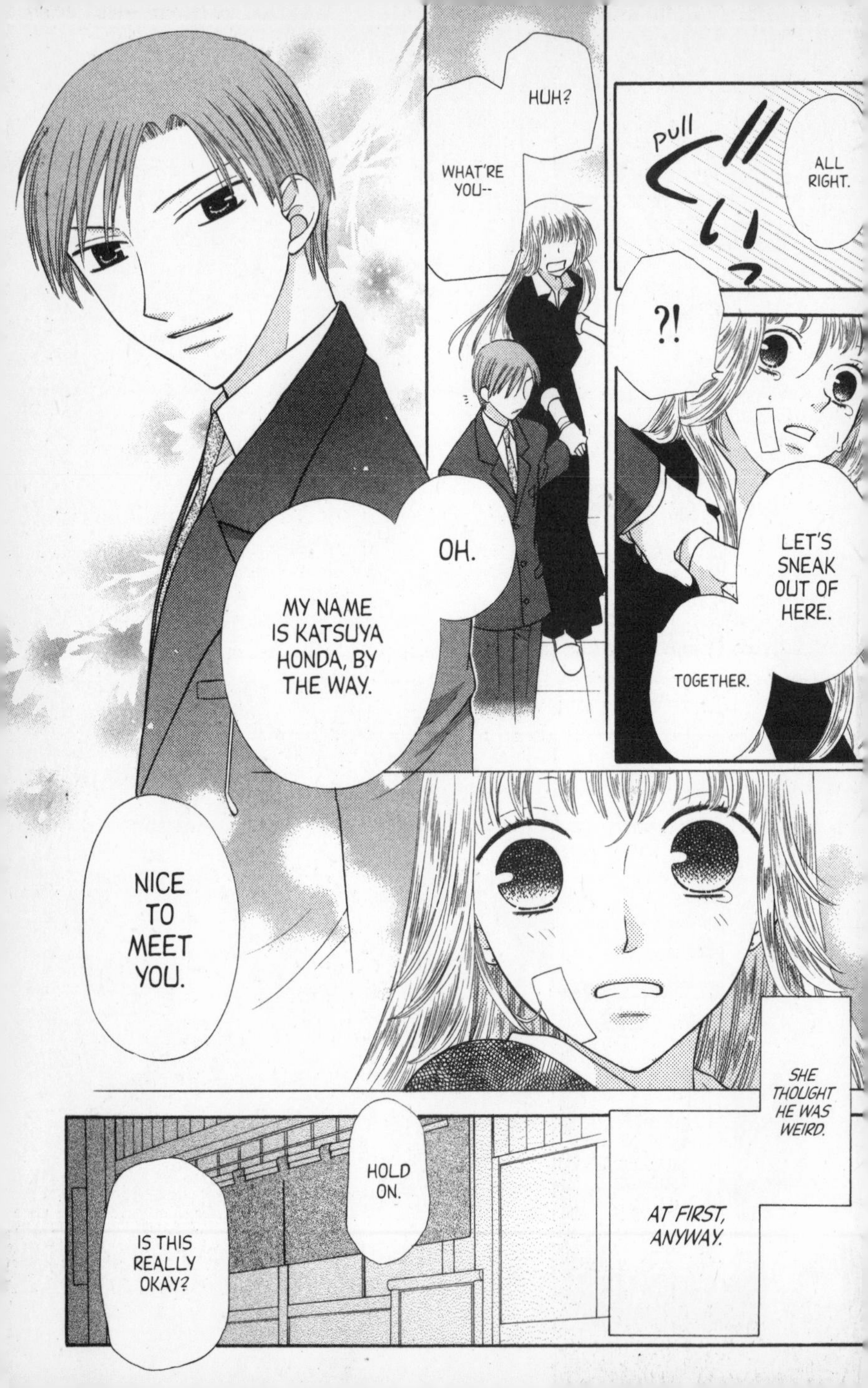
pull
ALL RIGHT.
?!
LET'S SNEAK OUT OF HERE.
TOGETHER.
HUH?
WHAT'RE YOU--
OH.
MY NAME IS KATSUYA HONDA, BY THE WAY.
NICE TO MEET YOU.
SHE THOUGHT HE WAS WEIRD.
AT FIRST, ANYWAY.
HOLD ON.
IS THIS REALLY OKAY?

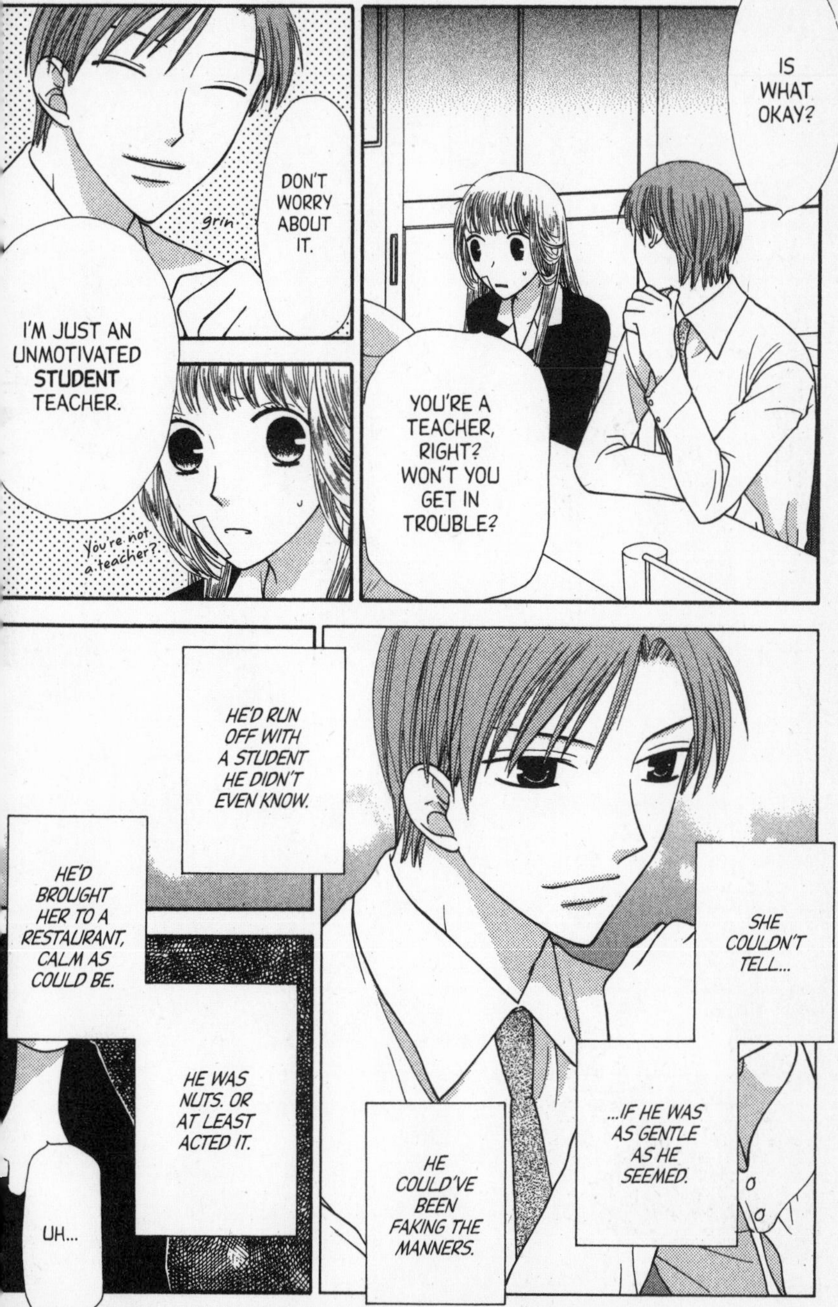
IS WHAT OKAY?
YOU'RE A TEACHER, RIGHT? WON'T YOU GET IN TROUBLE?
DON'T WORRY ABOUT IT.
grin
I'M JUST AN UNMOTIVATED **STUDENT** TEACHER.
You're not a teacher?
SHE COULDN'T TELL...
...IF HE WAS AS GENTLE AS HE SEEMED.
HE COULD'VE BEEN FAKING THE MANNERS.
HE'D RUN OFF WITH A STUDENT HE DIDN'T EVEN KNOW.
HE'D BROUGHT HER TO A RESTAURANT, CALM AS COULD BE.
HE WAS NUTS. OR AT LEAST ACTED IT.
UH...

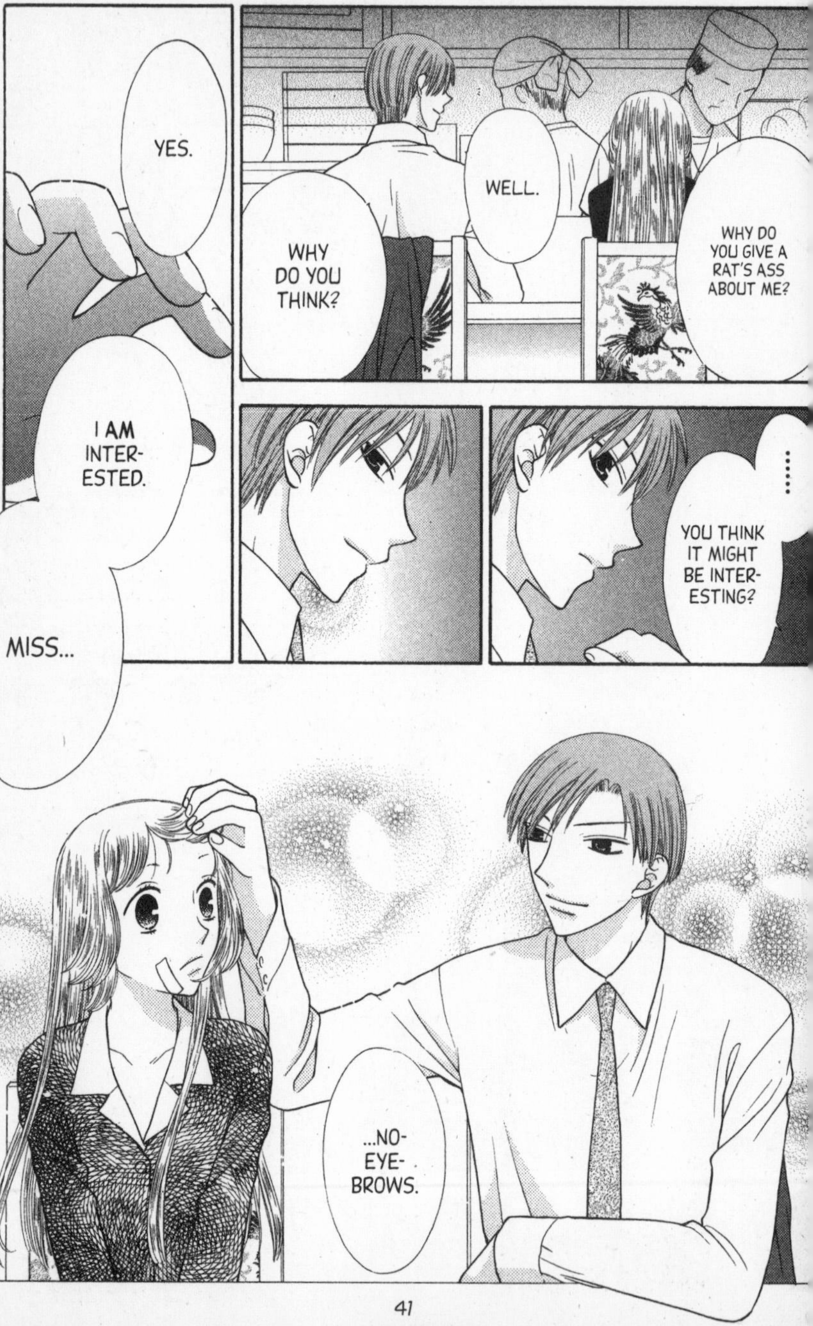
WHY DO YOU GIVE A RAT'S ASS ABOUT ME?
WELL.
WHY DO YOU THINK?
......
YOU THINK IT MIGHT BE INTER-ESTING?
YES.
I AM INTER-ESTED.
MISS...
...NO-EYE-BROWS.

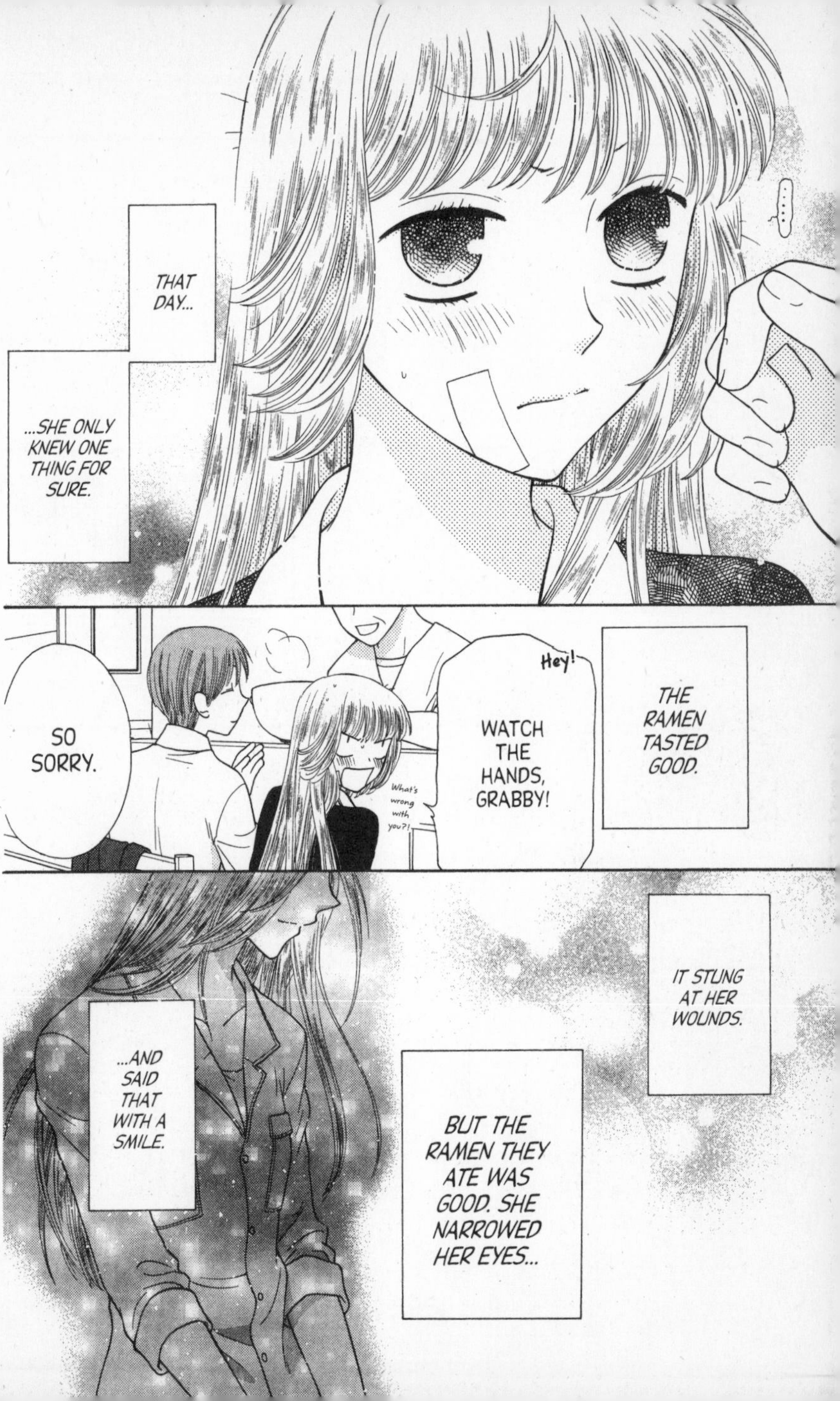
......
THAT DAY...
...SHE ONLY KNEW ONE THING FOR SURE.
THE RAMEN TASTED GOOD.
Hey!
WATCH THE HANDS, GRABBY!
What's wrong with you?!
SO SORRY.
IT STUNG AT HER WOUNDS.
BUT THE RAMEN THEY ATE WAS GOOD. SHE NARROWED HER EYES...
...AND SAID THAT WITH A SMILE.

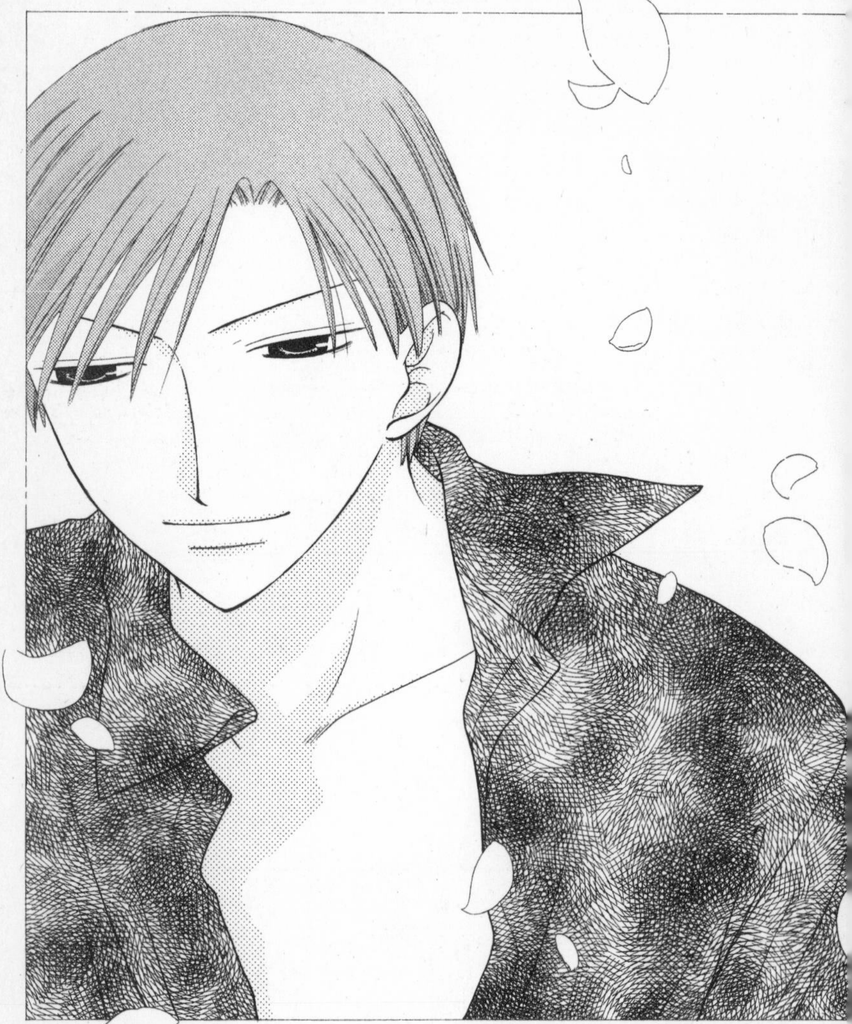

Chapter 91

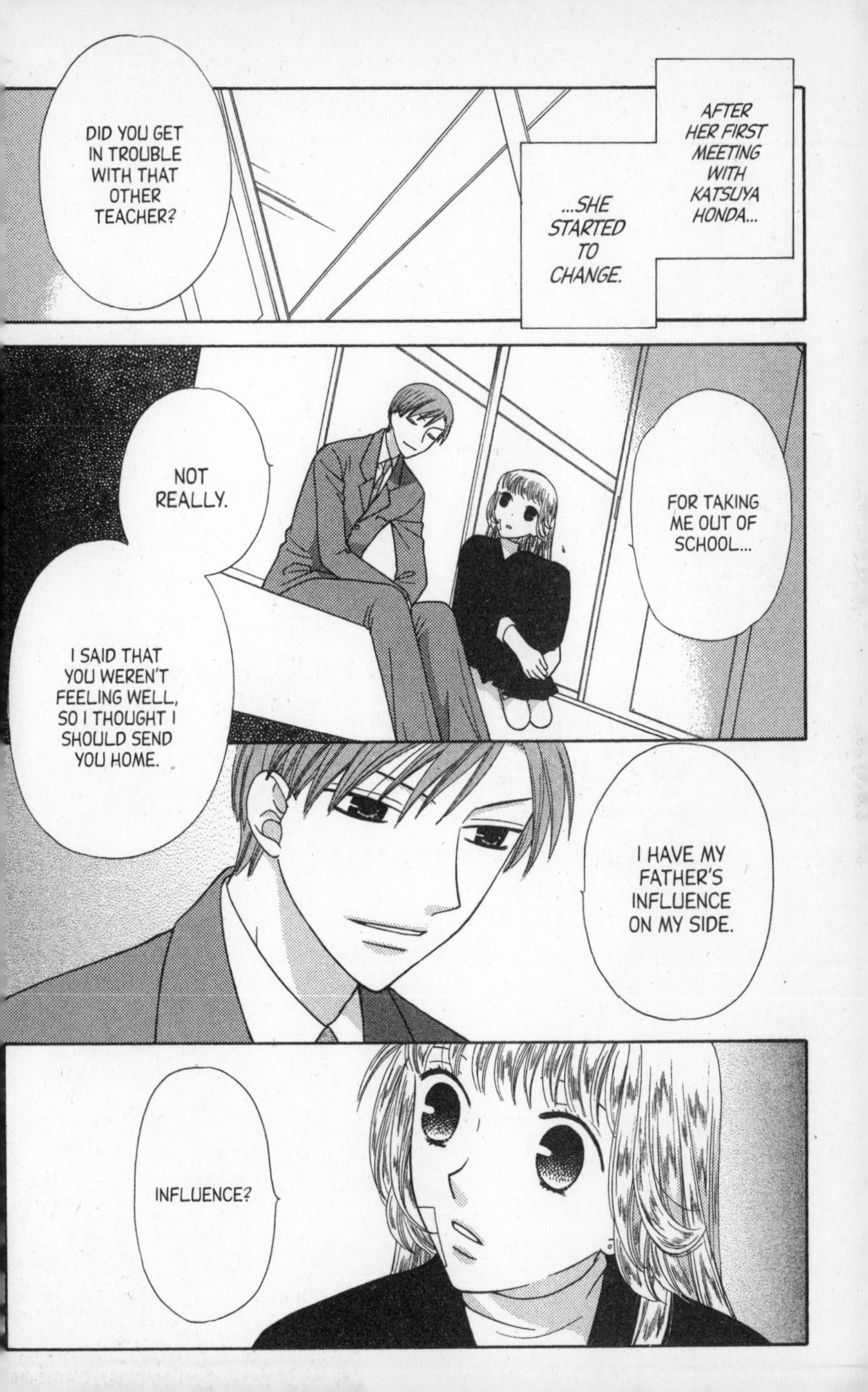
AFTER HER FIRST MEETING WITH KATSUYA HONDA...
...SHE STARTED TO CHANGE.
DID YOU GET IN TROUBLE WITH THAT OTHER TEACHER?
FOR TAKING ME OUT OF SCHOOL...
NOT REALLY.
I SAID THAT YOU WEREN'T FEELING WELL, SO I THOUGHT I SHOULD SEND YOU HOME.
I HAVE MY FATHER'S INFLUENCE ON MY SIDE.
INFLUENCE?

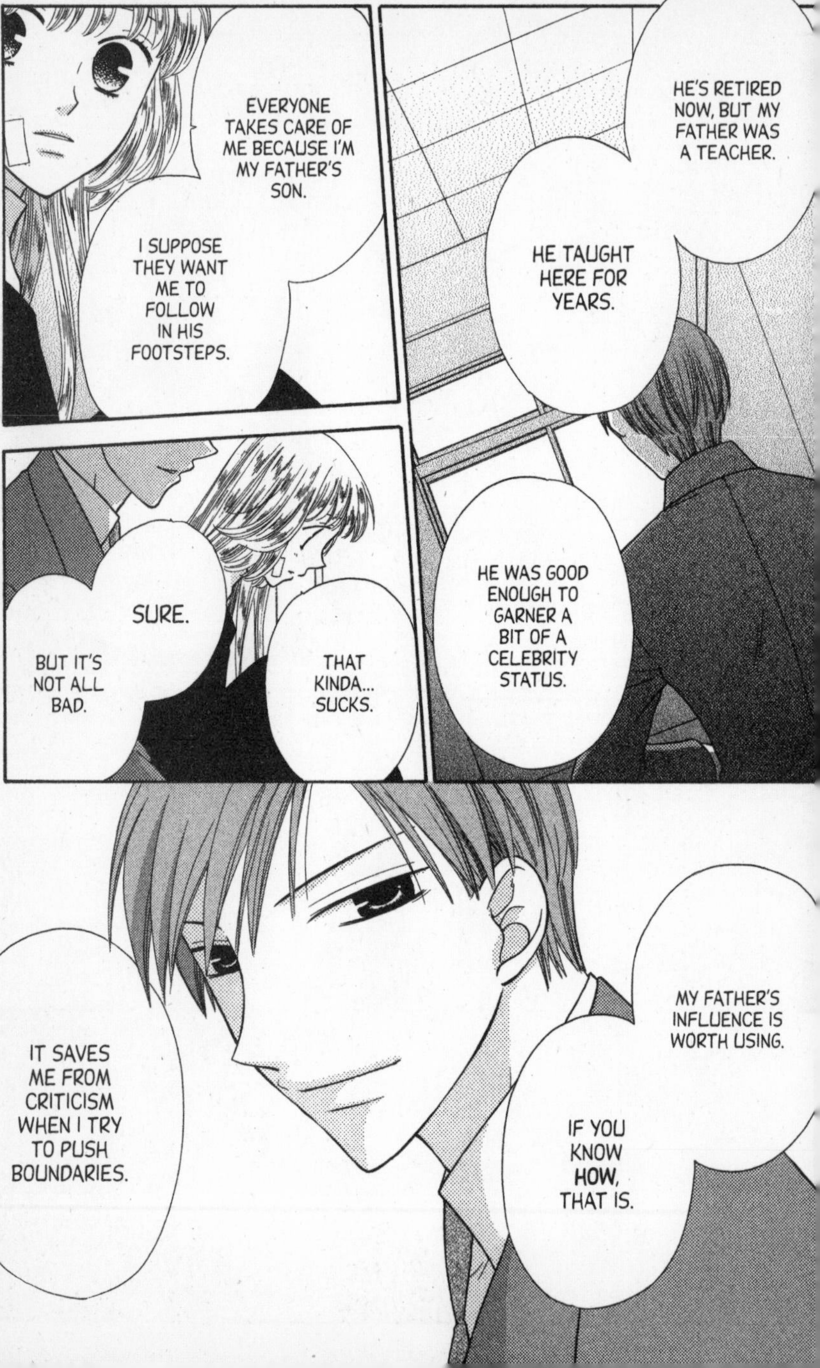
HE'S RETIRED NOW, BUT MY FATHER WAS A TEACHER.
HE TAUGHT HERE FOR YEARS.
HE WAS GOOD ENOUGH TO GARNER A BIT OF A CELEBRITY STATUS.
EVERYONE TAKES CARE OF ME BECAUSE I'M MY FATHER'S SON.
I SUPPOSE THEY WANT ME TO FOLLOW IN HIS FOOTSTEPS.
THAT KINDA... SUCKS.
SURE.
BUT IT'S NOT ALL BAD.
MY FATHER'S INFLUENCE IS WORTH USING.
IF YOU KNOW HOW, THAT IS.
IT SAVES ME FROM CRITICISM WHEN I TRY TO PUSH BOUNDARIES.

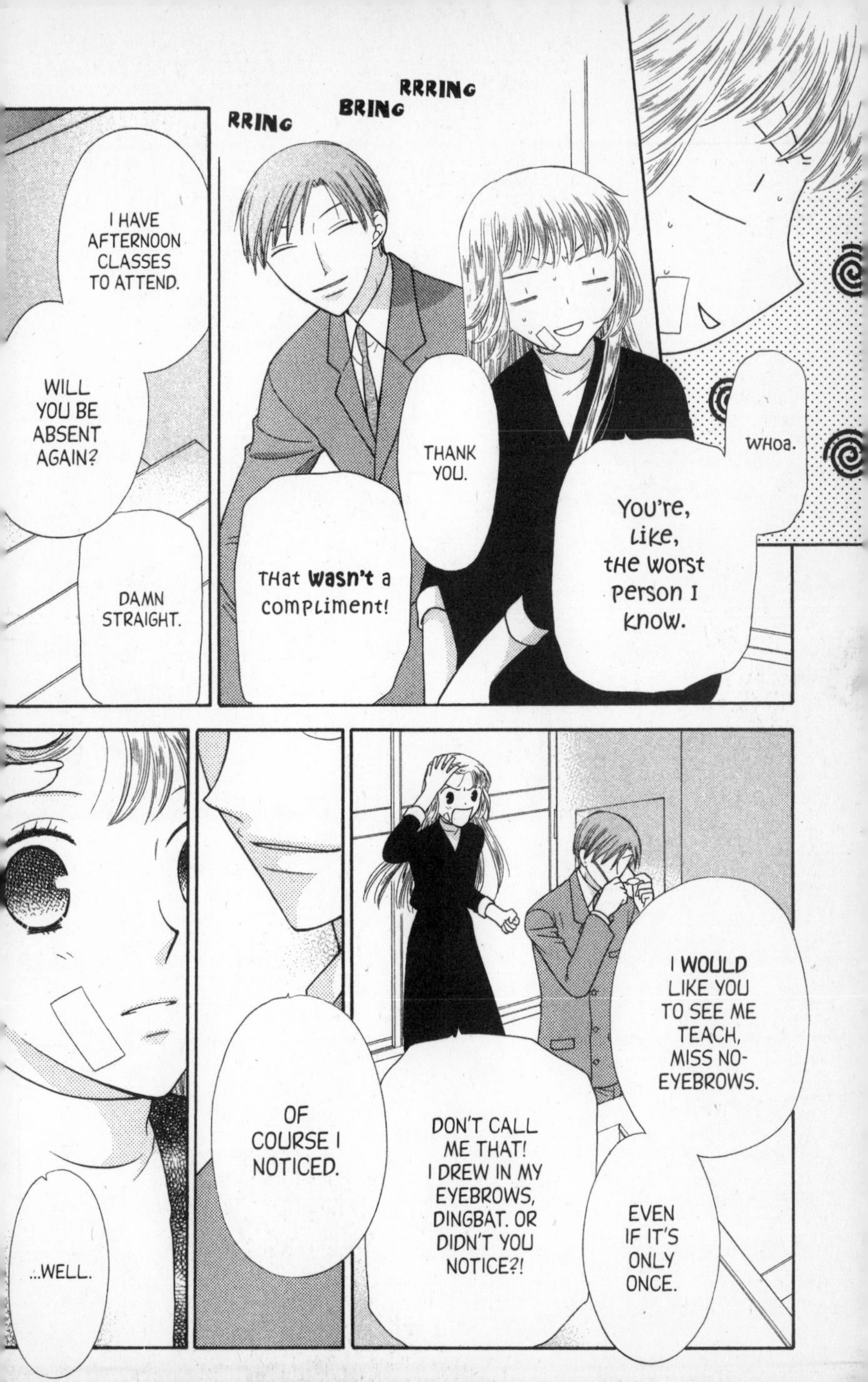

RRRING
BRING
RRING
Whoa.
You're, like, the worst person I know.
THANK YOU.
That **wasn't** a compliment!
I HAVE AFTERNOON CLASSES TO ATTEND.
WILL YOU BE ABSENT AGAIN?
DAMN STRAIGHT.
I **WOULD** LIKE YOU TO SEE ME TEACH, MISS NO-EYEBROWS.
EVEN IF IT'S ONLY ONCE.
DON'T CALL ME THAT! I DREW IN MY EYEBROWS, DINGBAT. OR DIDN'T YOU NOTICE?!
OF COURSE I NOTICED.
...WELL.

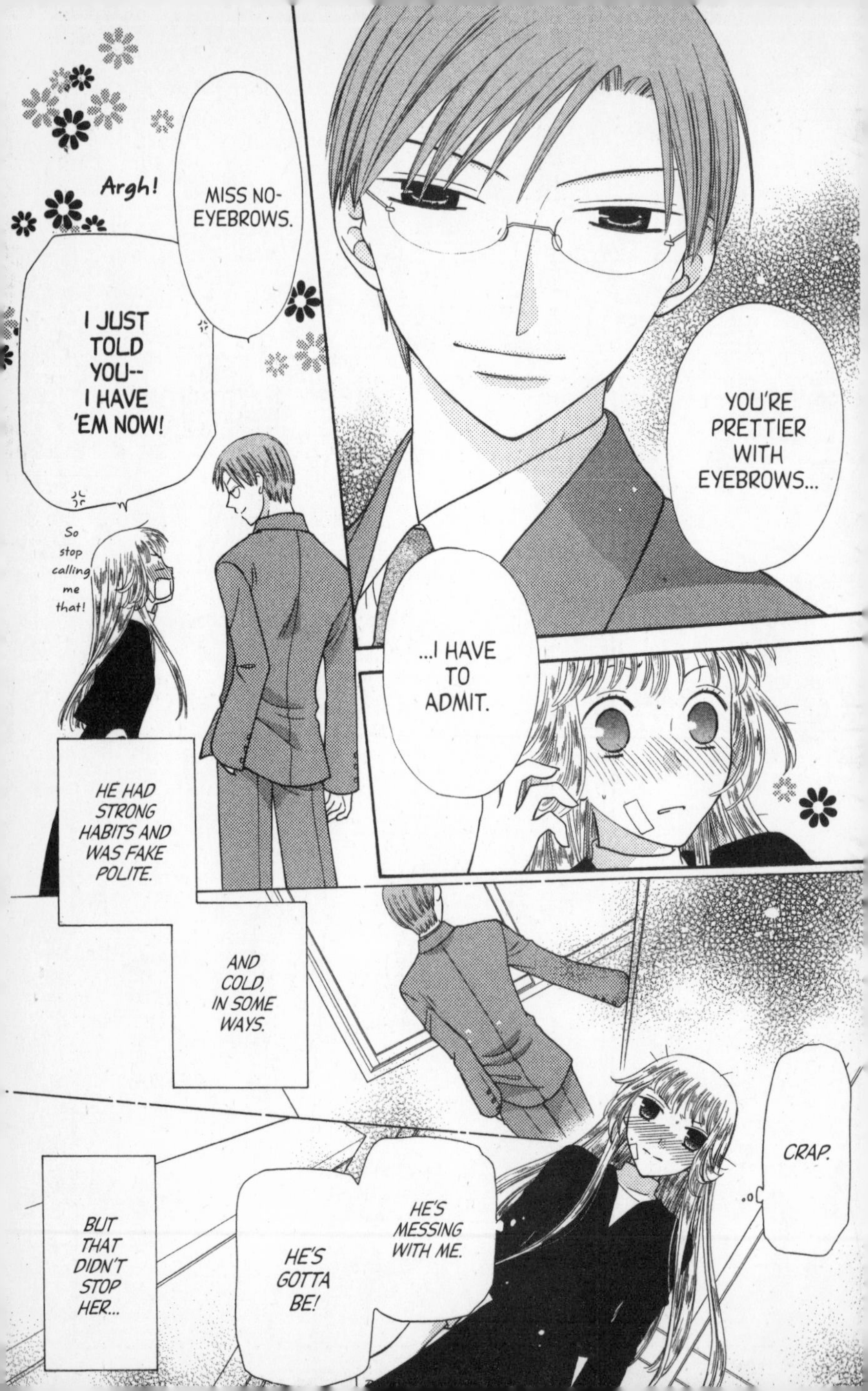

YOU'RE PRETTIER WITH EYEBROWS...
...I HAVE TO ADMIT.
MISS NO-EYEBROWS.
Argh!
I JUST TOLD YOU-- I HAVE 'EM NOW!
So stop calling me that!
HE HAD STRONG HABITS AND WAS FAKE POLITE.
AND COLD, IN SOME WAYS.
CRAP.
HE'S MESSING WITH ME.
HE'S GOTTA BE!
BUT THAT DIDN'T STOP HER...

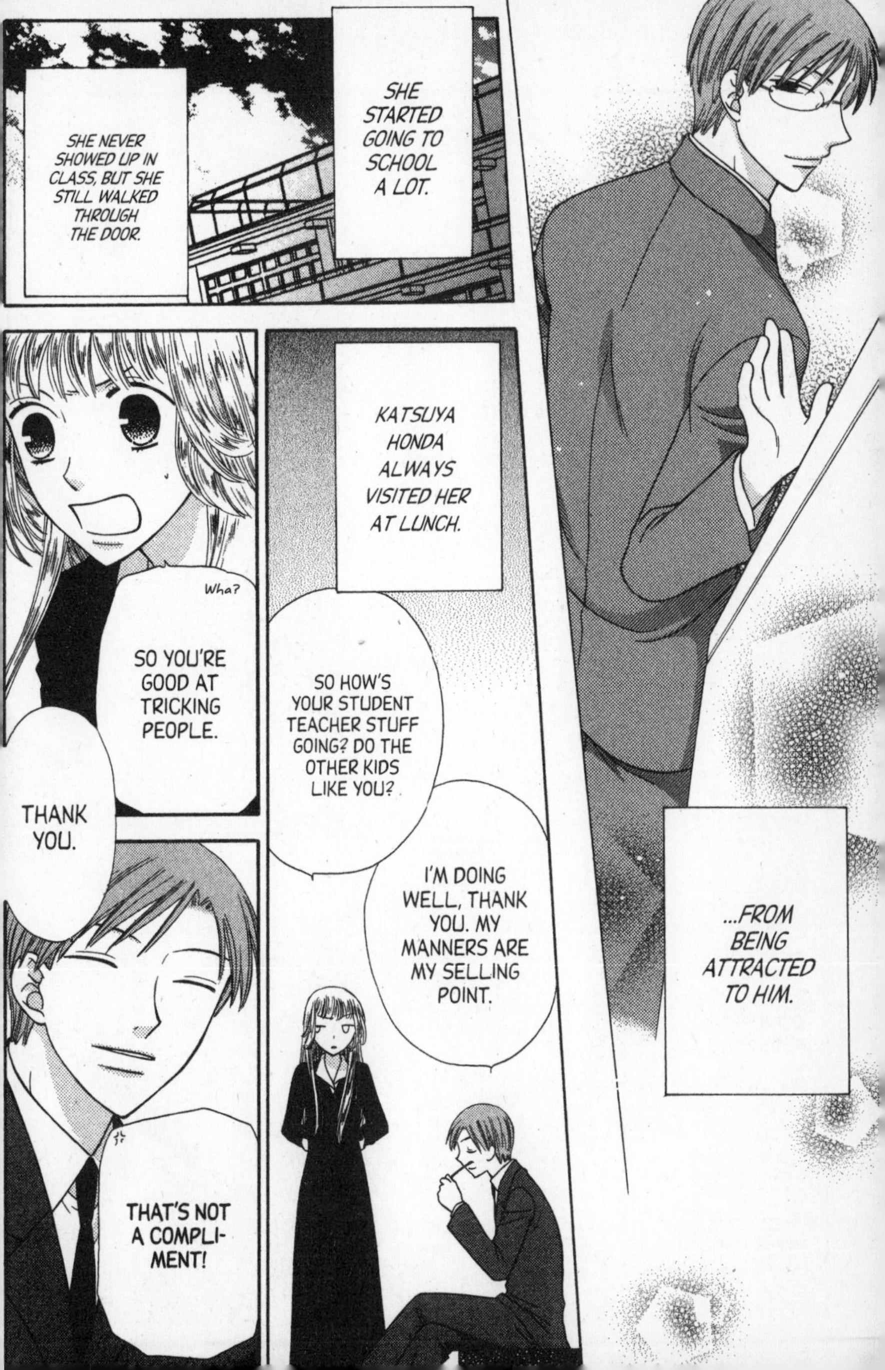
...FROM BEING ATTRACTED TO HIM.
SHE STARTED GOING TO SCHOOL A LOT.
SHE NEVER SHOWED UP IN CLASS, BUT SHE STILL WALKED THROUGH THE DOOR.
KATSUYA HONDA ALWAYS VISITED HER AT LUNCH.
SO HOW'S YOUR STUDENT TEACHER STUFF GOING? DO THE OTHER KIDS LIKE YOU?
I'M DOING WELL, THANK YOU. MY MANNERS ARE MY SELLING POINT.
Wha?
SO YOU'RE GOOD AT TRICKING PEOPLE.
THANK YOU.
THAT'S NOT A COMPLIMENT!

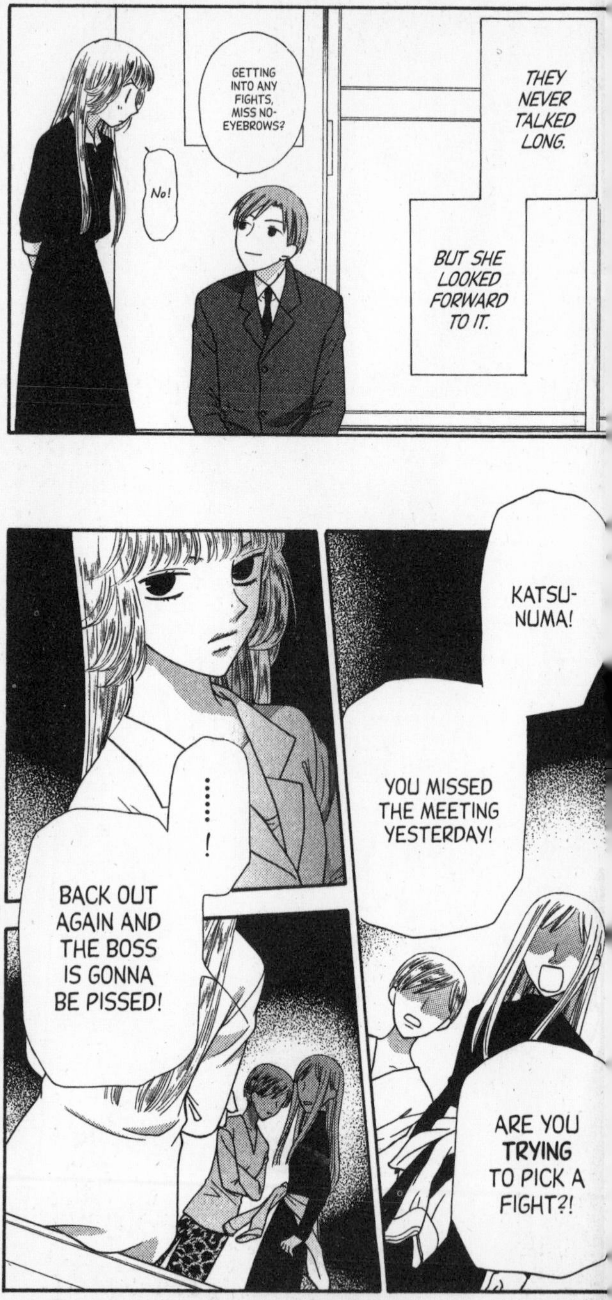
THEY NEVER TALKED LONG.
BUT SHE LOOKED FORWARD TO IT.
GETTING INTO ANY FIGHTS, MISS NO-EYEBROWS?
No!
KATSU-NUMA!
YOU MISSED THE MEETING YESTERDAY!
ARE YOU TRYING TO PICK A FIGHT?!
......!
BACK OUT AGAIN AND THE BOSS IS GONNA BE PISSED!

Why is it so fun drawing girly girls...?

Kagura

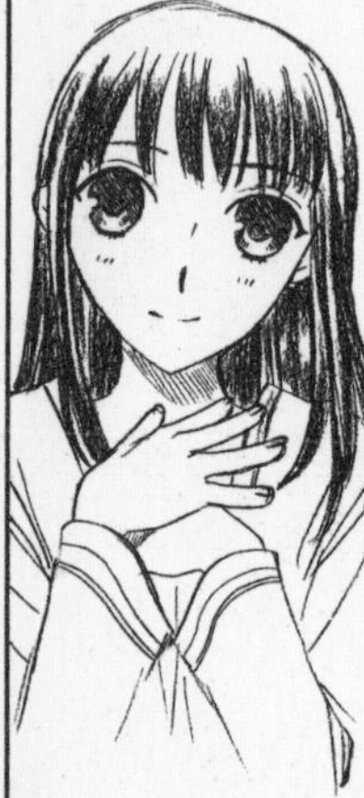

With her father and mother, Kagura's in a family of three.

As of Volume 16, she's a sophomore in junior college...right?

Her parents love her very much.

Kagura's house is more independent than the houses of the other members of the Zodiac.

Essentially, she's an older sister type who's always ready to help.

She gets along with everybody. Rin is the only one she's awkward with, but that's a matter of Rin's feelings.

She gets along especially well with Ritchan.

←To be continued

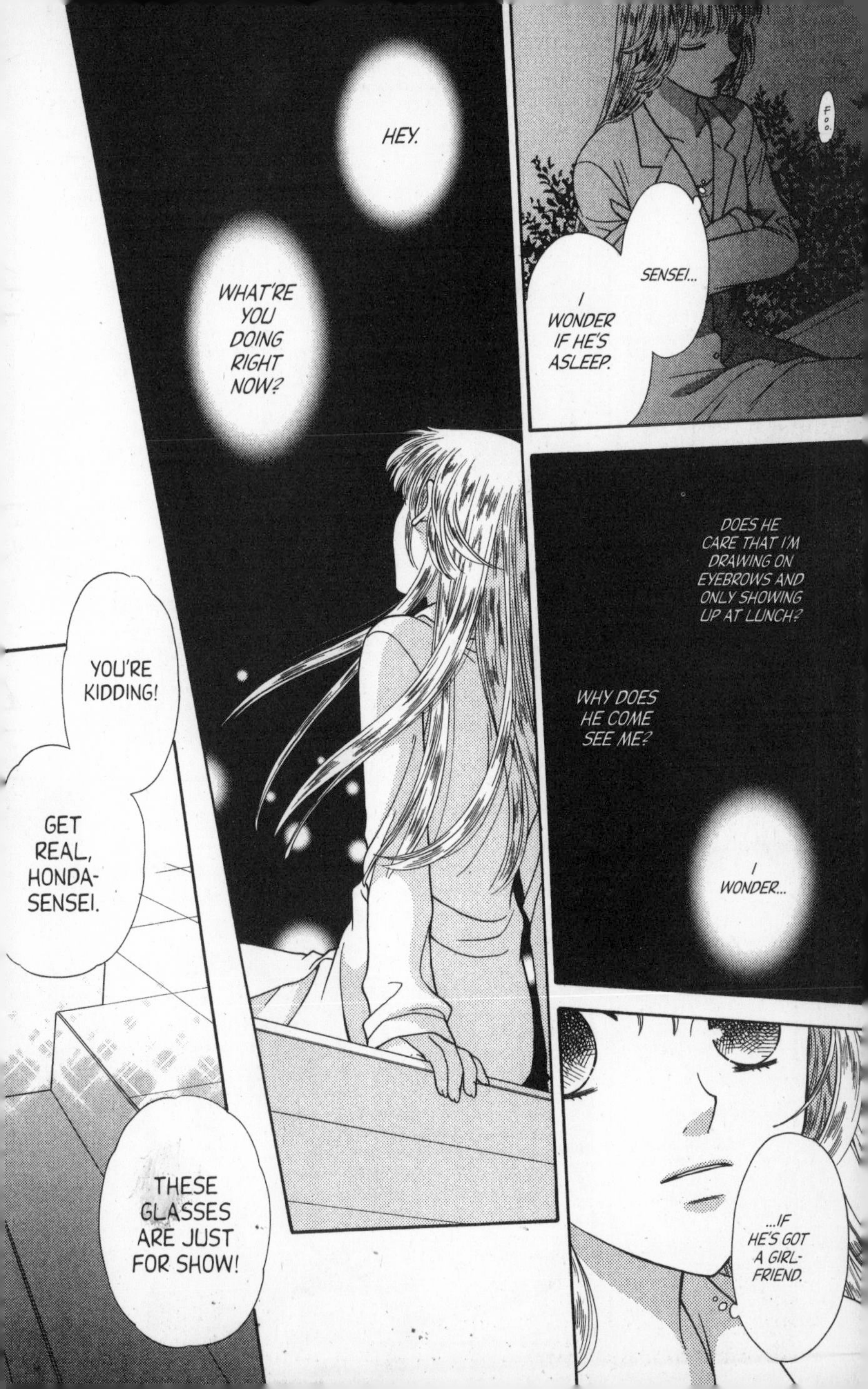
Foo.
SENSEI...
I WONDER IF HE'S ASLEEP.
DOES HE CARE THAT I'M DRAWING ON EYEBROWS AND ONLY SHOWING UP AT LUNCH?
WHY DOES HE COME SEE ME?
I WONDER...
...IF HE'S GOT A GIRL-FRIEND.
HEY.
WHAT'RE YOU DOING RIGHT NOW?
YOU'RE KIDDING!
GET REAL, HONDA-SENSEI.
THESE GLASSES ARE JUST FOR SHOW!

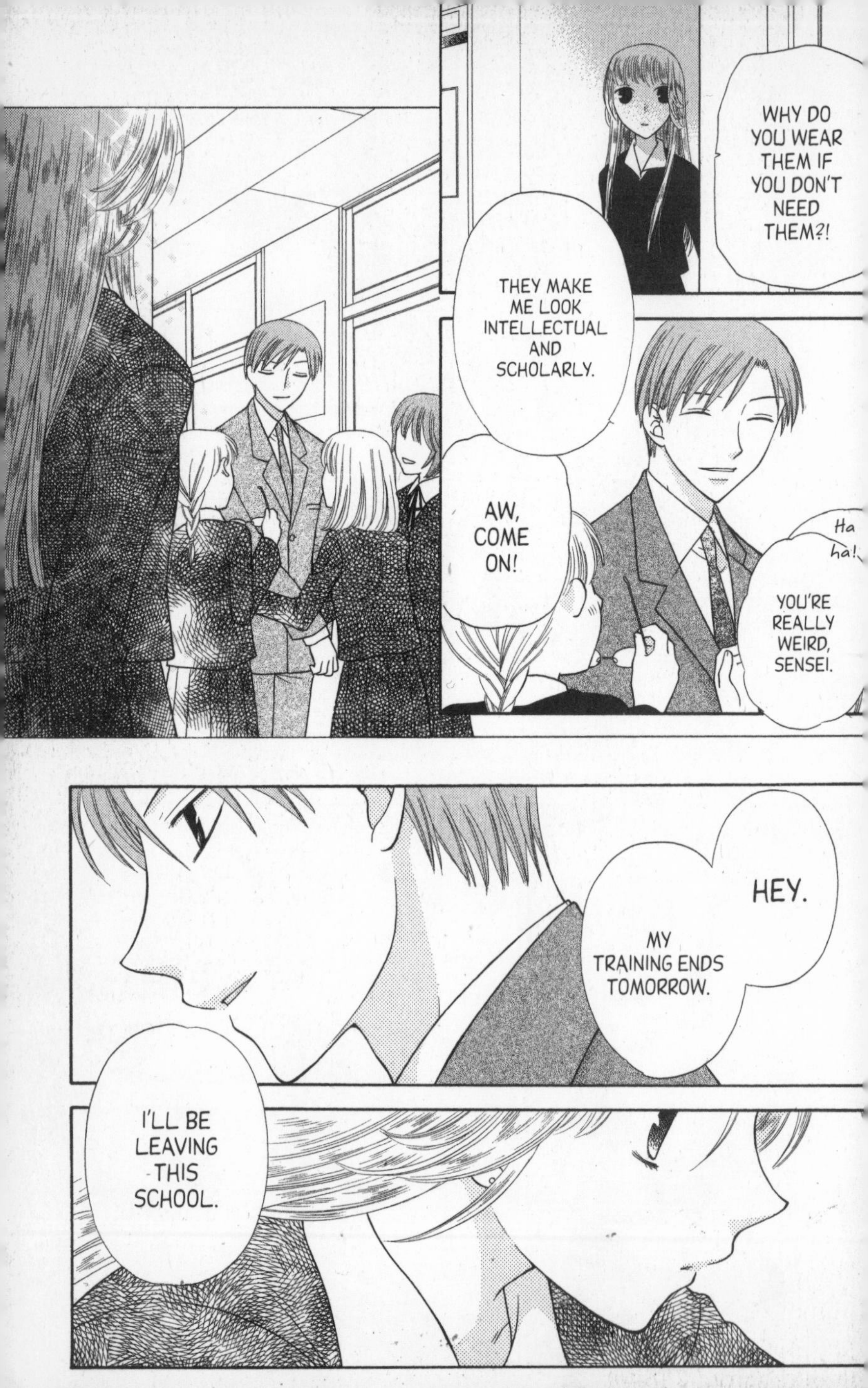
WHY DO YOU WEAR THEM IF YOU DON'T NEED THEM?!
THEY MAKE ME LOOK INTELLECTUAL AND SCHOLARLY.
AW, COME ON!
Ha ha!
YOU'RE REALLY WEIRD, SENSEI.
HEY.
MY TRAINING ENDS TOMORROW.
I'LL BE LEAVING THIS SCHOOL.

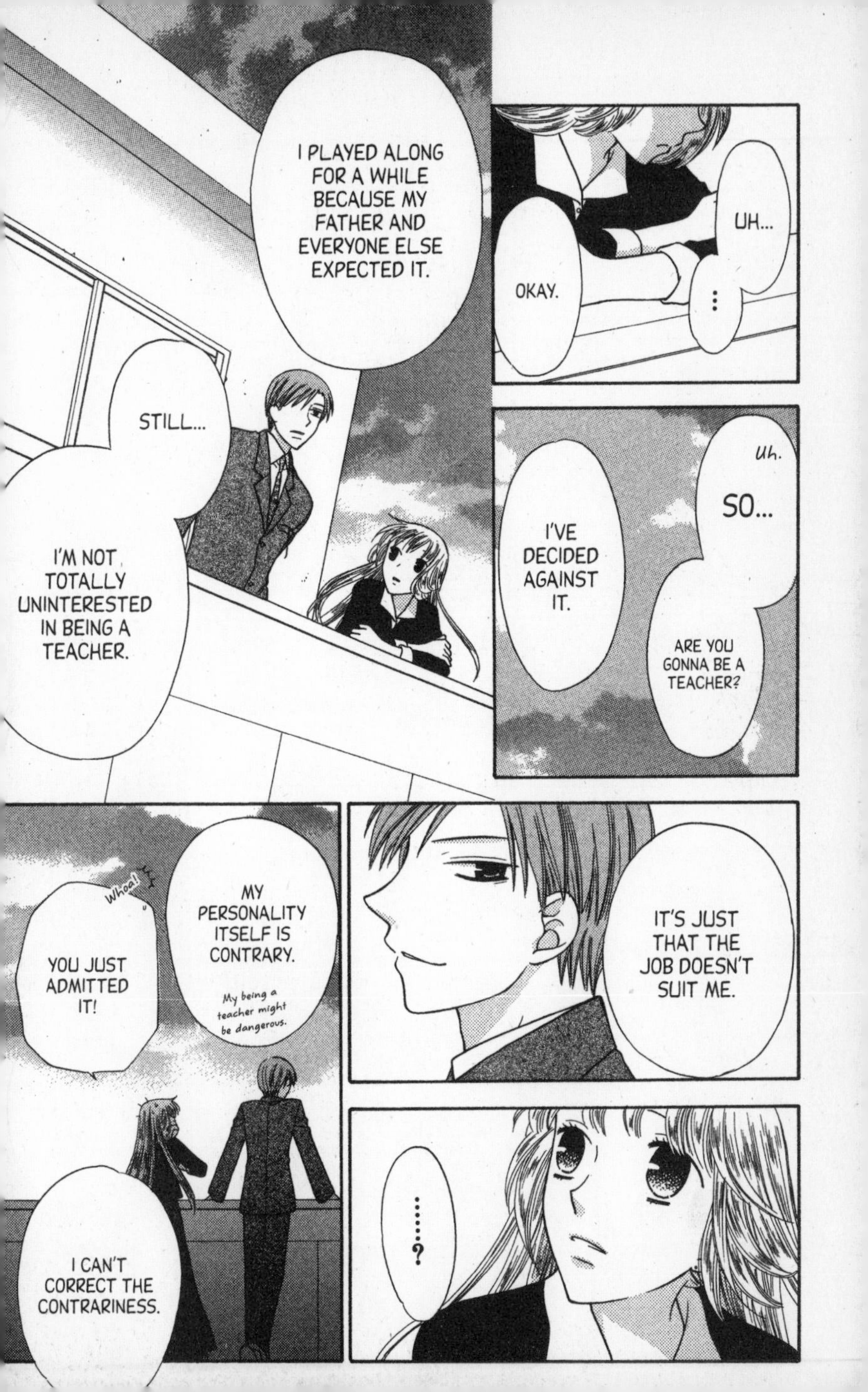
UH...
...
OKAY.
Uh.
SO...
ARE YOU GONNA BE A TEACHER?
I'VE DECIDED AGAINST IT.
I PLAYED ALONG FOR A WHILE BECAUSE MY FATHER AND EVERYONE ELSE EXPECTED IT.
STILL...
I'M NOT TOTALLY UNINTERESTED IN BEING A TEACHER.
IT'S JUST THAT THE JOB DOESN'T SUIT ME.
......?
MY PERSONALITY ITSELF IS CONTRARY.
My being a teacher might be dangerous.
Whoa!
YOU JUST ADMITTED IT!
I CAN'T CORRECT THE CONTRARINESS.

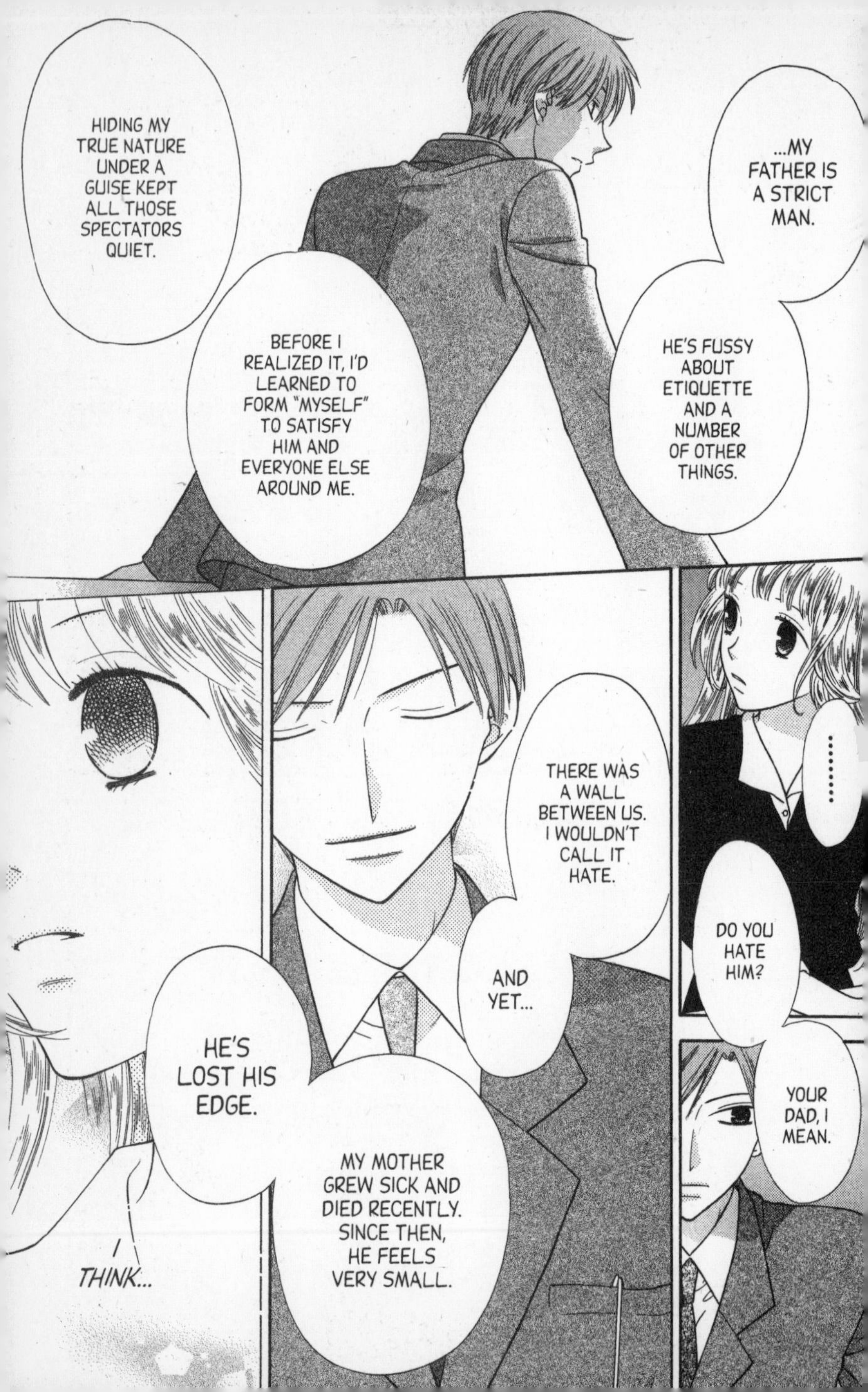
...MY FATHER IS A STRICT MAN.
HE'S FUSSY ABOUT ETIQUETTE AND A NUMBER OF OTHER THINGS.
BEFORE I REALIZED IT, I'D LEARNED TO FORM "MYSELF" TO SATISFY HIM AND EVERYONE ELSE AROUND ME.
HIDING MY TRUE NATURE UNDER A GUISE KEPT ALL THOSE SPECTATORS QUIET.
......
DO YOU HATE HIM?
YOUR DAD, I MEAN.
THERE WAS A WALL BETWEEN US. I WOULDN'T CALL IT HATE.
AND YET...
HE'S LOST HIS EDGE.
MY MOTHER GREW SICK AND DIED RECENTLY. SINCE THEN, HE FEELS VERY SMALL.
I THINK...

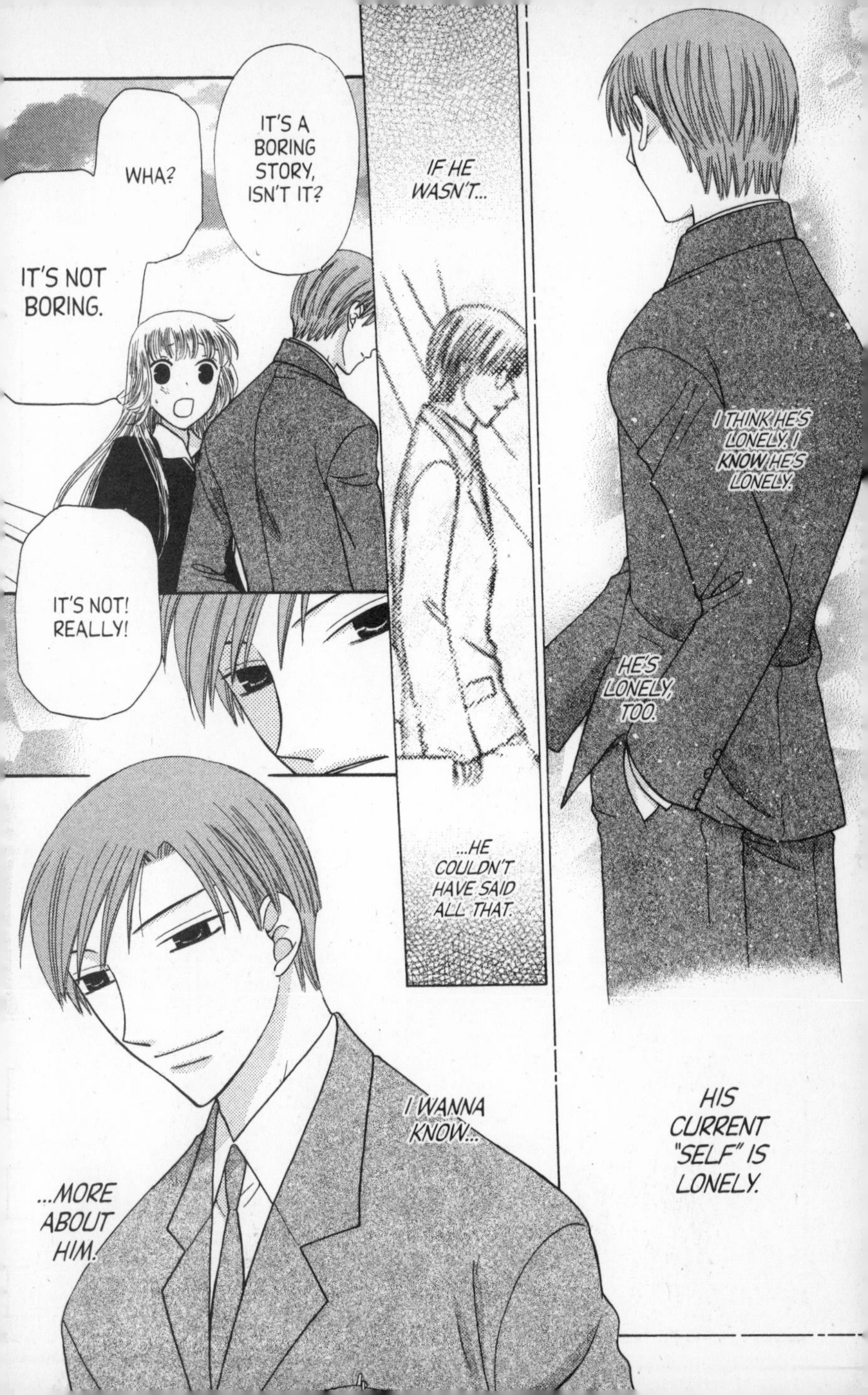
I THINK HE'S LONELY. I KNOW HE'S LONELY.
HE'S LONELY, TOO.
HIS CURRENT "SELF" IS LONELY.
IF HE WASN'T...
...HE COULDN'T HAVE SAID ALL THAT.
IT'S A BORING STORY, ISN'T IT?
WHA?
IT'S NOT BORING.
IT'S NOT! REALLY!
I WANNA KNOW...
...MORE ABOUT HIM.

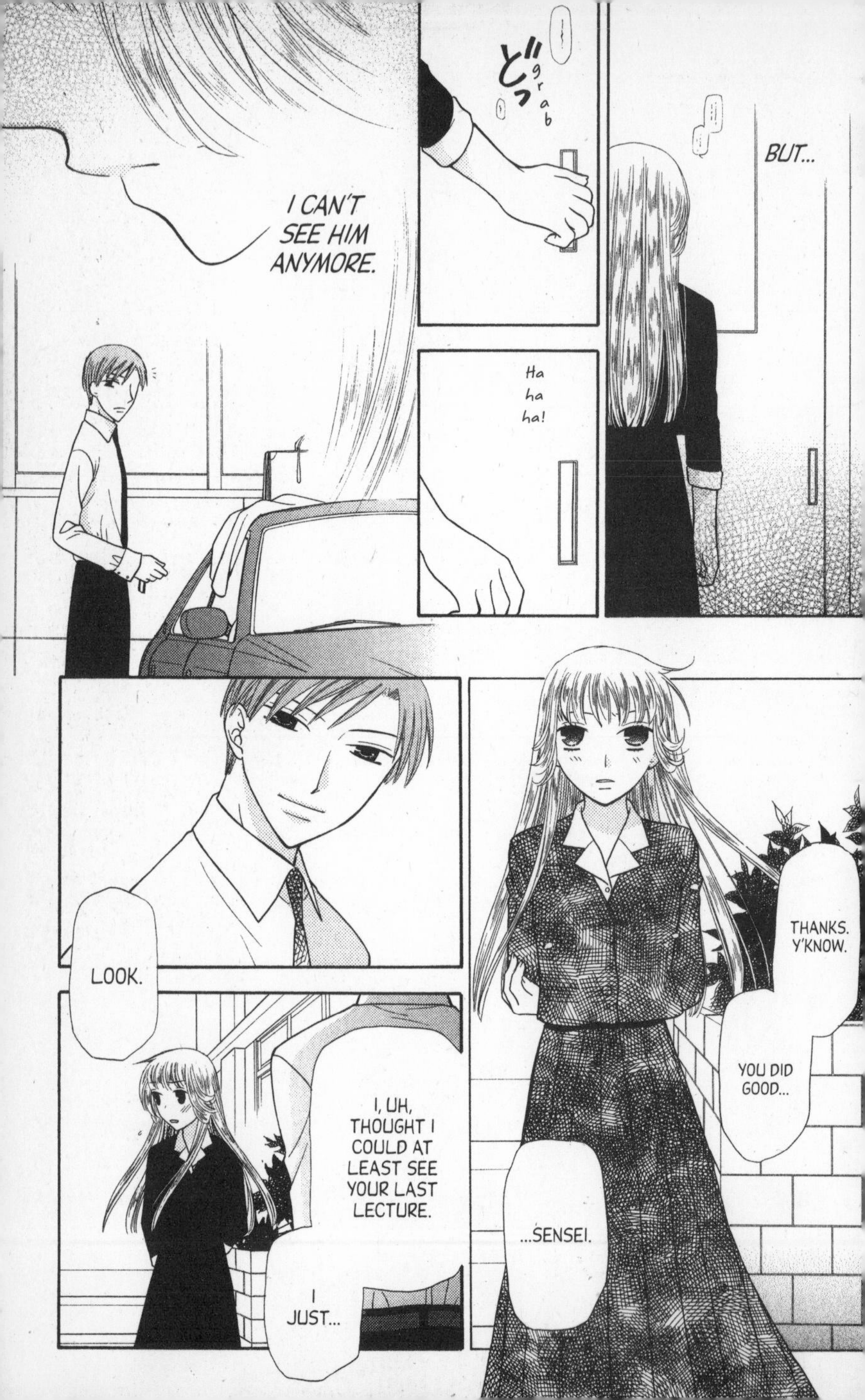
BUT...
!
どっ grab
Ha ha ha!
I CAN'T SEE HIM ANYMORE.
THANKS. Y'KNOW.
YOU DID GOOD...
...SENSEI.
LOOK.
I, UH, THOUGHT I COULD AT LEAST SEE YOUR LAST LECTURE.
I JUST...

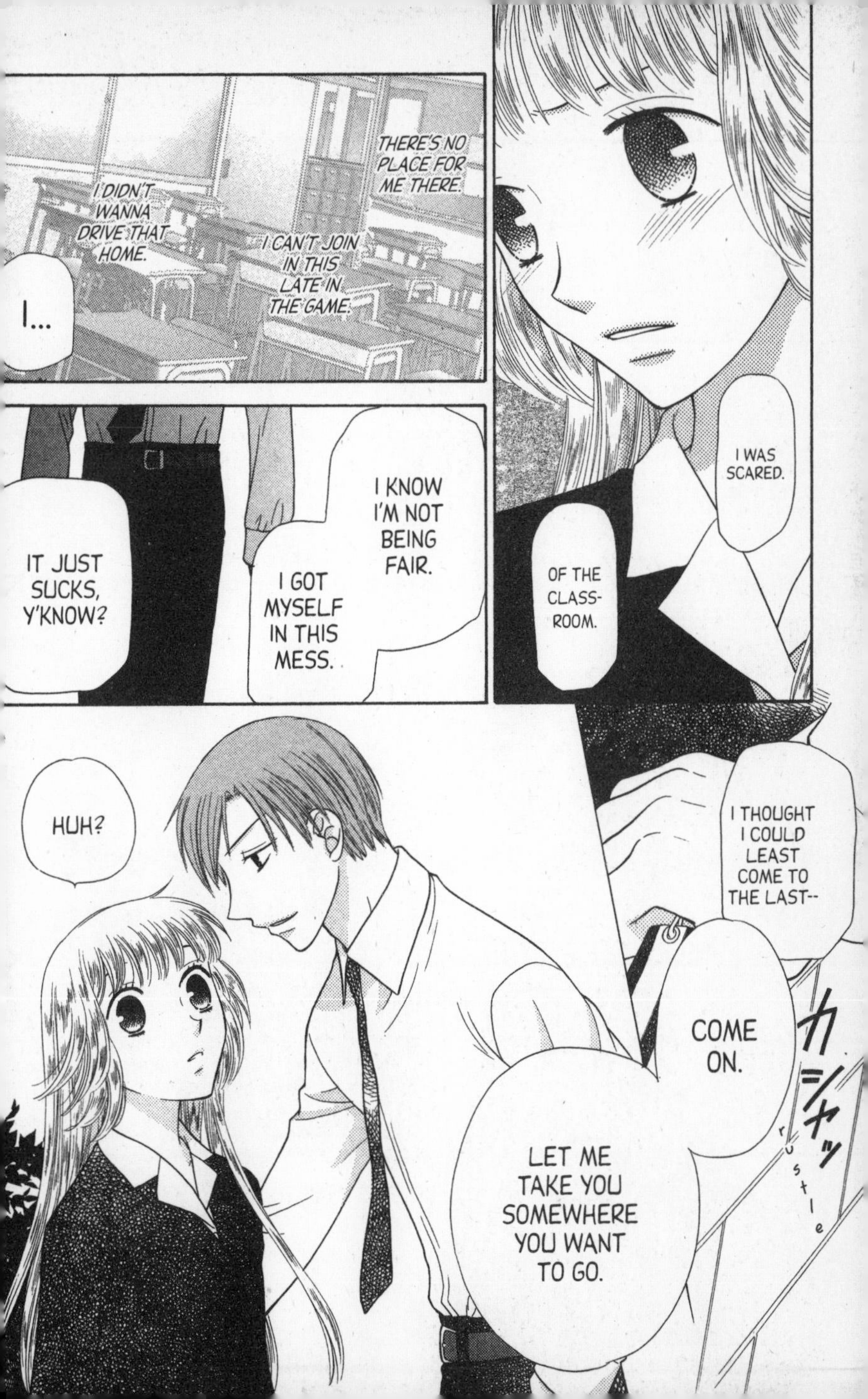
I WAS SCARED.
OF THE CLASS-ROOM.
THERE'S NO PLACE FOR ME THERE.
I CAN'T JOIN IN THIS LATE IN THE GAME.
I DIDN'T WANNA DRIVE THAT HOME.
I...
I KNOW I'M NOT BEING FAIR.
I GOT MYSELF IN THIS MESS.
IT JUST SUCKS, Y'KNOW?
I THOUGHT I COULD LEAST COME TO THE LAST--
rustle
COME ON.
LET ME TAKE YOU SOMEWHERE YOU WANT TO GO.
HUH?

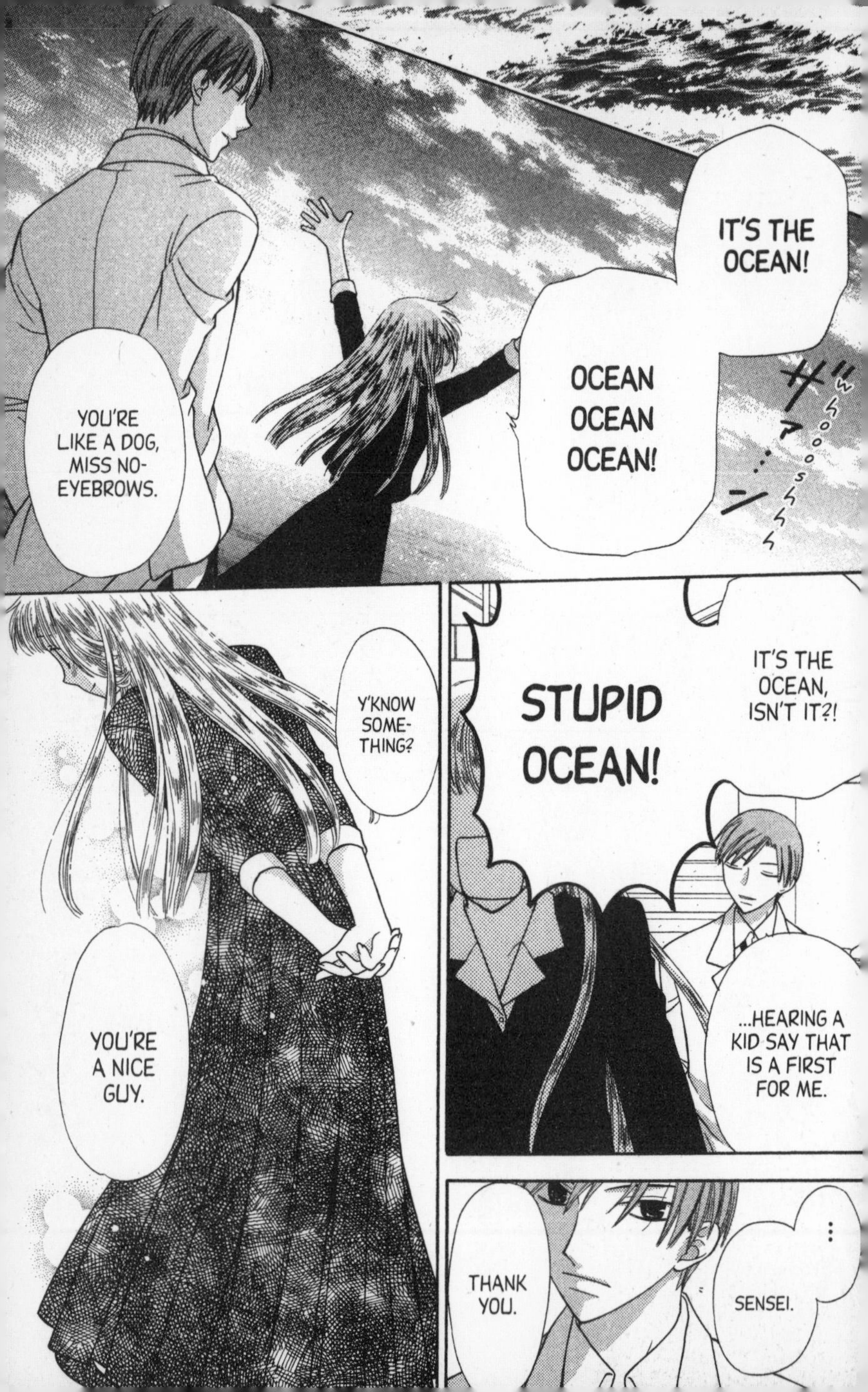
IT'S THE OCEAN!
OCEAN OCEAN OCEAN!
ザァ…ン
whooosshhhh
YOU'RE LIKE A DOG, MISS NO-EYEBROWS.
IT'S THE OCEAN, ISN'T IT?!
STUPID OCEAN!
...HEARING A KID SAY THAT IS A FIRST FOR ME.
...
SENSEI.
THANK YOU.
Y'KNOW SOMETHING?
YOU'RE A NICE GUY.

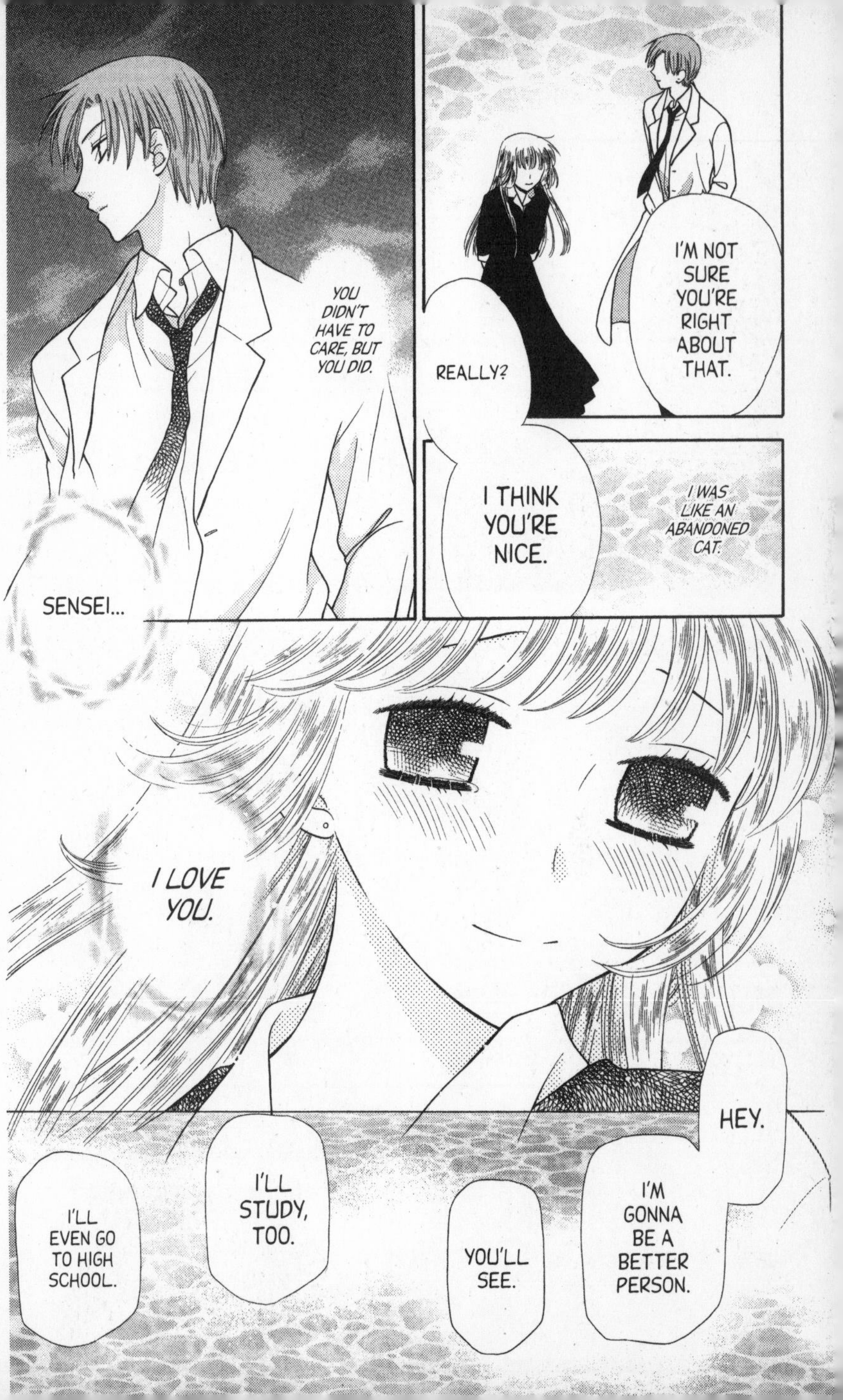
I'M NOT SURE YOU'RE RIGHT ABOUT THAT.
REALLY?
I WAS LIKE AN ABANDONED CAT.
I THINK YOU'RE NICE.
YOU DIDN'T HAVE TO CARE, BUT YOU DID.
SENSEI...
I LOVE YOU.
HEY.
I'M GONNA BE A BETTER PERSON.
YOU'LL SEE.
I'LL STUDY, TOO.
I'LL EVEN GO TO HIGH SCHOOL.

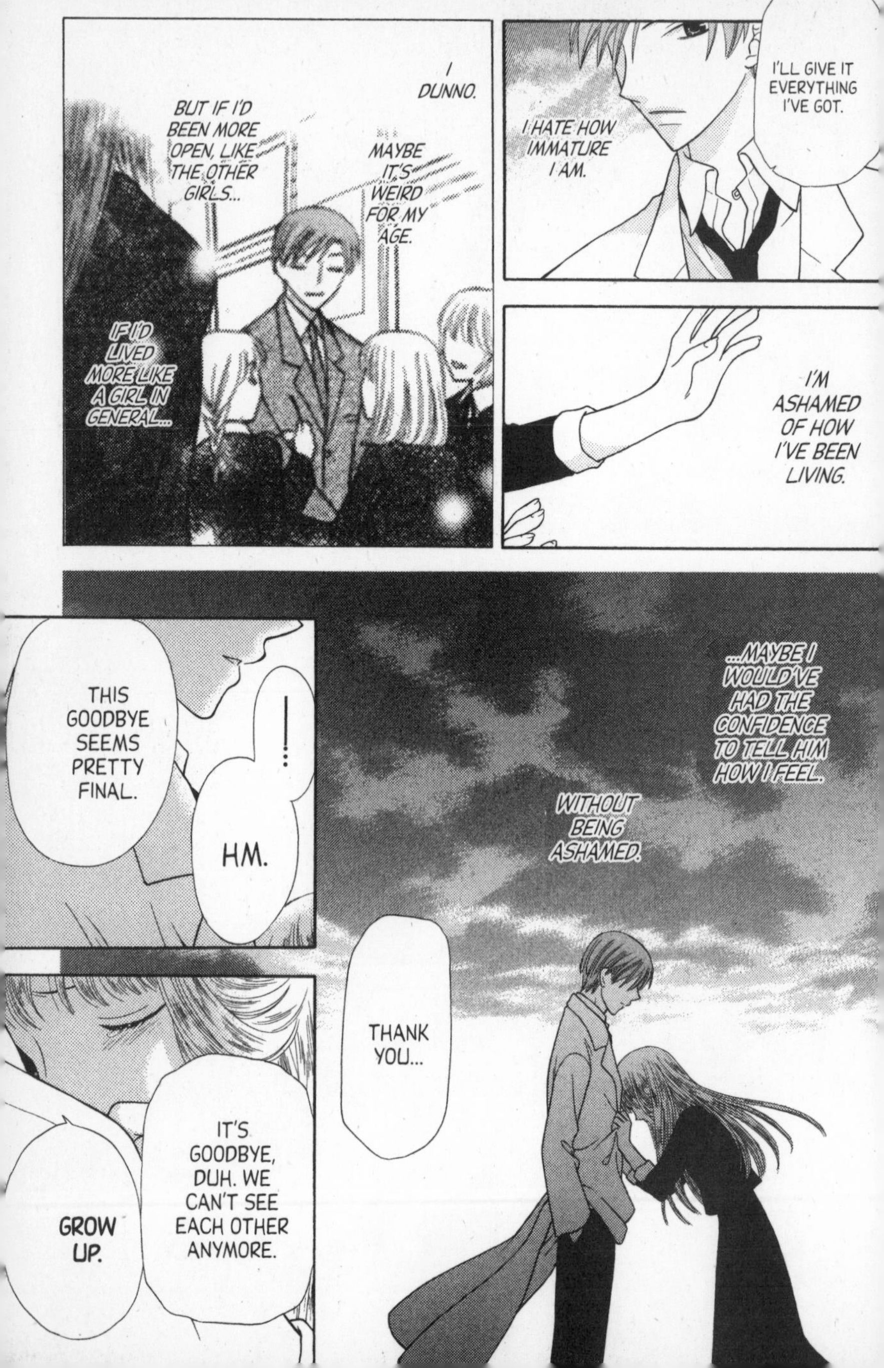
I'LL GIVE IT EVERYTHING I'VE GOT.
I HATE HOW IMMATURE I AM.
I'M ASHAMED OF HOW I'VE BEEN LIVING.
I DUNNO.
MAYBE IT'S WEIRD FOR MY AGE.
BUT IF I'D BEEN MORE OPEN, LIKE THE OTHER GIRLS...
IF I'D LIVED MORE LIKE A GIRL IN GENERAL...
...MAYBE I WOULD'VE HAD THE CONFIDENCE TO TELL HIM HOW I FEEL.
WITHOUT BEING ASHAMED.
THANK YOU...
THIS GOODBYE SEEMS PRETTY FINAL.
...!
HM.
IT'S GOODBYE, DUH. WE CAN'T SEE EACH OTHER ANYMORE.
GROW UP.

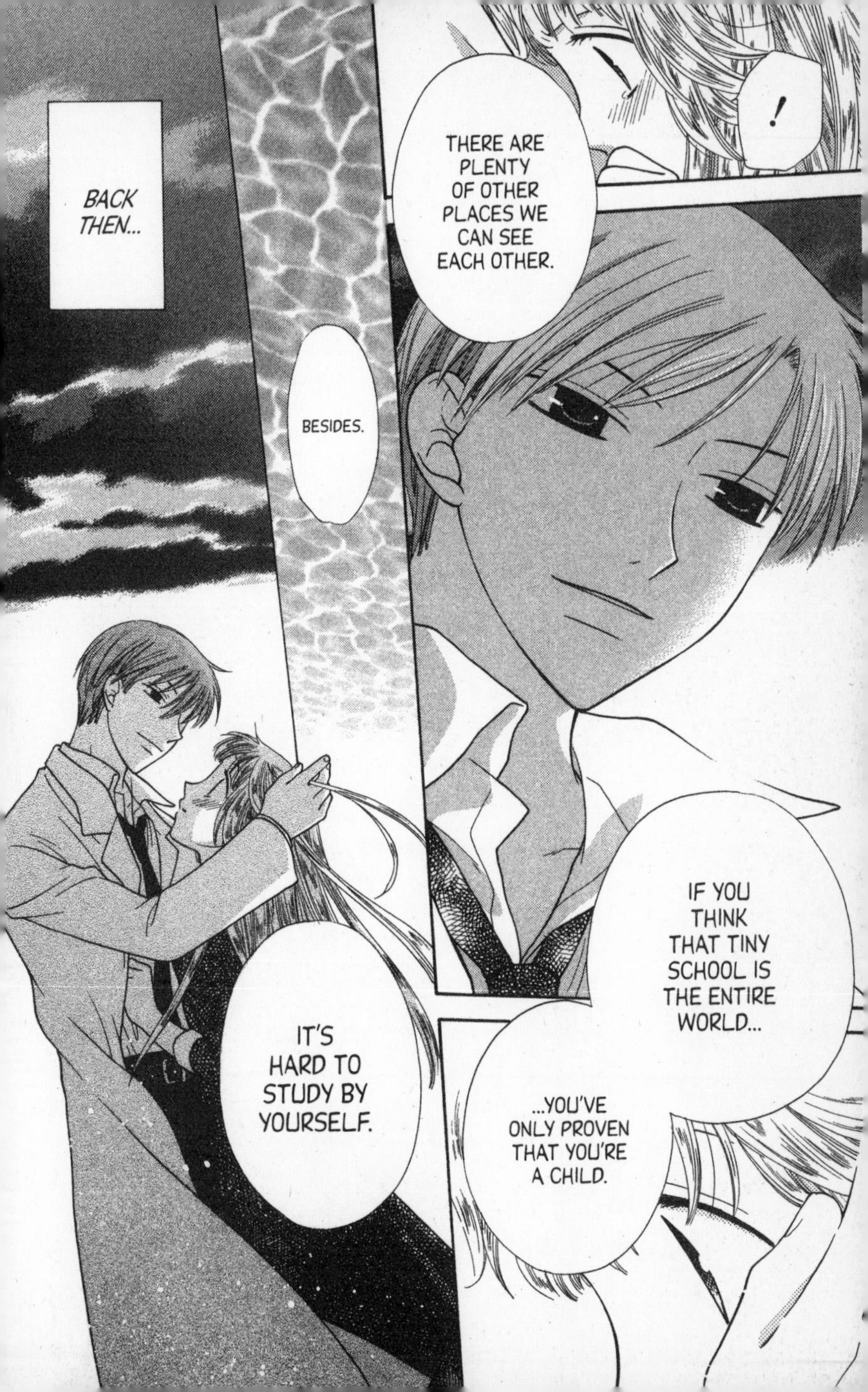
!
THERE ARE PLENTY OF OTHER PLACES WE CAN SEE EACH OTHER.
IF YOU THINK THAT TINY SCHOOL IS THE ENTIRE WORLD...
...YOU'VE ONLY PROVEN THAT YOU'RE A CHILD.
BESIDES.
BACK THEN...
IT'S HARD TO STUDY BY YOURSELF.

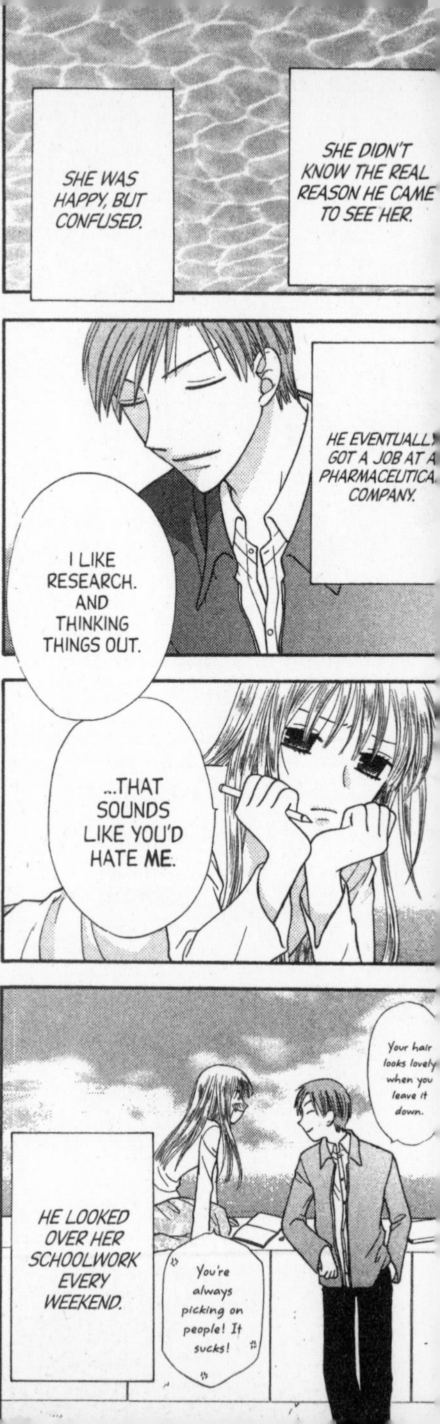
SHE DIDN'T KNOW THE REAL REASON HE CAME TO SEE HER.
SHE WAS HAPPY, BUT CONFUSED.
HE EVENTUALL GOT A JOB AT A PHARMACEUTICA COMPANY.
I LIKE RESEARCH. AND THINKING THINGS OUT.
...THAT SOUNDS LIKE YOU'D HATE ME.
Your hair looks lovely when you leave it down.
HE LOOKED OVER HER SCHOOLWORK EVERY WEEKEND.
You're always picking on people! It sucks!

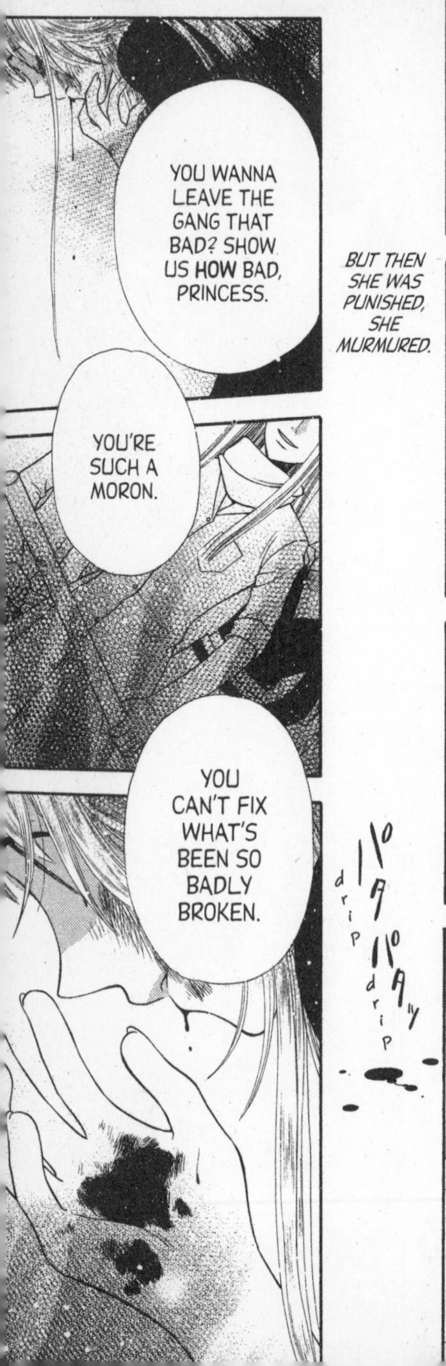
BUT THEN SHE WAS PUNISHED, SHE MURMURED.
YOU WANNA LEAVE THE GANG THAT BAD? SHOW US HOW BAD, PRINCESS.
YOU'RE SUCH A MORON.
YOU CAN'T FIX WHAT'S BEEN SO BADLY BROKEN.
drip
drip

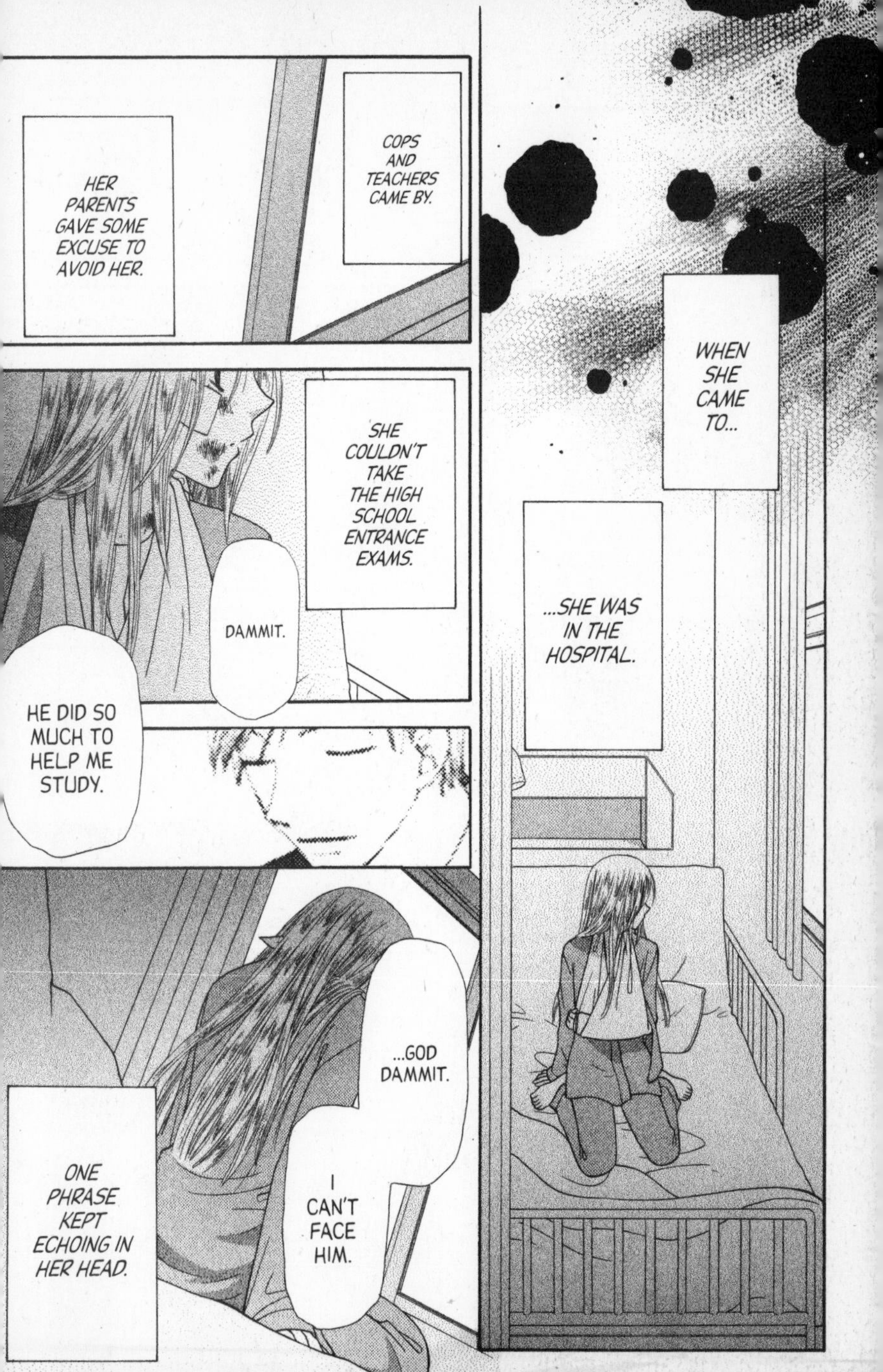
WHEN SHE CAME TO...
...SHE WAS IN THE HOSPITAL.
COPS AND TEACHERS CAME BY.
HER PARENTS GAVE SOME EXCUSE TO AVOID HER.
SHE COULDN'T TAKE THE HIGH SCHOOL ENTRANCE EXAMS.
DAMMIT.
HE DID SO MUCH TO HELP ME STUDY.
...GOD DAMMIT.
I CAN'T FACE HIM.
ONE PHRASE KEPT ECHOING IN HER HEAD.

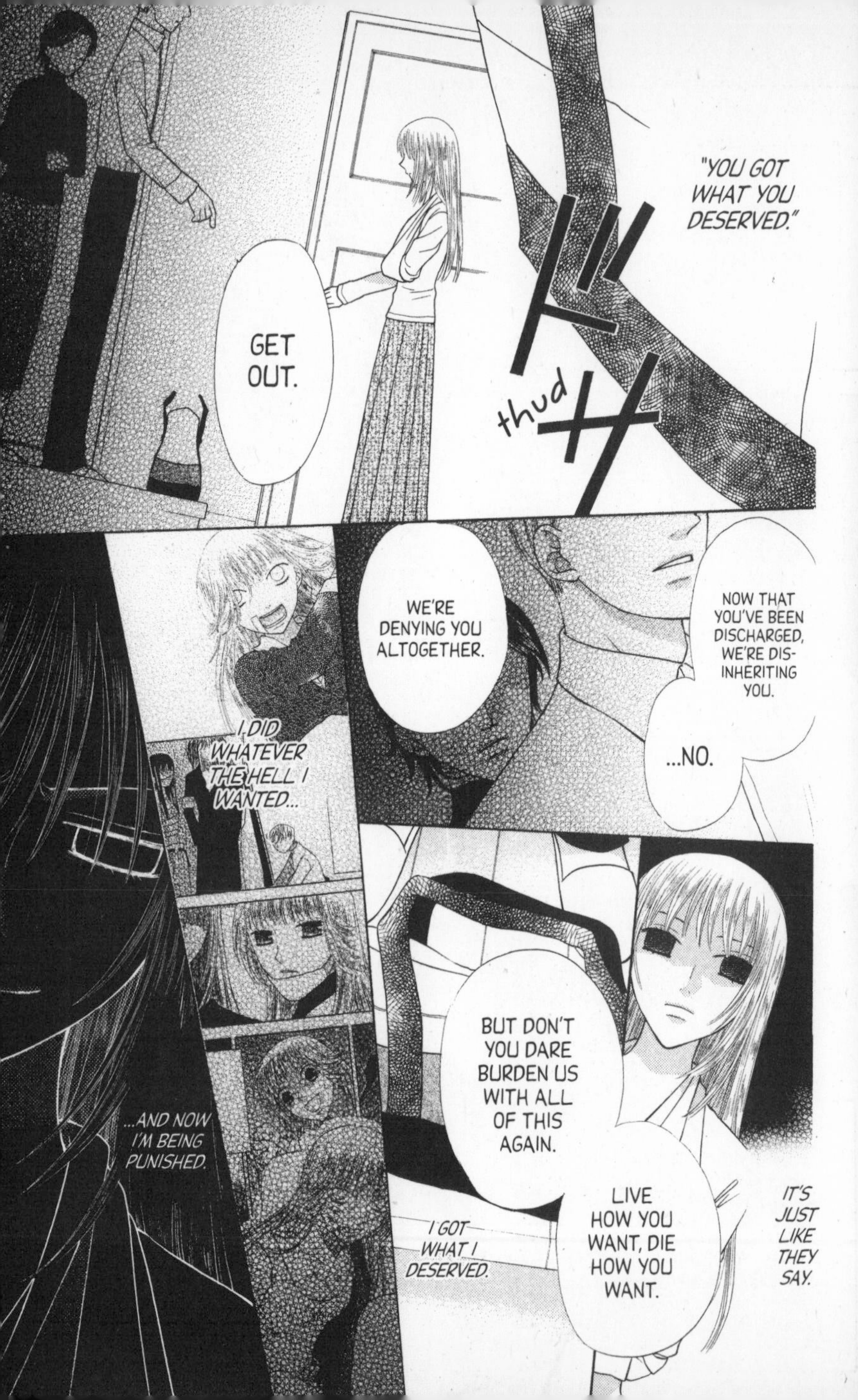
"YOU GOT WHAT YOU DESERVED."
thud
GET OUT.
NOW THAT YOU'VE BEEN DISCHARGED, WE'RE DIS-INHERITING YOU.
...NO.
WE'RE DENYING YOU ALTOGETHER.
IT'S JUST LIKE THEY SAY.
LIVE HOW YOU WANT, DIE HOW YOU WANT.
BUT DON'T YOU DARE BURDEN US WITH ALL OF THIS AGAIN.
I GOT WHAT I DESERVED.
I DID WHATEVER THE HELL I WANTED...
...AND NOW I'M BEING PUNISHED.

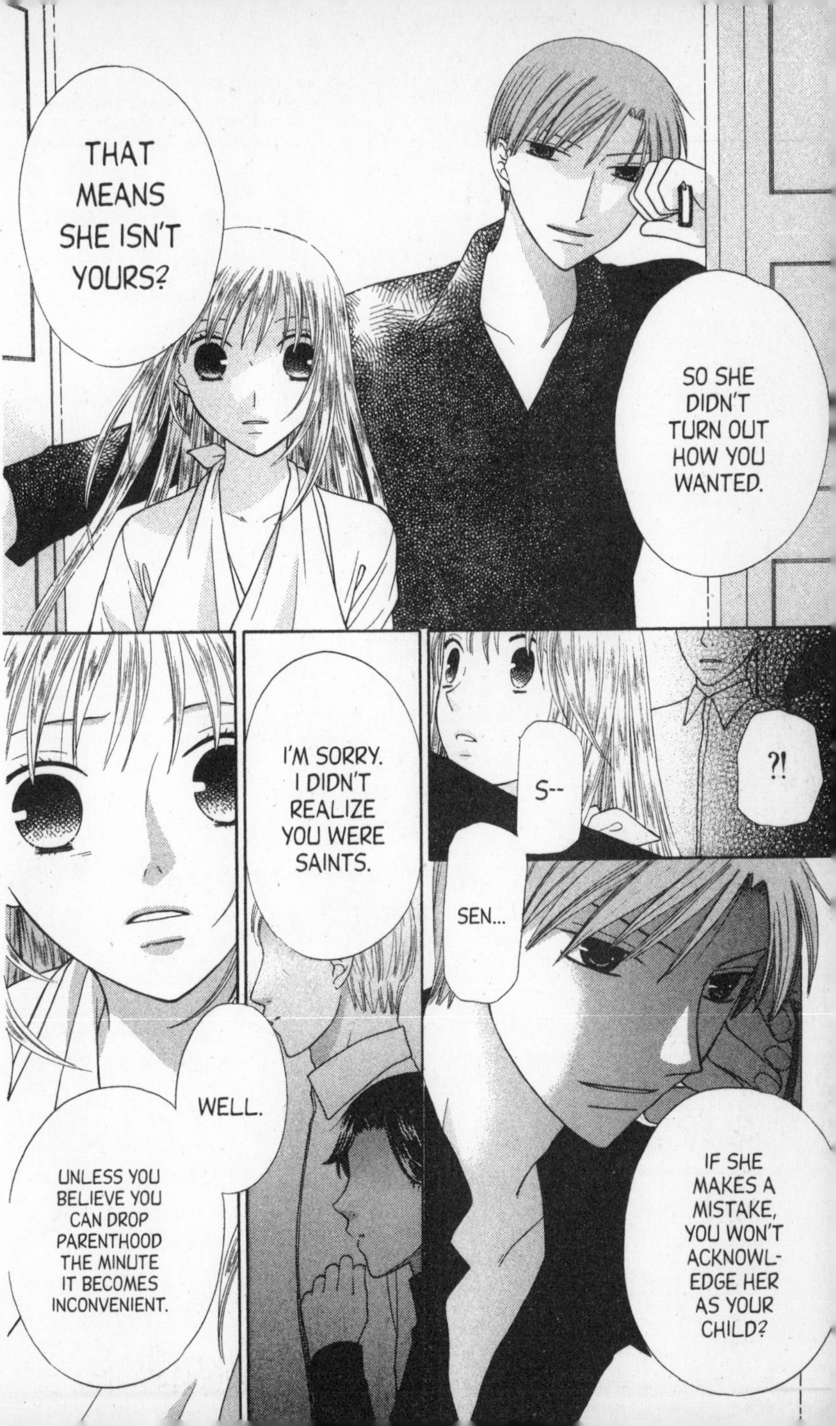
SO SHE DIDN'T TURN OUT HOW YOU WANTED.
THAT MEANS SHE ISN'T YOURS?
?!
S--
SEN...
IF SHE MAKES A MISTAKE, YOU WON'T ACKNOWL-EDGE HER AS YOUR CHILD?
I'M SORRY. I DIDN'T REALIZE YOU WERE SAINTS.
WELL.
UNLESS YOU BELIEVE YOU CAN DROP PARENTHOOD THE MINUTE IT BECOMES INCONVENIENT.

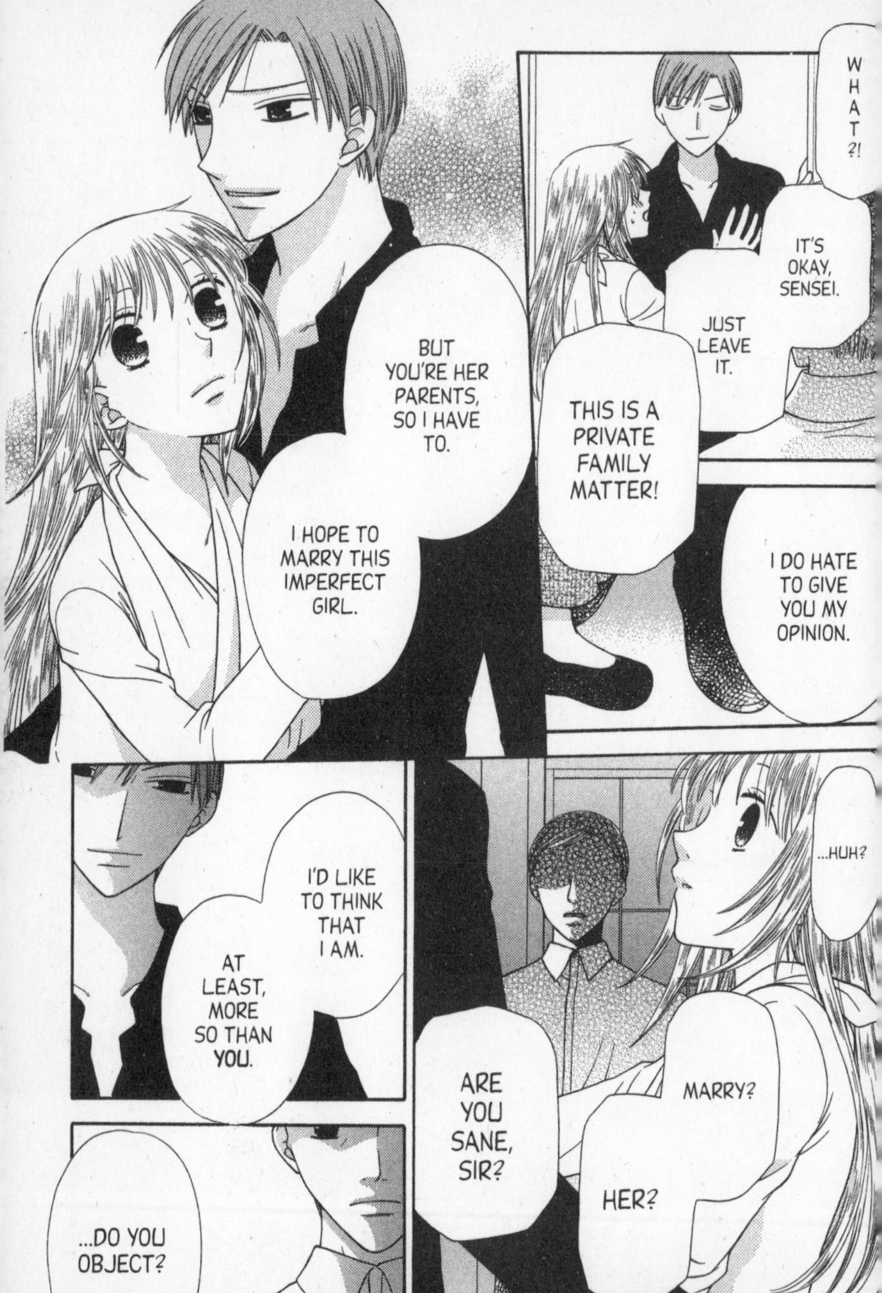
WHAT?!
IT'S OKAY, SENSEI.
JUST LEAVE IT.
THIS IS A PRIVATE FAMILY MATTER!
I DO HATE TO GIVE YOU MY OPINION.
BUT YOU'RE HER PARENTS, SO I HAVE TO.
I HOPE TO MARRY THIS IMPERFECT GIRL.
...HUH?
MARRY?
HER?
ARE YOU SANE, SIR?
I'D LIKE TO THINK THAT I AM.
AT LEAST, MORE SO THAN YOU.
...DO YOU OBJECT?

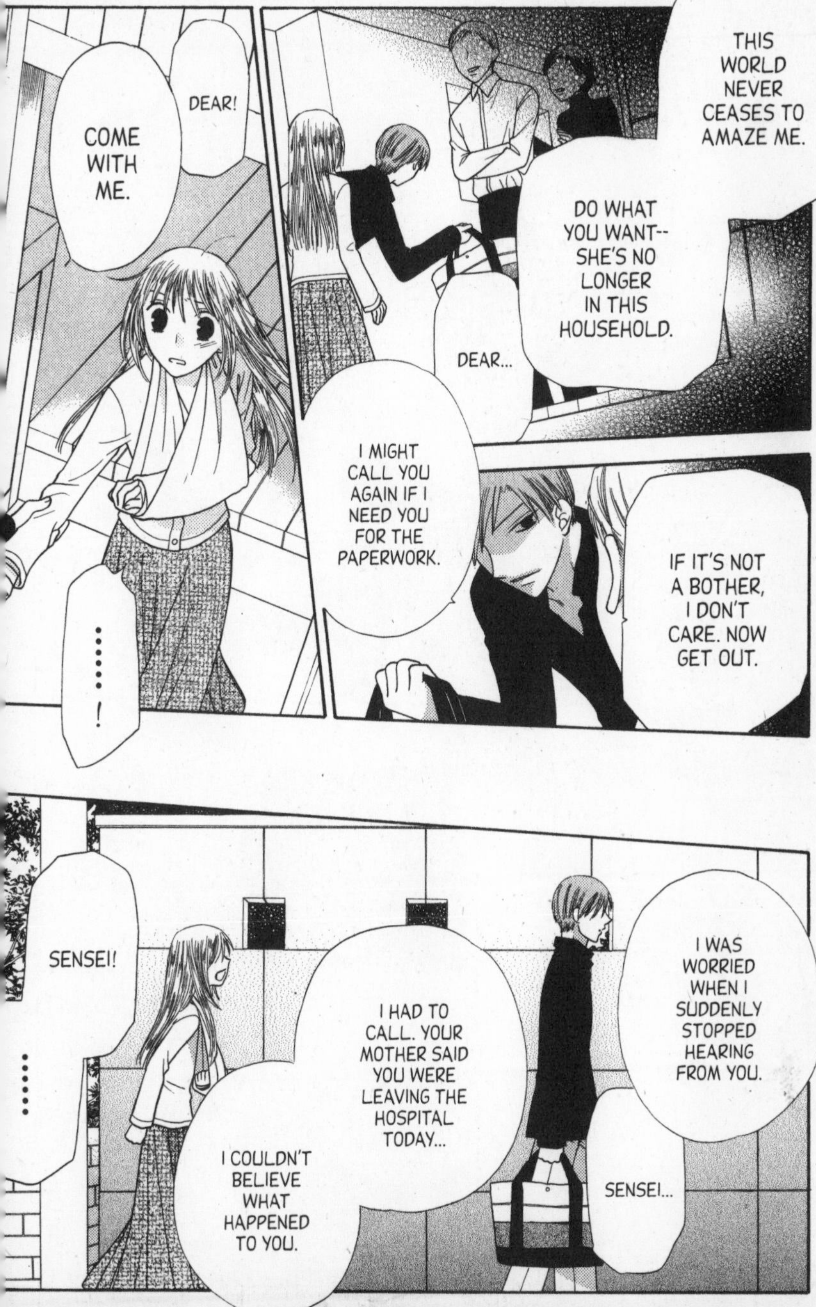
THIS WORLD NEVER CEASES TO AMAZE ME.
DO WHAT YOU WANT-- SHE'S NO LONGER IN THIS HOUSEHOLD.
DEAR...
I MIGHT CALL YOU AGAIN IF I NEED YOU FOR THE PAPERWORK.
IF IT'S NOT A BOTHER, I DON'T CARE. NOW GET OUT.
DEAR!
COME WITH ME.
......!
I WAS WORRIED WHEN I SUDDENLY STOPPED HEARING FROM YOU.
SENSEI...
I HAD TO CALL. YOUR MOTHER SAID YOU WERE LEAVING THE HOSPITAL TODAY...
I COULDN'T BELIEVE WHAT HAPPENED TO YOU.
SENSEI!
......

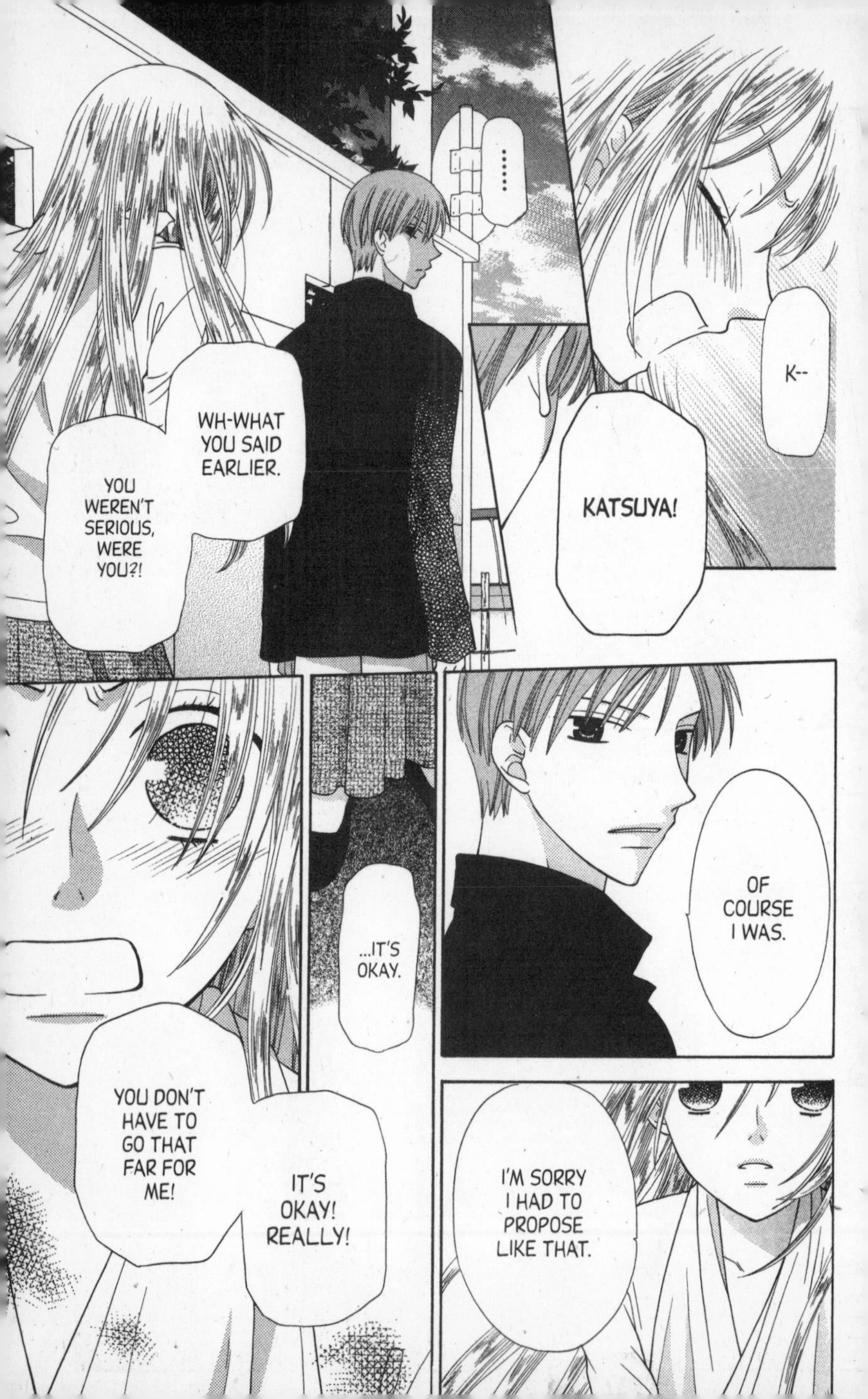
K--
KATSUYA!
......
WH-WHAT YOU SAID EARLIER.
YOU WEREN'T SERIOUS, WERE YOU?!
OF COURSE I WAS.
I'M SORRY I HAD TO PROPOSE LIKE THAT.
...IT'S OKAY.
YOU DON'T HAVE TO GO THAT FAR FOR ME!
IT'S OKAY! REALLY!

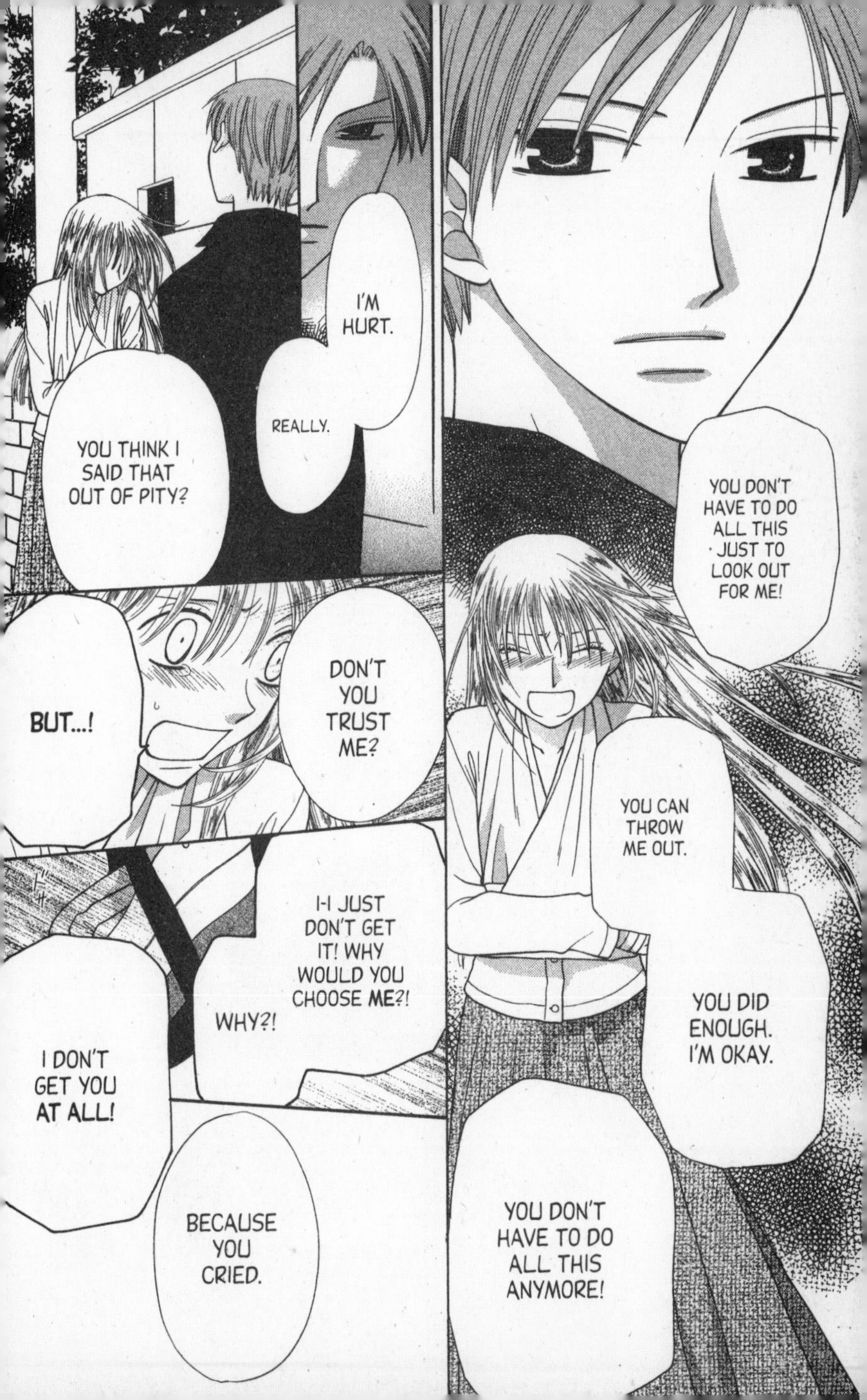
YOU DON'T HAVE TO DO ALL THIS JUST TO LOOK OUT FOR ME!
YOU CAN THROW ME OUT.
YOU DID ENOUGH. I'M OKAY.
YOU DON'T HAVE TO DO ALL THIS ANYMORE!
I'M HURT.
REALLY.
YOU THINK I SAID THAT OUT OF PITY?
DON'T YOU TRUST ME?
BUT...!
I-I JUST DON'T GET IT! WHY WOULD YOU CHOOSE ME?!
WHY?!
I DON'T GET YOU AT ALL!
BECAUSE YOU CRIED.

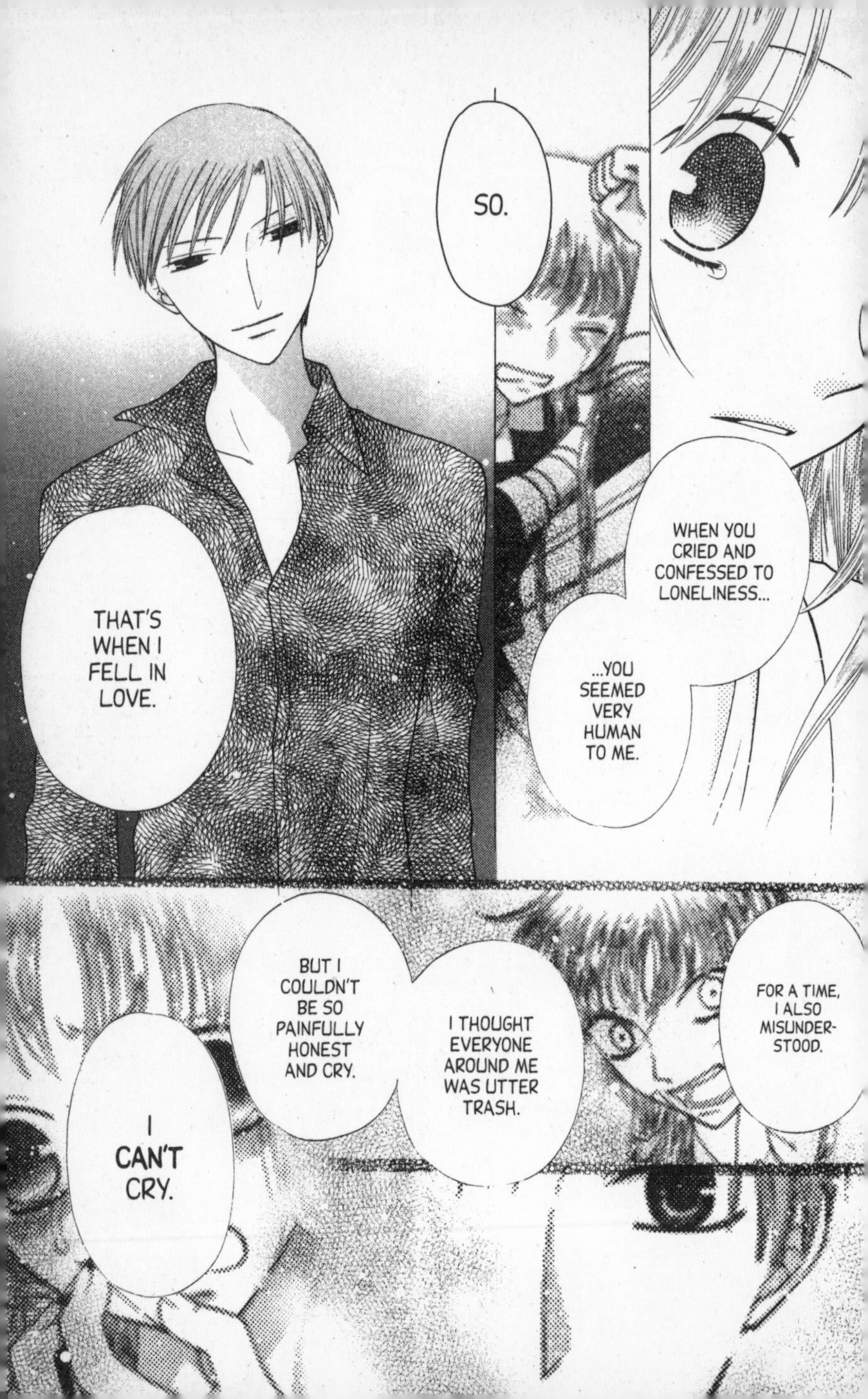
WHEN YOU CRIED AND CONFESSED TO LONELINESS...
...YOU SEEMED VERY HUMAN TO ME.
SO.
THAT'S WHEN I FELL IN LOVE.
FOR A TIME, I ALSO MISUNDERSTOOD.
I THOUGHT EVERYONE AROUND ME WAS UTTER TRASH.
BUT I COULDN'T BE SO PAINFULLY HONEST AND CRY.
I CAN'T CRY.

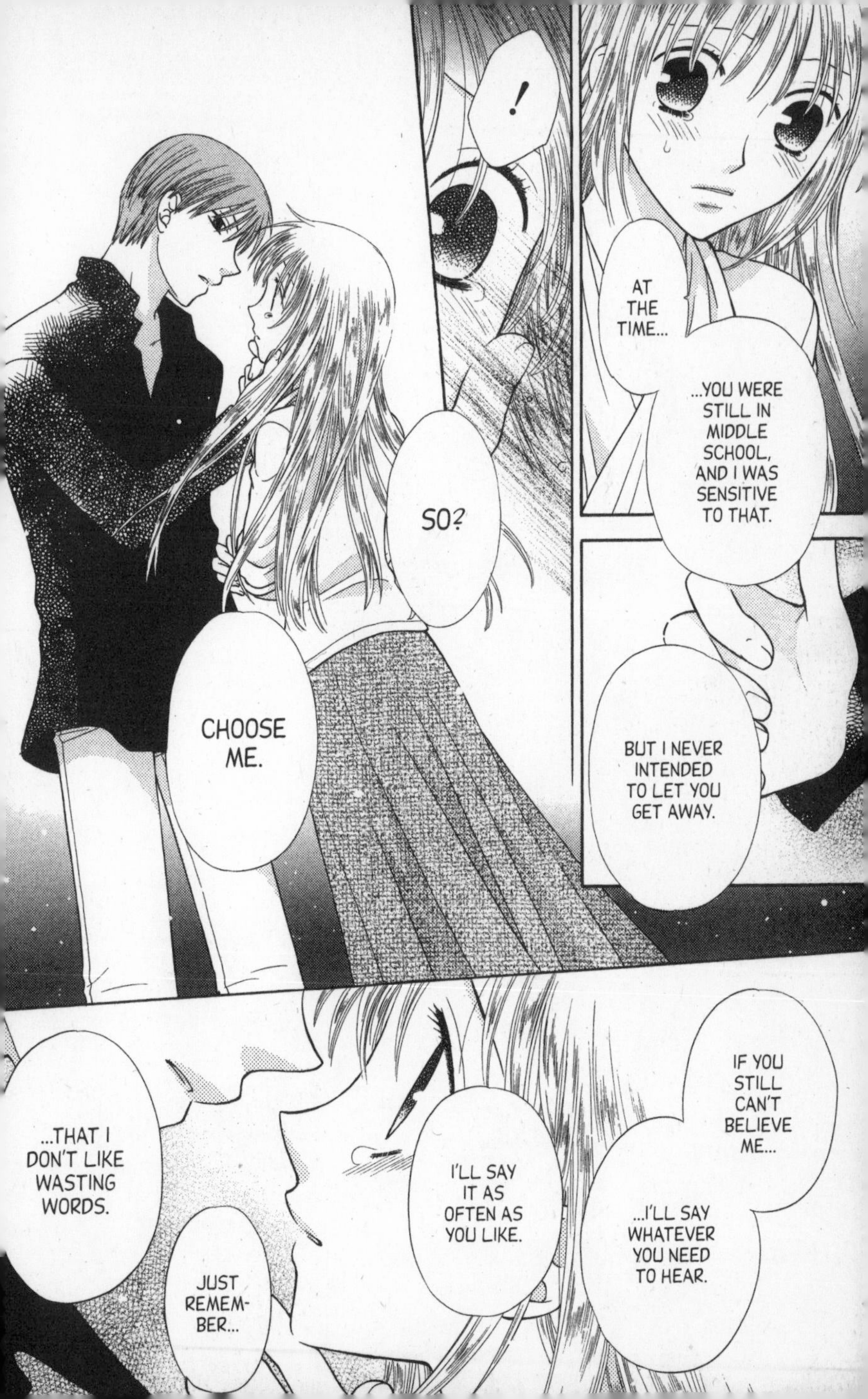
AT THE TIME...
...YOU WERE STILL IN MIDDLE SCHOOL, AND I WAS SENSITIVE TO THAT.
BUT I NEVER INTENDED TO LET YOU GET AWAY.
!
SO?
CHOOSE ME.
IF YOU STILL CAN'T BELIEVE ME...
...I'LL SAY WHATEVER YOU NEED TO HEAR.
I'LL SAY IT AS OFTEN AS YOU LIKE.
JUST REMEMBER...
...THAT I DON'T LIKE WASTING WORDS.

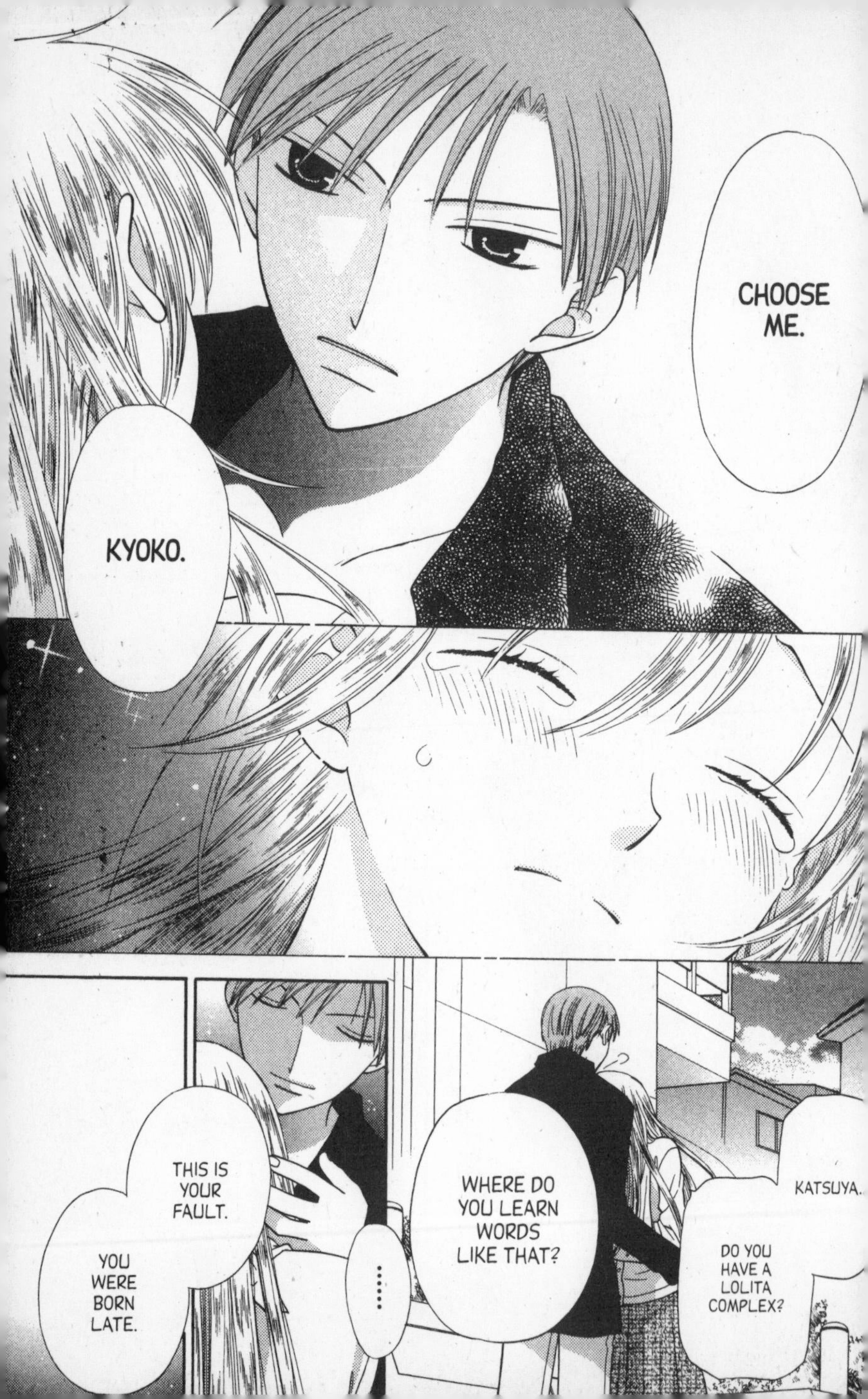

CHOOSE ME.
KYOKO.
KATSUYA...
DO YOU HAVE A LOLITA COMPLEX?
WHERE DO YOU LEARN WORDS LIKE THAT?
......
THIS IS YOUR FAULT.
YOU WERE BORN LATE.

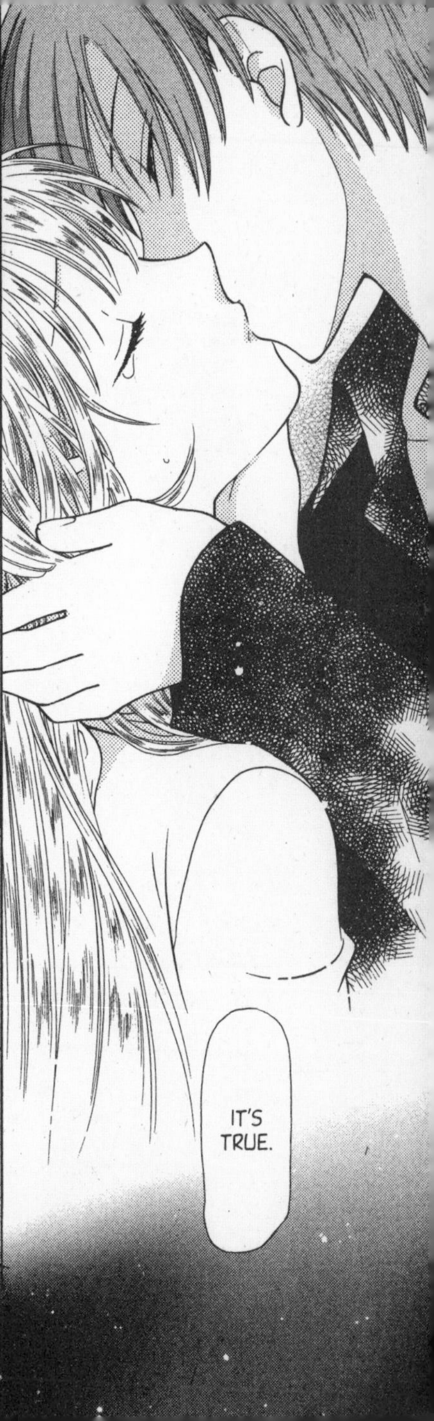
IT'S TRUE.

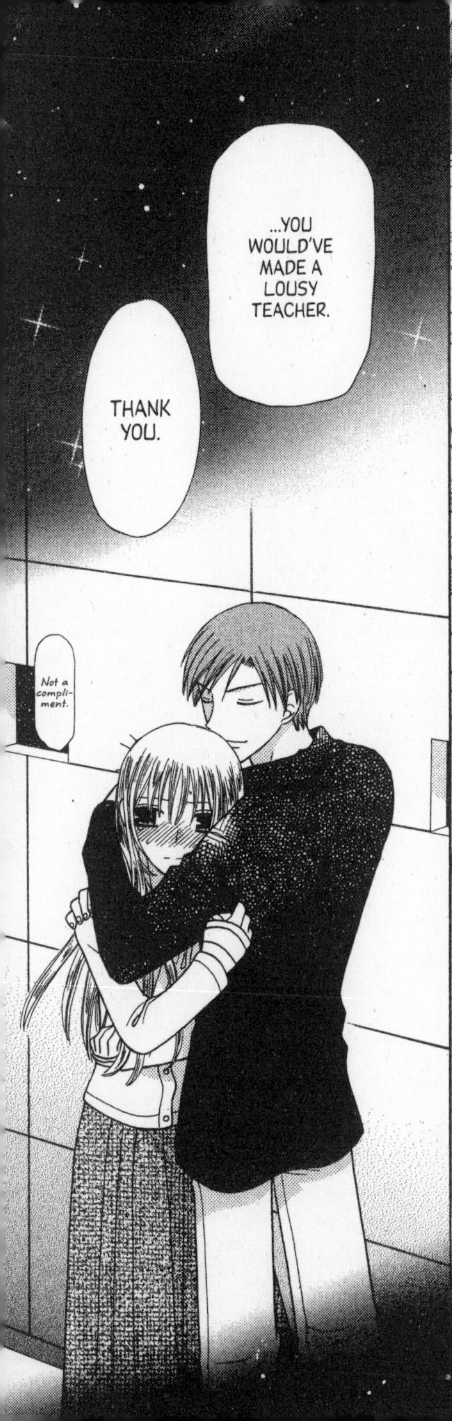
...YOU WOULD'VE MADE A LOUSY TEACHER.
THANK YOU.
Not a compli-ment.

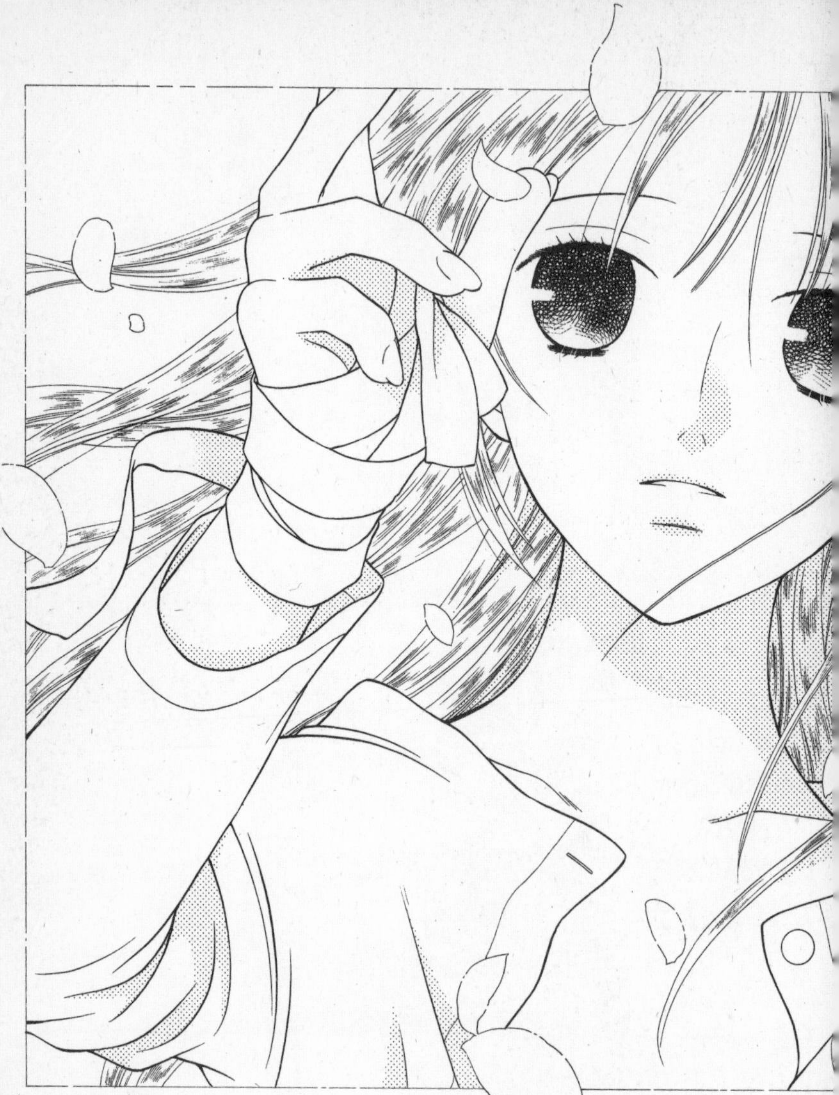

Chapter 92

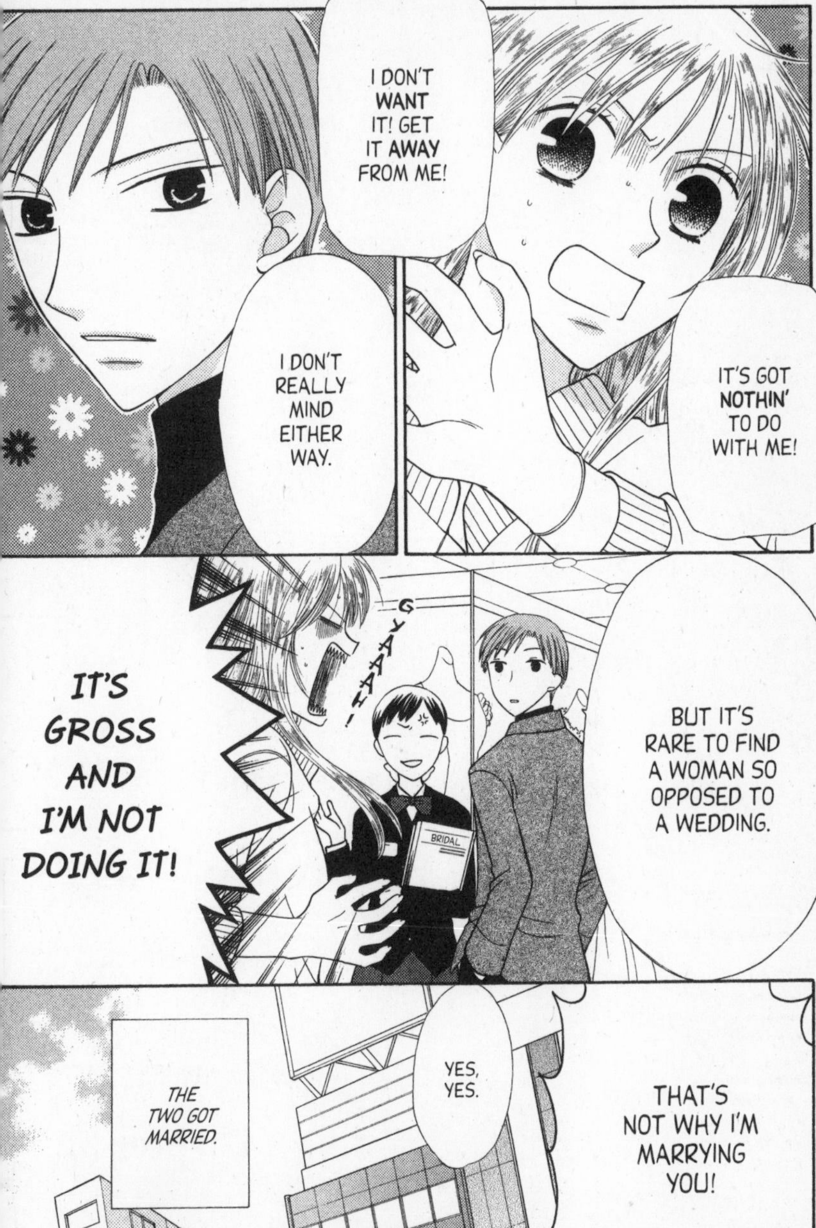
I DON'T WANT IT! GET IT AWAY FROM ME!
IT'S GOT NOTHIN' TO DO WITH ME!
I DON'T REALLY MIND EITHER WAY.
BUT IT'S RARE TO FIND A WOMAN SO OPPOSED TO A WEDDING.
GYAAAAH!
BRIDAL
IT'S GROSS AND I'M NOT DOING IT!
THAT'S NOT WHY I'M MARRYING YOU!
YES, YES.
THE TWO GOT MARRIED.

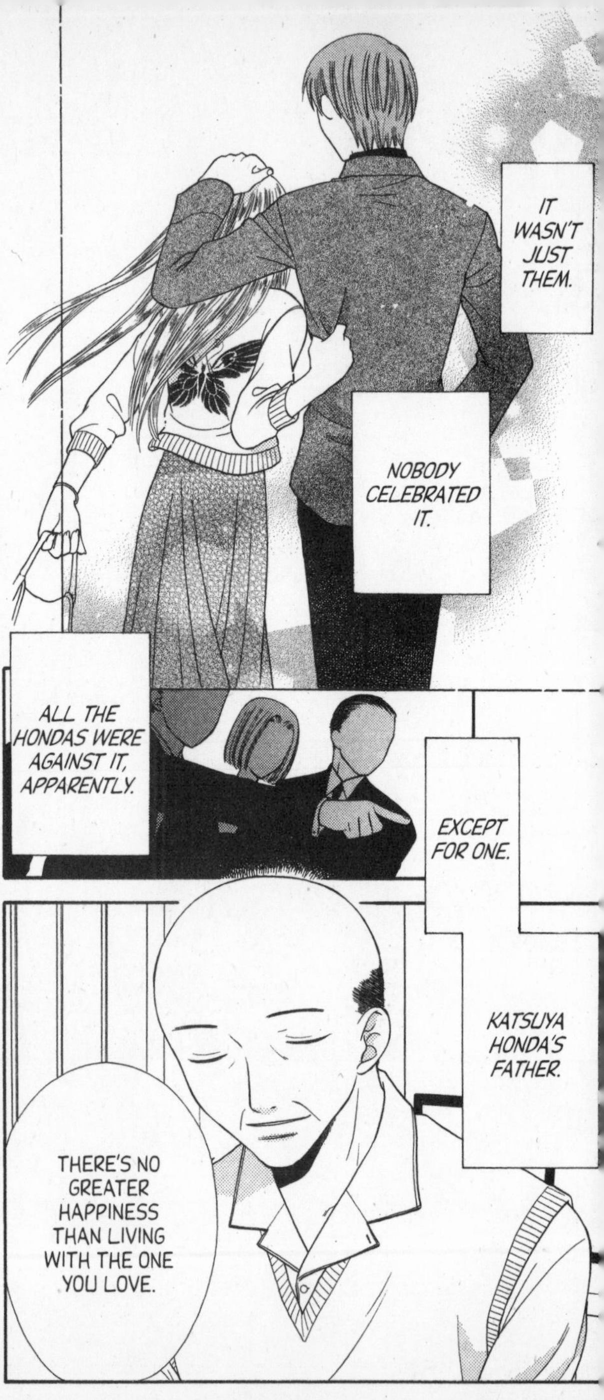
IT WASN'T JUST THEM.
NOBODY CELEBRATED IT.
ALL THE HONDAS WERE AGAINST IT, APPARENTLY.
EXCEPT FOR ONE.
KATSUYA HONDA'S FATHER.
THERE'S NO GREATER HAPPINESS THAN LIVING WITH THE ONE YOU LOVE.

Continued →

- Kagura still loves Kyon. It's probably not something you can change easily.
- She's fighting with that side of herself.
- Her dream is to work at a day-care. It's a dream she can't reach the way she is now.

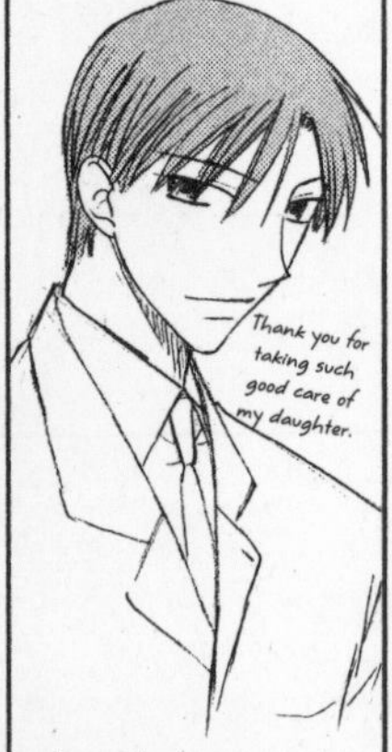
Thank you for taking such good care of my daughter.

I knew he was going to die, and I can't change that, but drawing him was really sad.

Katsuya-papa

- With his father, mother (died of an illness), and younger sister, Katsuya has a family of four. Had.
- As long as you love each other, age doesn't matter...! (There's an eight-year difference between him and Kyoko-san.)
- As a child he was contrary, which he's mentioned himself.

← To be continued

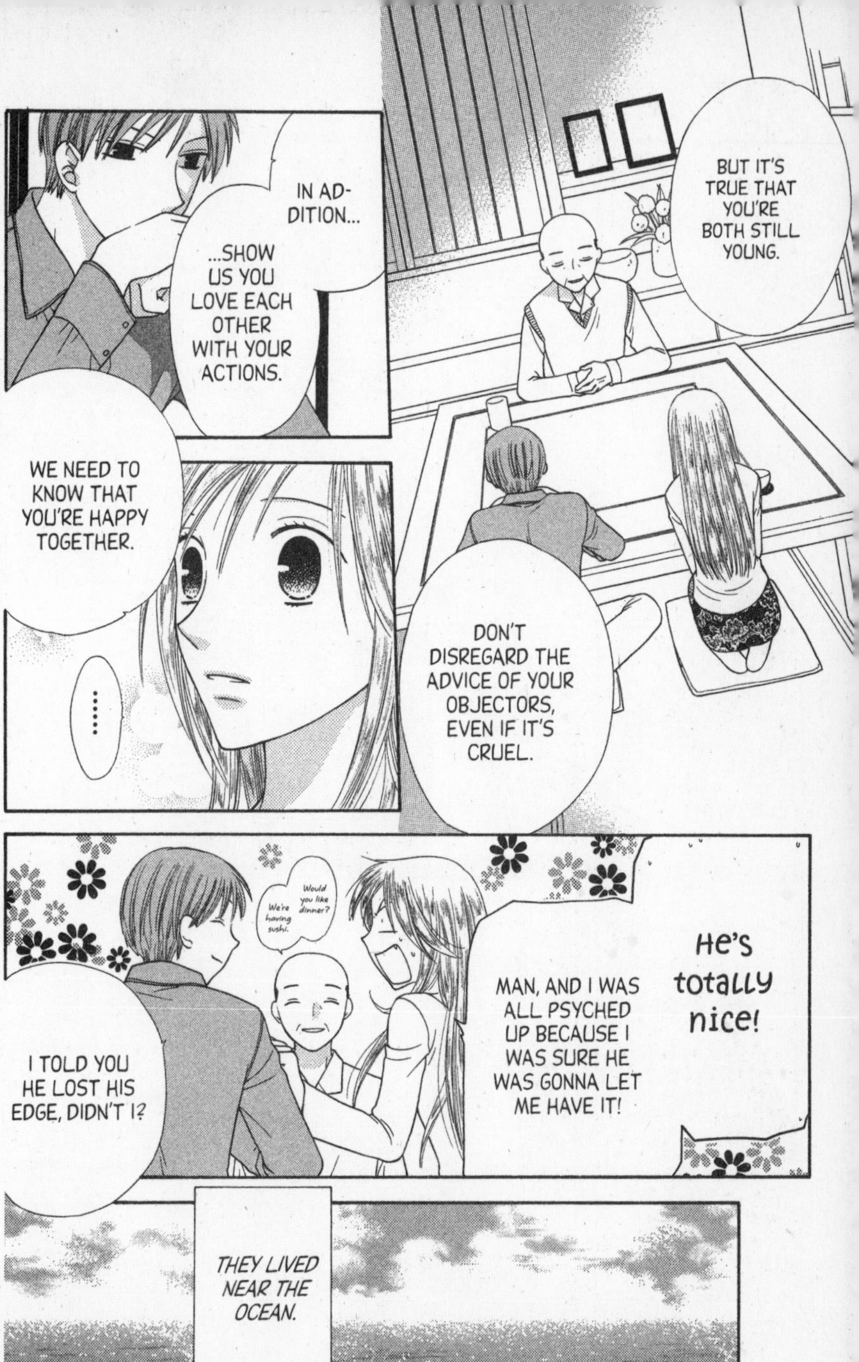
BUT IT'S TRUE THAT YOU'RE BOTH STILL YOUNG.
DON'T DISREGARD THE ADVICE OF YOUR OBJECTORS, EVEN IF IT'S CRUEL.
IN ADDITION...
...SHOW US YOU LOVE EACH OTHER WITH YOUR ACTIONS.
WE NEED TO KNOW THAT YOU'RE HAPPY TOGETHER.
......
He's totally nice!
MAN, AND I WAS ALL PSYCHED UP BECAUSE I WAS SURE HE WAS GONNA LET ME HAVE IT!
Would you like dinner?
We're having sushi.
I TOLD YOU HE LOST HIS EDGE, DIDN'T I?
THEY LIVED NEAR THE OCEAN.

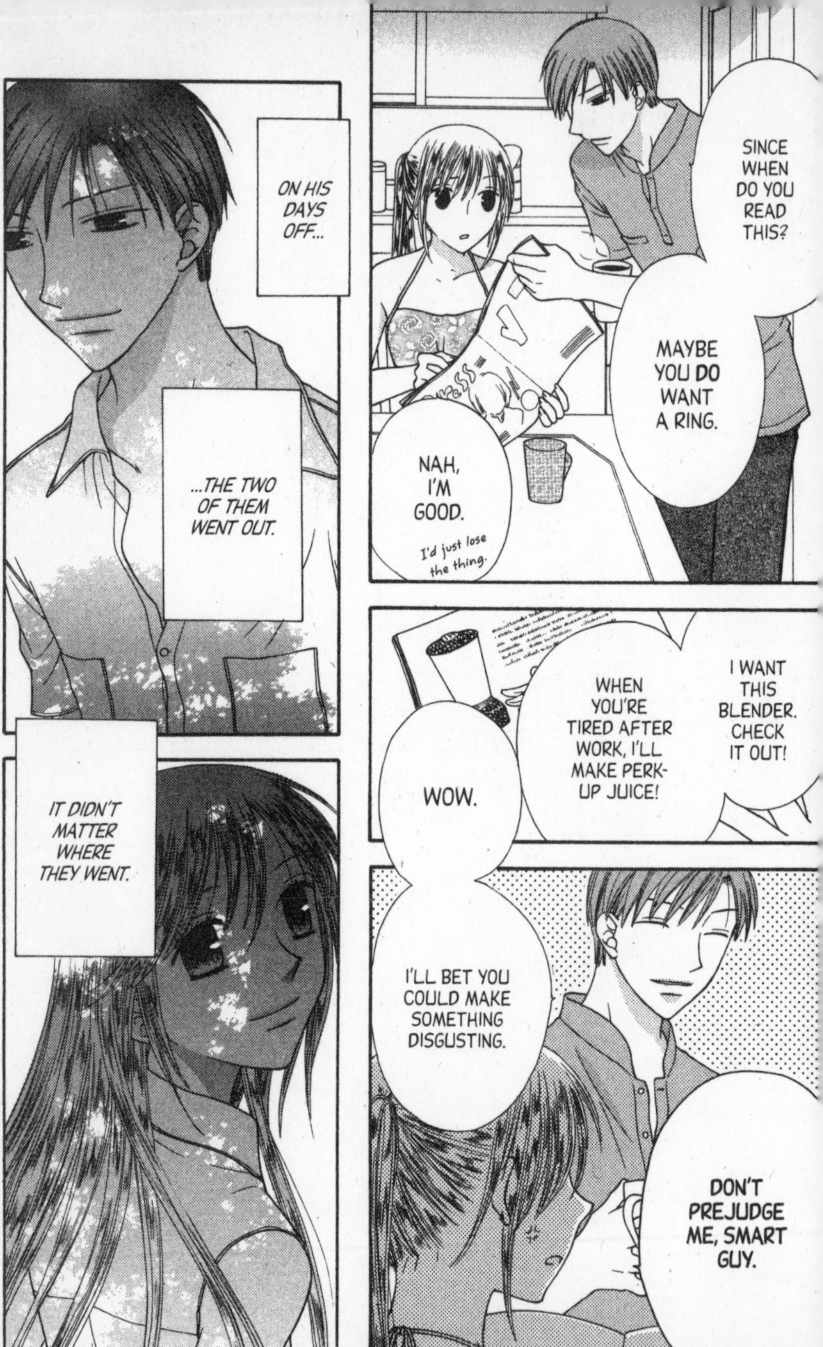
SINCE WHEN DO YOU READ THIS?
MAYBE YOU DO WANT A RING.
NAH, I'M GOOD.
I'd just lose the thing.
I WANT THIS BLENDER. CHECK IT OUT!
WHEN YOU'RE TIRED AFTER WORK, I'LL MAKE PERK-UP JUICE!
WOW.
I'LL BET YOU COULD MAKE SOMETHING DISGUSTING.
DON'T PREJUDGE ME, SMART GUY.
ON HIS DAYS OFF...
...THE TWO OF THEM WENT OUT.
IT DIDN'T MATTER WHERE THEY WENT.

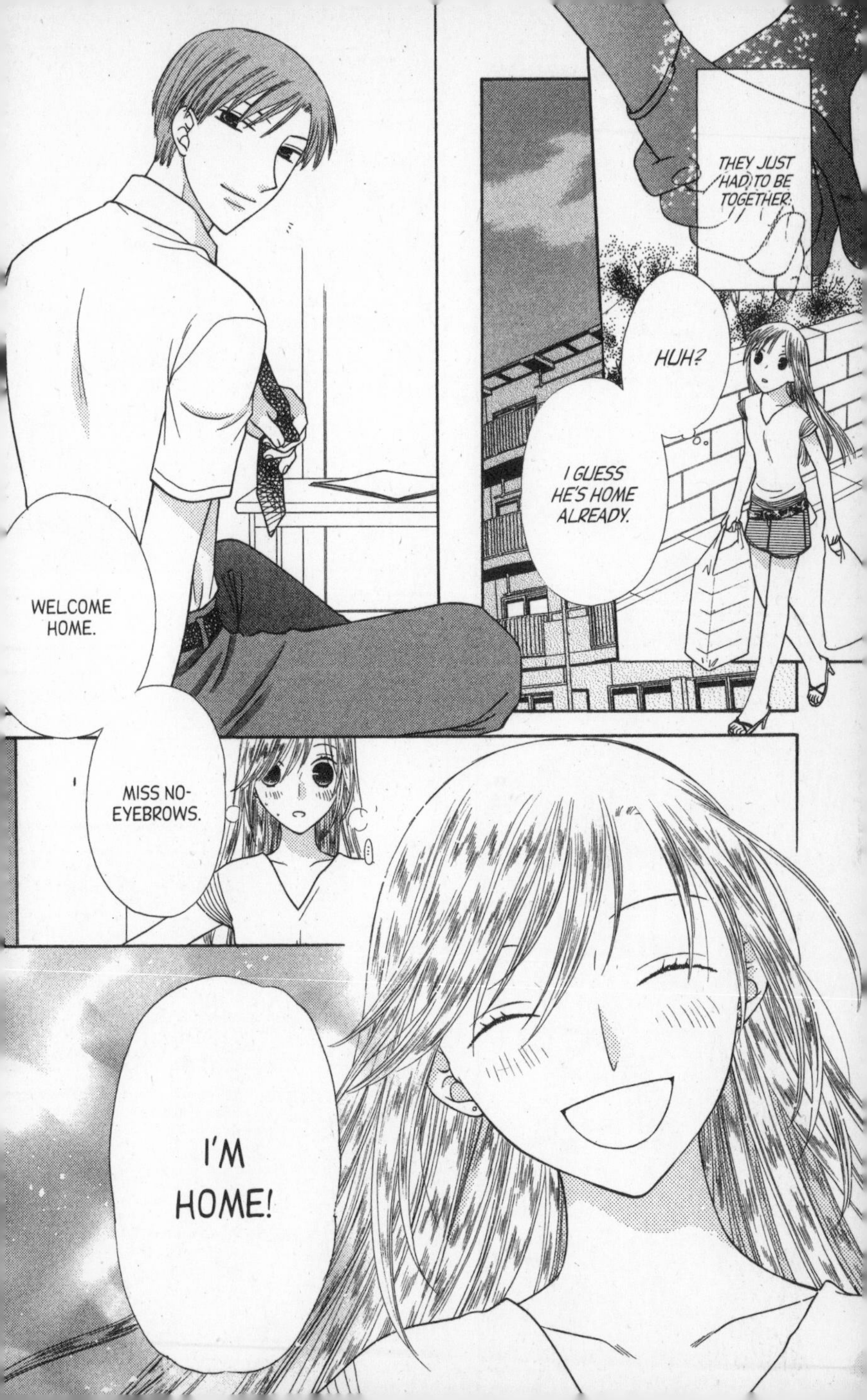

THEY JUST HAD TO BE TOGETHER.
HUH?
I GUESS HE'S HOME ALREADY.
WELCOME HOME.
MISS NO-EYEBROWS.
I'M HOME!

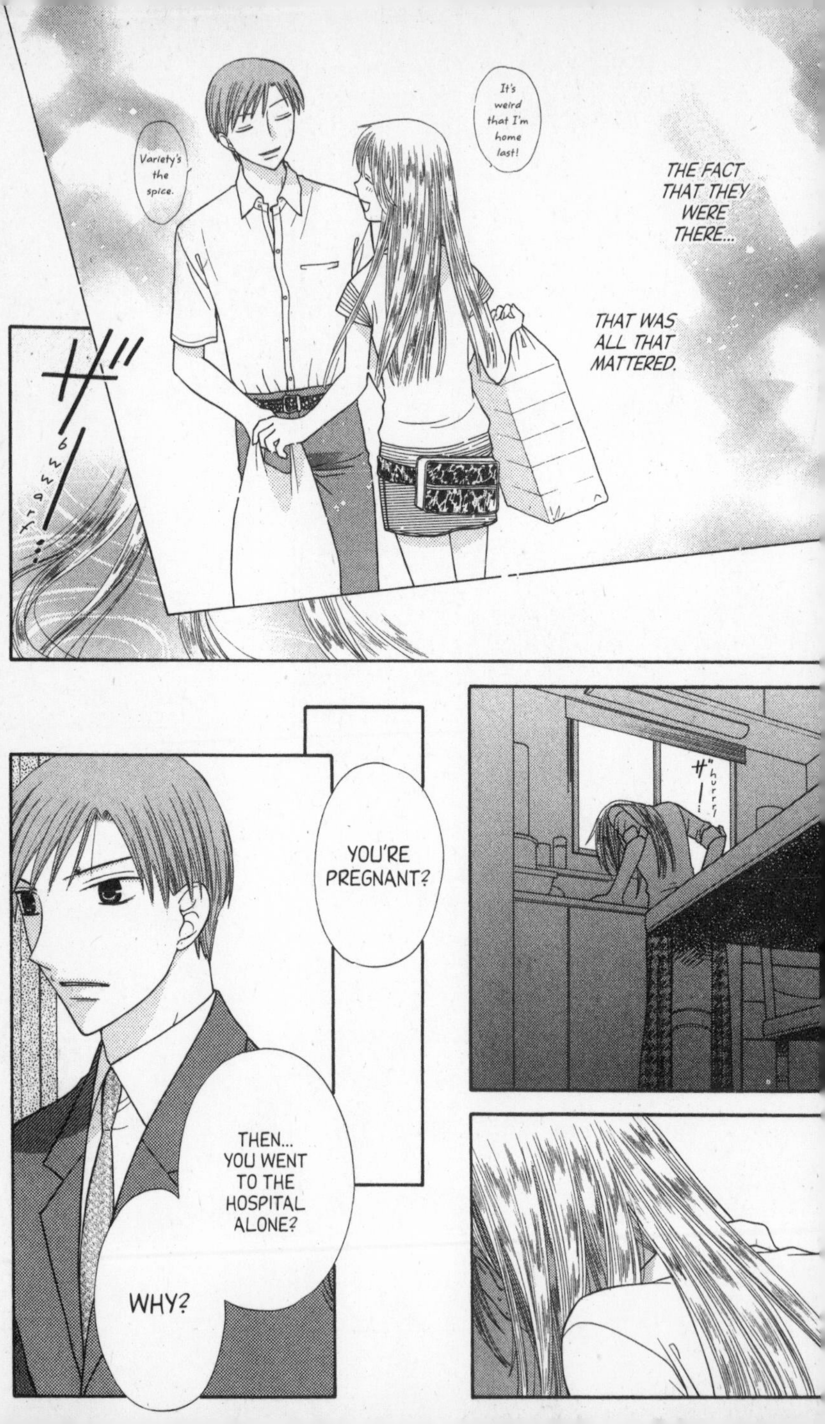
THE FACT THAT THEY WERE THERE...
It's weird that I'm home last!
Variety's the spice.
THAT WAS ALL THAT MATTERED.
ザー
bwwarf...
ザー!
hurrrl
YOU'RE PREGNANT?
THEN... YOU WENT TO THE HOSPITAL ALONE?
WHY?

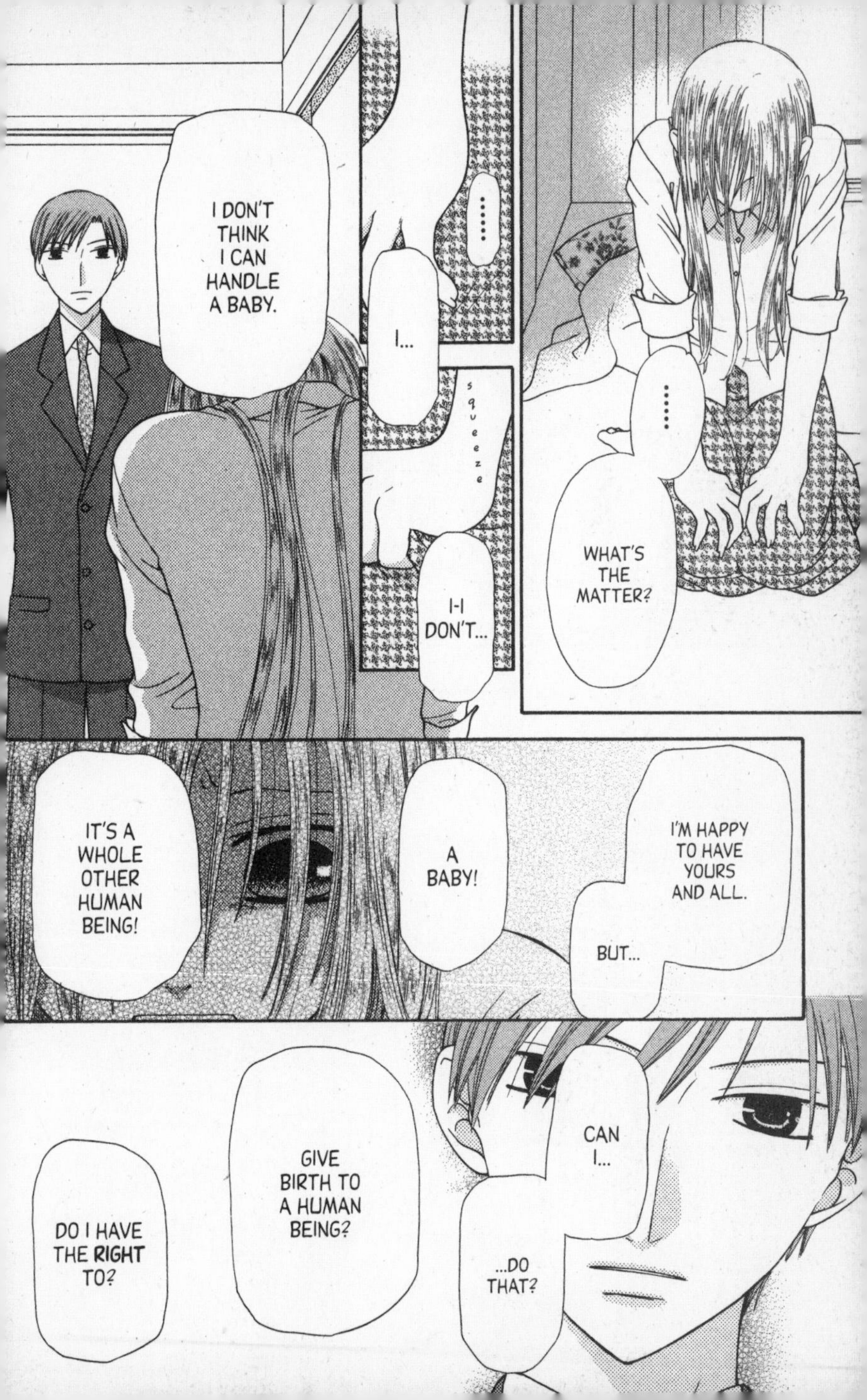
......
WHAT'S THE MATTER?
......
I...
squeeze
I-I DON'T...
I DON'T THINK I CAN HANDLE A BABY.
I'M HAPPY TO HAVE YOURS AND ALL.
BUT...
A BABY!
IT'S A WHOLE OTHER HUMAN BEING!
CAN I...
...DO THAT?
GIVE BIRTH TO A HUMAN BEING?
DO I HAVE THE **RIGHT** TO?

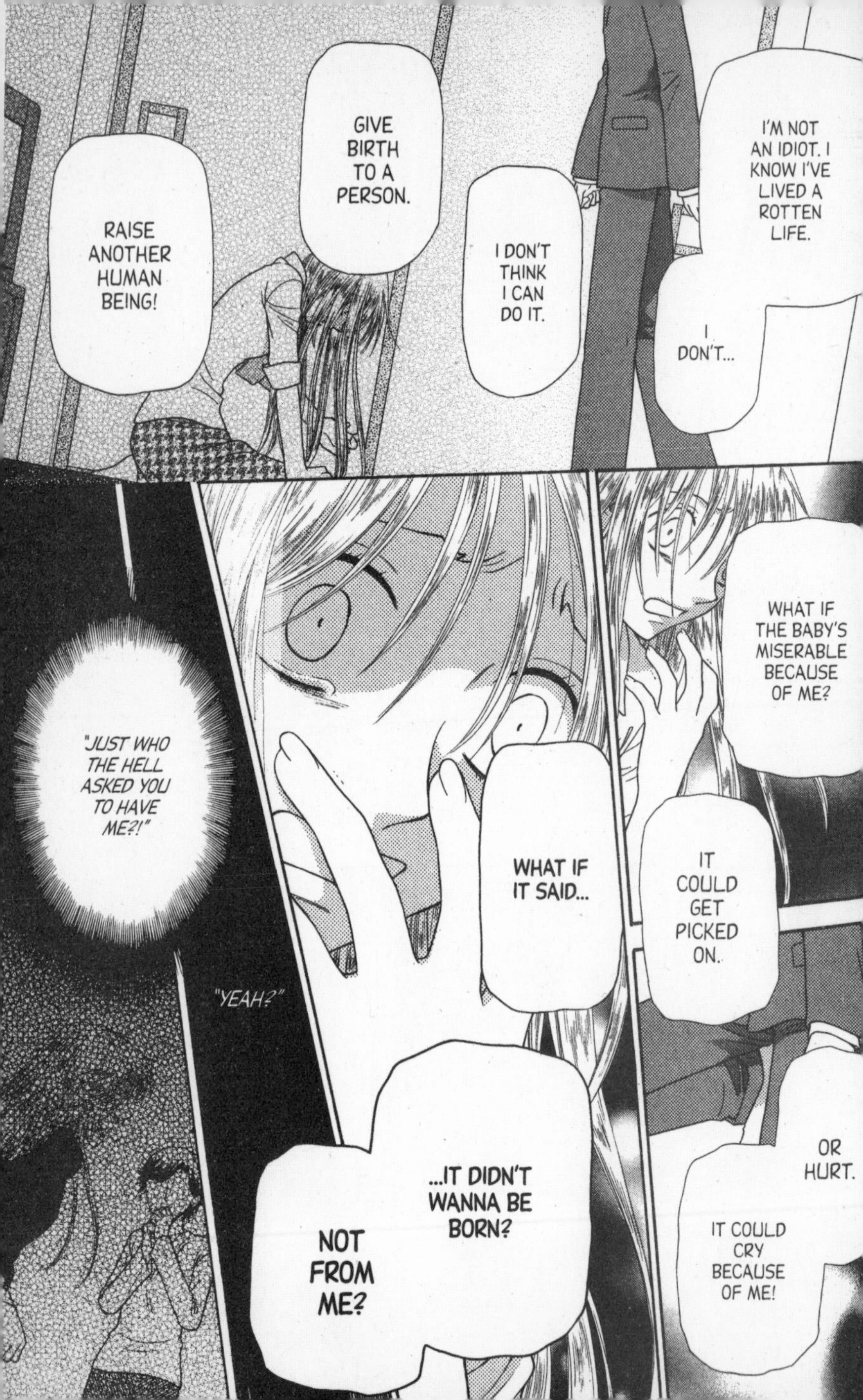
I'M NOT AN IDIOT. I KNOW I'VE LIVED A ROTTEN LIFE.
I DON'T...
I DON'T THINK I CAN DO IT.
GIVE BIRTH TO A PERSON.
RAISE ANOTHER HUMAN BEING!
WHAT IF THE BABY'S MISERABLE BECAUSE OF ME?
IT COULD GET PICKED ON.
OR HURT.
IT COULD CRY BECAUSE OF ME!
WHAT IF IT SAID...
...IT DIDN'T WANNA BE BORN?
NOT FROM ME?
"JUST WHO THE HELL ASKED YOU TO HAVE ME?!"
"YEAH?"

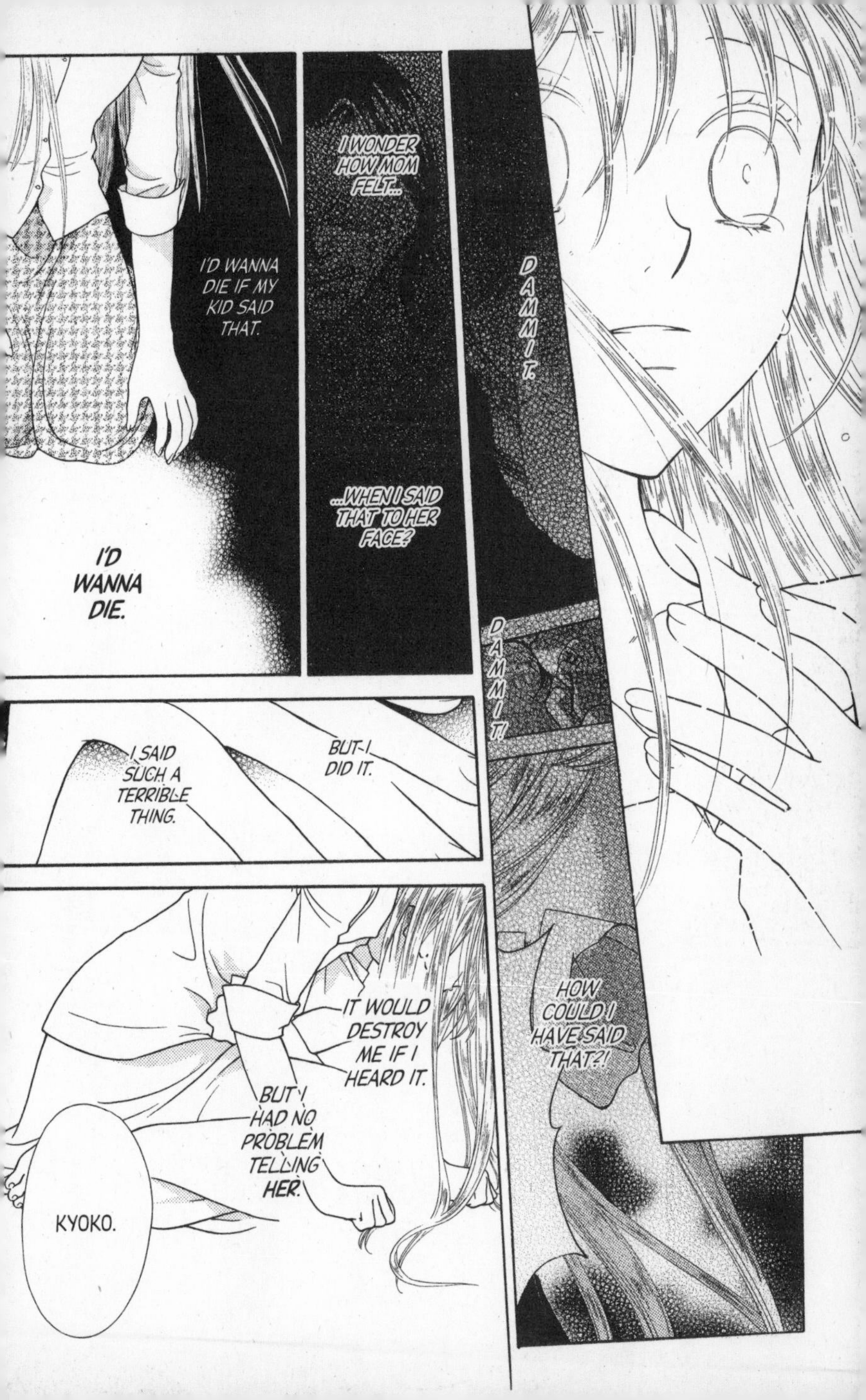
DAMMIT.
DAMMIT!
HOW COULD I HAVE SAID THAT?!
I WONDER HOW MOM FELT...
...WHEN I SAID THAT TO HER FACE?
I'D WANNA DIE IF MY KID SAID THAT.
I'D WANNA DIE.
BUT-I DID IT.
I SAID SUCH A TERRIBLE THING.
IT WOULD DESTROY ME IF I HEARD IT.
BUT I HAD NO PROBLEM TELLING HER.
KYOKO.

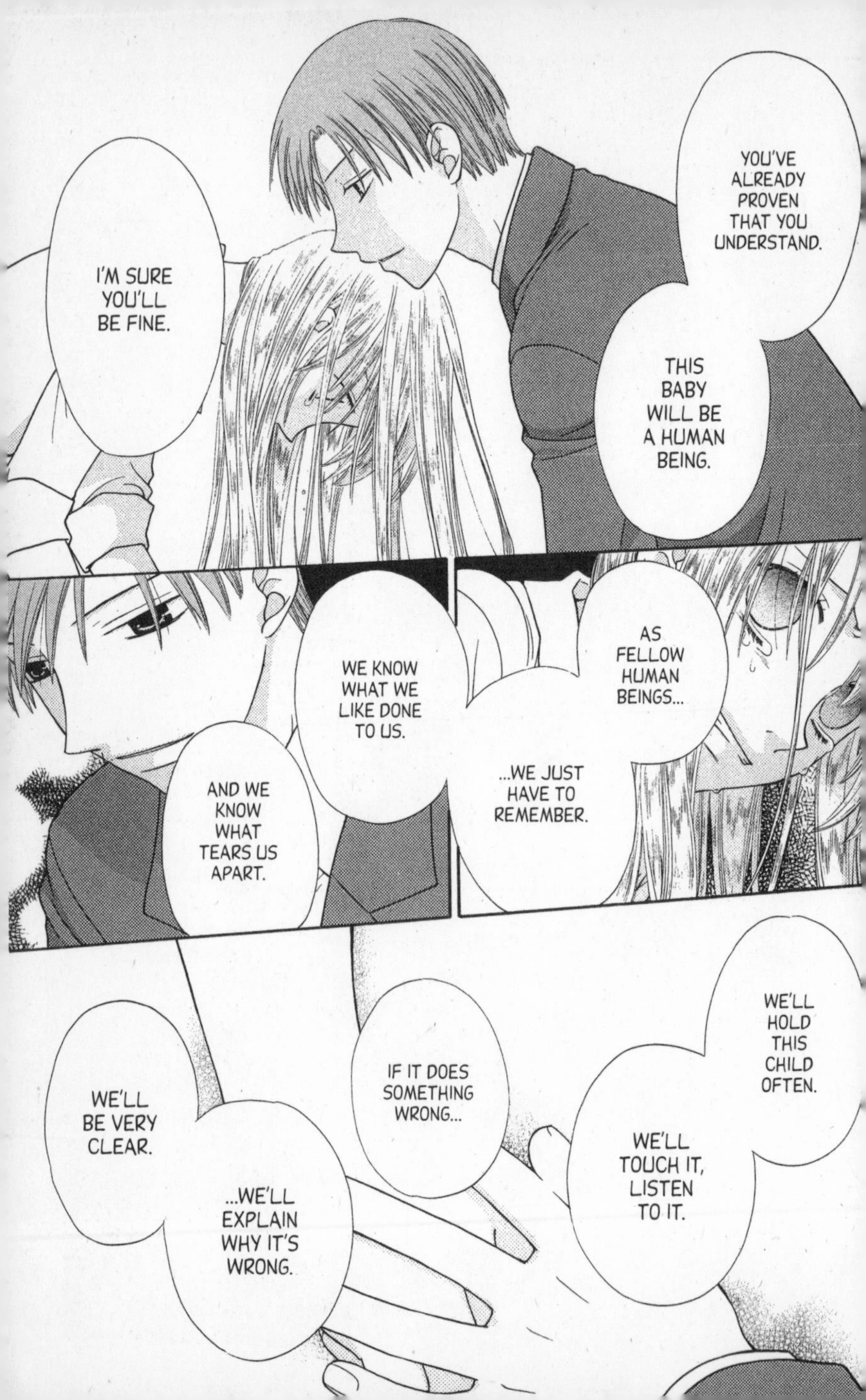
YOU'VE ALREADY PROVEN THAT YOU UNDERSTAND.
THIS BABY WILL BE A HUMAN BEING.
I'M SURE YOU'LL BE FINE.
AS FELLOW HUMAN BEINGS...
...WE JUST HAVE TO REMEMBER.
WE KNOW WHAT WE LIKE DONE TO US.
AND WE KNOW WHAT TEARS US APART.
WE'LL HOLD THIS CHILD OFTEN.
WE'LL TOUCH IT, LISTEN TO IT.
IF IT DOES SOMETHING WRONG...
...WE'LL EXPLAIN WHY IT'S WRONG.
WE'LL BE VERY CLEAR.

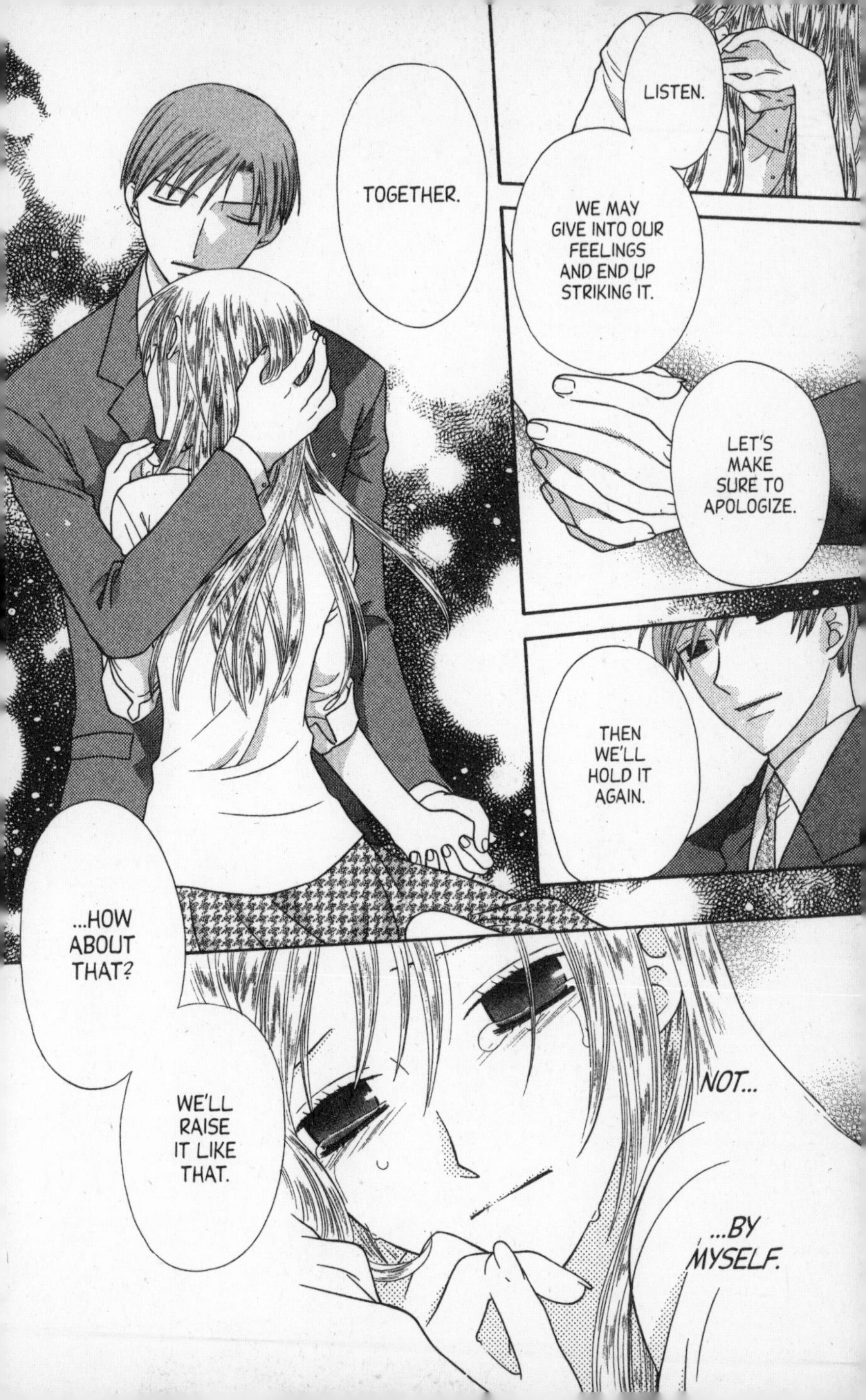
LISTEN.
WE MAY GIVE INTO OUR FEELINGS AND END UP STRIKING IT.
LET'S MAKE SURE TO APOLOGIZE.
THEN WE'LL HOLD IT AGAIN.
TOGETHER.
...HOW ABOUT THAT?
WE'LL RAISE IT LIKE THAT.
NOT...
...BY MYSELF.

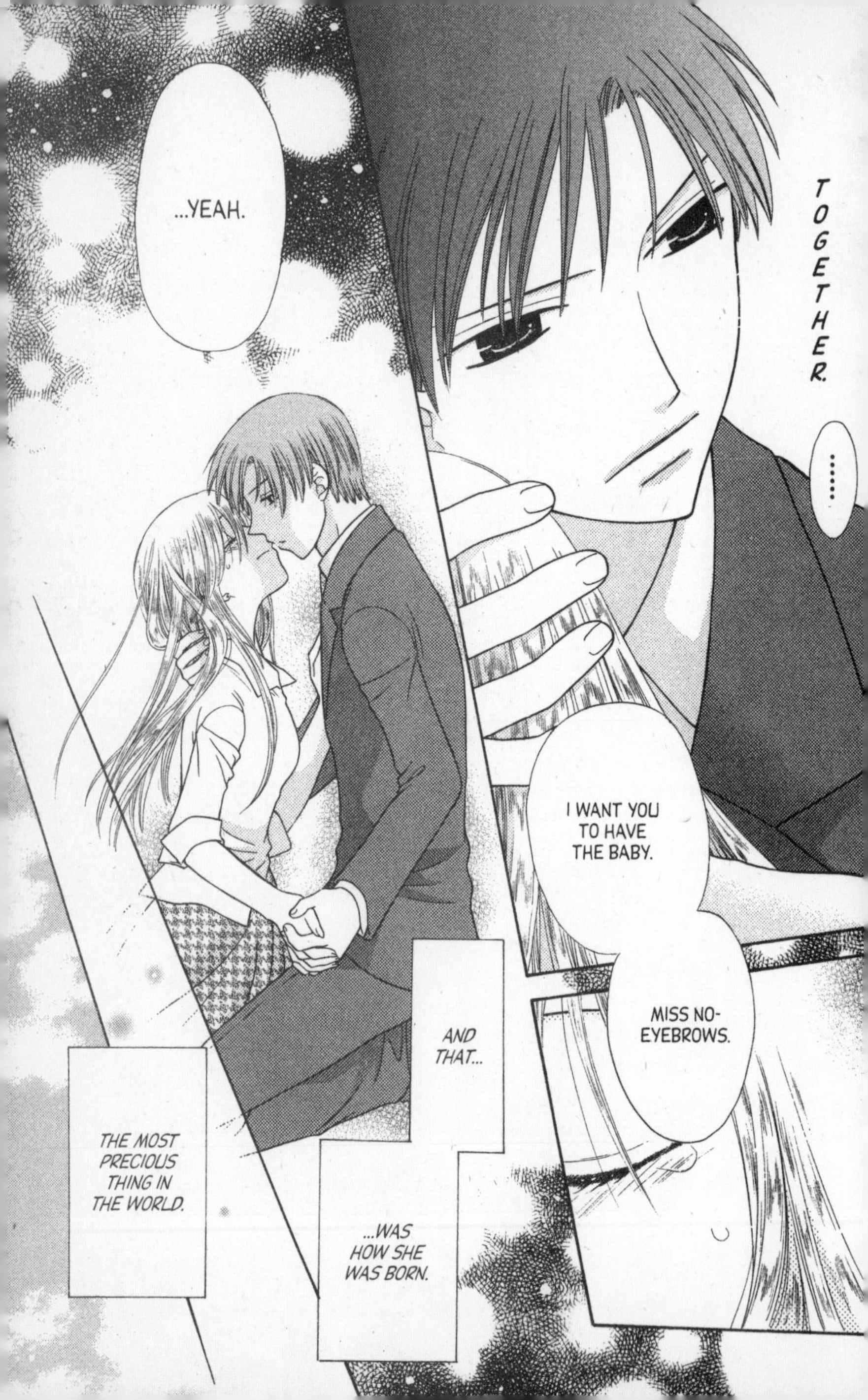
TOGETHER.
......
I WANT YOU TO HAVE THE BABY.
MISS NO-EYEBROWS.
...YEAH.
AND THAT...
...WAS HOW SHE WAS BORN.
THE MOST PRECIOUS THING IN THE WORLD.

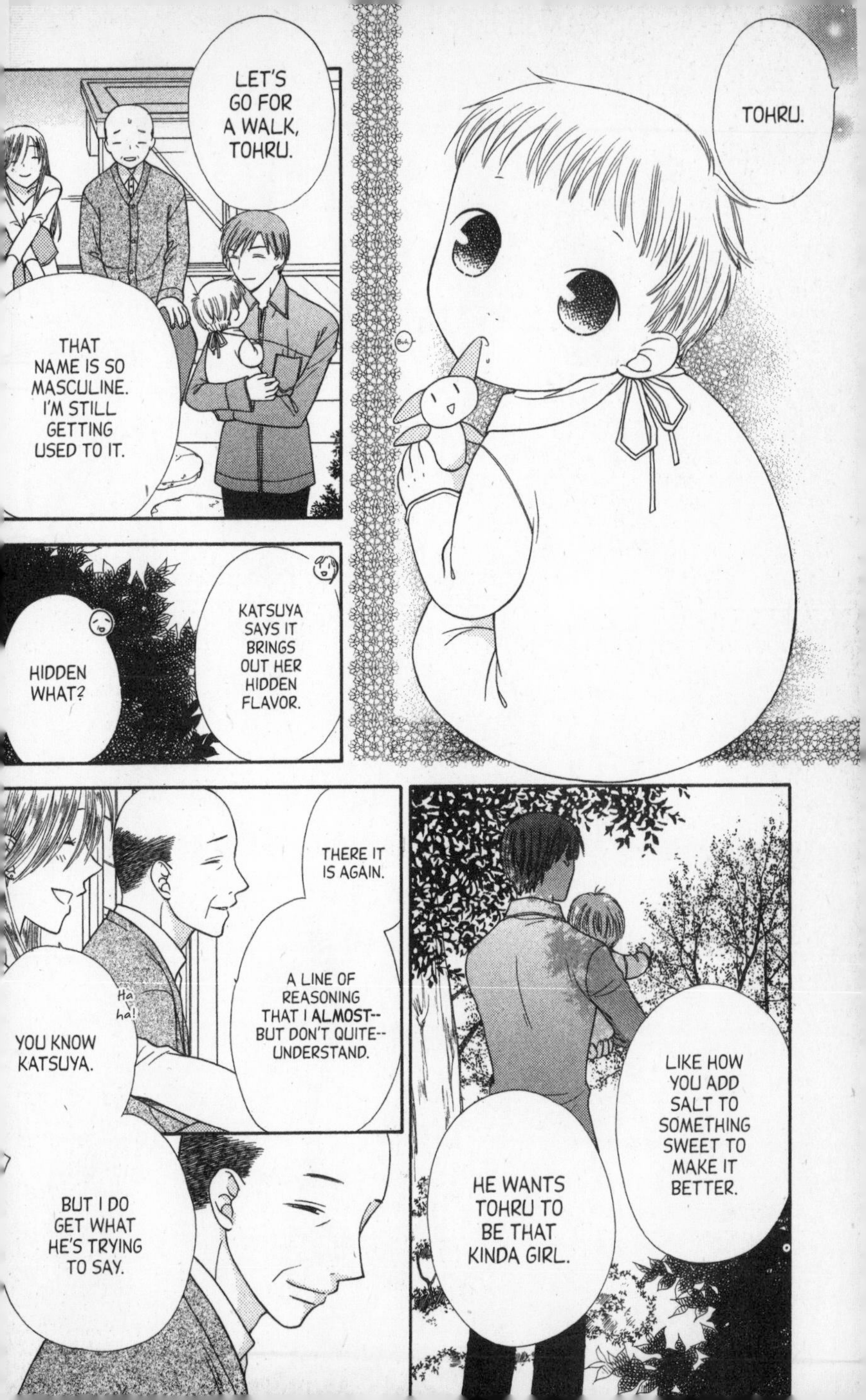
TOHRU.
LET'S GO FOR A WALK, TOHRU.
THAT NAME IS SO MASCULINE. I'M STILL GETTING USED TO IT.
KATSUYA SAYS IT BRINGS OUT HER HIDDEN FLAVOR.
HIDDEN WHAT?
LIKE HOW YOU ADD SALT TO SOMETHING SWEET TO MAKE IT BETTER.
HE WANTS TOHRU TO BE THAT KINDA GIRL.
THERE IT IS AGAIN.
A LINE OF REASONING THAT I **ALMOST**-- BUT DON'T QUITE-- UNDERSTAND.
Ha ha!
YOU KNOW KATSUYA.
BUT I DO GET WHAT HE'S TRYING TO SAY.

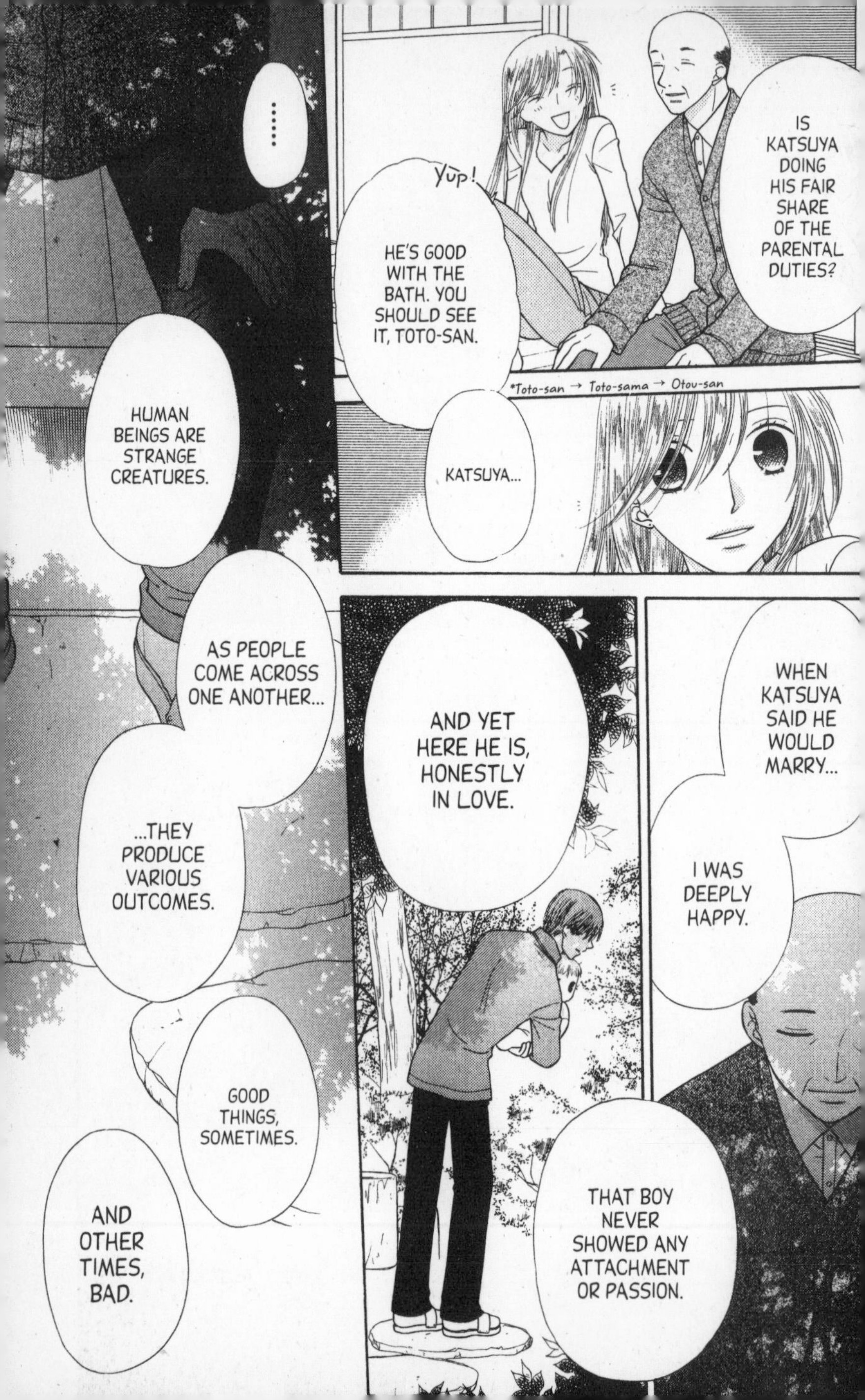
IS KATSUYA DOING HIS FAIR SHARE OF THE PARENTAL DUTIES?
Yup!
HE'S GOOD WITH THE BATH. YOU SHOULD SEE IT, TOTO-SAN.
*Toto-san → Toto-sama → Otou-san
KATSUYA...
WHEN KATSUYA SAID HE WOULD MARRY...
I WAS DEEPLY HAPPY.
THAT BOY NEVER SHOWED ANY ATTACHMENT OR PASSION.
AND YET HERE HE IS, HONESTLY IN LOVE.
......
HUMAN BEINGS ARE STRANGE CREATURES.
AS PEOPLE COME ACROSS ONE ANOTHER...
...THEY PRODUCE VARIOUS OUTCOMES.
GOOD THINGS, SOMETIMES.
AND OTHER TIMES, BAD.

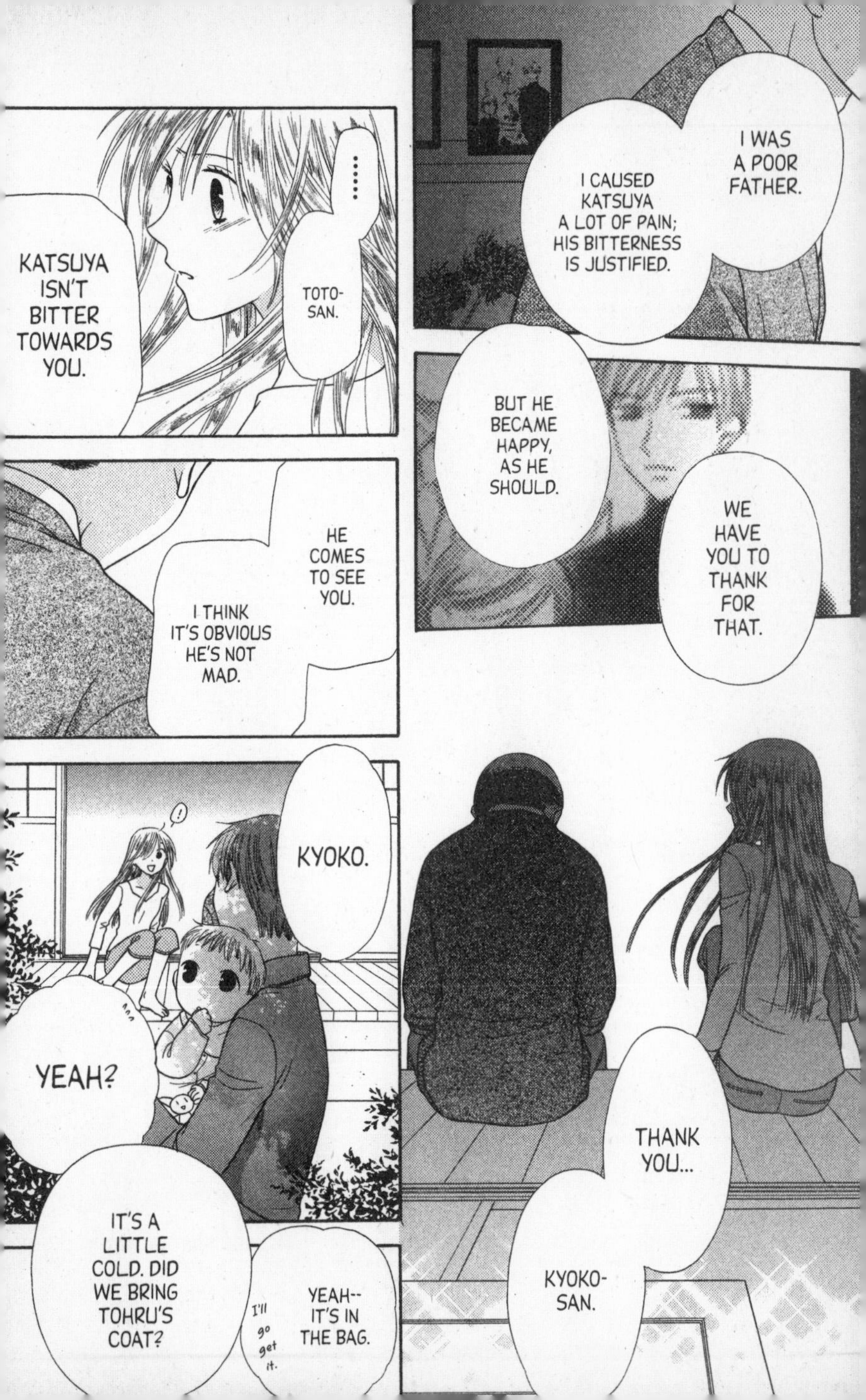

I WAS A POOR FATHER.
I CAUSED KATSUYA A LOT OF PAIN; HIS BITTERNESS IS JUSTIFIED.
BUT HE BECAME HAPPY, AS HE SHOULD.
WE HAVE YOU TO THANK FOR THAT.
THANK YOU...
KYOKO-SAN.
......
TOTO-SAN.
KATSUYA ISN'T BITTER TOWARDS YOU.
HE COMES TO SEE YOU.
I THINK IT'S OBVIOUS HE'S NOT MAD.
KYOKO.
!
YEAH?
IT'S A LITTLE COLD. DID WE BRING TOHRU'S COAT?
YEAH-- IT'S IN THE BAG.
I'll go get it.

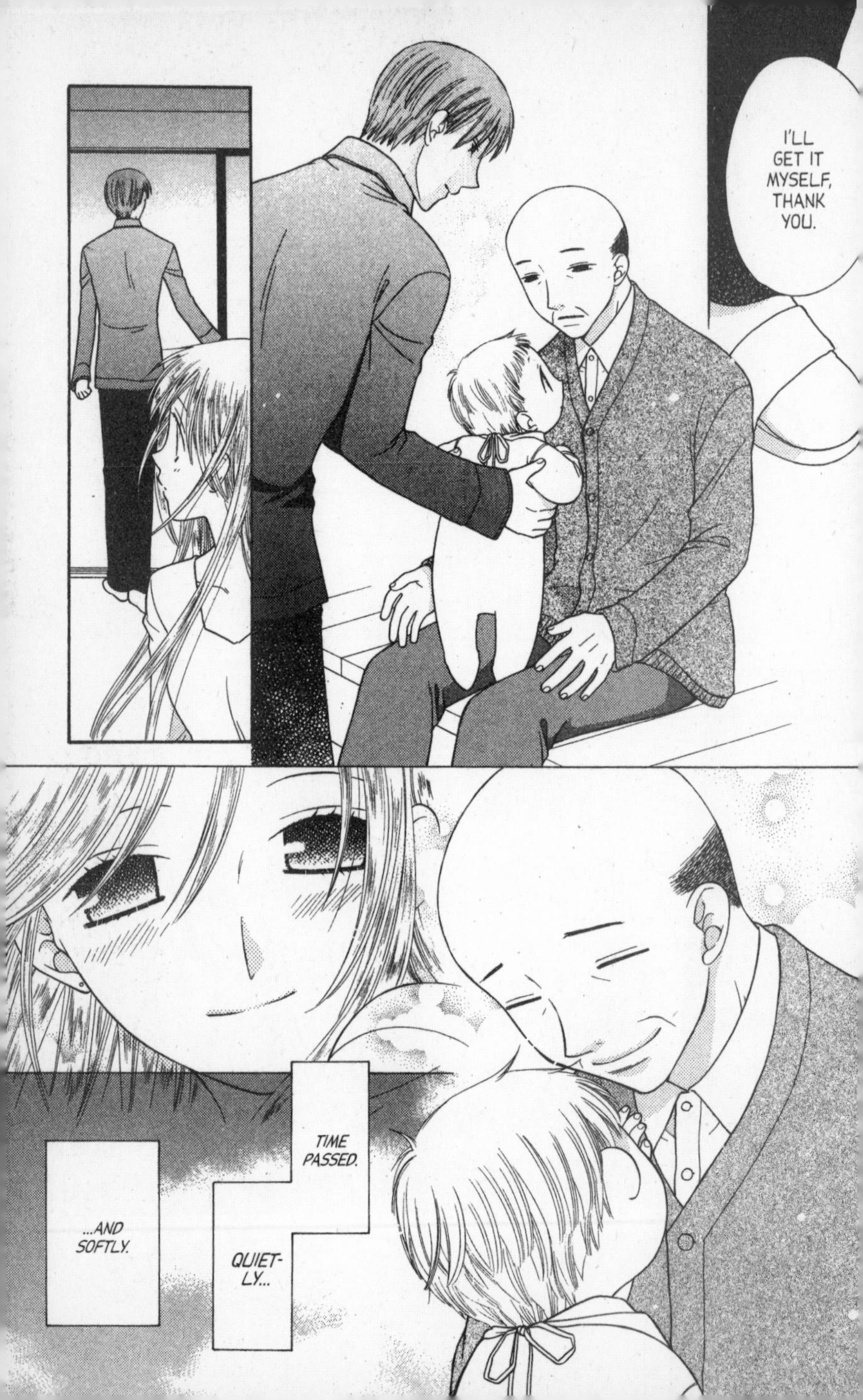
I'LL GET IT MYSELF, THANK YOU.
TIME PASSED.
QUIET-LY...
...AND SOFTLY.

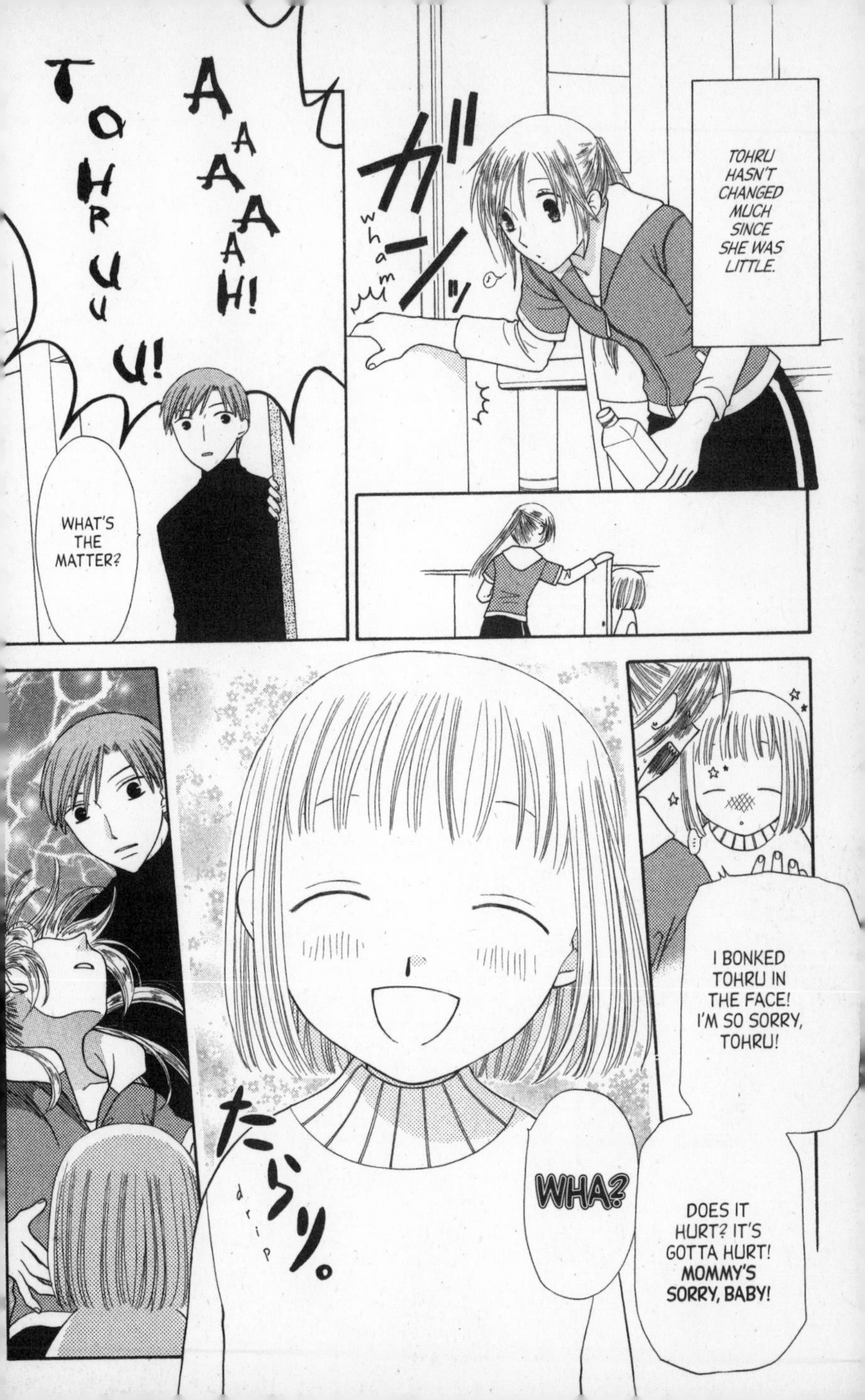
TOHRU HASN'T CHANGED MUCH SINCE SHE WAS LITTLE.
ガーン
wham
AAAAAH!
TOHRUUU!
WHAT'S THE MATTER?
I BONKED TOHRU IN THE FACE! I'M SO SORRY, TOHRU!
DOES IT HURT? IT'S GOTTA HURT! MOMMY'S SORRY, BABY!
WHA?
たらり。
drip

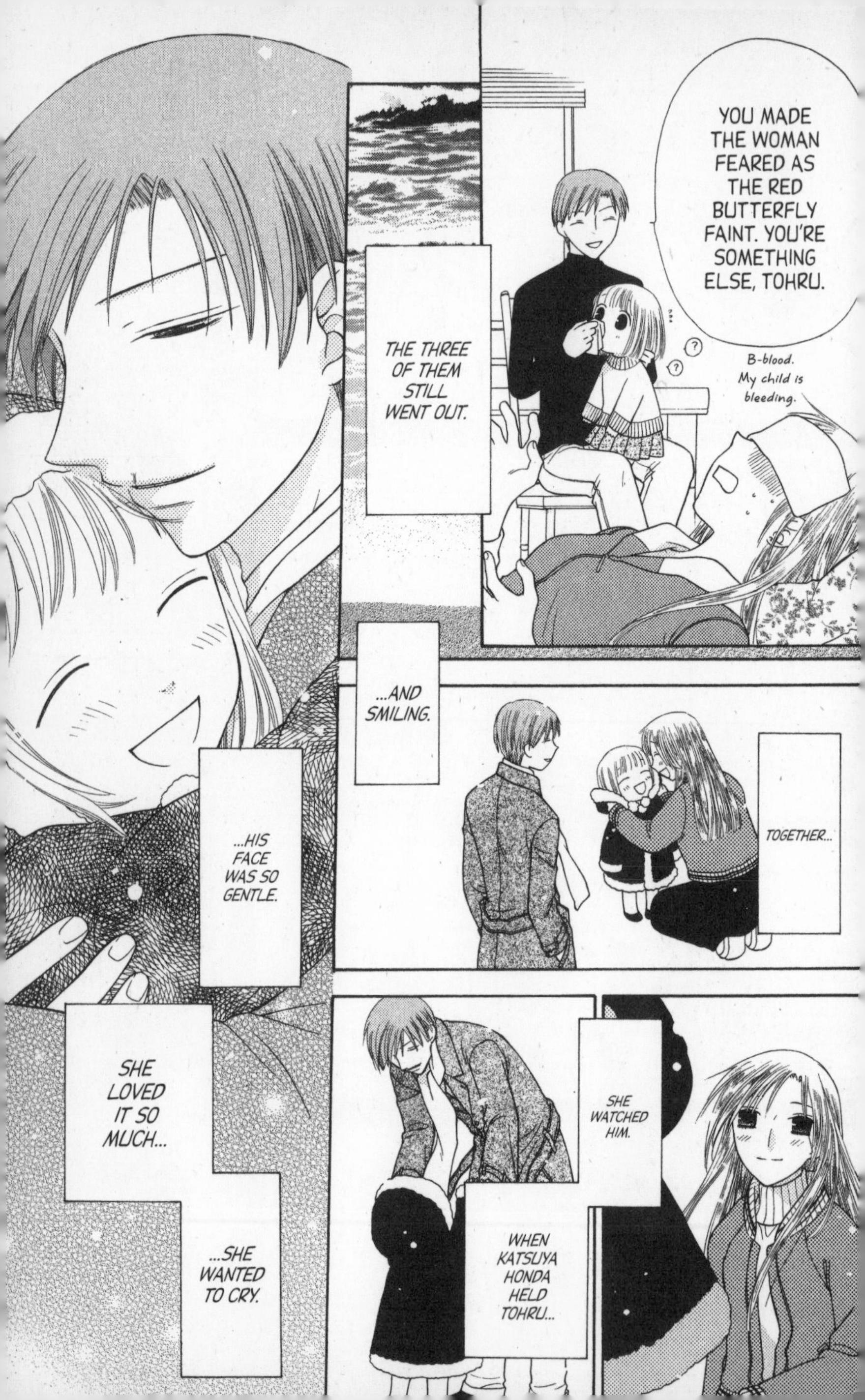

YOU MADE THE WOMAN FEARED AS THE RED BUTTERFLY FAINT. YOU'RE SOMETHING ELSE, TOHRU.
B-blood. My child is bleeding.
?
?
THE THREE OF THEM STILL WENT OUT.
TOGETHER...
...AND SMILING.
...HIS FACE WAS SO GENTLE.
SHE WATCHED HIM.
WHEN KATSUYA HONDA HELD TOHRU...
SHE LOVED IT SO MUCH...
...SHE WANTED TO CRY.

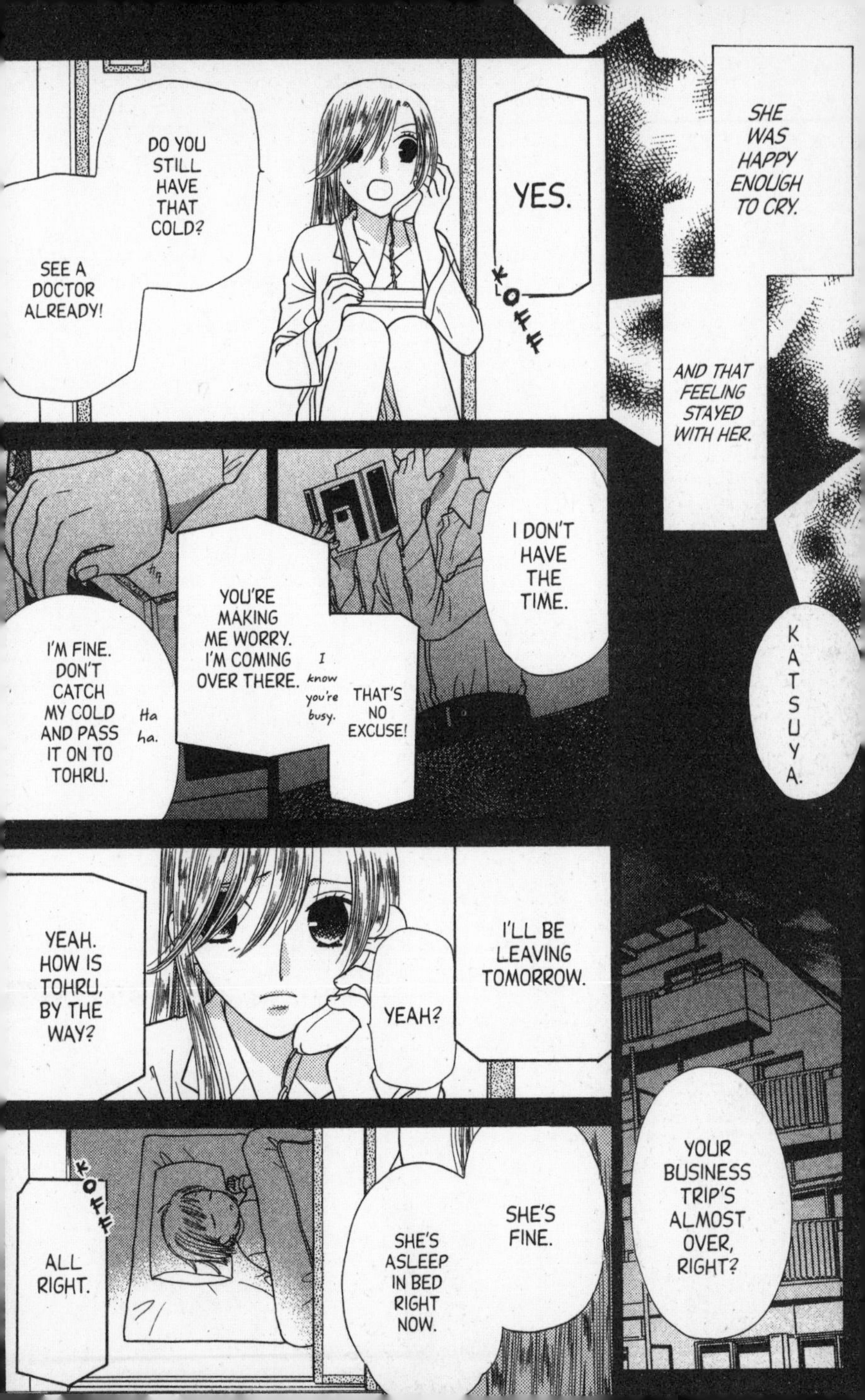
SHE WAS HAPPY ENOUGH TO CRY.
AND THAT FEELING STAYED WITH HER.
KATSUYA.
YOUR BUSINESS TRIP'S ALMOST OVER, RIGHT?
YES.
KOFF
DO YOU STILL HAVE THAT COLD?
SEE A DOCTOR ALREADY!
I DON'T HAVE THE TIME.
YOU'RE MAKING ME WORRY. I'M COMING OVER THERE.
THAT'S NO EXCUSE!
I know you're busy.
Ha ha.
I'M FINE. DON'T CATCH MY COLD AND PASS IT ON TO TOHRU.
I'LL BE LEAVING TOMORROW.
YEAH?
YEAH. HOW IS TOHRU, BY THE WAY?
SHE'S FINE.
SHE'S ASLEEP IN BED RIGHT NOW.
KOFF
ALL RIGHT.

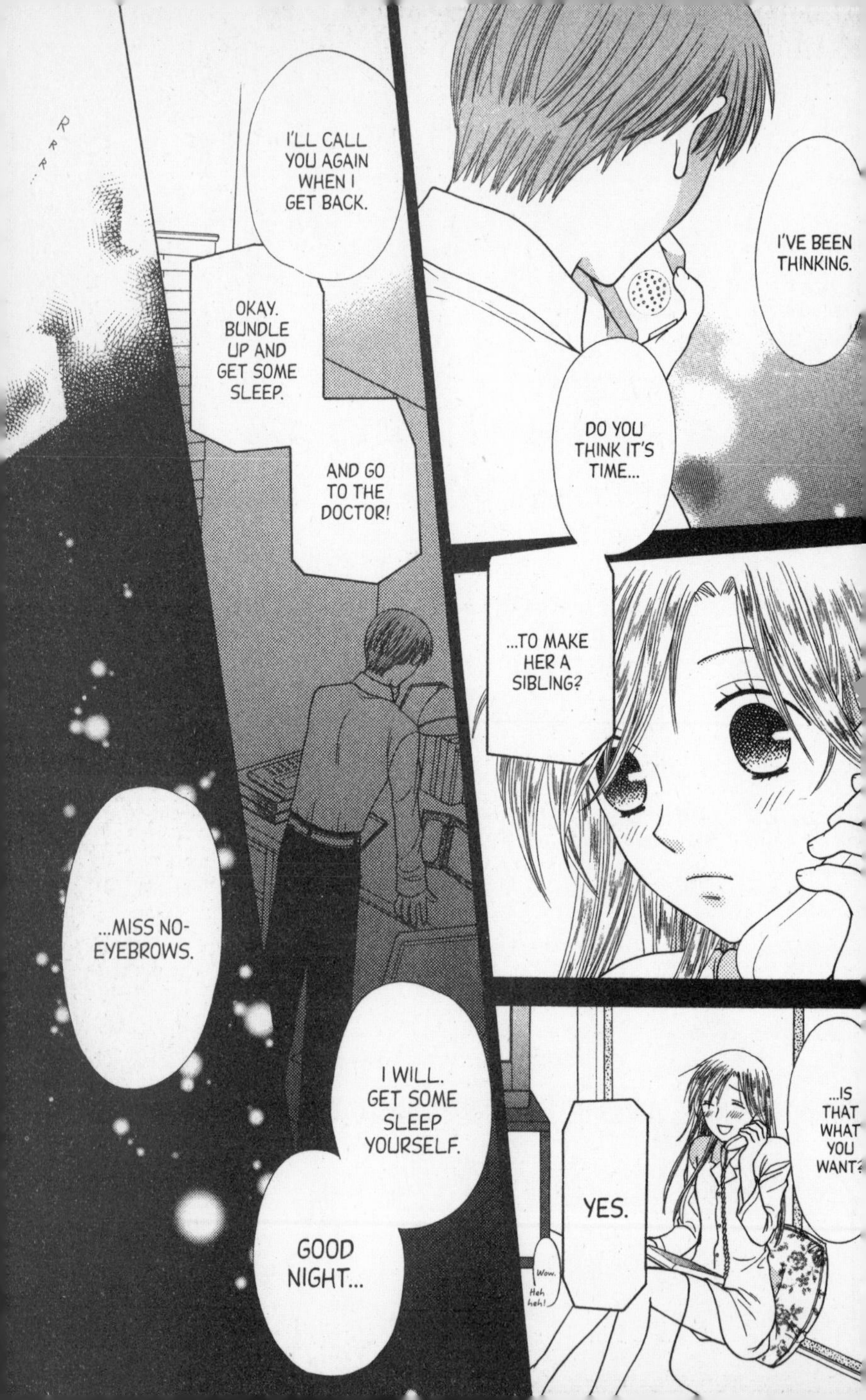
I'VE BEEN THINKING.
DO YOU THINK IT'S TIME...
...TO MAKE HER A SIBLING?
...IS THAT WHAT YOU WANT?
YES.
Wow.
Heh heh!
I'LL CALL YOU AGAIN WHEN I GET BACK.
OKAY. BUNDLE UP AND GET SOME SLEEP.
AND GO TO THE DOCTOR!
I WILL. GET SOME SLEEP YOURSELF.
GOOD NIGHT...
RRR...
...MISS NO-EYEBROWS.

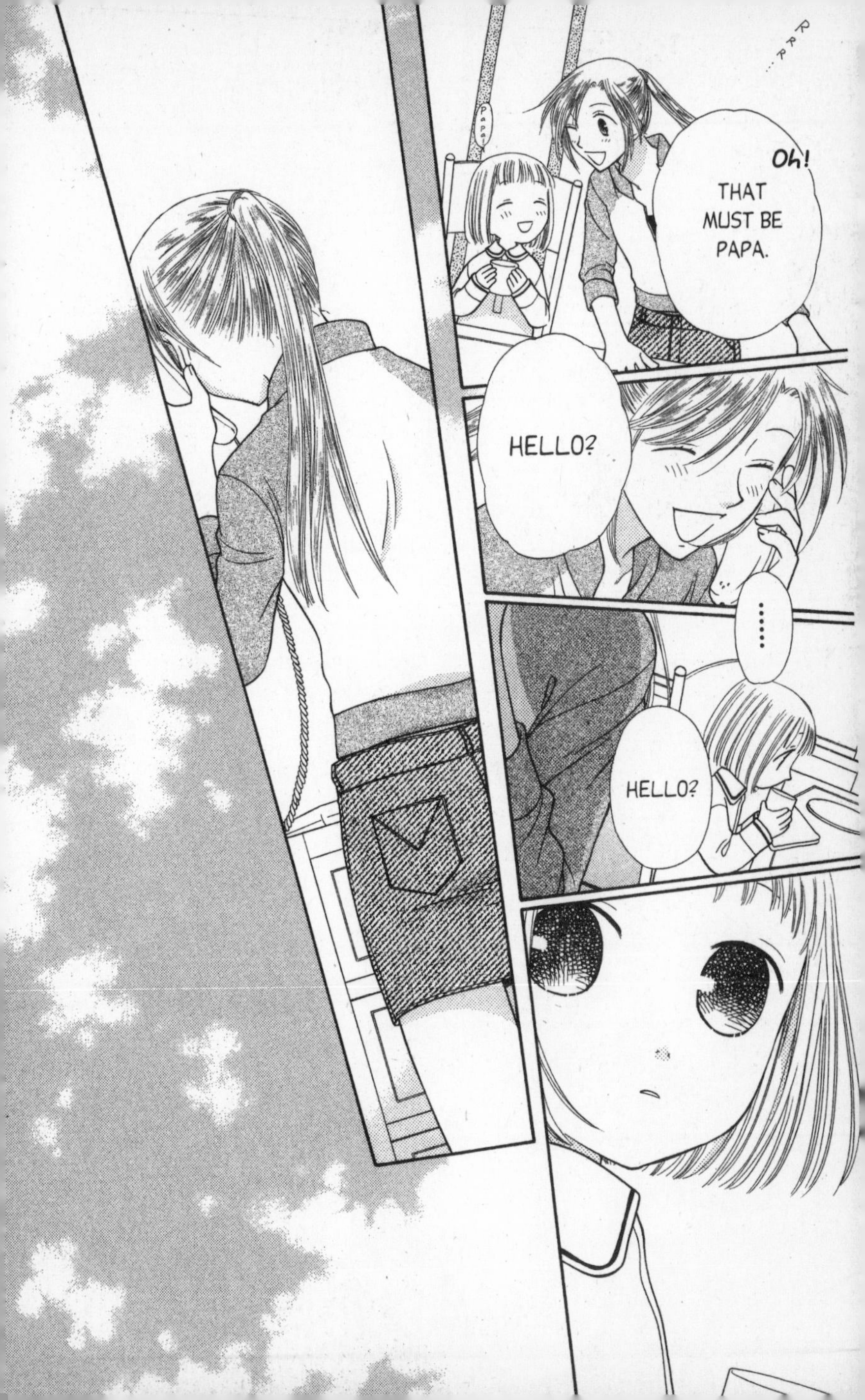
RRRR...
Papa!
Oh! THAT MUST BE PAPA.
HELLO?
......
HELLO?

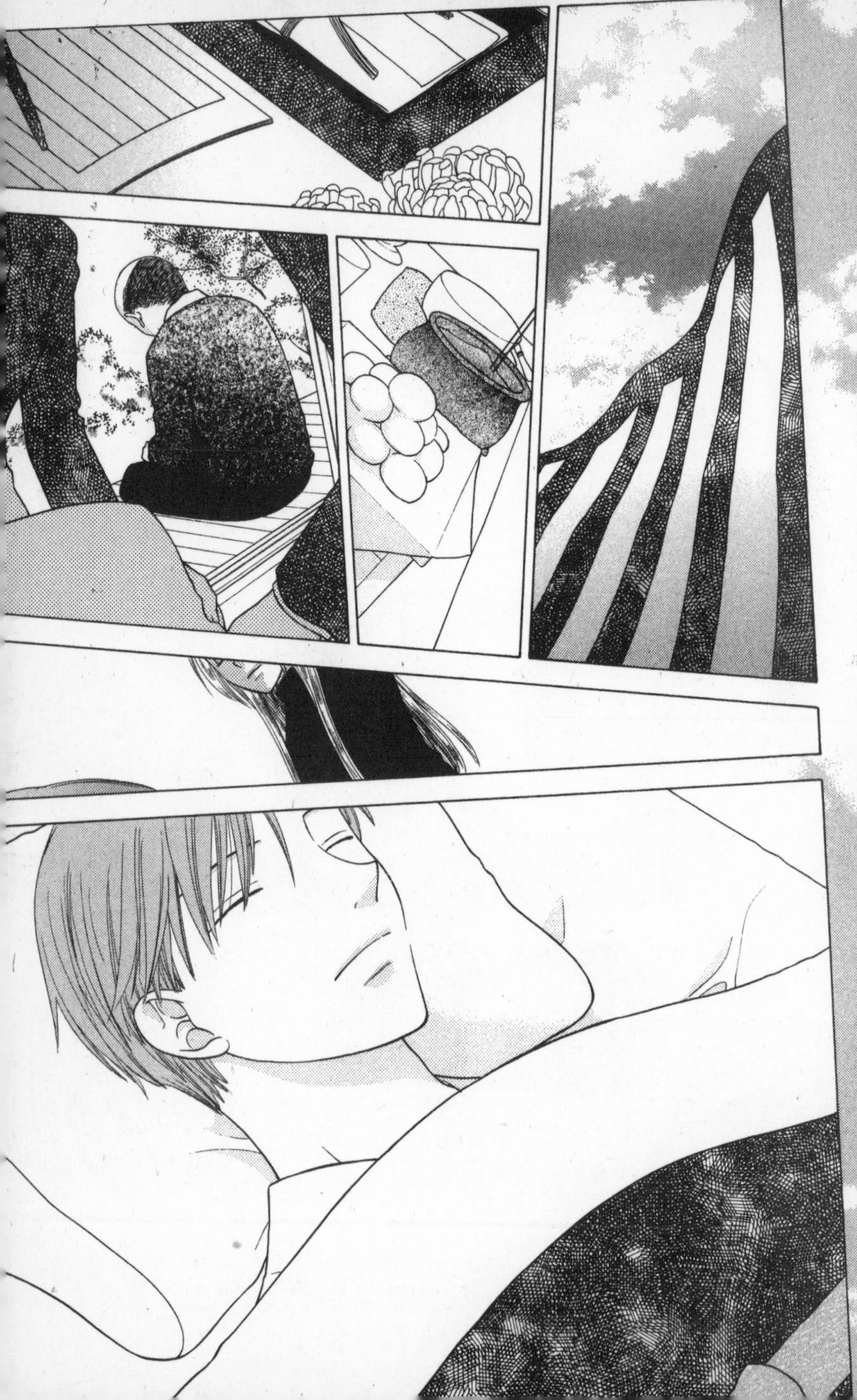

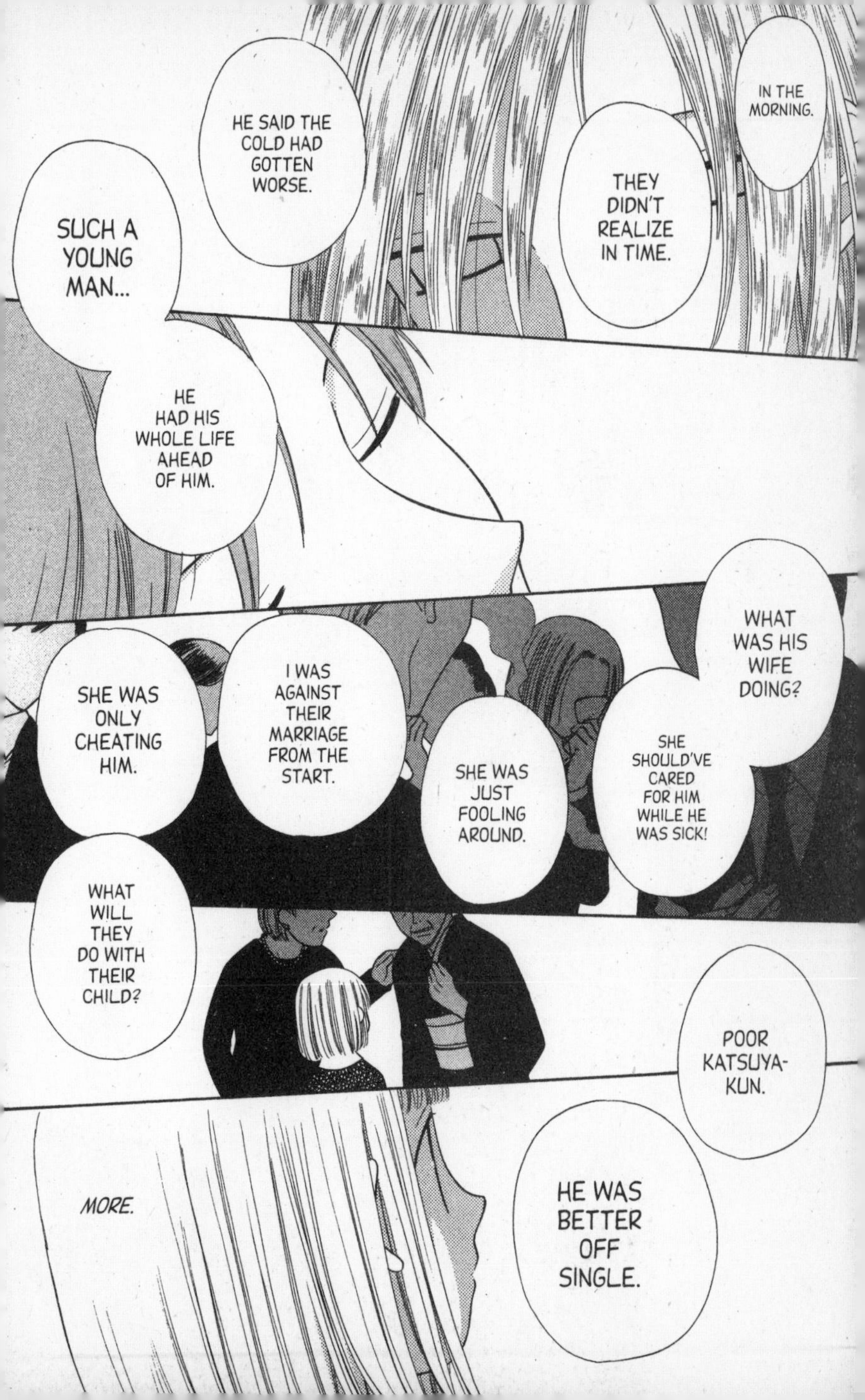
IN THE MORNING.
THEY DIDN'T REALIZE IN TIME.
HE SAID THE COLD HAD GOTTEN WORSE.
SUCH A YOUNG MAN...
HE HAD HIS WHOLE LIFE AHEAD OF HIM.
WHAT WAS HIS WIFE DOING?
SHE SHOULD'VE CARED FOR HIM WHILE HE WAS SICK!
SHE WAS JUST FOOLING AROUND.
I WAS AGAINST THEIR MARRIAGE FROM THE START.
SHE WAS ONLY CHEATING HIM.
POOR KATSUYA-KUN.
WHAT WILL THEY DO WITH THEIR CHILD?
HE WAS BETTER OFF SINGLE.
MORE.

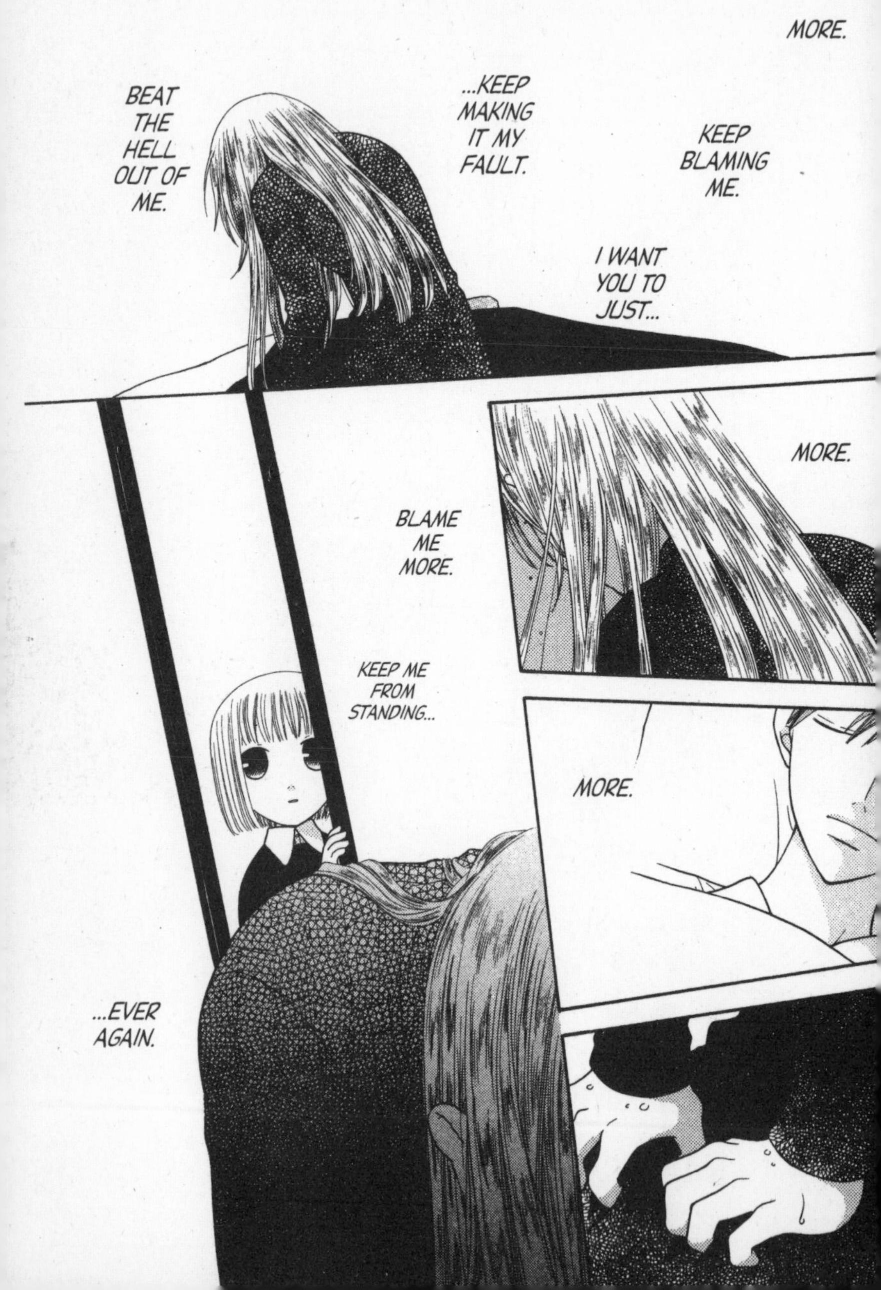
MORE.
KEEP BLAMING ME.
I WANT YOU TO JUST...
...KEEP MAKING IT MY FAULT.
BEAT THE HELL OUT OF ME.
MORE.
MORE.
BLAME ME MORE.
KEEP ME FROM STANDING...
...EVER AGAIN.

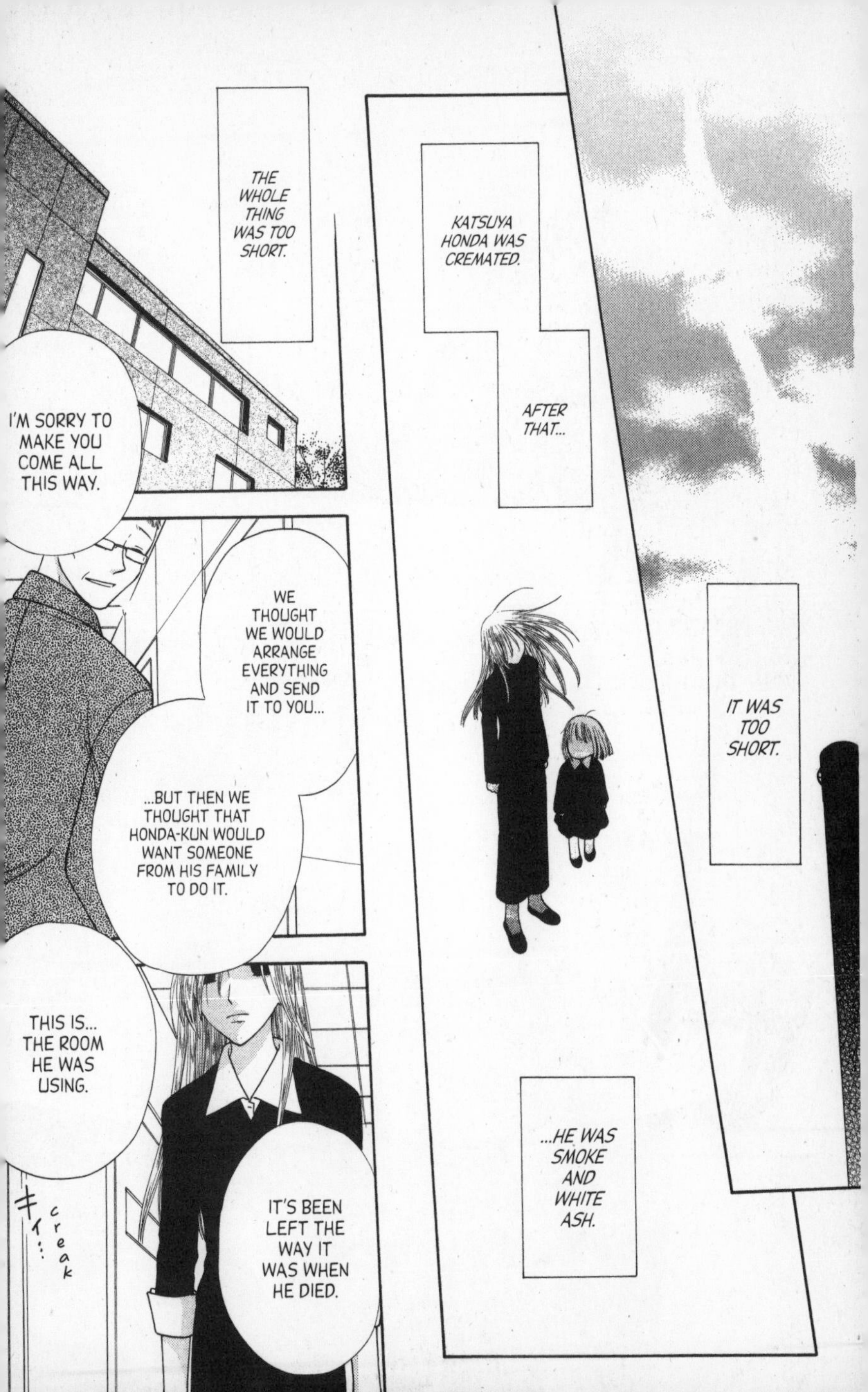
KATSUYA HONDA WAS CREMATED.
AFTER THAT...
IT WAS TOO SHORT.
...HE WAS SMOKE AND WHITE ASH.
THE WHOLE THING WAS TOO SHORT.
I'M SORRY TO MAKE YOU COME ALL THIS WAY.
WE THOUGHT WE WOULD ARRANGE EVERYTHING AND SEND IT TO YOU...
...BUT THEN WE THOUGHT THAT HONDA-KUN WOULD WANT SOMEONE FROM HIS FAMILY TO DO IT.
THIS IS... THE ROOM HE WAS USING.
IT'S BEEN LEFT THE WAY IT WAS WHEN HE DIED.
キイ...
creak

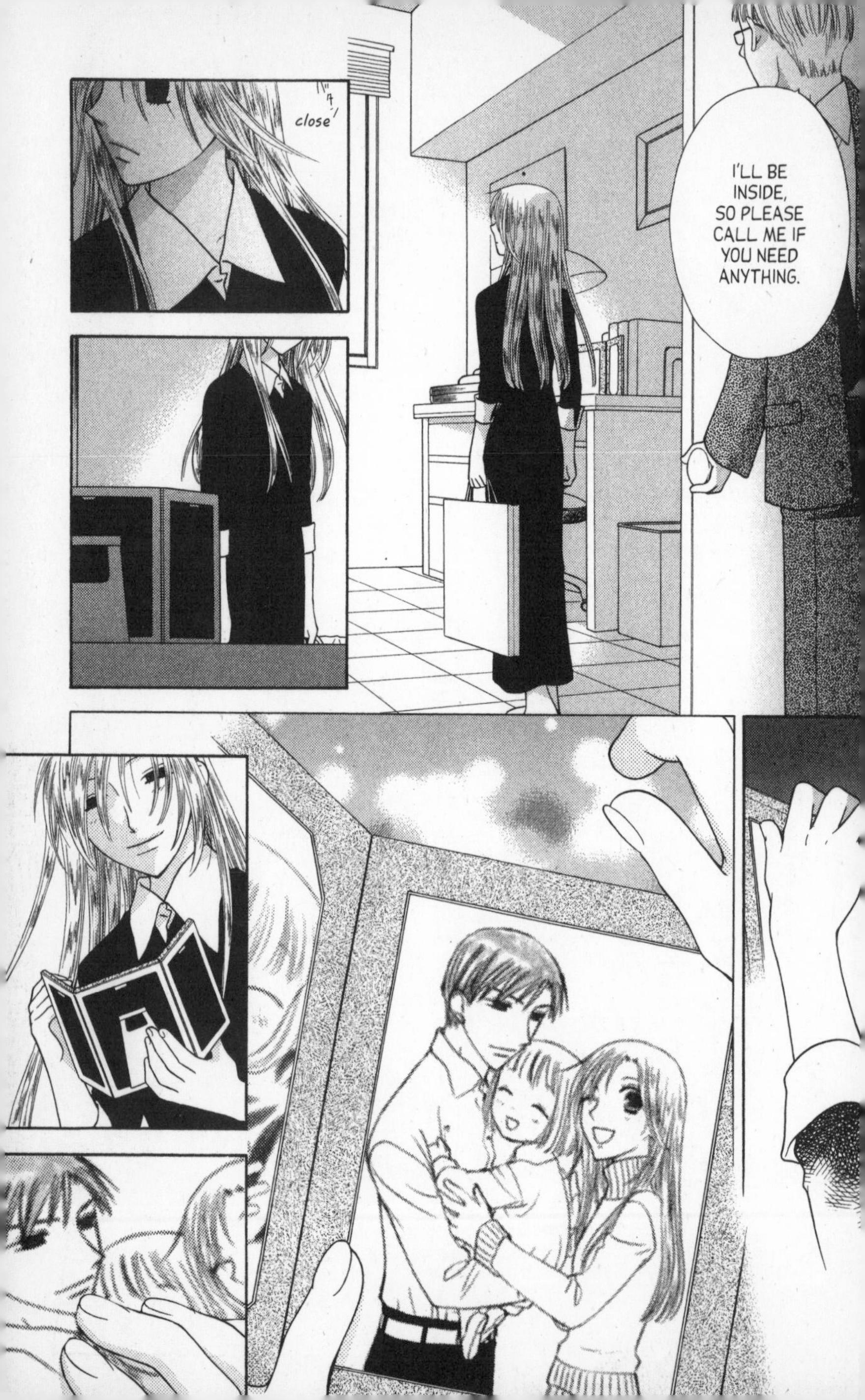
I'LL BE INSIDE, SO PLEASE CALL ME IF YOU NEED ANYTHING.
close

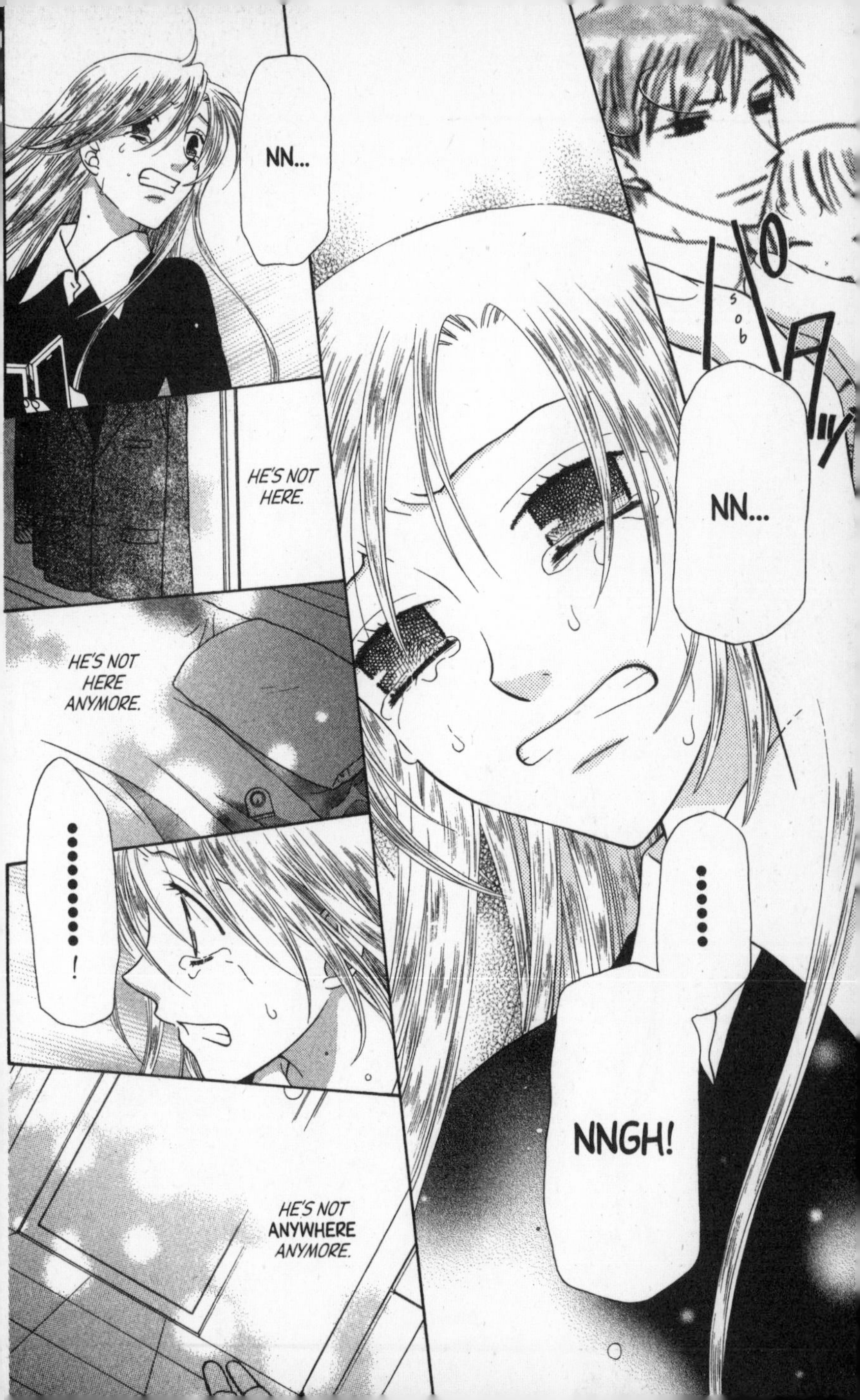
sob
NN...
......
NNGH!
NN...
HE'S NOT HERE.
HE'S NOT HERE ANYMORE.
......!
HE'S NOT ANYWHERE ANYMORE.

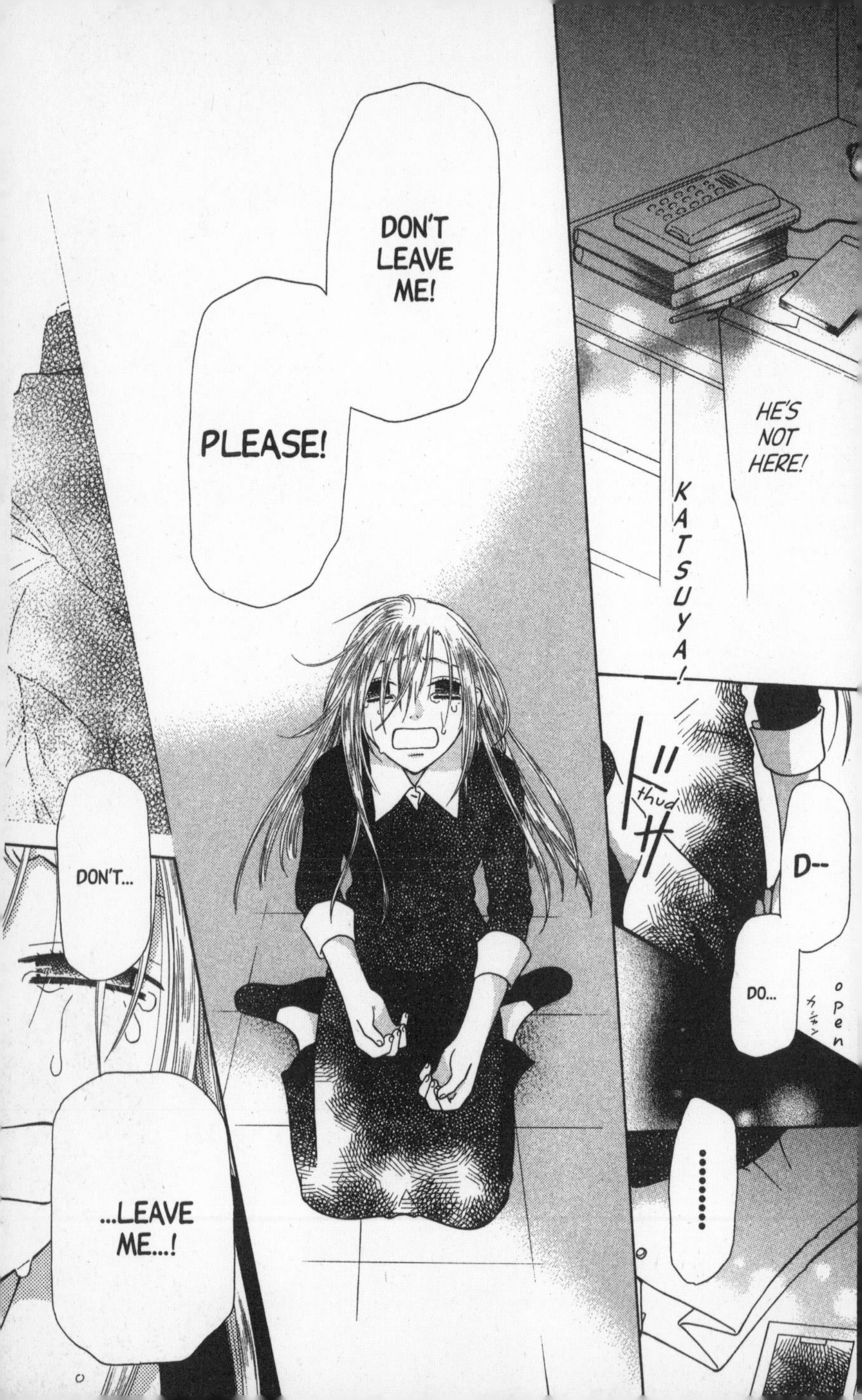
HE'S NOT HERE!
KATSUYA!
thud
D--
DO...
open
........!
DON'T LEAVE ME!
PLEASE!
DON'T...
...LEAVE ME...!

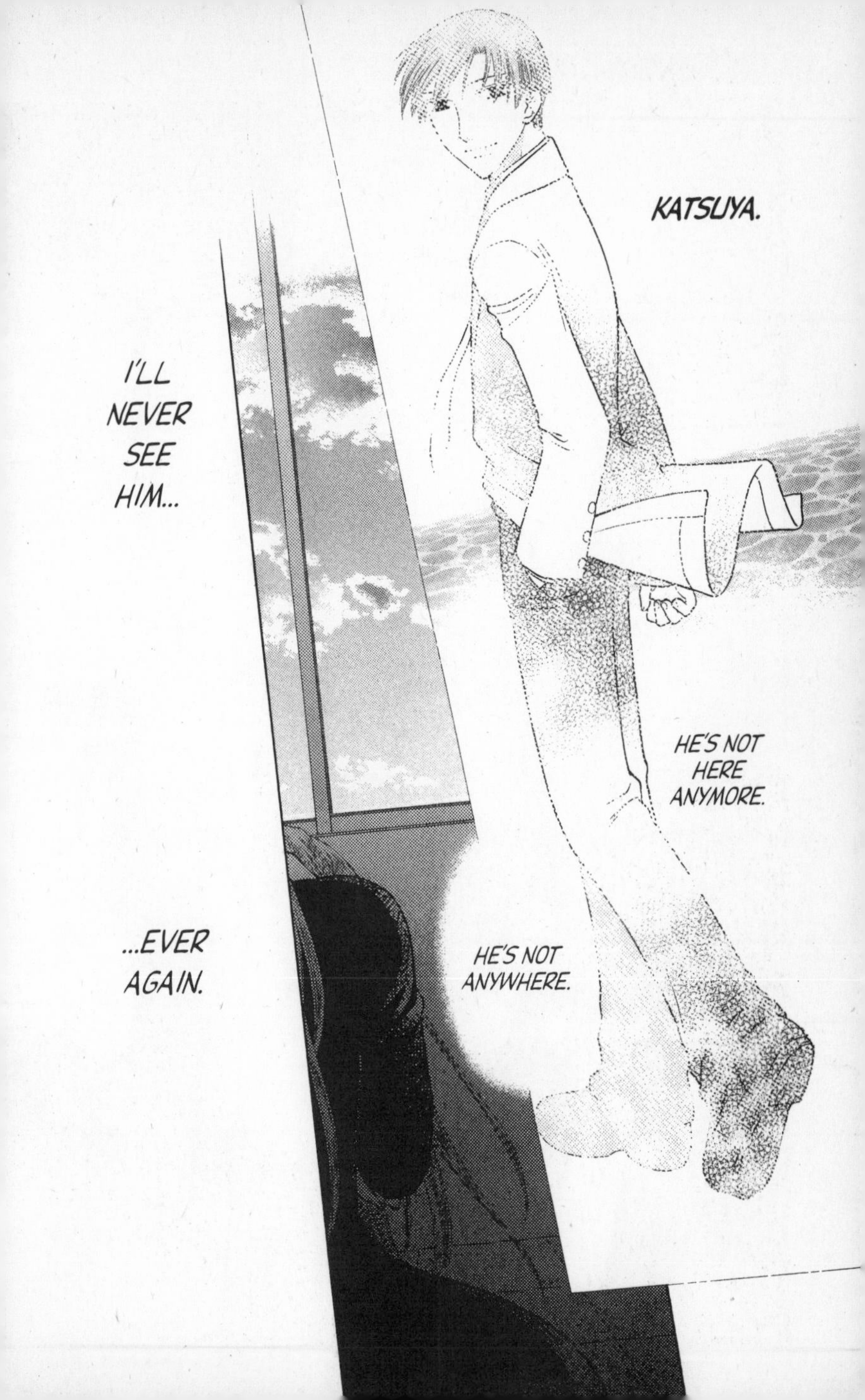
KATSUYA.
HE'S NOT HERE ANYMORE.
HE'S NOT ANYWHERE.
I'LL NEVER SEE HIM...
...EVER AGAIN.

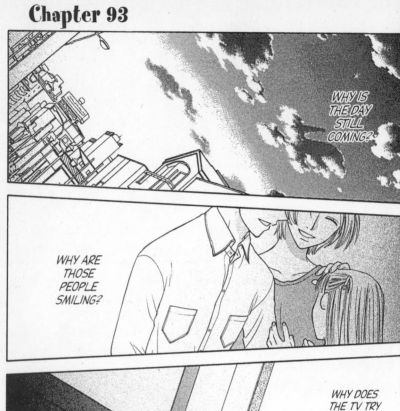

WHY IS THE DAY STILL COMING?

WHY ARE THOSE PEOPLE SMILING?

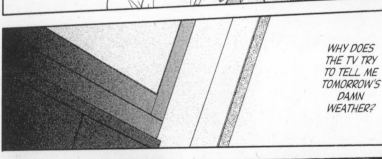

WHY DOES THE TV TRY TO TELL ME TOMORROW'S DAMN WEATHER?

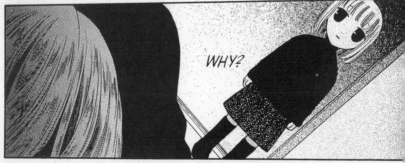

WHY?

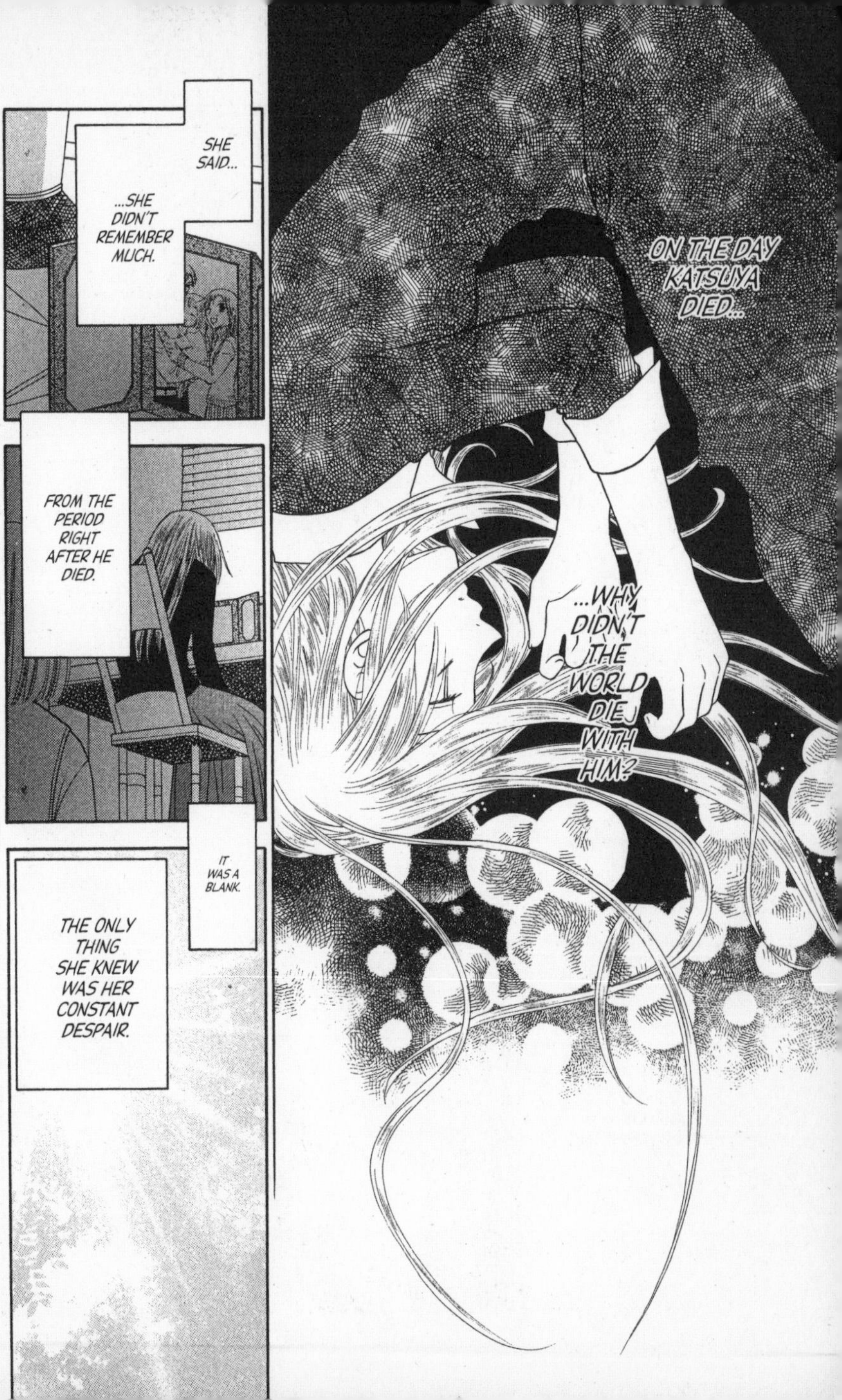
ON THE DAY KATSUYA DIED...
...WHY DIDN'T THE WORLD DIE WITH HIM?
SHE SAID...
...SHE DIDN'T REMEMBER MUCH.
FROM THE PERIOD RIGHT AFTER HE DIED.
IT WAS A BLANK.
THE ONLY THING SHE KNEW WAS HER CONSTANT DESPAIR.

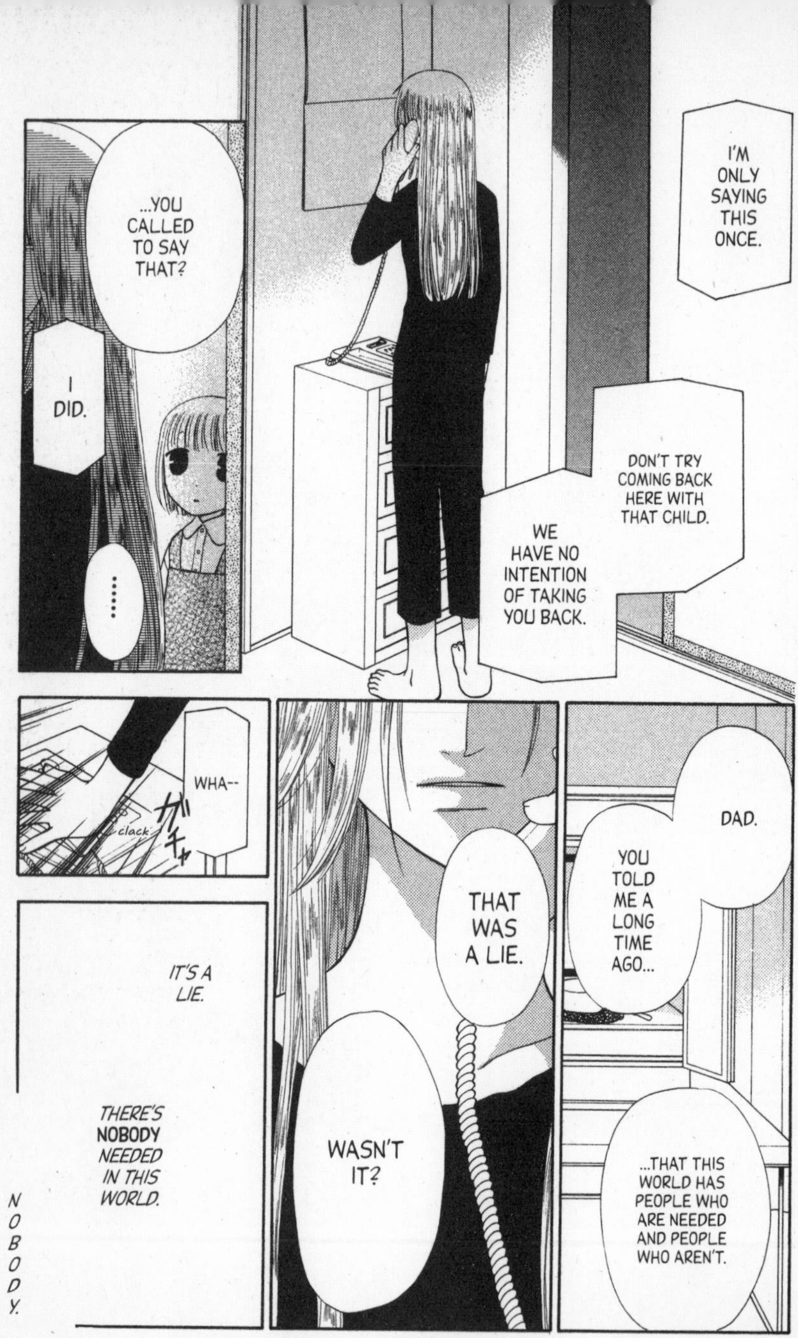
I'M ONLY SAYING THIS ONCE.
DON'T TRY COMING BACK HERE WITH THAT CHILD.
WE HAVE NO INTENTION OF TAKING YOU BACK.
...YOU CALLED TO SAY THAT?
I DID.
......
DAD.
YOU TOLD ME A LONG TIME AGO...
...THAT THIS WORLD HAS PEOPLE WHO ARE NEEDED AND PEOPLE WHO AREN'T.
THAT WAS A LIE.
WASN'T IT?
WHA--
ガチャ
clack
IT'S A LIE.
THERE'S NOBODY NEEDED IN THIS WORLD.
NOBODY.

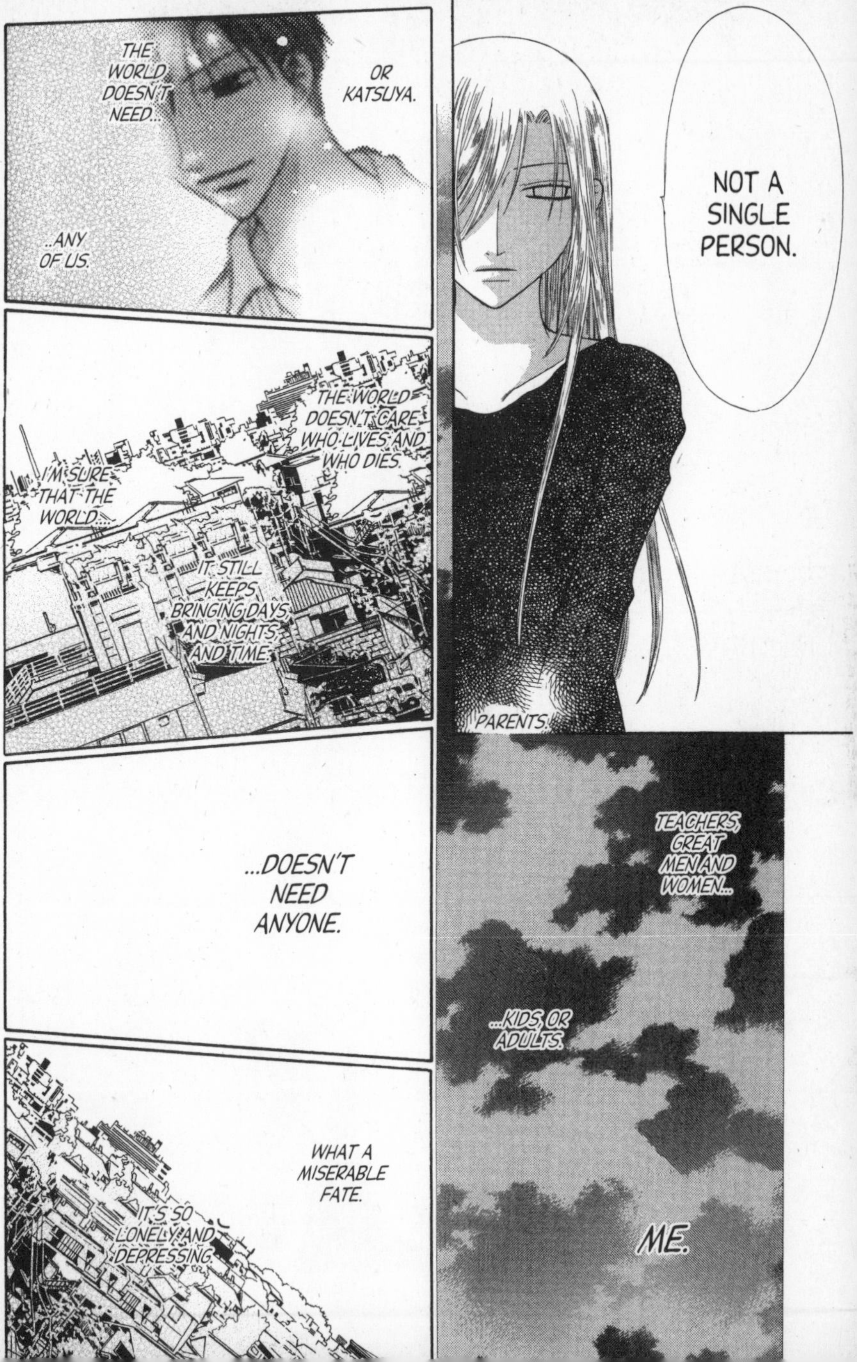
NOT A SINGLE PERSON.
PARENTS.
TEACHERS, GREAT MEN AND WOMEN...
...KIDS, OR ADULTS.
ME.
OR KATSUYA.
THE WORLD DOESN'T NEED...
..ANY OF US.
THE WORLD DOESN'T CARE WHO LIVES AND WHO DIES.
I'M SURE THAT THE WORLD...
IT STILL KEEPS BRINGING DAYS AND NIGHTS AND TIME.
...DOESN'T NEED ANYONE.
WHAT A MISERABLE FATE.
IT'S SO LONELY AND DEPRESSING.

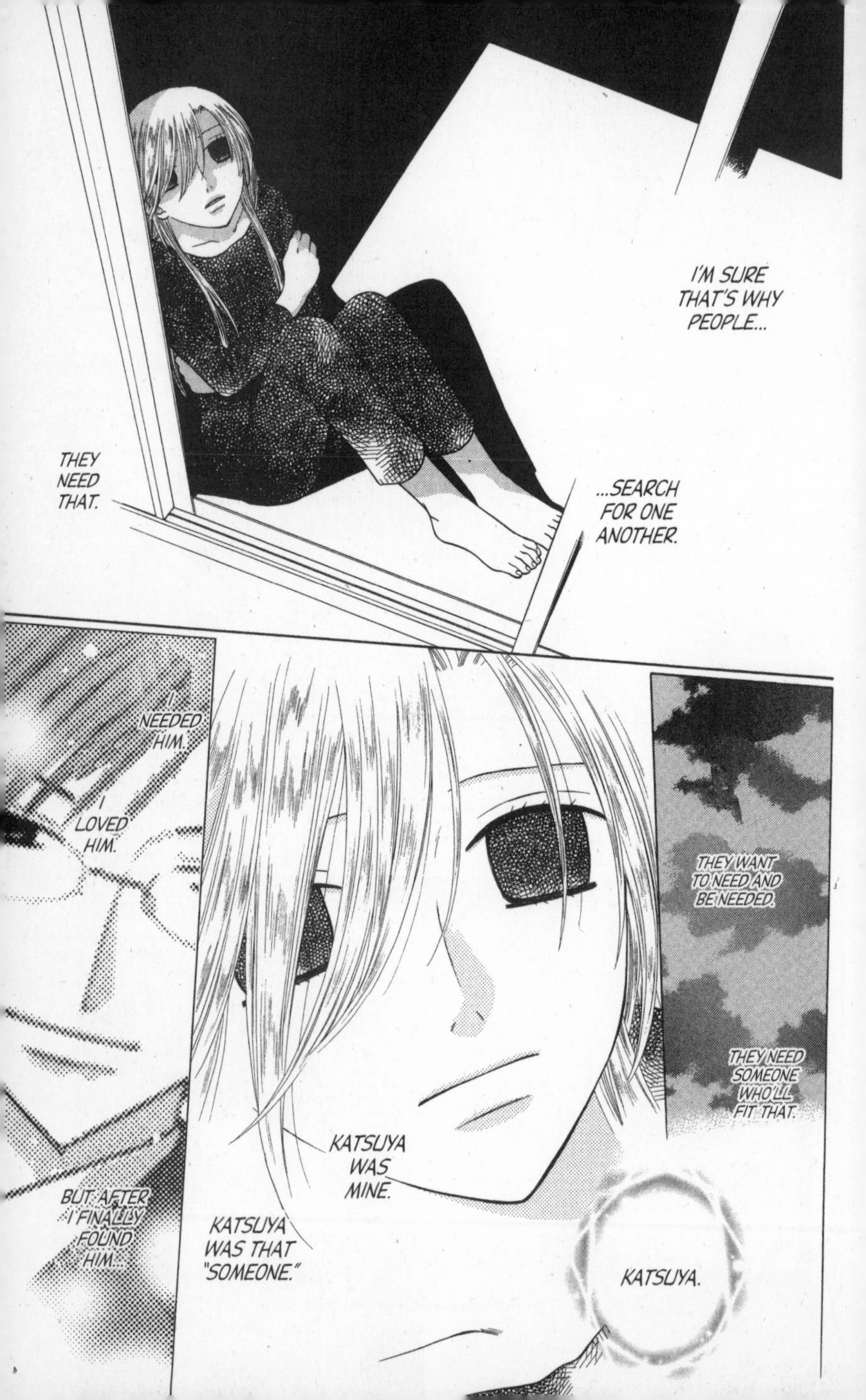
I'M SURE THAT'S WHY PEOPLE...
...SEARCH FOR ONE ANOTHER.
THEY NEED THAT.
THEY WANT TO NEED AND BE NEEDED.
THEY NEED SOMEONE WHO'LL FIT THAT.
KATSUYA WAS MINE.
KATSUYA WAS THAT "SOMEONE."
KATSUYA.
I NEEDED HIM.
I LOVED HIM.
BUT AFTER I FINALLY FOUND HIM...

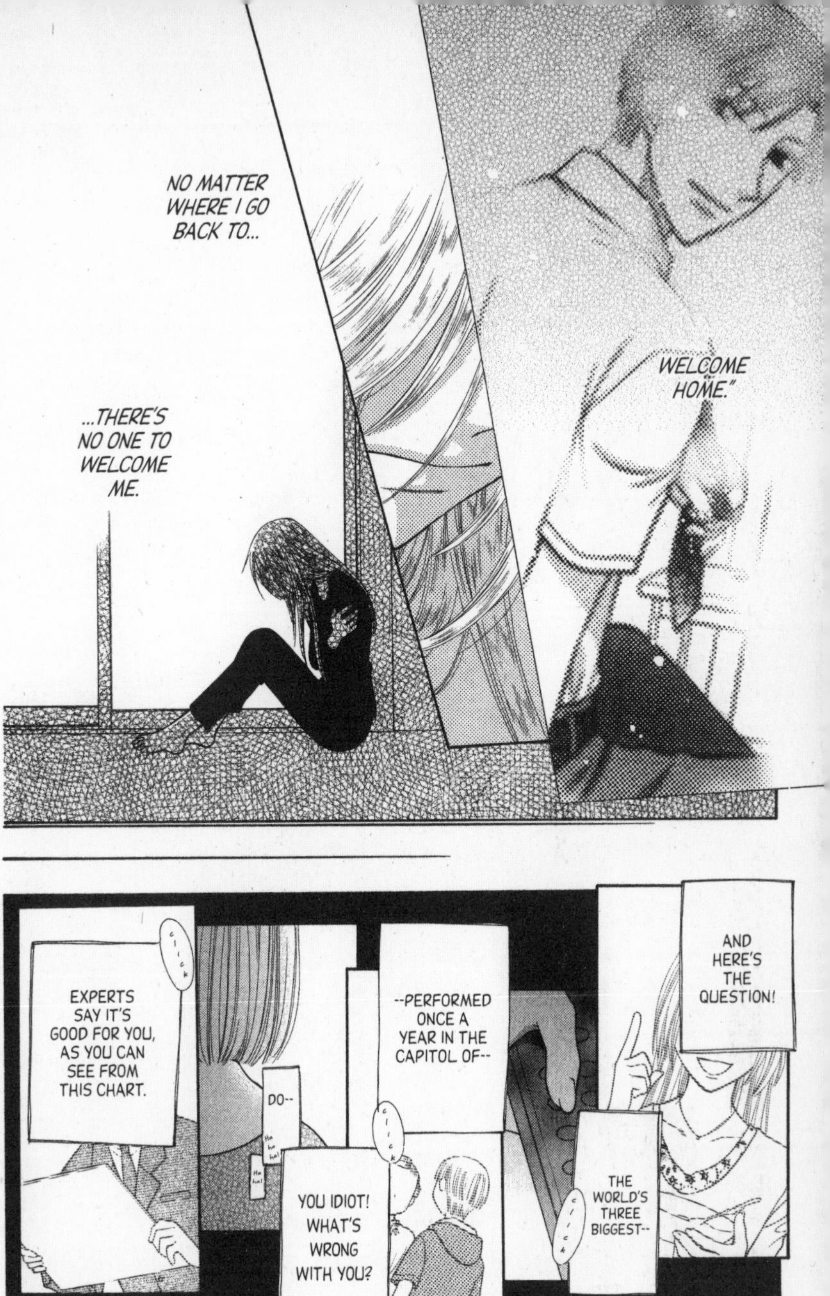
WELCOME HOME."
NO MATTER WHERE I GO BACK TO...
...THERE'S NO ONE TO WELCOME ME.
AND HERE'S THE QUESTION!
THE WORLD'S THREE BIGGEST--
click
--PERFORMED ONCE A YEAR IN THE CAPITOL OF--
YOU IDIOT! WHAT'S WRONG WITH YOU?
click
DO--
Ha ha ha!
Ha ha!
EXPERTS SAY IT'S GOOD FOR YOU, AS YOU CAN SEE FROM THIS CHART.
click

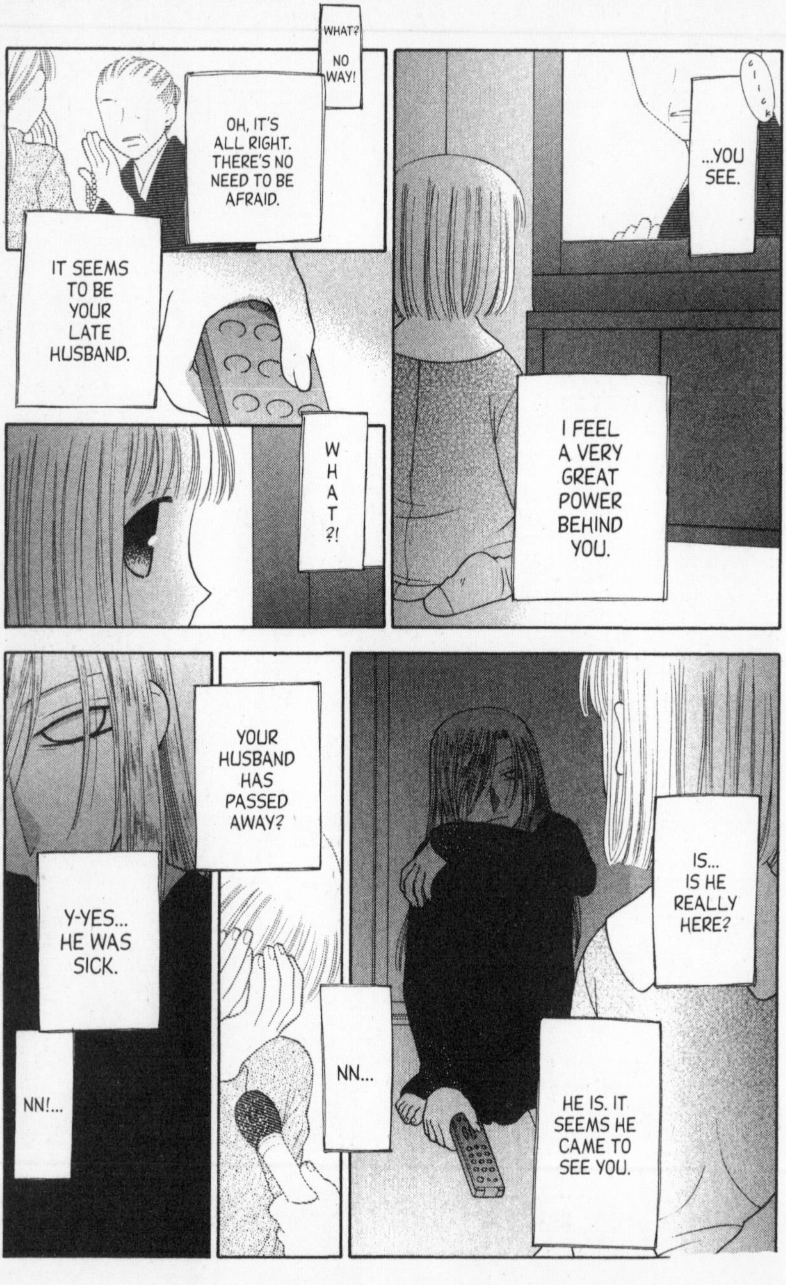
c l i c k
...YOU SEE.
I FEEL A VERY GREAT POWER BEHIND YOU.
WHAT? NO WAY!
OH, IT'S ALL RIGHT. THERE'S NO NEED TO BE AFRAID.
IT SEEMS TO BE YOUR LATE HUSBAND.
WHAT?!
IS... IS HE REALLY HERE?
HE IS. IT SEEMS HE CAME TO SEE YOU.
YOUR HUSBAND HAS PASSED AWAY?
NN...
Y-YES... HE WAS SICK.
NN!...

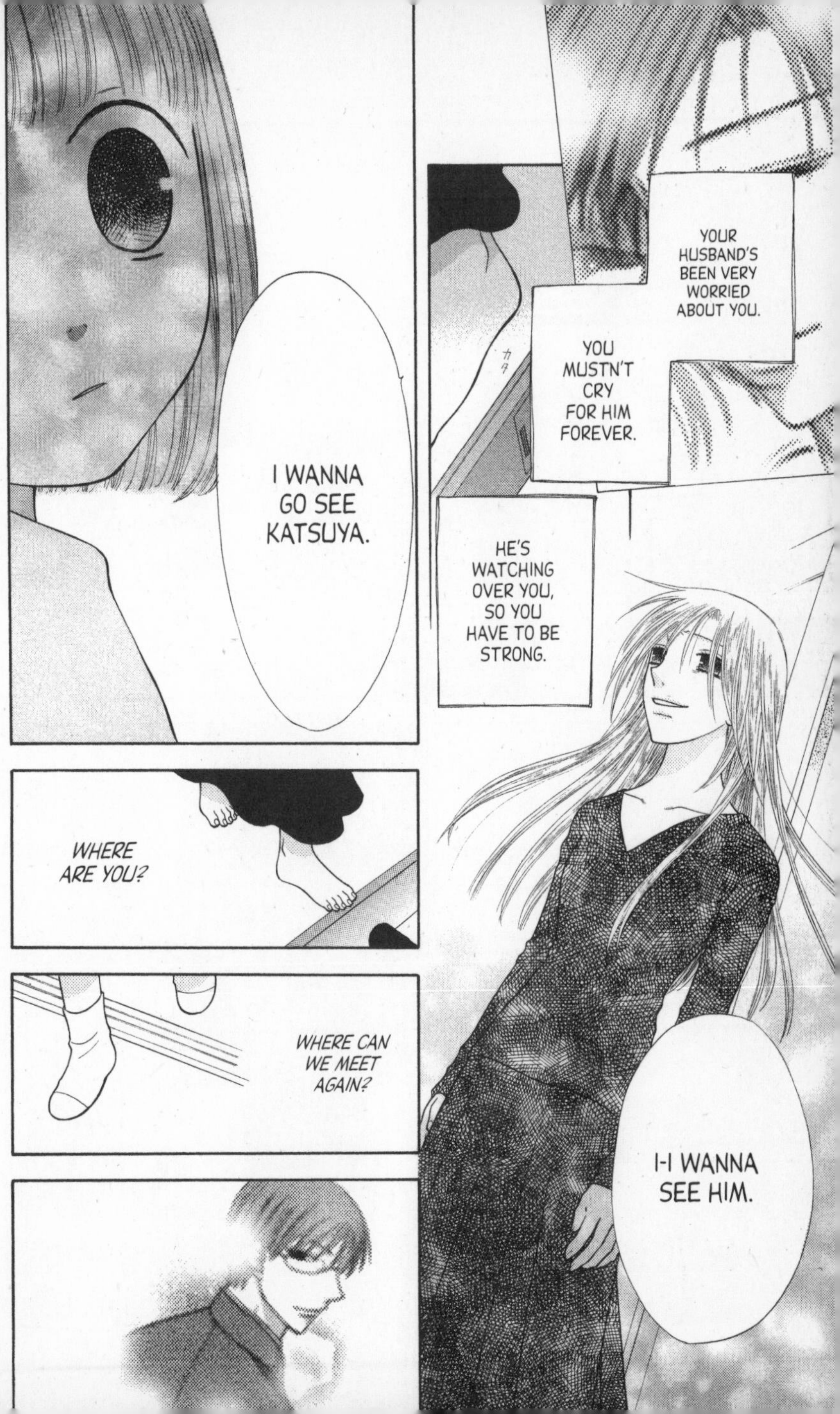
YOUR HUSBAND'S BEEN VERY WORRIED ABOUT YOU.
YOU MUSTN'T CRY FOR HIM FOREVER.
カタ
HE'S WATCHING OVER YOU, SO YOU HAVE TO BE STRONG.
I-I WANNA SEE HIM.
I WANNA GO SEE KATSUYA.
WHERE ARE YOU?
WHERE CAN WE MEET AGAIN?

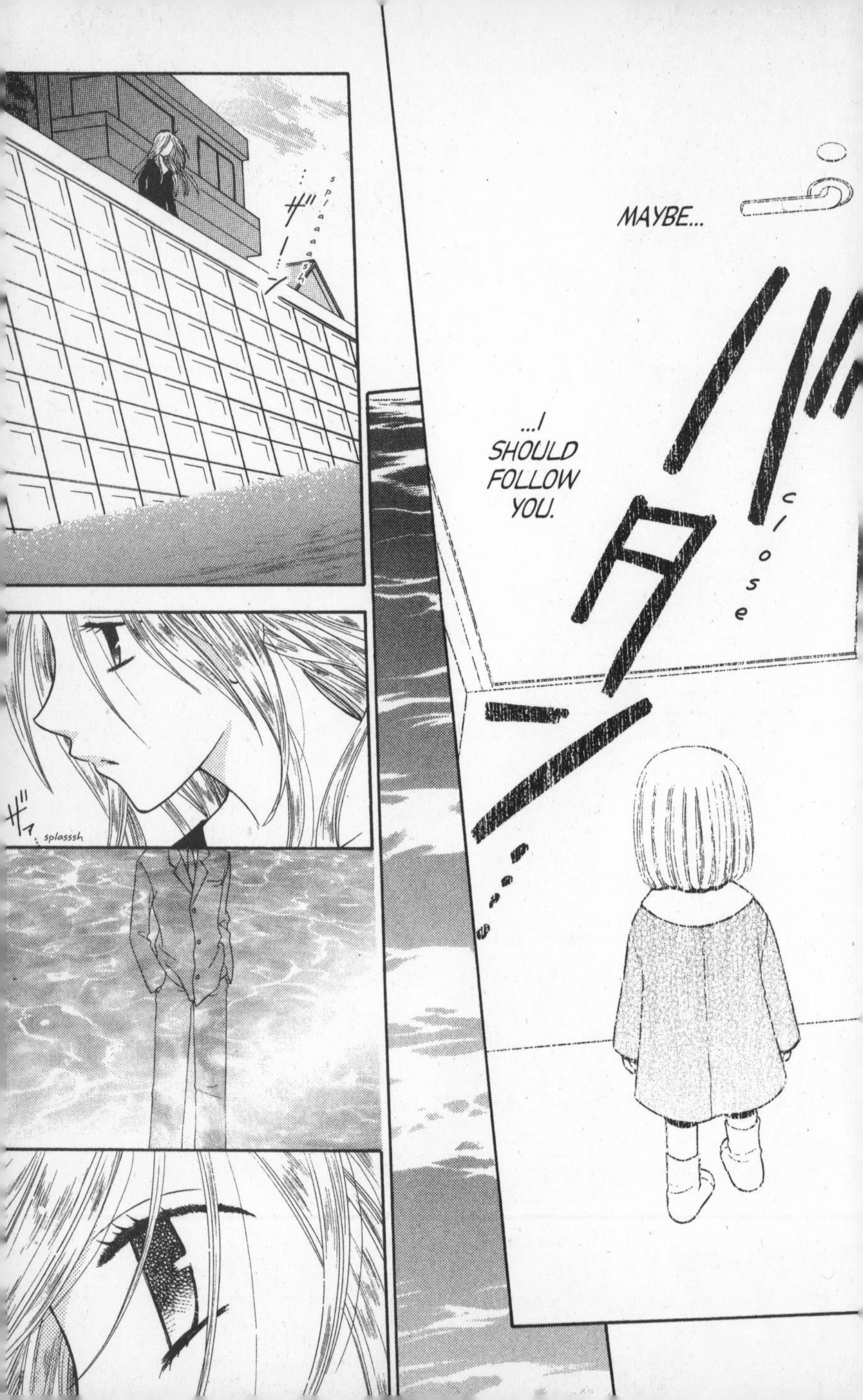
MAYBE...
...I SHOULD FOLLOW YOU.
close
splaaaash
splasssh

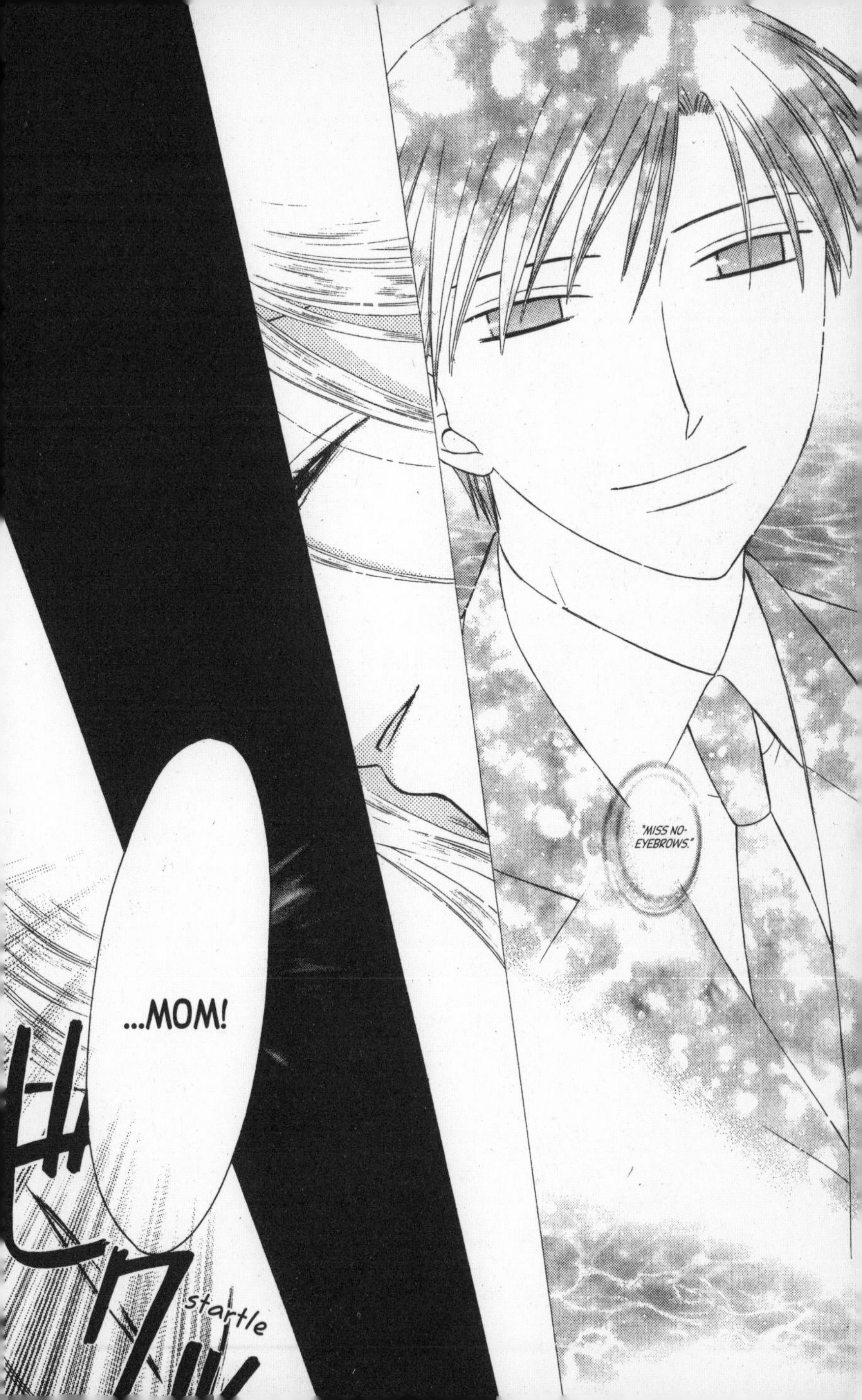
"MISS NO-EYEBROWS."
...MOM!
startle

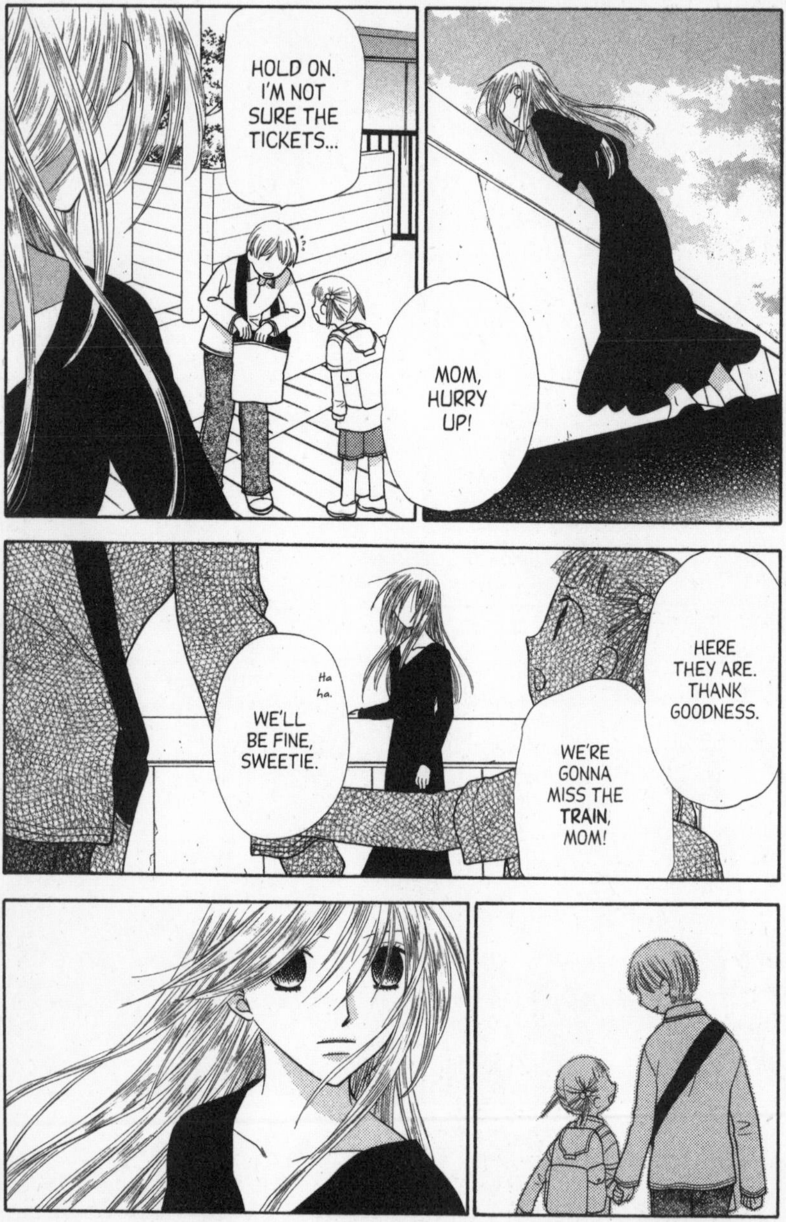
HOLD ON. I'M NOT SURE THE TICKETS...
MOM, HURRY UP!
HERE THEY ARE. THANK GOODNESS.
WE'RE GONNA MISS THE TRAIN, MOM!
Ha ha.
WE'LL BE FINE, SWEETIE.

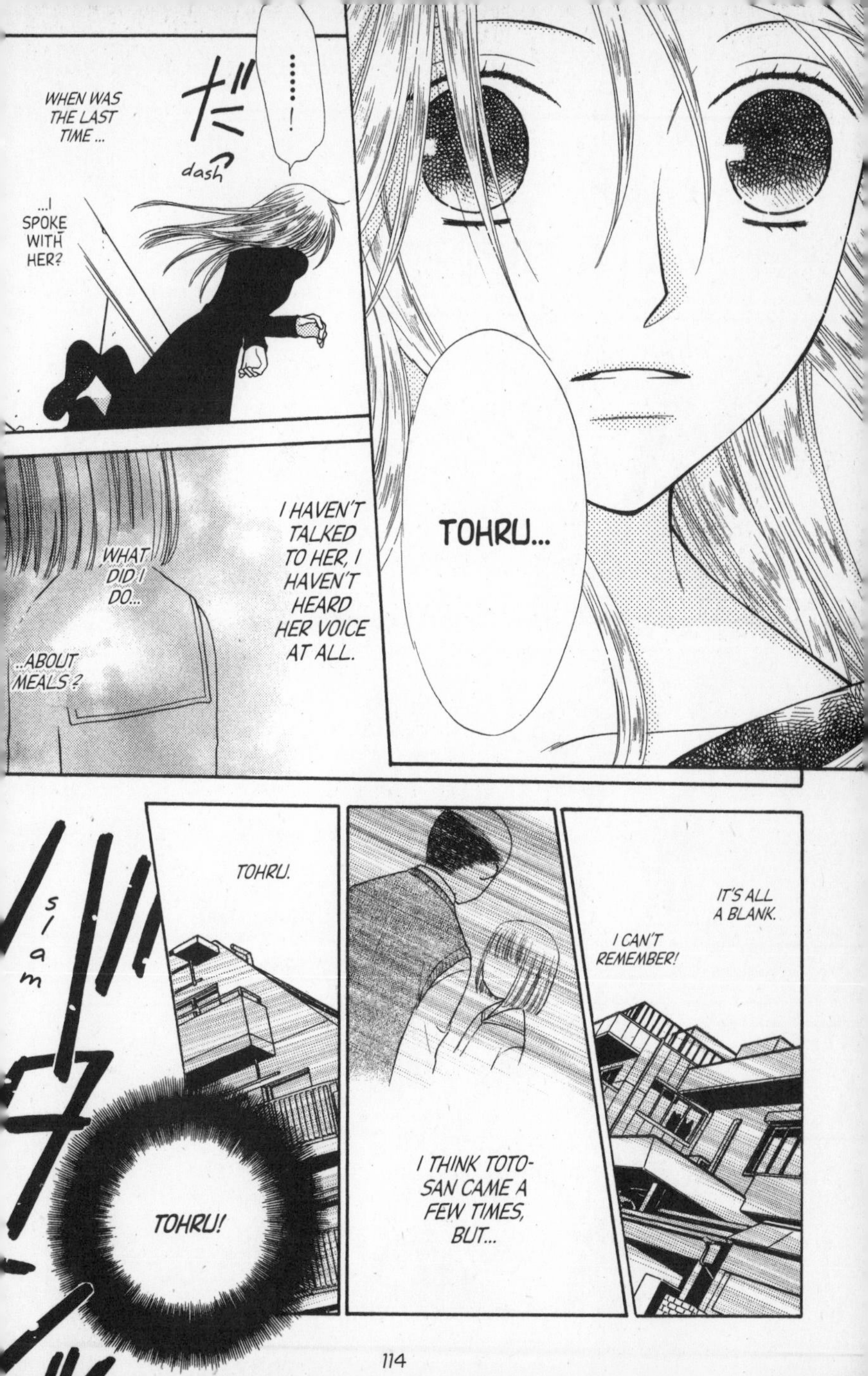
TOHRU...
......!
dash
WHEN WAS THE LAST TIME ...
...I SPOKE WITH HER?
I HAVEN'T TALKED TO HER, I HAVEN'T HEARD HER VOICE AT ALL.
WHAT DID I DO...
...ABOUT MEALS?
IT'S ALL A BLANK.
I CAN'T REMEMBER!
I THINK TOTO-SAN CAME A FEW TIMES, BUT...
TOHRU.
slam
TOHRU!

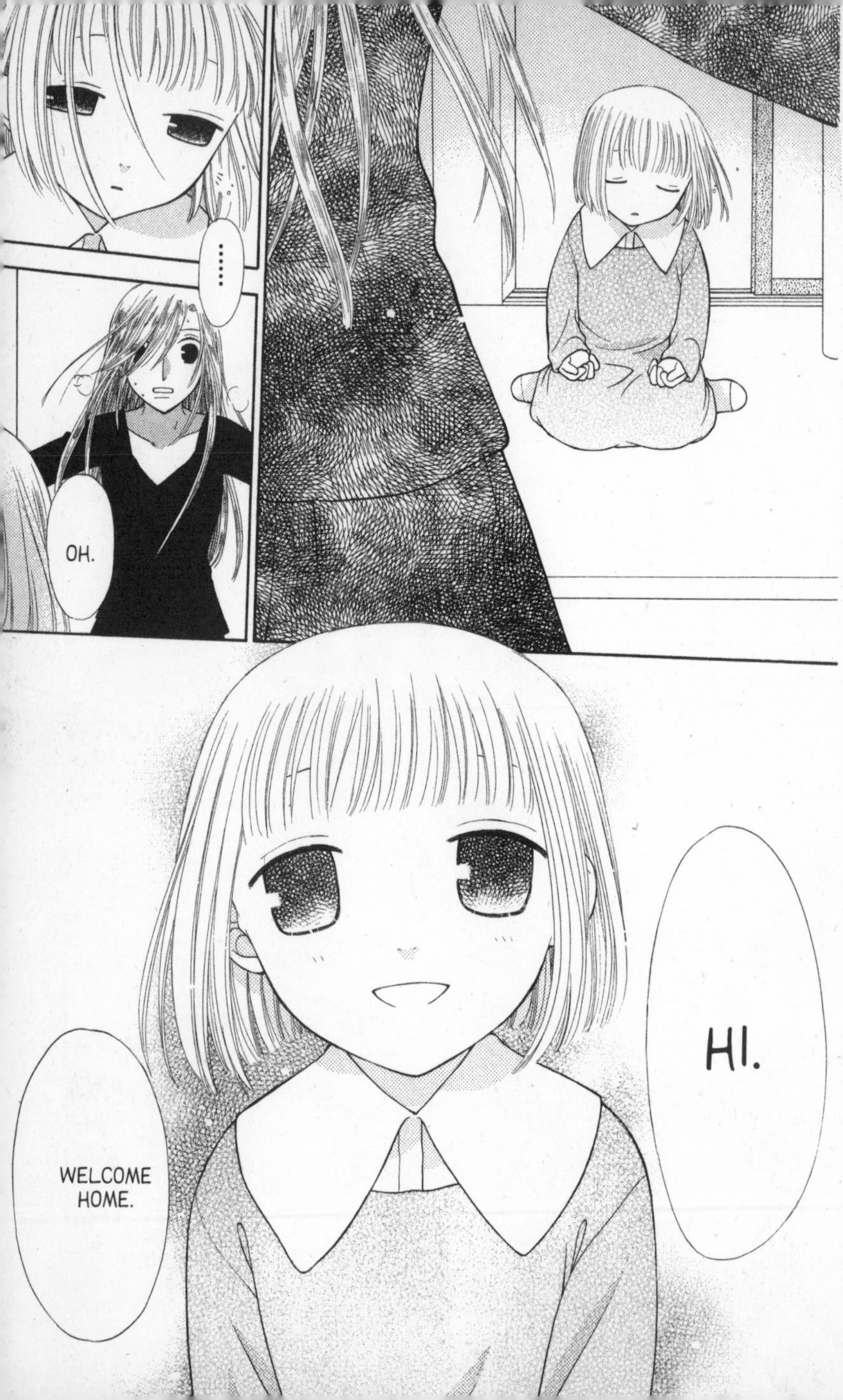
......
OH.
HI.
WELCOME HOME.

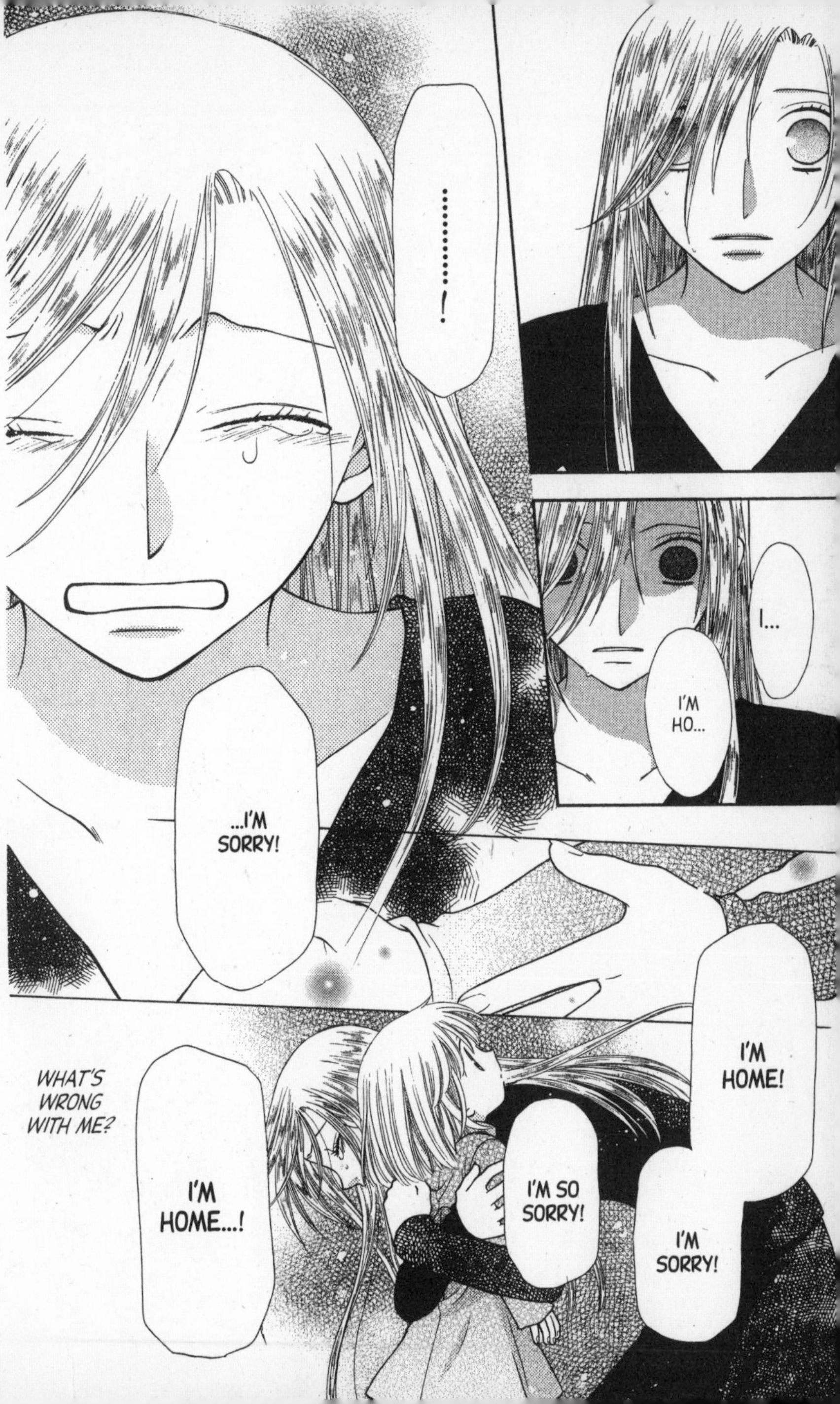
I...
I'M HO...
......!
...I'M SORRY!
I'M HOME!
I'M SORRY!
I'M SO SORRY!
I'M HOME...!
WHAT'S WRONG WITH ME?

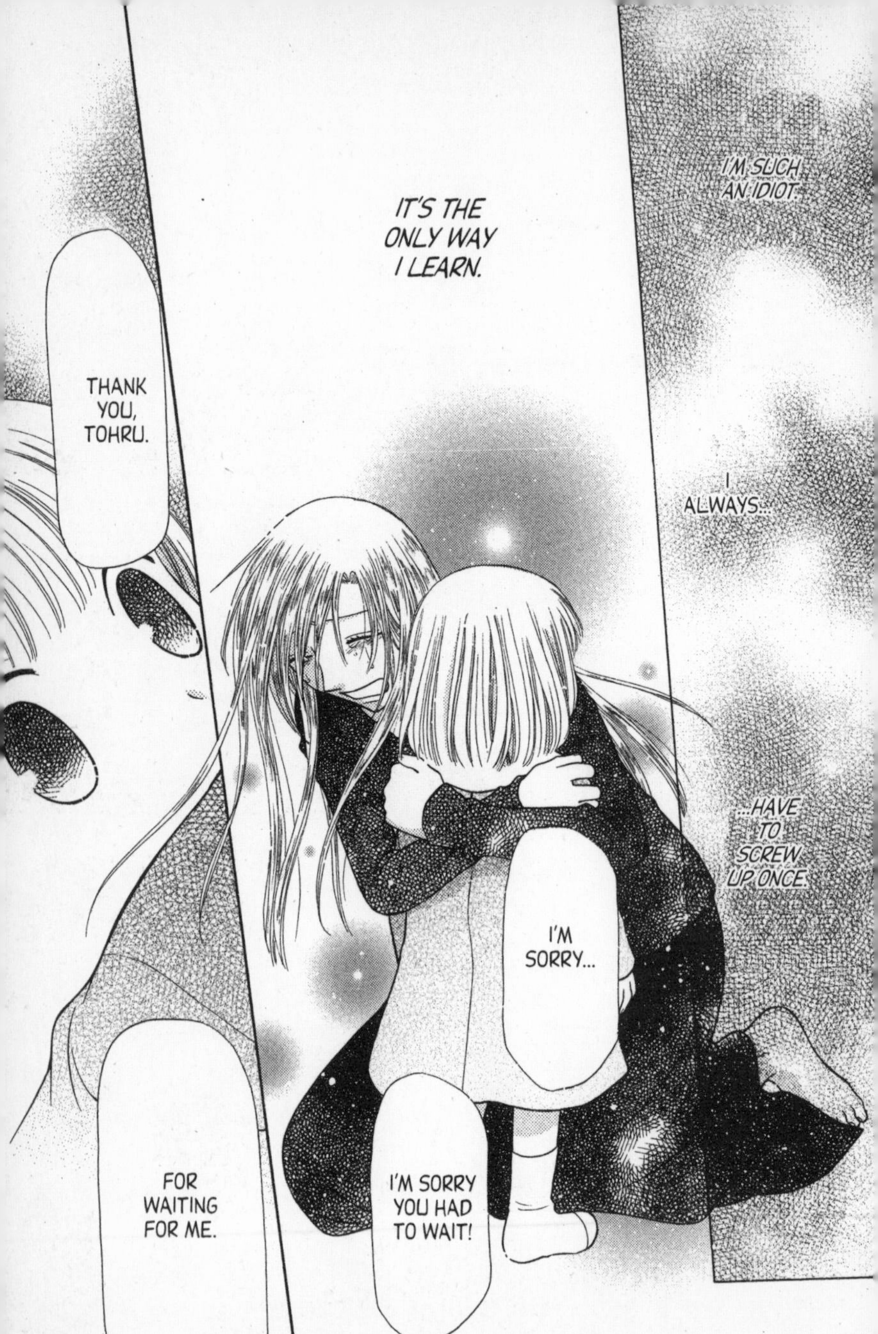
I'M SUCH AN IDIOT.
I ALWAYS...
...HAVE TO SCREW UP ONCE.
IT'S THE ONLY WAY I LEARN.
I'M SORRY...
I'M SORRY YOU HAD TO WAIT!
THANK YOU, TOHRU.
FOR WAITING FOR ME.

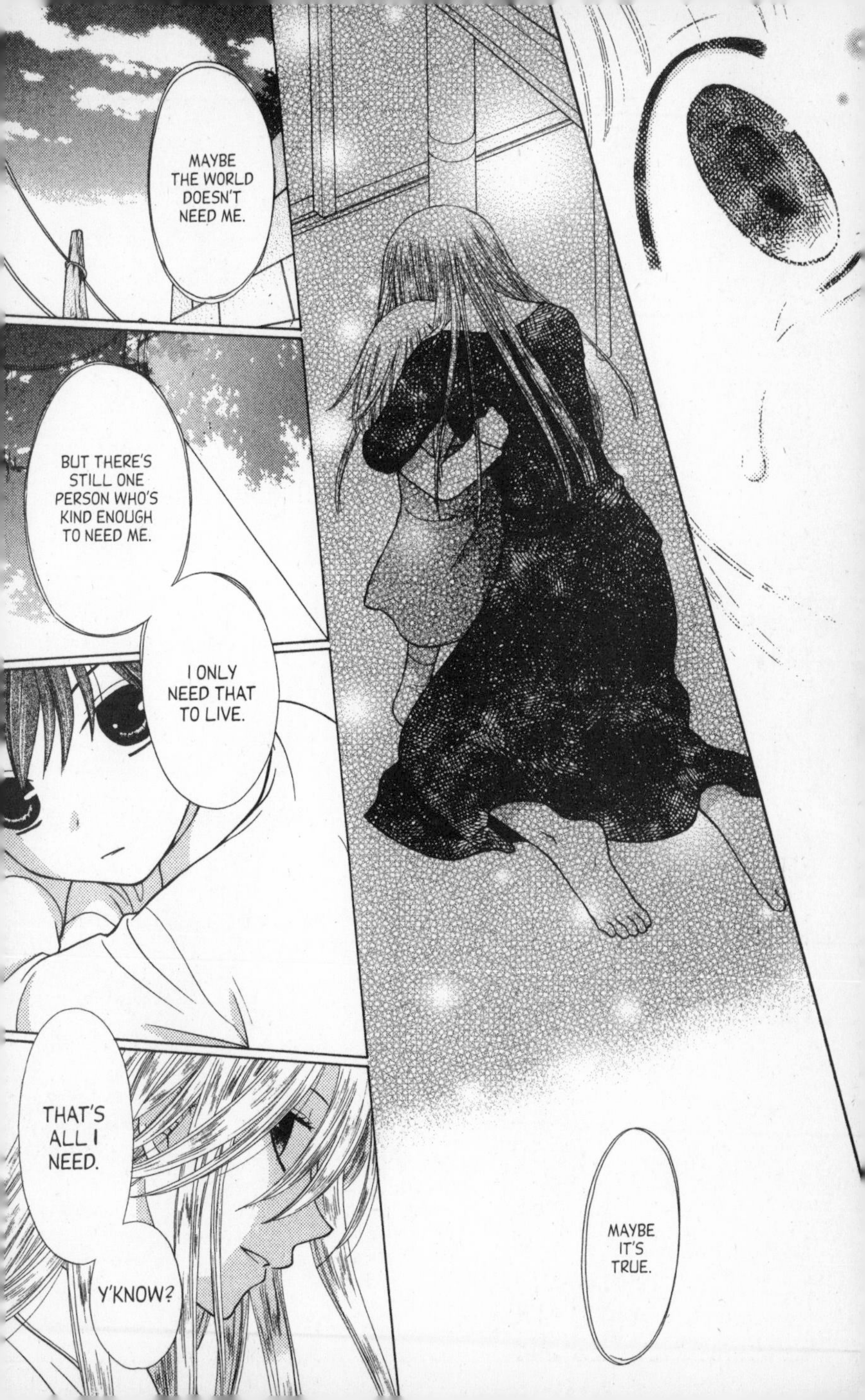
MAYBE IT'S TRUE.
MAYBE THE WORLD DOESN'T NEED ME.
BUT THERE'S STILL ONE PERSON WHO'S KIND ENOUGH TO NEED ME.
I ONLY NEED THAT TO LIVE.
THAT'S ALL I NEED.
Y'KNOW?

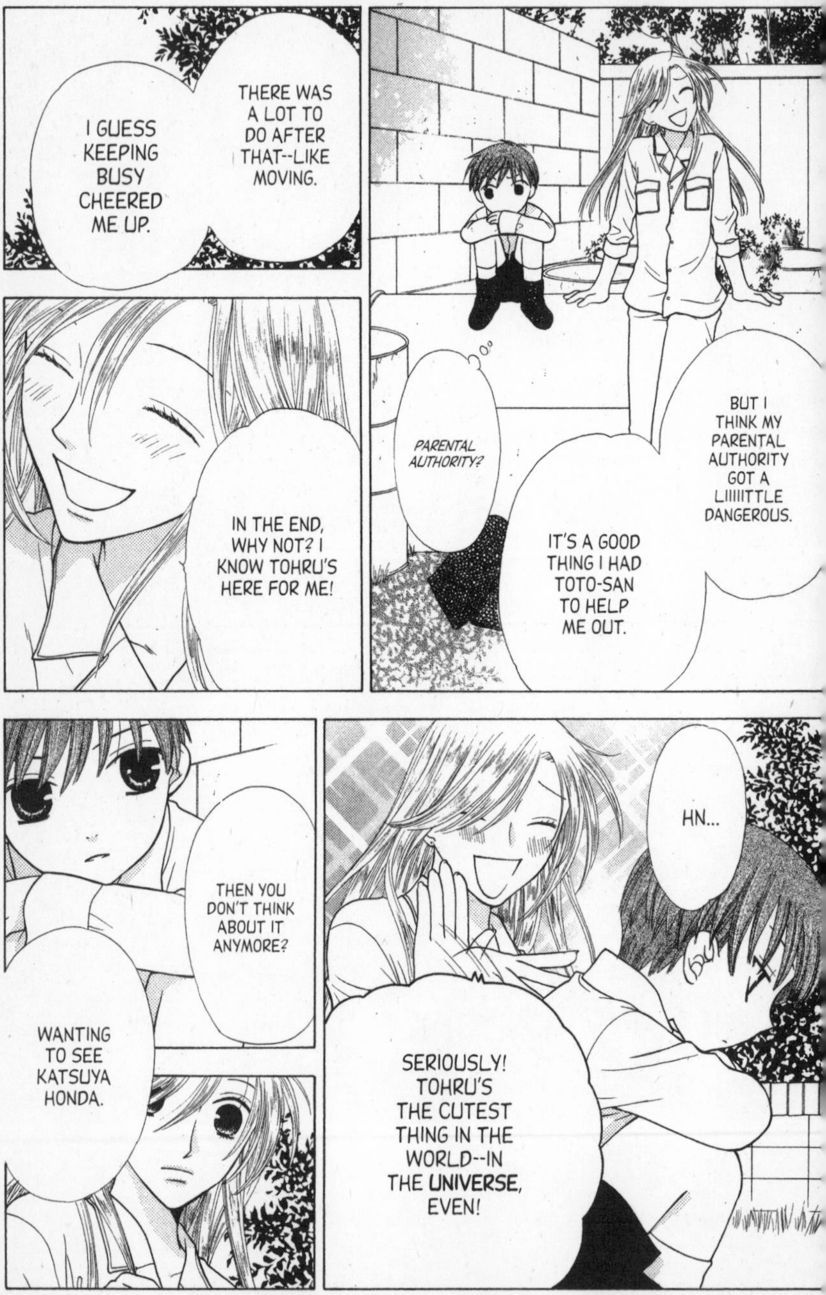
BUT I THINK MY PARENTAL AUTHORITY GOT A LIIIIITTLE DANGEROUS.
PARENTAL AUTHORITY?
IT'S A GOOD THING I HAD TOTO-SAN TO HELP ME OUT.
THERE WAS A LOT TO DO AFTER THAT--LIKE MOVING.
I GUESS KEEPING BUSY CHEERED ME UP.
IN THE END, WHY NOT? I KNOW TOHRU'S HERE FOR ME!
HN...
SERIOUSLY! TOHRU'S THE CUTEST THING IN THE WORLD--IN THE **UNIVERSE**, EVEN!
THEN YOU DON'T THINK ABOUT IT ANYMORE?
WANTING TO SEE KATSUYA HONDA.

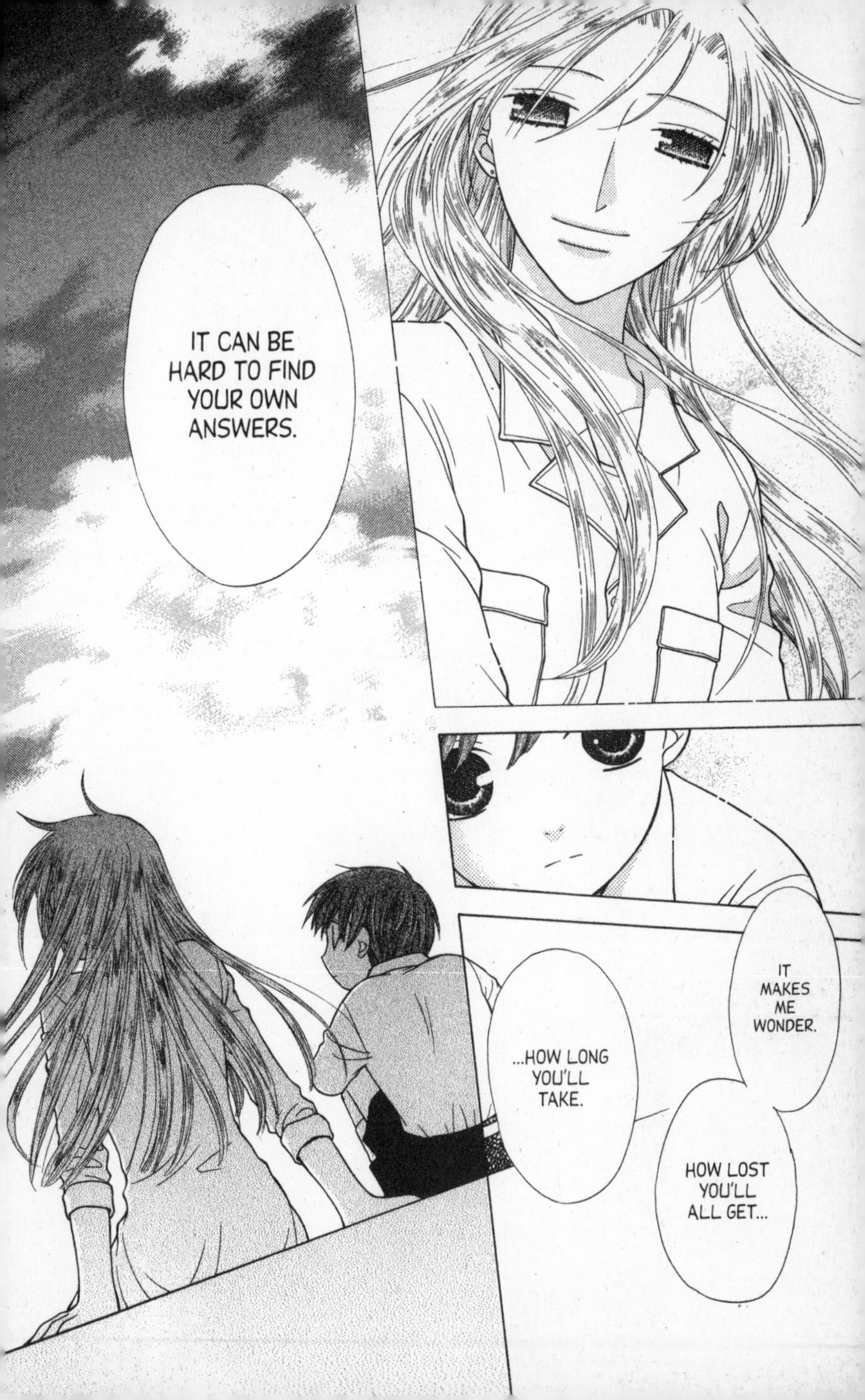
IT CAN BE HARD TO FIND YOUR OWN ANSWERS.
IT MAKES ME WONDER.
HOW LOST YOU'LL ALL GET...
...HOW LONG YOU'LL TAKE.

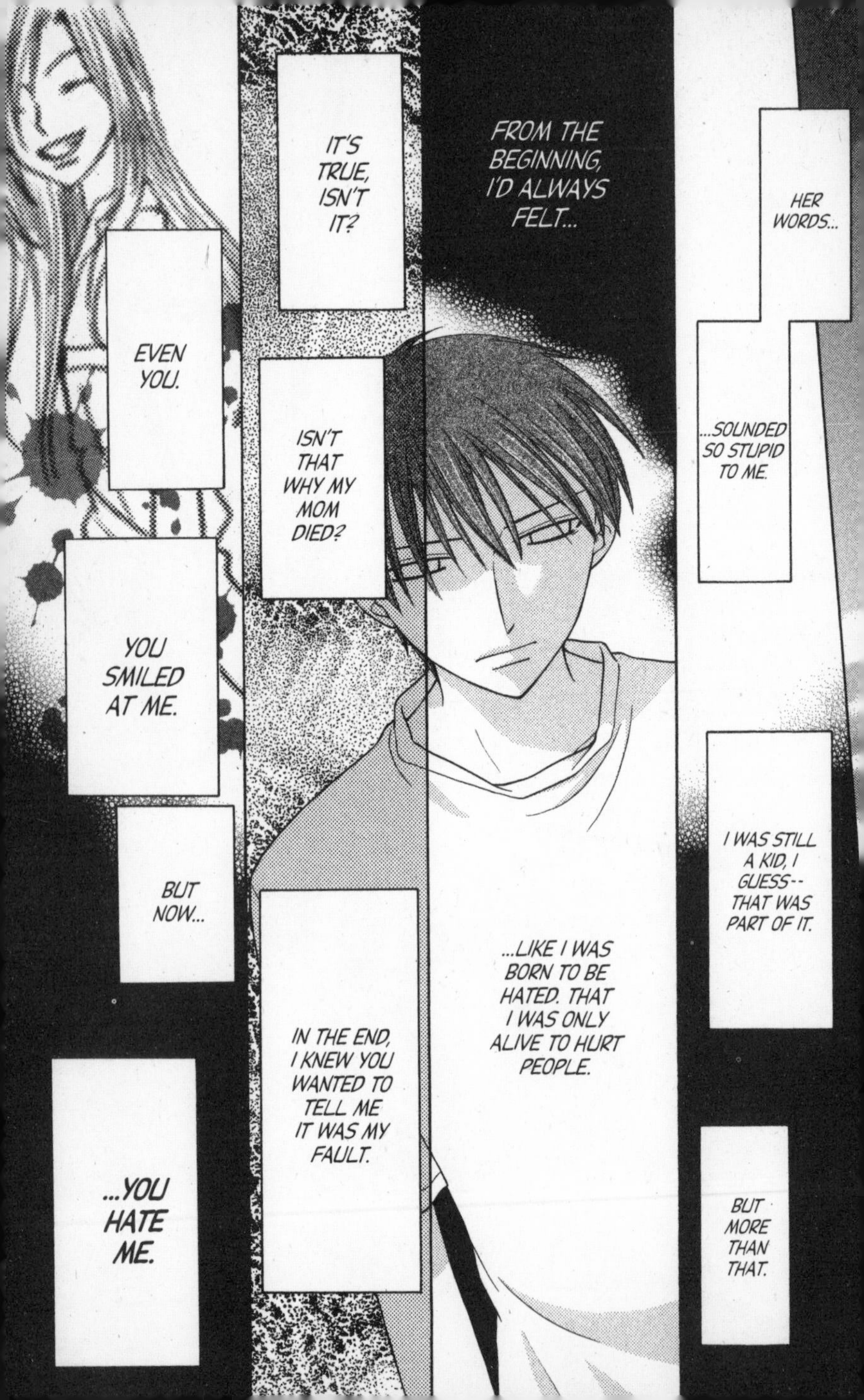
HER WORDS...
...SOUNDED SO STUPID TO ME.
I WAS STILL A KID, I GUESS-- THAT WAS PART OF IT.
BUT MORE THAN THAT.
FROM THE BEGINNING, I'D ALWAYS FELT...
...LIKE I WAS BORN TO BE HATED. THAT I WAS ONLY ALIVE TO HURT PEOPLE.
IT'S TRUE, ISN'T IT?
ISN'T THAT WHY MY MOM DIED?
IN THE END, I KNEW YOU WANTED TO TELL ME IT WAS MY FAULT.
EVEN YOU.
YOU SMILED AT ME.
BUT NOW...
...YOU HATE ME.

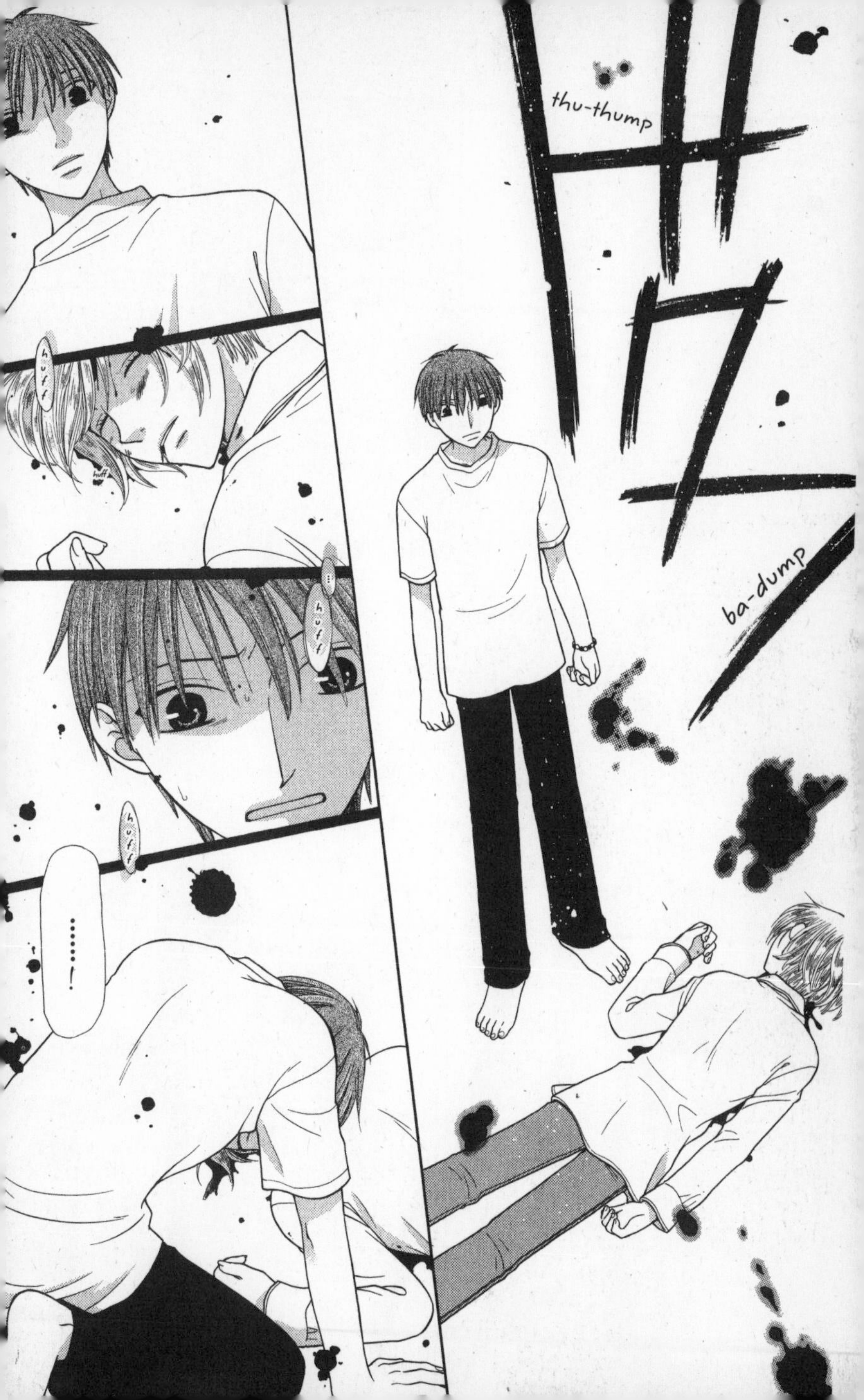

thu-thump
ba-dump
huff
huff
...
huff
huff
......!

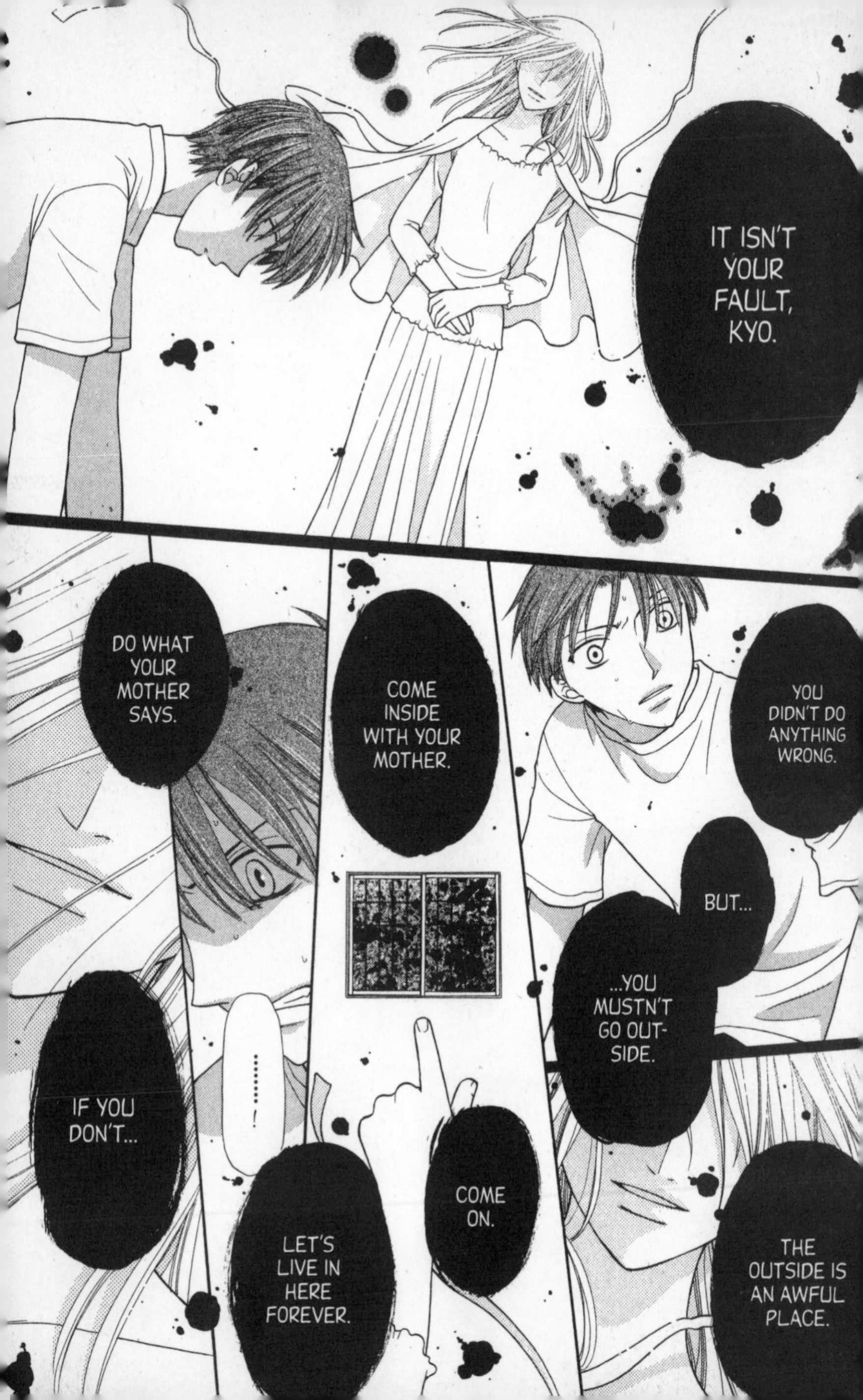
IT ISN'T YOUR FAULT, KYO.
YOU DIDN'T DO ANYTHING WRONG.
BUT...
...YOU MUSTN'T GO OUT-SIDE.
THE OUTSIDE IS AN AWFUL PLACE.
COME INSIDE WITH YOUR MOTHER.
COME ON.
LET'S LIVE IN HERE FOREVER.
DO WHAT YOUR MOTHER SAYS.
......!
IF YOU DON'T...

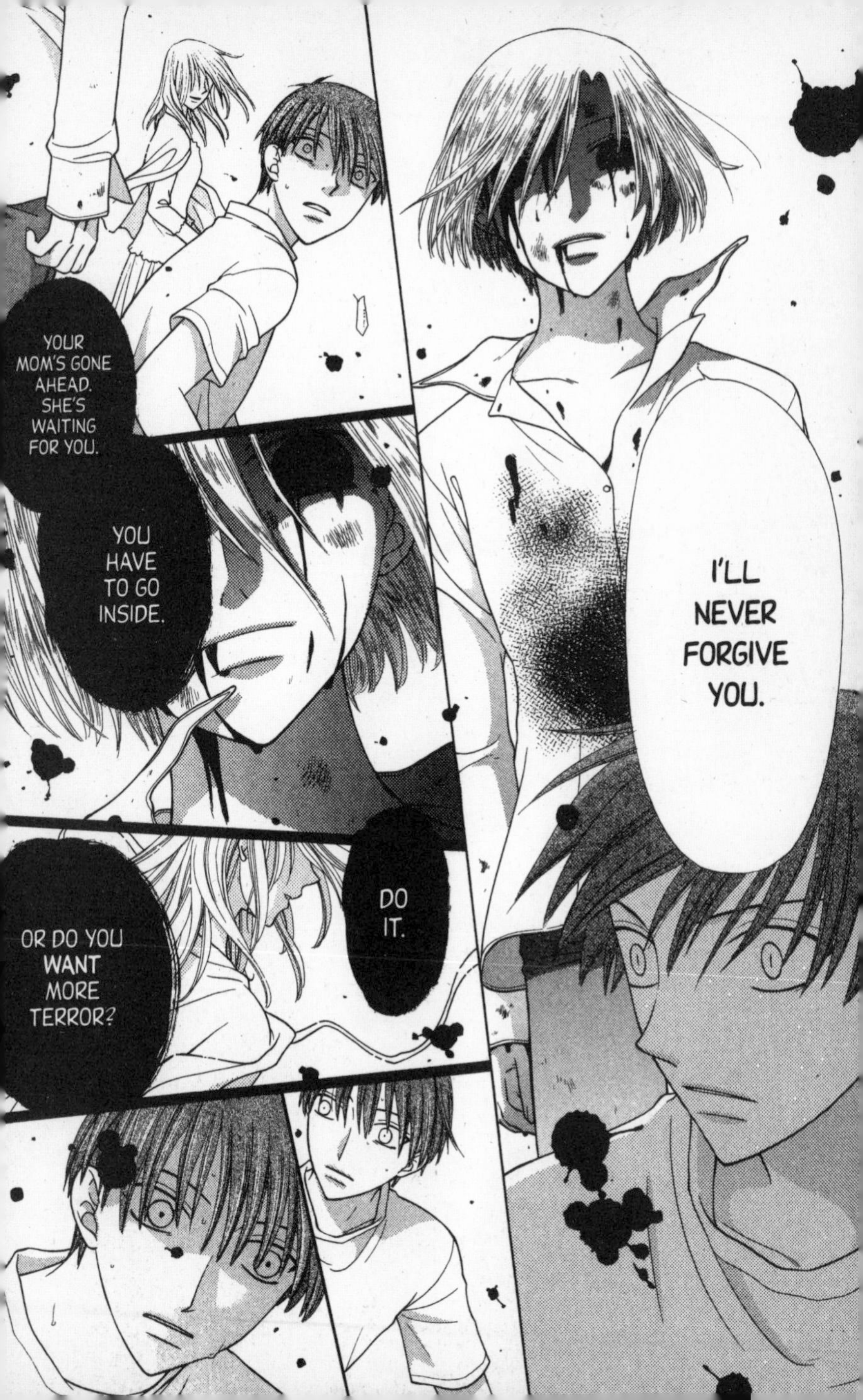
I'LL NEVER FORGIVE YOU.
YOUR MOM'S GONE AHEAD. SHE'S WAITING FOR YOU.
YOU HAVE TO GO INSIDE.
DO IT.
OR DO YOU WANT MORE TERROR?

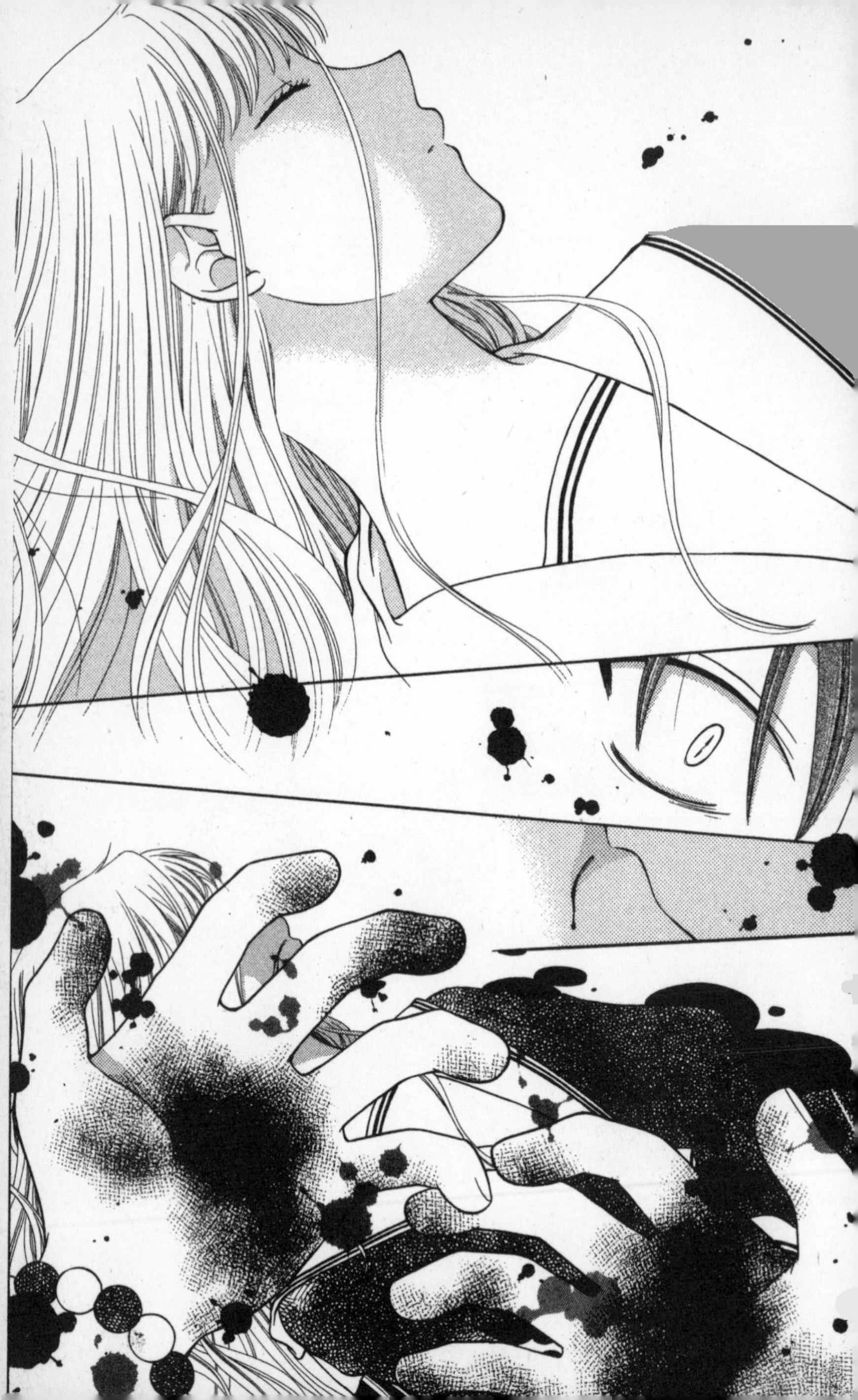

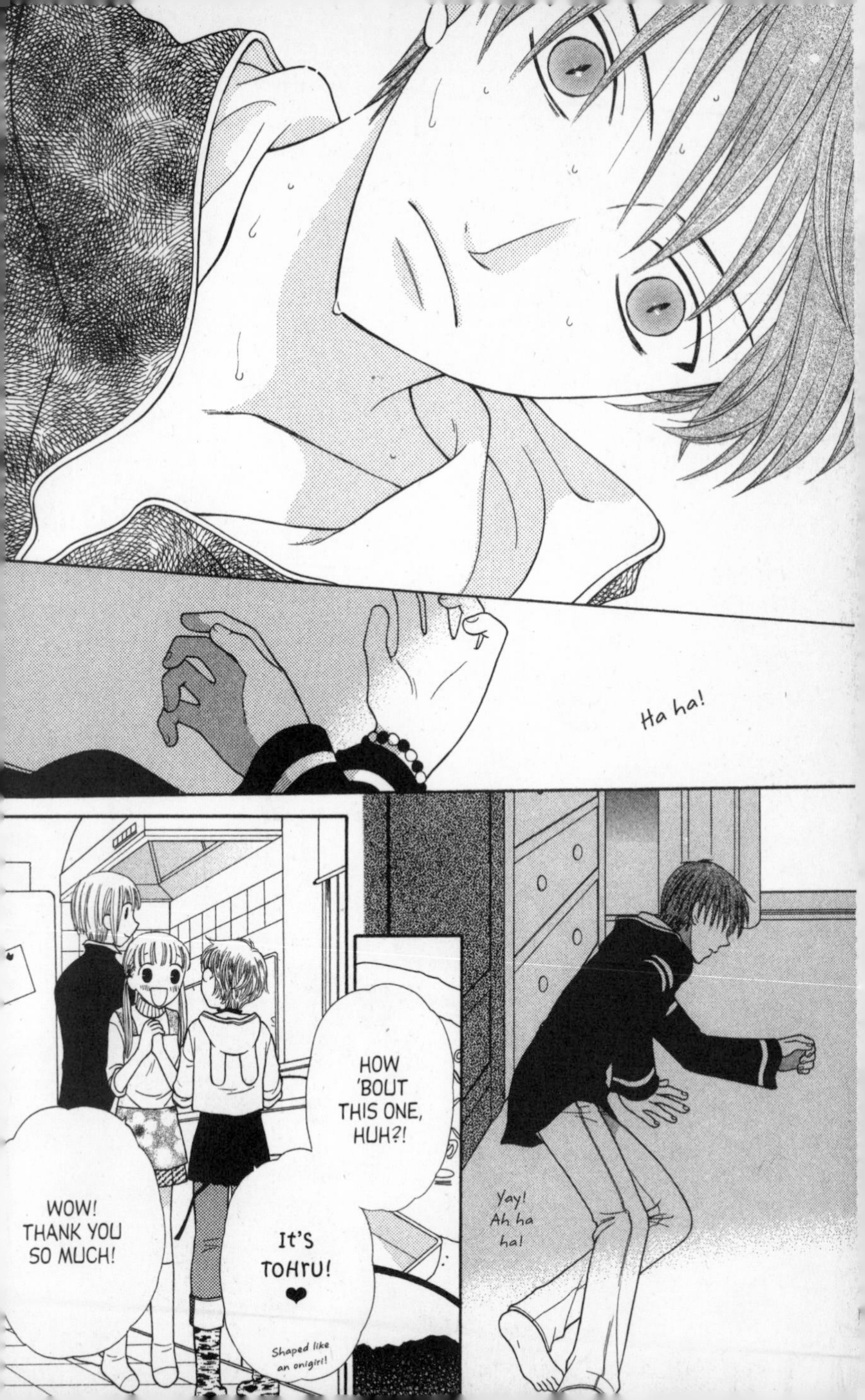
Ha ha!
Yay! Ah ha ha!
HOW 'BOUT THIS ONE, HUH?!
It's TOHRU! ❤
Shaped like an onigiri!
WOW! THANK YOU SO MUCH!

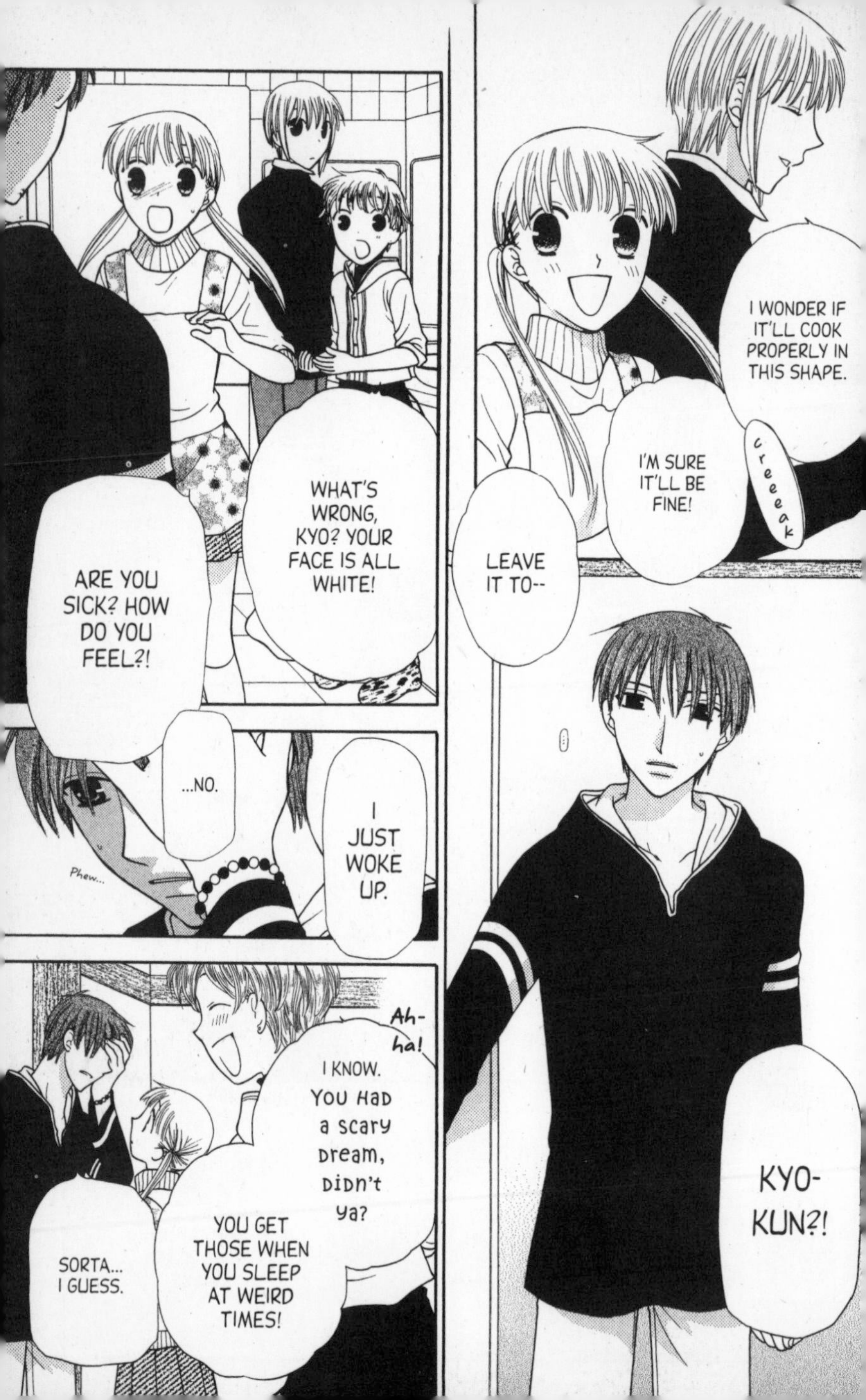
I WONDER IF IT'LL COOK PROPERLY IN THIS SHAPE.
creeeak
I'M SURE IT'LL BE FINE!
LEAVE IT TO--
...
KYO-KUN?!
WHAT'S WRONG, KYO? YOUR FACE IS ALL WHITE!
ARE YOU SICK? HOW DO YOU FEEL?!
...NO.
I JUST WOKE UP.
Phew...
Ah-ha!
I KNOW. You had a scary Dream, Didn't ya?
YOU GET THOSE WHEN YOU SLEEP AT WEIRD TIMES!
SORTA... I GUESS.

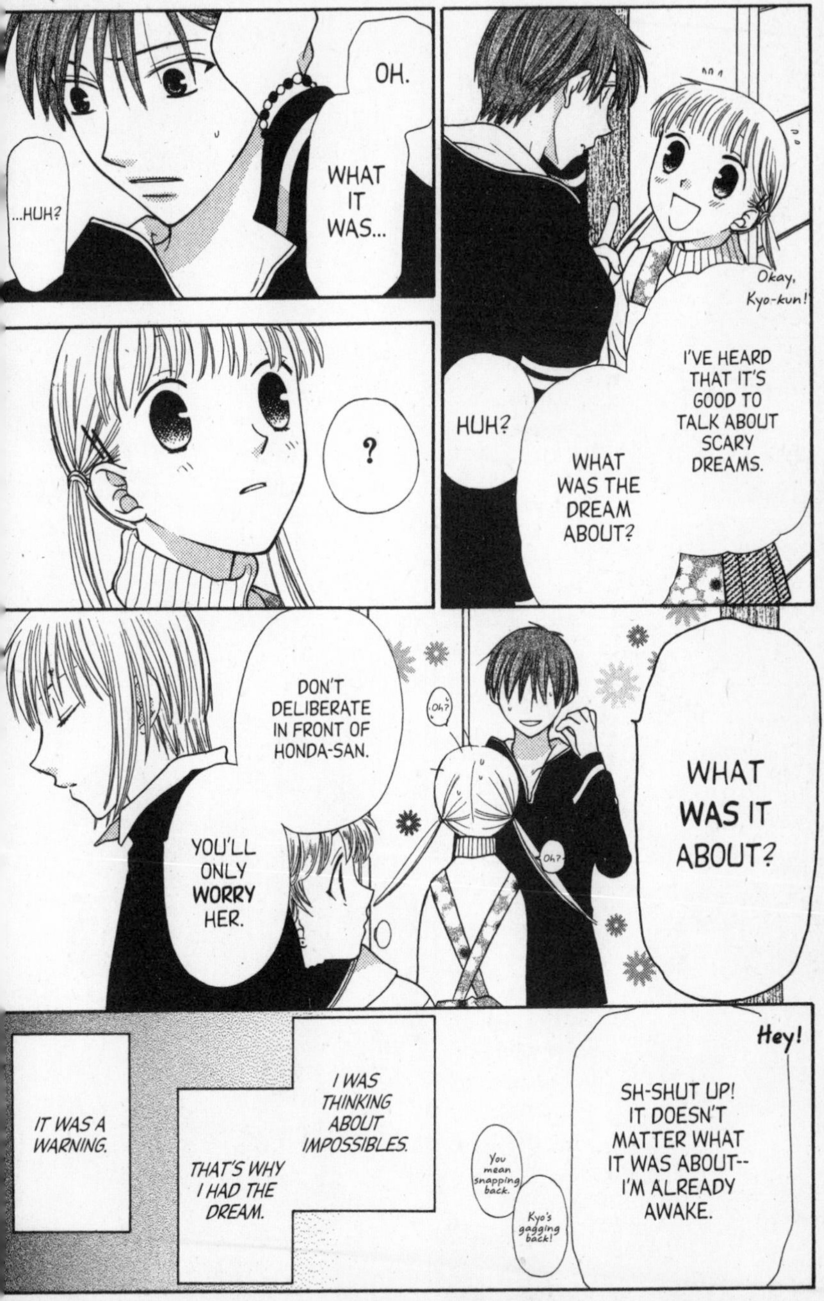
Okay, Kyo-kun!
I'VE HEARD THAT IT'S GOOD TO TALK ABOUT SCARY DREAMS.
WHAT WAS THE DREAM ABOUT?
HUH?
OH.
WHAT IT WAS...
...HUH?
?
WHAT WAS IT ABOUT?
Oh?
Oh?
DON'T DELIBERATE IN FRONT OF HONDA-SAN.
YOU'LL ONLY WORRY HER.
Hey!
SH-SHUT UP! IT DOESN'T MATTER WHAT IT WAS ABOUT-- I'M ALREADY AWAKE.
Kyo's gagging back!
You mean snapping back.
I WAS THINKING ABOUT IMPOSSIBLES.
THAT'S WHY I HAD THE DREAM.
IT WAS A WARNING.

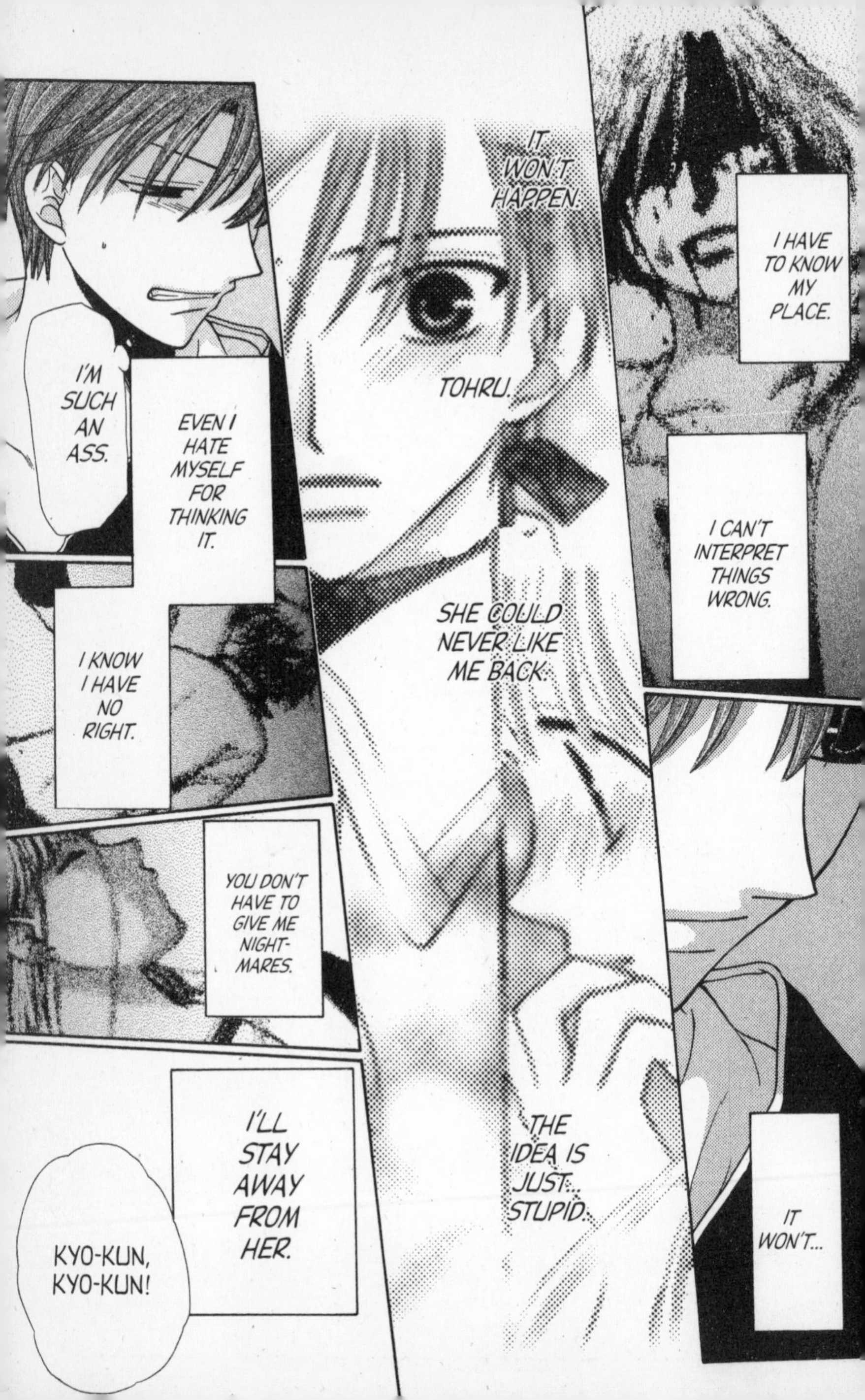

I HAVE TO KNOW MY PLACE.
I CAN'T INTERPRET THINGS WRONG.
IT WON'T...
IT WON'T HAPPEN.
TOHRU.
SHE COULD NEVER LIKE ME BACK.
THE IDEA IS JUST... STUPID.
EVEN I HATE MYSELF FOR THINKING IT.
I'M SUCH AN ASS.
I KNOW I HAVE NO RIGHT.
YOU DON'T HAVE TO GIVE ME NIGHT-MARES.
I'LL STAY AWAY FROM HER.
KYO-KUN, KYO-KUN!

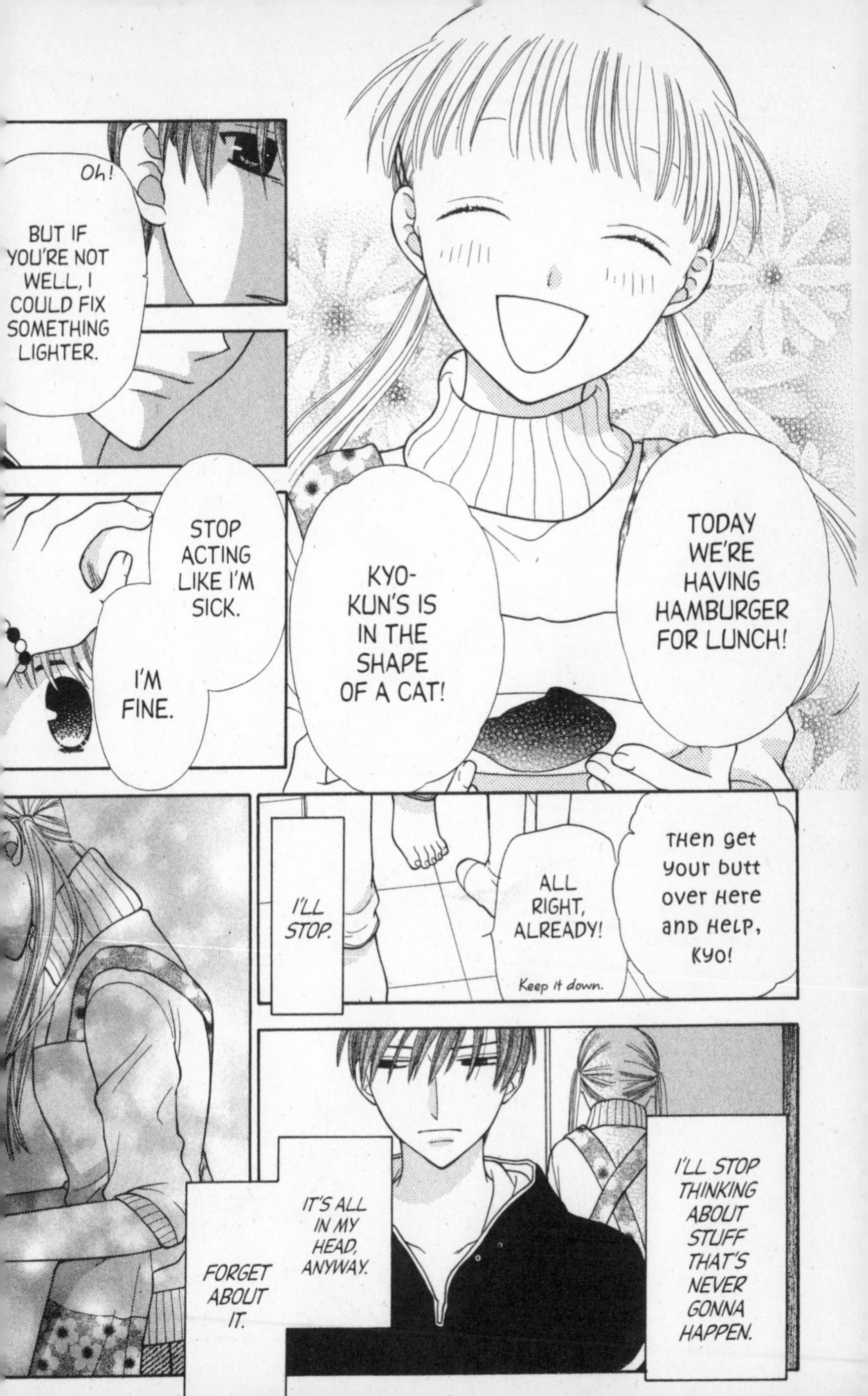
TODAY WE'RE HAVING HAMBURGER FOR LUNCH!
KYO-KUN'S IS IN THE SHAPE OF A CAT!
Oh!
BUT IF YOU'RE NOT WELL, I COULD FIX SOMETHING LIGHTER.
STOP ACTING LIKE I'M SICK.
I'M FINE.
Then get your butt over here and help, Kyo!
ALL RIGHT, ALREADY!
Keep it down.
I'LL STOP.
I'LL STOP THINKING ABOUT STUFF THAT'S NEVER GONNA HAPPEN.
IT'S ALL IN MY HEAD, ANYWAY.
FORGET ABOUT IT.

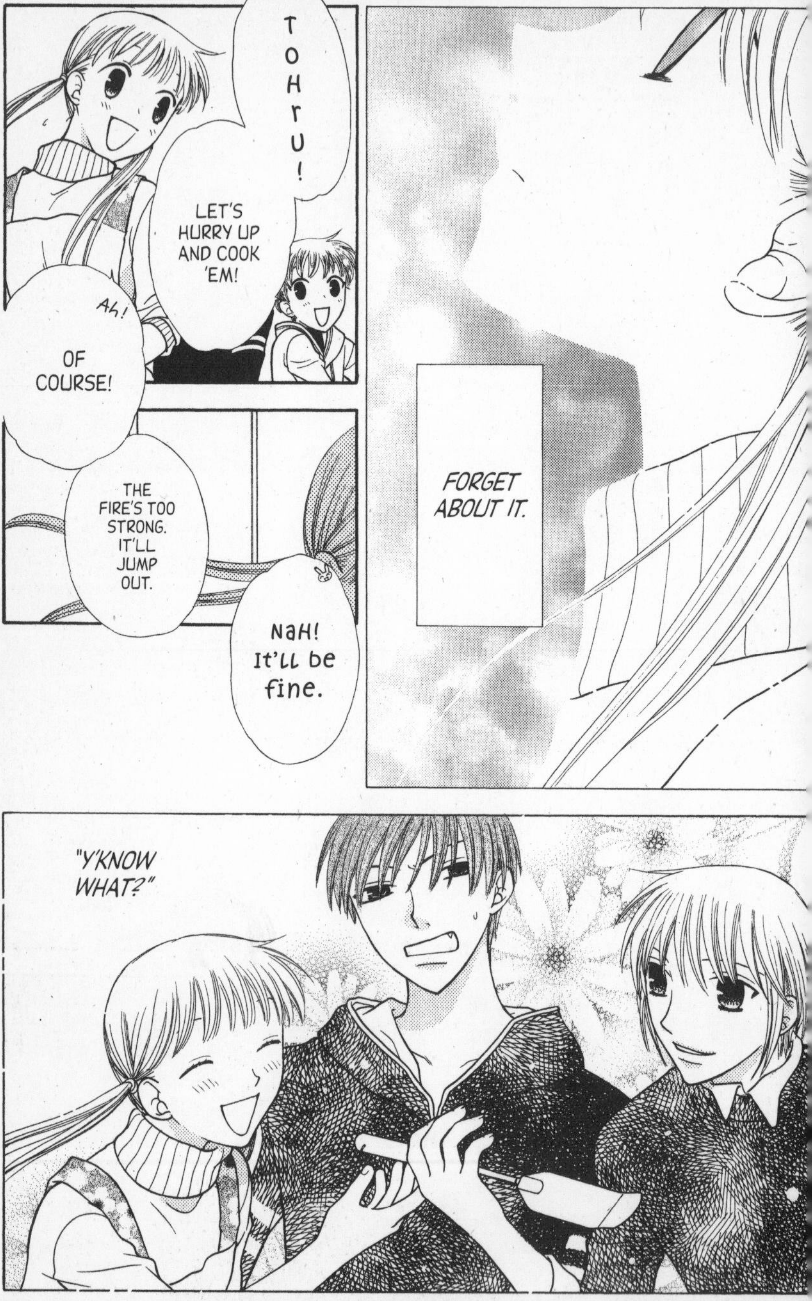
FORGET ABOUT IT.
TOHrU!
LET'S HURRY UP AND COOK 'EM!
AH! OF COURSE!
THE FIRE'S TOO STRONG. IT'LL JUMP OUT.
NaH! It'll be fine.
"Y'KNOW WHAT?"

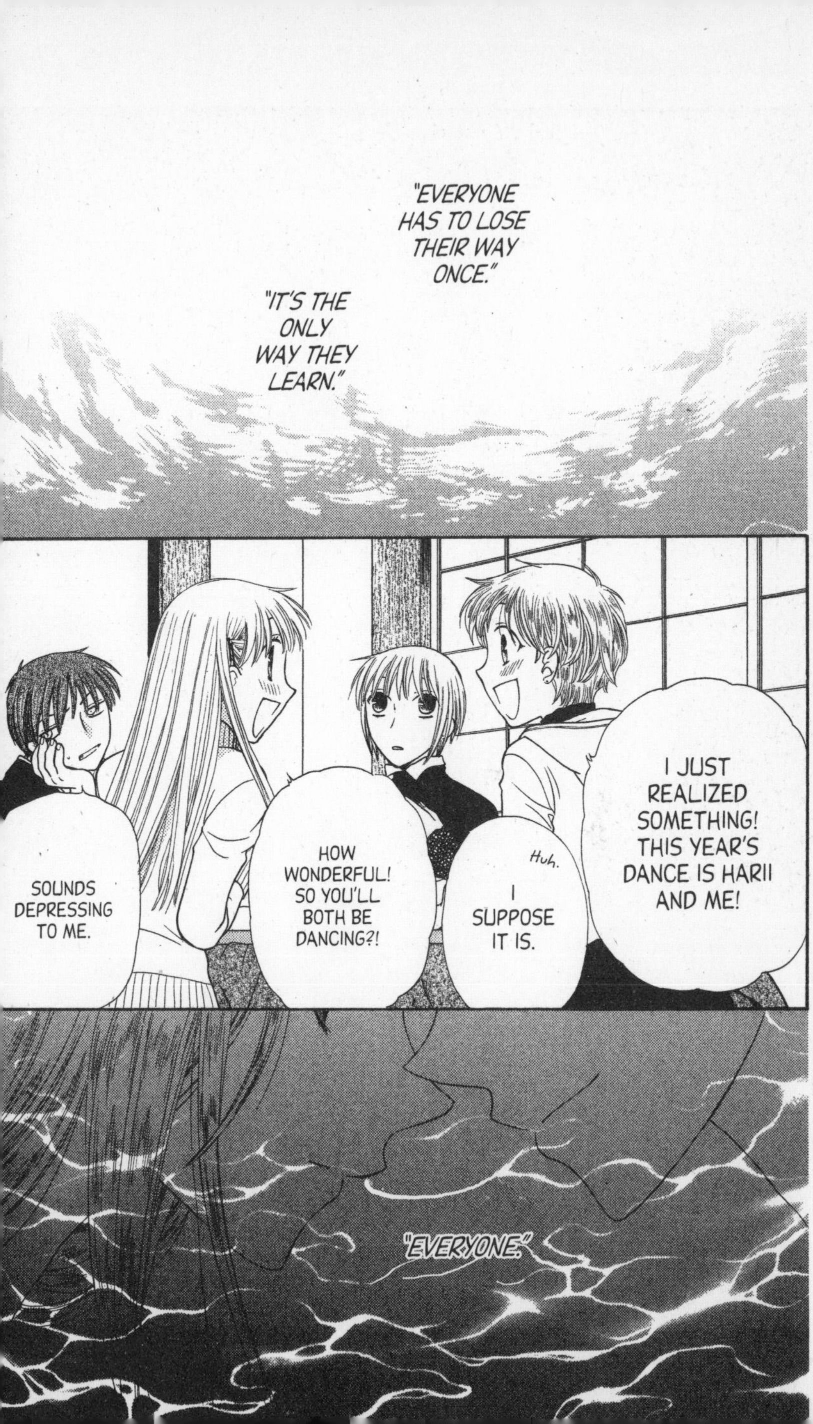
"EVERYONE HAS TO LOSE THEIR WAY ONCE."
"IT'S THE ONLY WAY THEY LEARN."
I JUST REALIZED SOMETHING! THIS YEAR'S DANCE IS HARII AND ME!
Huh.
I SUPPOSE IT IS.
HOW WONDERFUL! SO YOU'LL BOTH BE DANCING?!
SOUNDS DEPRESSING TO ME.
"EVERYONE."

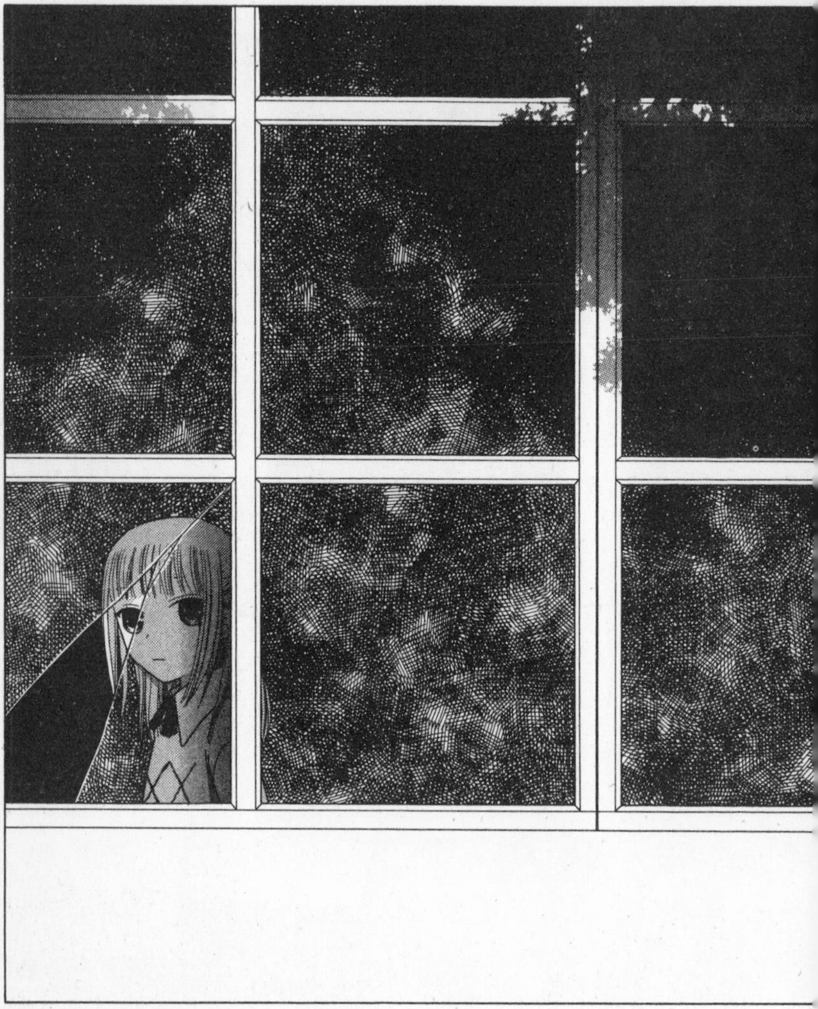

Chapter 94

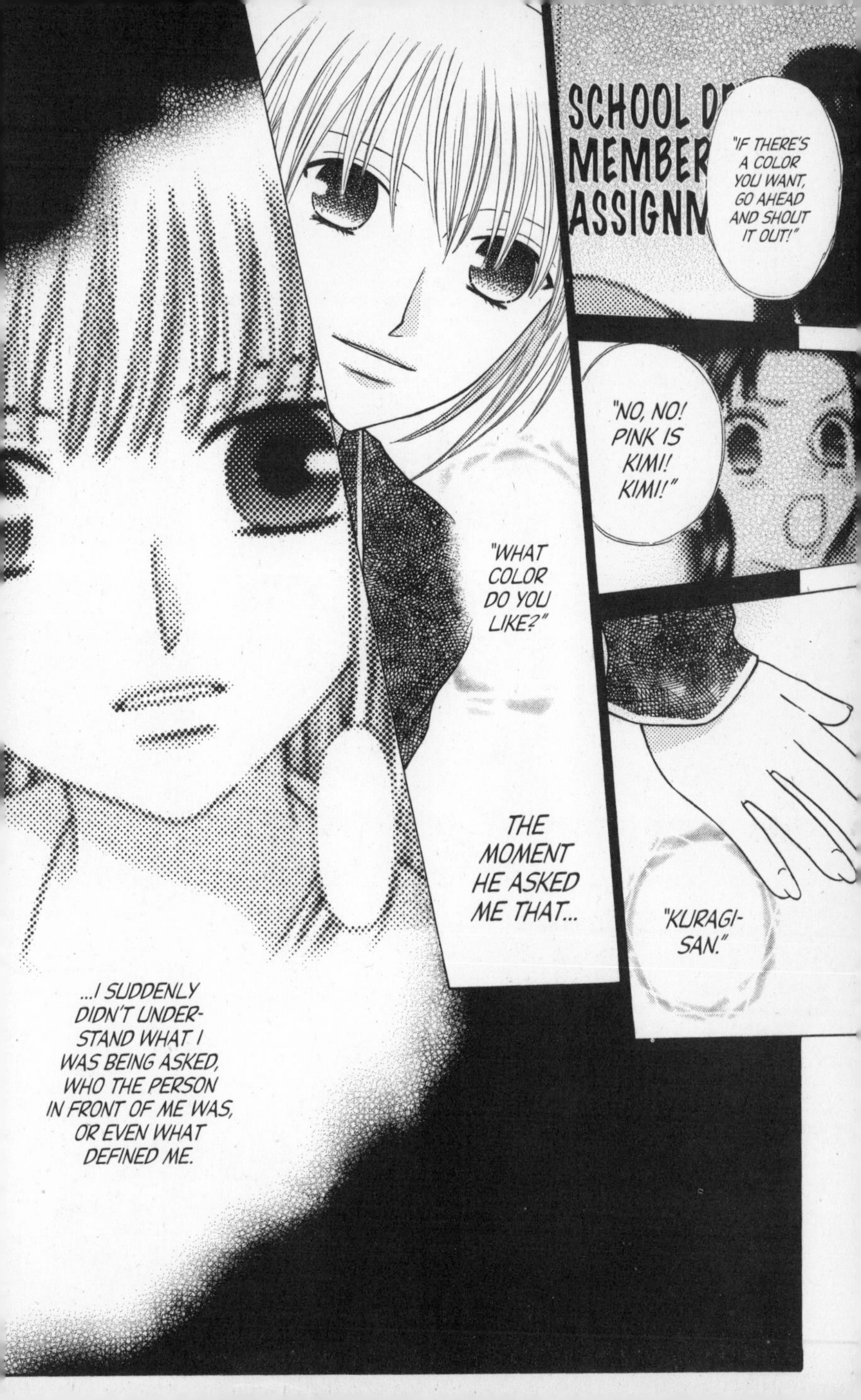
SCHOOL DE
MEMBER
ASSIGNM
"IF THERE'S A COLOR YOU WANT, GO AHEAD AND SHOUT IT OUT!"
"NO, NO! PINK IS KIMI! KIMI!"
"KURAGI-SAN."
"WHAT COLOR DO YOU LIKE?"
THE MOMENT HE ASKED ME THAT...
...I SUDDENLY DIDN'T UNDER-STAND WHAT I WAS BEING ASKED, WHO THE PERSON IN FRONT OF ME WAS, OR EVEN WHAT DEFINED ME.

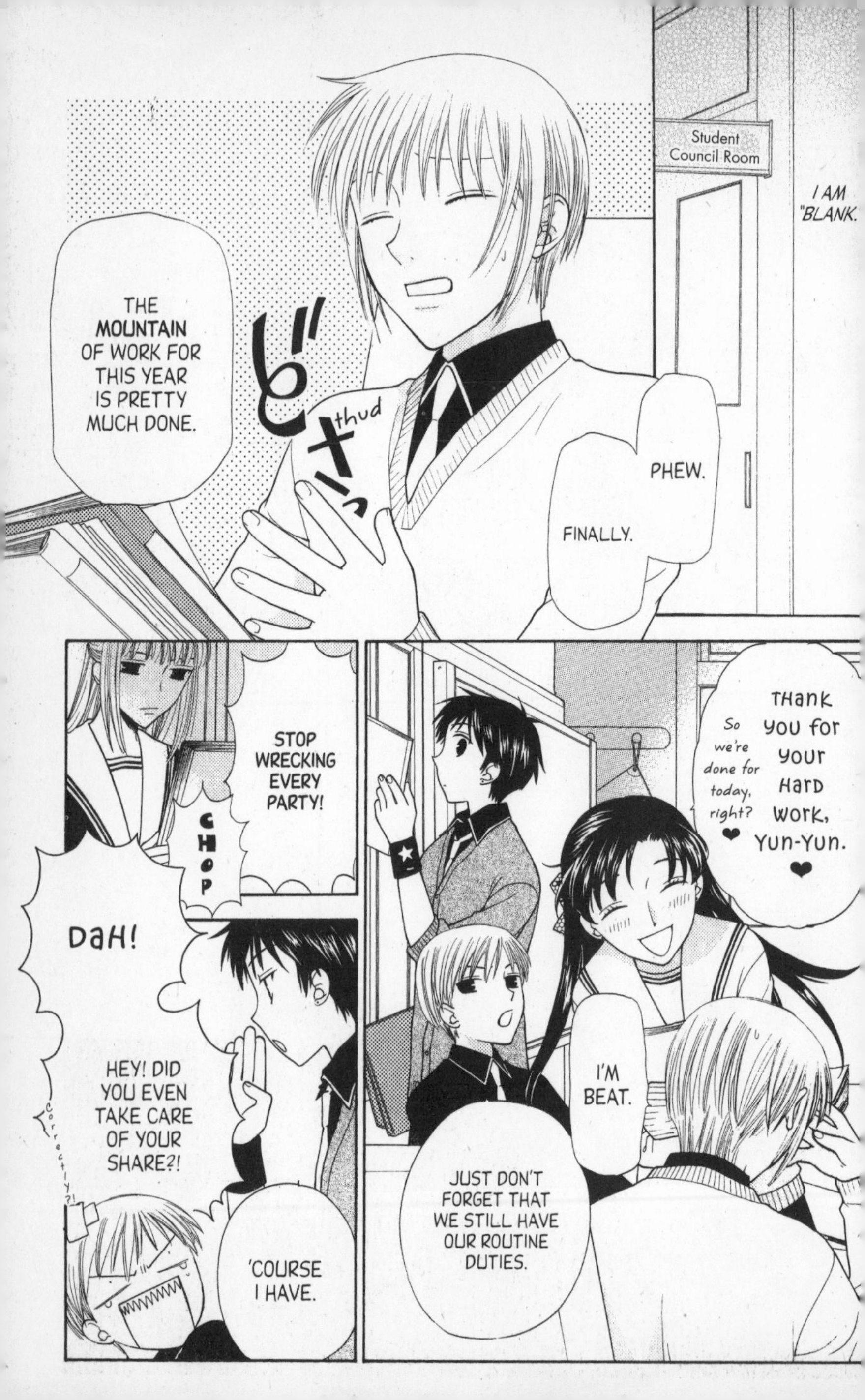
Student Council Room
I AM "BLANK.
PHEW.
FINALLY.
thud
THE MOUNTAIN OF WORK FOR THIS YEAR IS PRETTY MUCH DONE.
Thank you for your hard work, Yun-Yun. ❤
So we're done for today, right? ❤
I'M BEAT.
JUST DON'T FORGET THAT WE STILL HAVE OUR ROUTINE DUTIES.
STOP WRECKING EVERY PARTY!
CHOP
DAH!
HEY! DID YOU EVEN TAKE CARE OF YOUR SHARE?!
'COURSE I HAVE.
Correctly?!

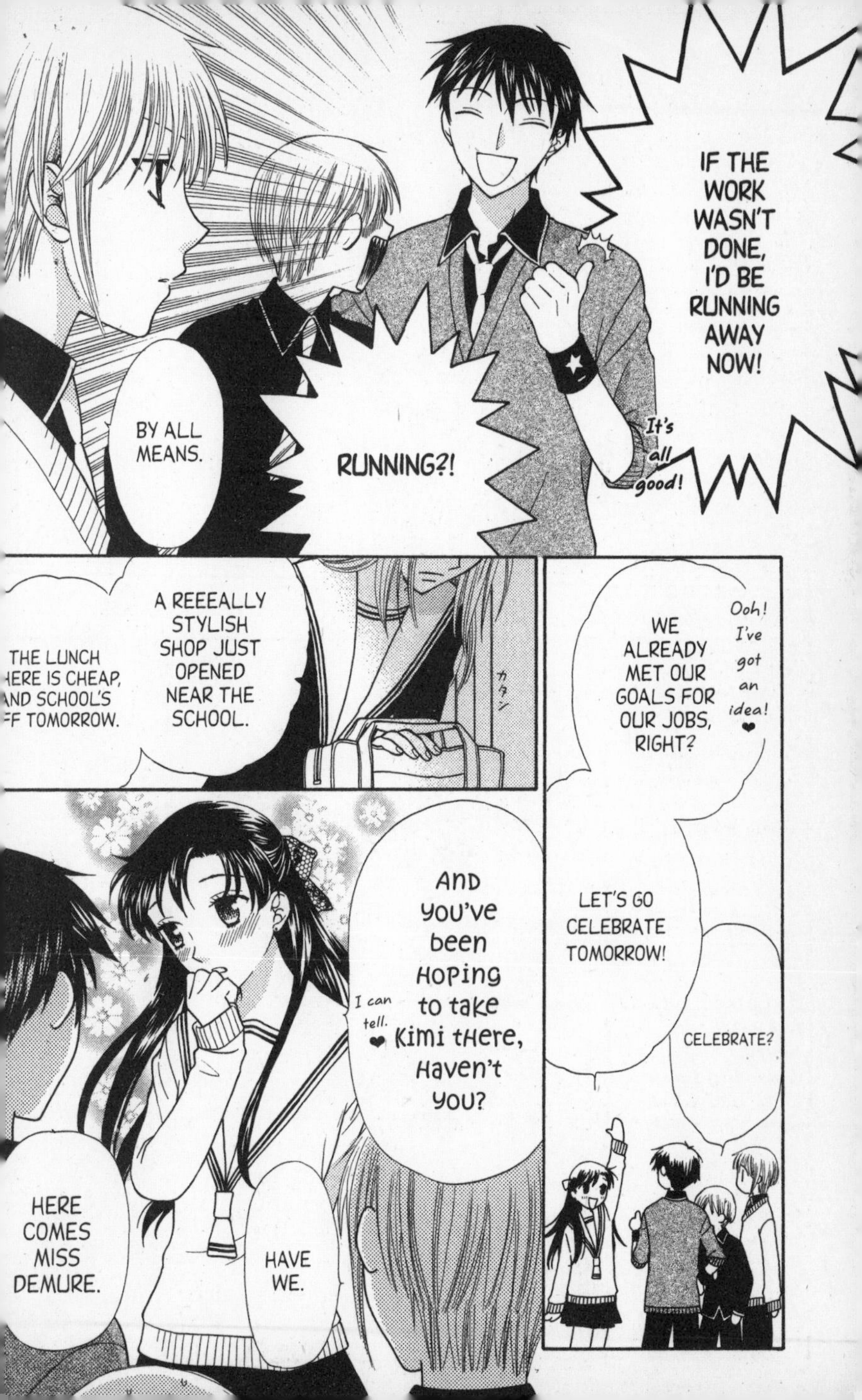
IF THE WORK WASN'T DONE, I'D BE RUNNING AWAY NOW!
It's all good!
RUNNING?!
BY ALL MEANS.
Ooh! I've got an idea! ❤
WE ALREADY MET OUR GOALS FOR OUR JOBS, RIGHT?
LET'S GO CELEBRATE TOMORROW!
CELEBRATE?
A REEEALLY STYLISH SHOP JUST OPENED NEAR THE SCHOOL.
THE LUNCH HERE IS CHEAP, AND SCHOOL'S FF TOMORROW.
And you've been hoping to take Kimi there, haven't you?
I can tell. ❤
HAVE WE.
HERE COMES MISS DEMURE.

Continued →

He didn't really fight with his father, but there was a "rift" between them for a long time.

Even after his mother's death, he didn't have much contact with his father. When he took Kyoko-san to meet his father in Chapter 92, it was their first reunion in a long time.

The reason he went to work for a pharmaceutical company is that, in a corner of his mind, he thought of his mother (who died from an illness).

His father's head is smooth and shiny (laugh), so he thought he might also go bald in the future.

He just mused on it (laugh), but he didn't try to do anything about it.

Back when Katsuya's face never really appeared, I received anxious letters asking, "Is he actually Kyo's father? Are Kyo and Tohru siblings?!" Um, huh?

Since drawing Katsuya, I think I've developed a weakness for Papa characters. It even hits me when I play video games.

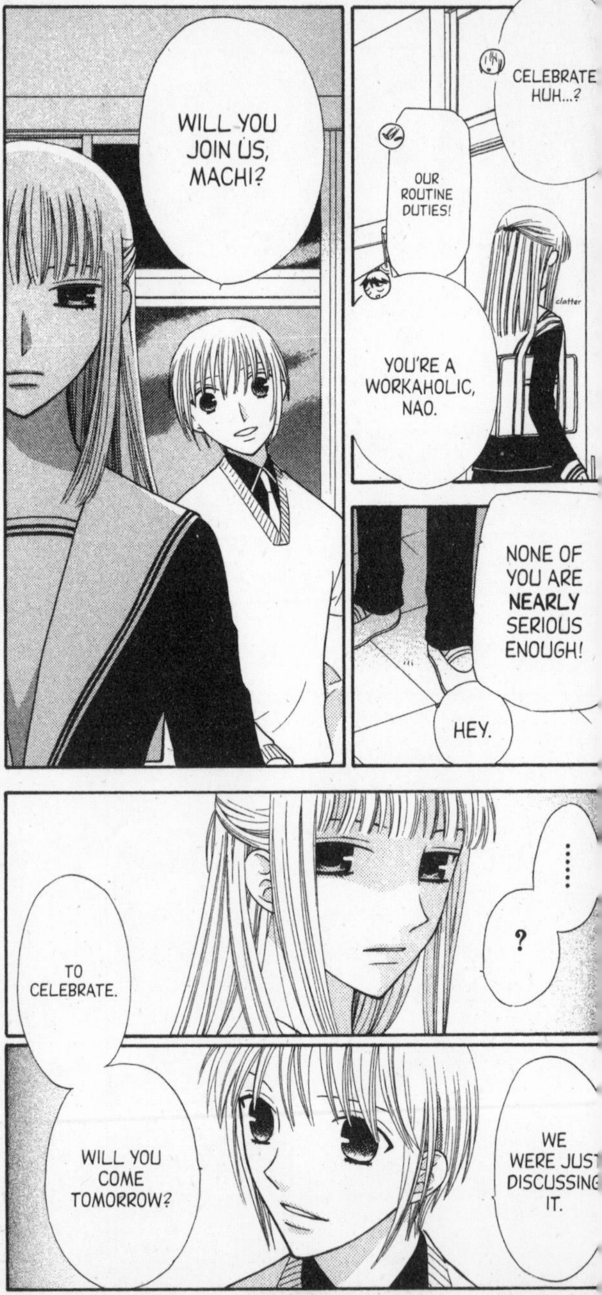
CELEBRATE HUH...?
OUR ROUTINE DUTIES!
YOU'RE A WORKAHOLIC, NAO.
clatter
NONE OF YOU ARE **NEARLY** SERIOUS ENOUGH!
HEY.
WILL YOU JOIN US, MACHI?
......
?
TO CELEBRATE.
WE WERE JUST DISCUSSING IT.
WILL YOU COME TOMORROW?

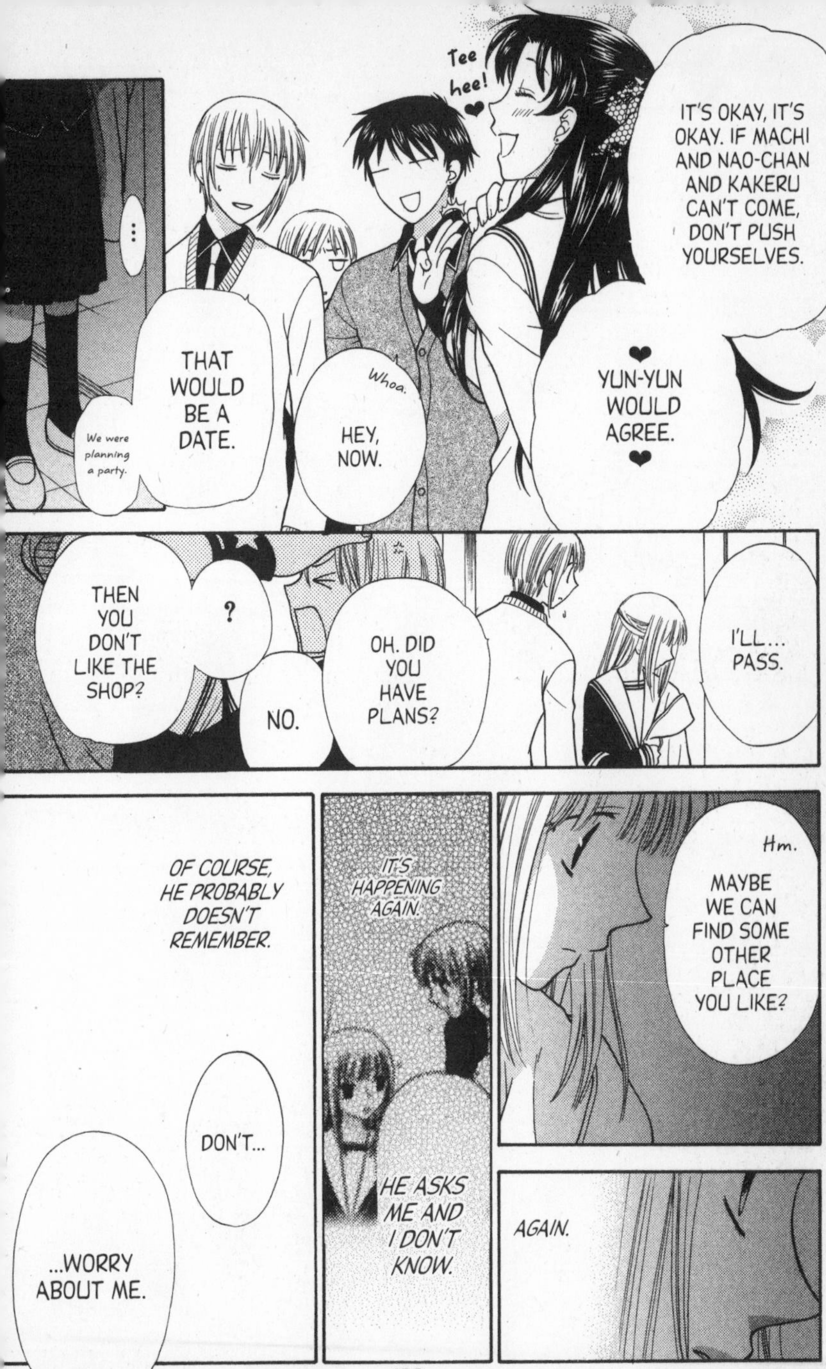
Tee hee!
IT'S OKAY, IT'S OKAY. IF MACHI AND NAO-CHAN AND KAKERU CAN'T COME, DON'T PUSH YOURSELVES.
YUN-YUN WOULD AGREE.
Whoa.
HEY, NOW.
THAT WOULD BE A DATE.
We were planning a party.
...
I'LL... PASS.
OH. DID YOU HAVE PLANS?
NO.
?
THEN YOU DON'T LIKE THE SHOP?
Hm.
MAYBE WE CAN FIND SOME OTHER PLACE YOU LIKE?
AGAIN.
IT'S HAPPENING AGAIN.
HE ASKS ME AND I DON'T KNOW.
OF COURSE, HE PROBABLY DOESN'T REMEMBER.
DON'T...
...WORRY ABOUT ME.

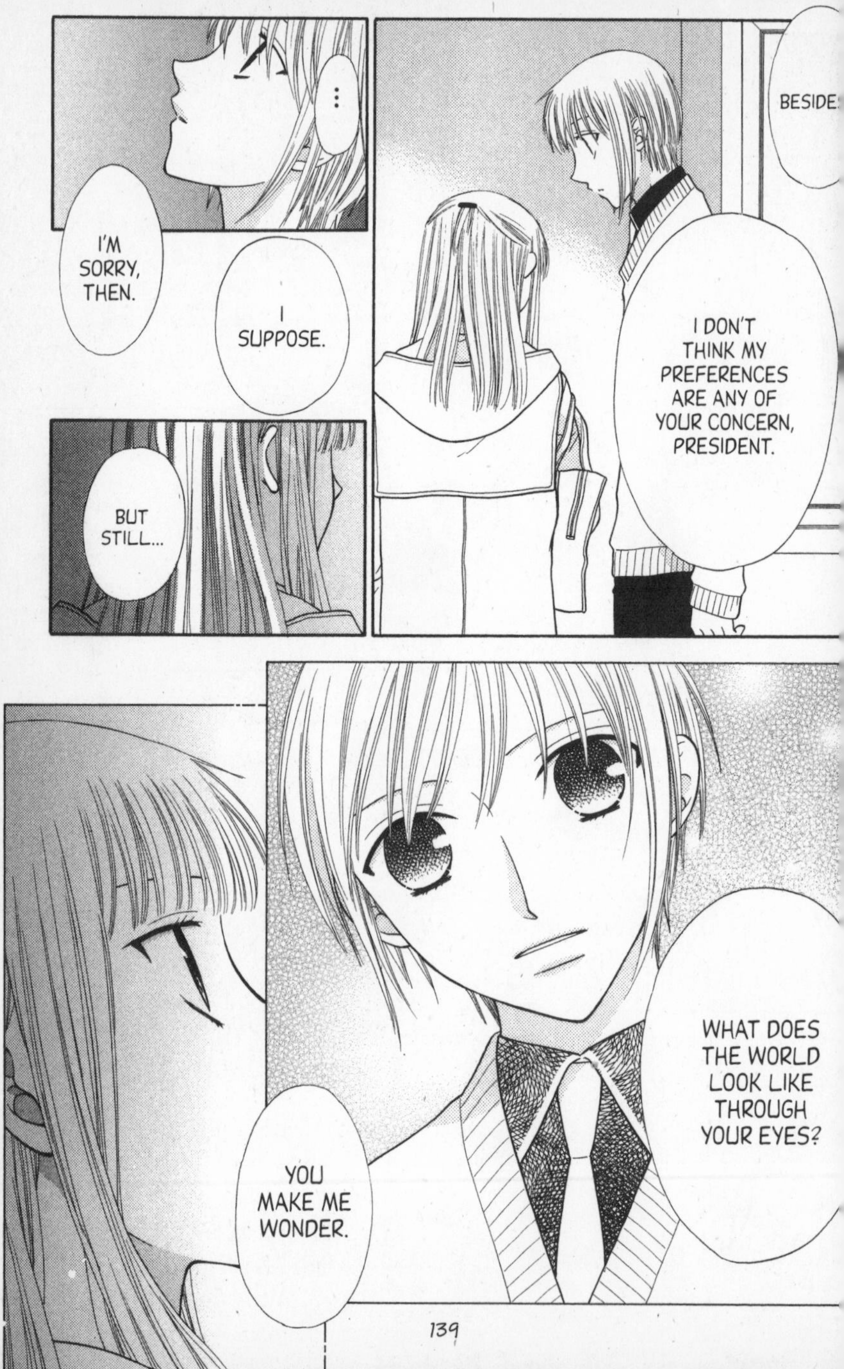
BESIDE
I DON'T THINK MY PREFERENCES ARE ANY OF YOUR CONCERN, PRESIDENT.
...
I SUPPOSE.
I'M SORRY, THEN.
BUT STILL...
WHAT DOES THE WORLD LOOK LIKE THROUGH YOUR EYES?
YOU MAKE ME WONDER.

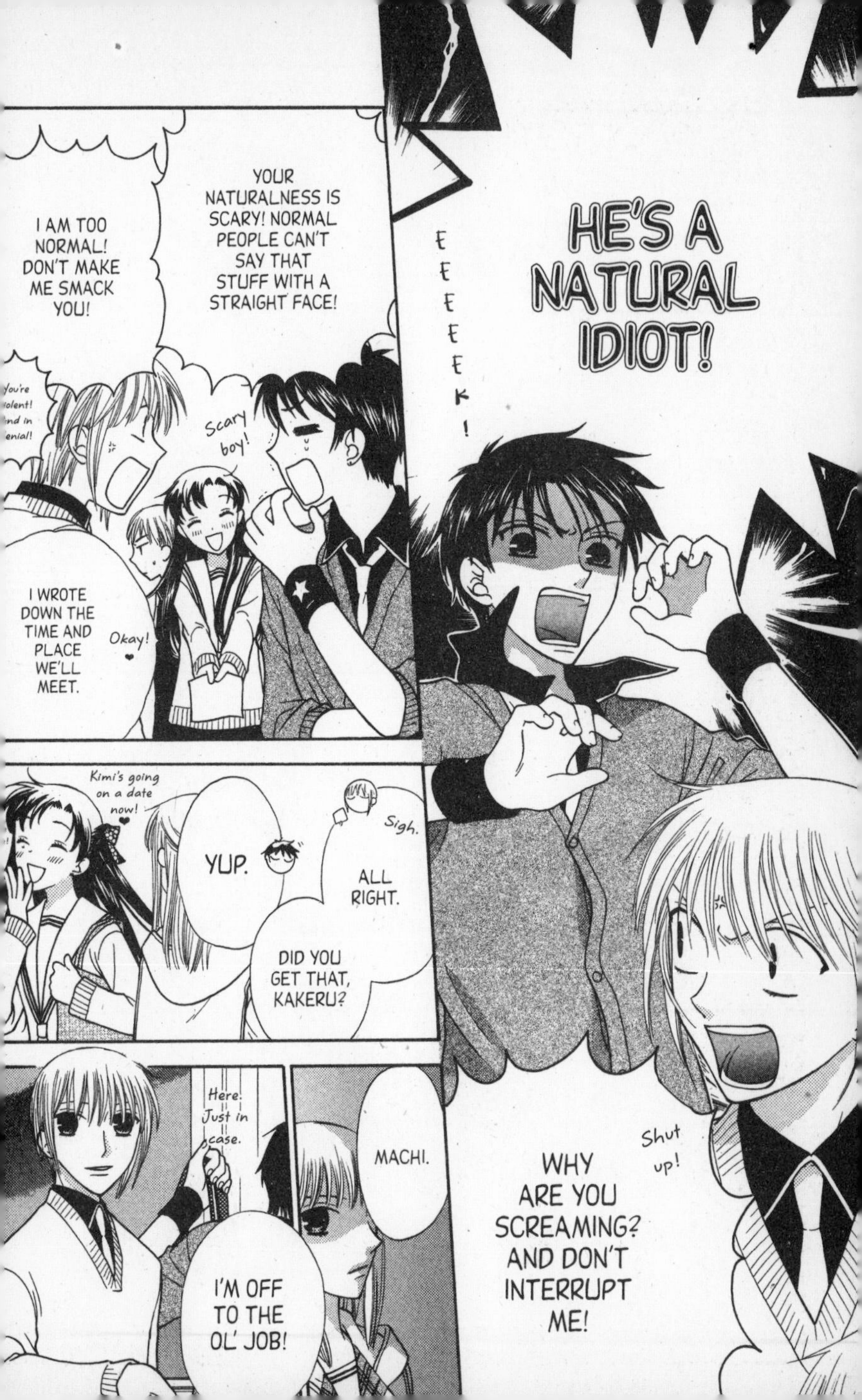
HE'S A NATURAL IDIOT!
EEEEEK!
Shut up!
WHY ARE YOU SCREAMING? AND DON'T INTERRUPT ME!
YOUR NATURALNESS IS SCARY! NORMAL PEOPLE CAN'T SAY THAT STUFF WITH A STRAIGHT FACE!
I AM TOO NORMAL! DON'T MAKE ME SMACK YOU!
Scary boy!
You're iolent! nd in enial!
I WROTE DOWN THE TIME AND PLACE WE'LL MEET.
Okay!
Kimi's going on a date now!
YUP.
Sigh.
ALL RIGHT.
DID YOU GET THAT, KAKERU?
MACHI.
I'M OFF TO THE OL' JOB!
Here. Just in case.

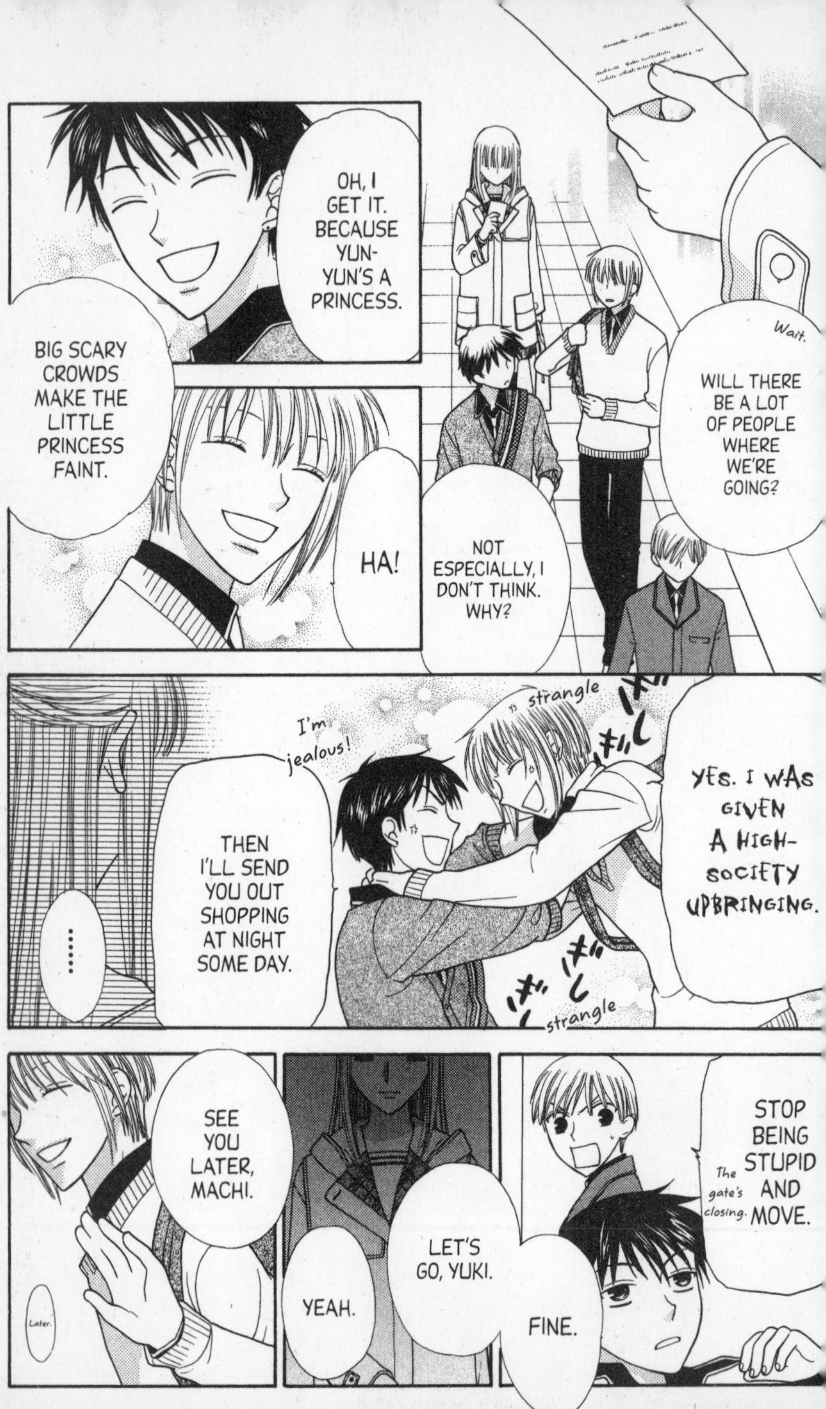
Wait.
WILL THERE BE A LOT OF PEOPLE WHERE WE'RE GOING?
NOT ESPECIALLY, I DON'T THINK. WHY?
OH, I GET IT. BECAUSE YUN-YUN'S A PRINCESS.
BIG SCARY CROWDS MAKE THE LITTLE PRINCESS FAINT.
HA!
YES. I WAS GIVEN A HIGH-SOCIETY UPBRINGING.
strangle
I'm jealous!
THEN I'LL SEND YOU OUT SHOPPING AT NIGHT SOME DAY.
strangle
......
STOP BEING STUPID AND MOVE.
The gate's closing.
FINE.
LET'S GO, YUKI.
YEAH.
SEE YOU LATER, MACHI.
Later.

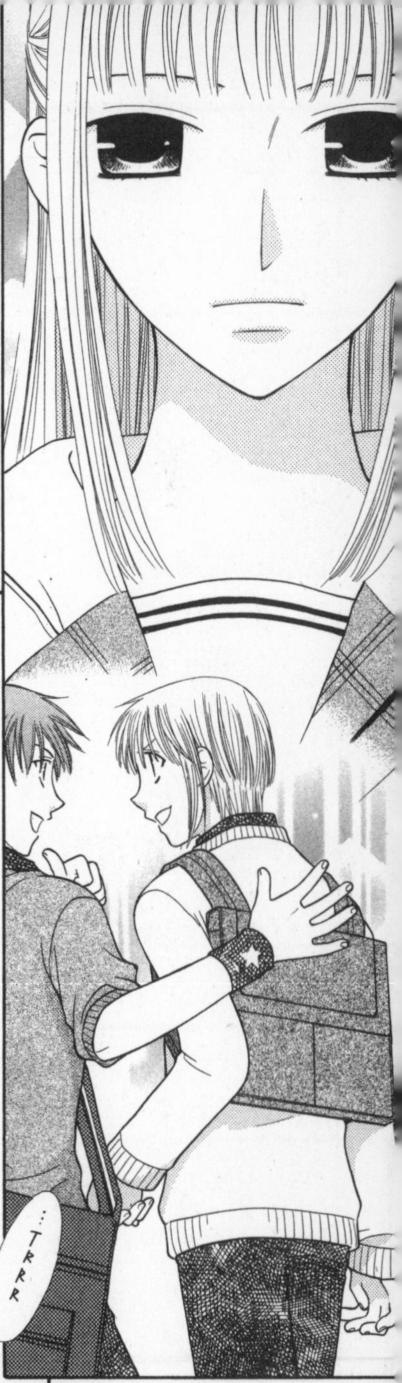
...TRRR

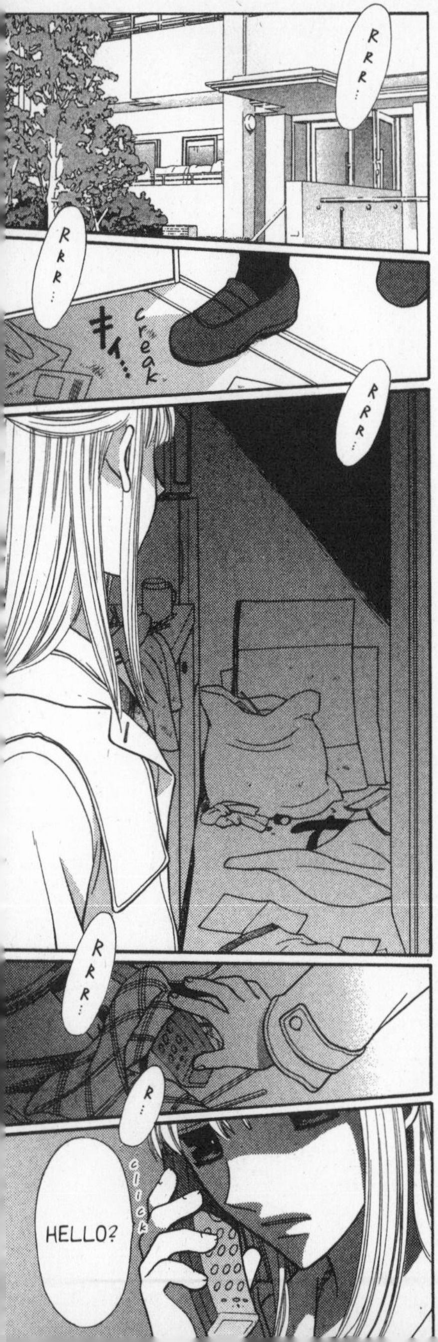
RRR...
Rrr...
キイ... creak
RRR...
RRR...
R...
click
HELLO?

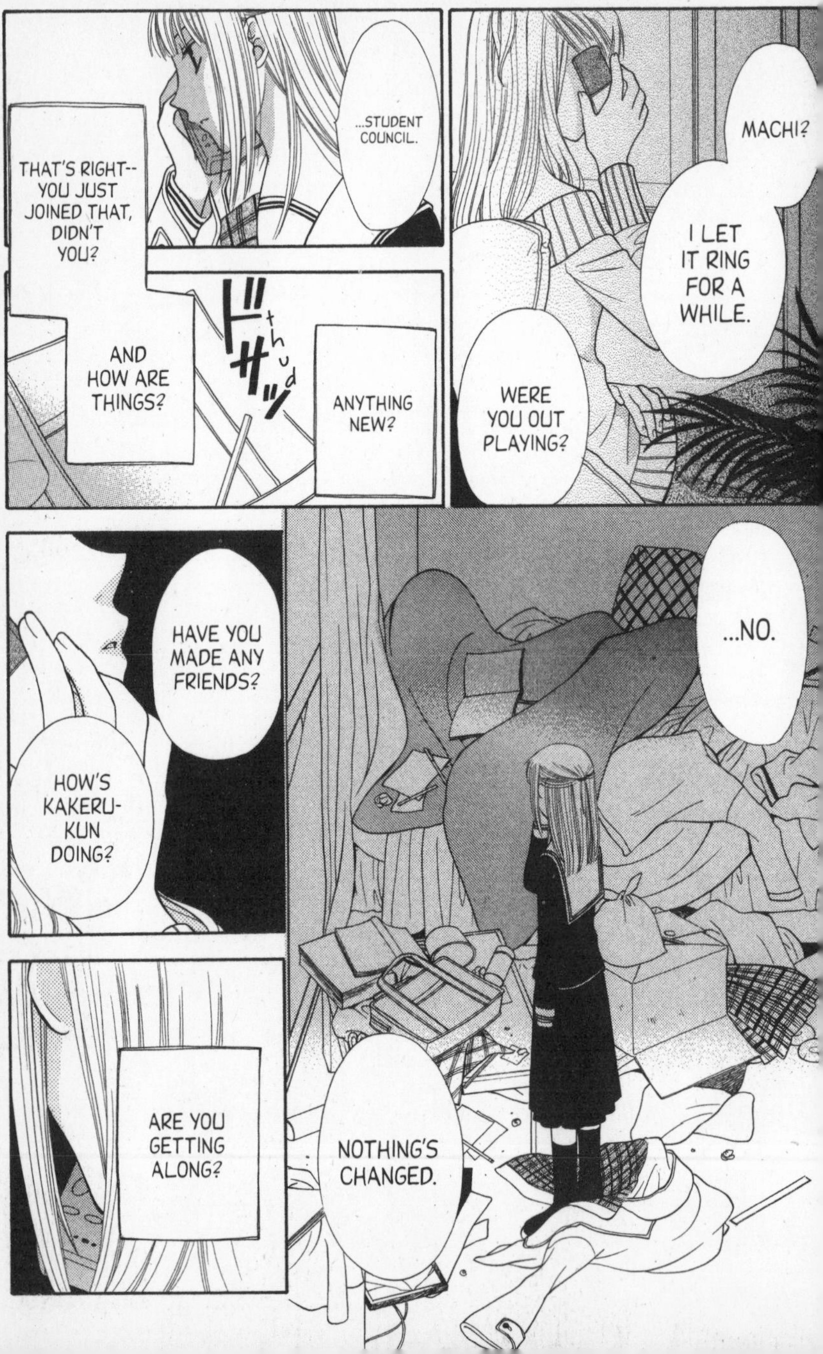
MACHI?
I LET IT RING FOR A WHILE.
WERE YOU OUT PLAYING?
...STUDENT COUNCIL.
THAT'S RIGHT-- YOU JUST JOINED THAT, DIDN'T YOU?
ANYTHING NEW?
ドザッ
thud
AND HOW ARE THINGS?
...NO.
NOTHING'S CHANGED.
HAVE YOU MADE ANY FRIENDS?
HOW'S KAKERU-KUN DOING?
ARE YOU GETTING ALONG?

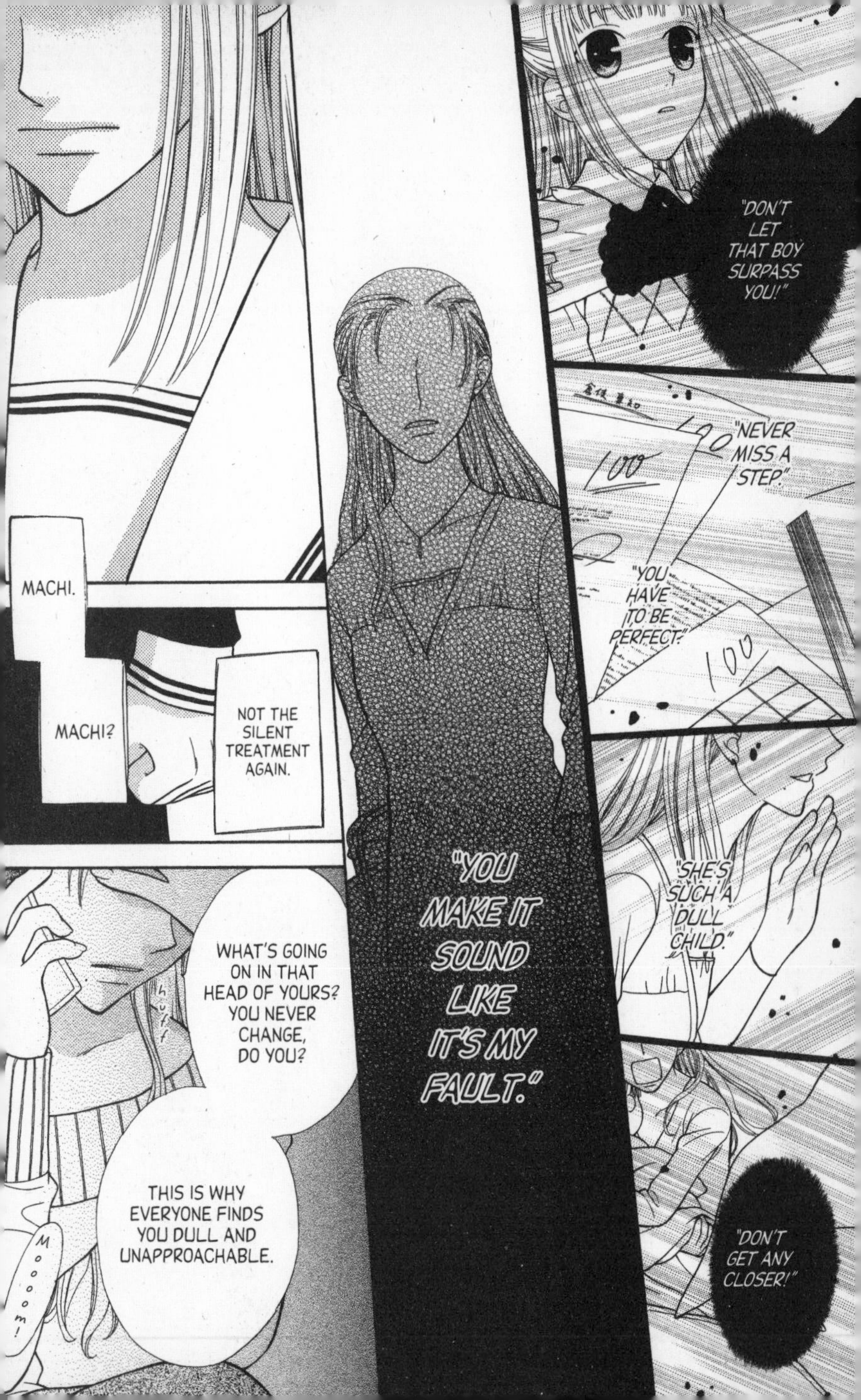
"DON'T LET THAT BOY SURPASS YOU!"
"NEVER MISS A STEP."
100
"YOU HAVE TO BE PERFECT."
100
"SHE'S SUCH A DULL CHILD."
"DON'T GET ANY CLOSER!"
"YOU MAKE IT SOUND LIKE IT'S MY FAULT."
MACHI.
NOT THE SILENT TREATMENT AGAIN.
MACHI?
WHAT'S GOING ON IN THAT HEAD OF YOURS? YOU NEVER CHANGE, DO YOU?
THIS IS WHY EVERYONE FINDS YOU DULL AND UNAPPROACHABLE.
Mooooom!

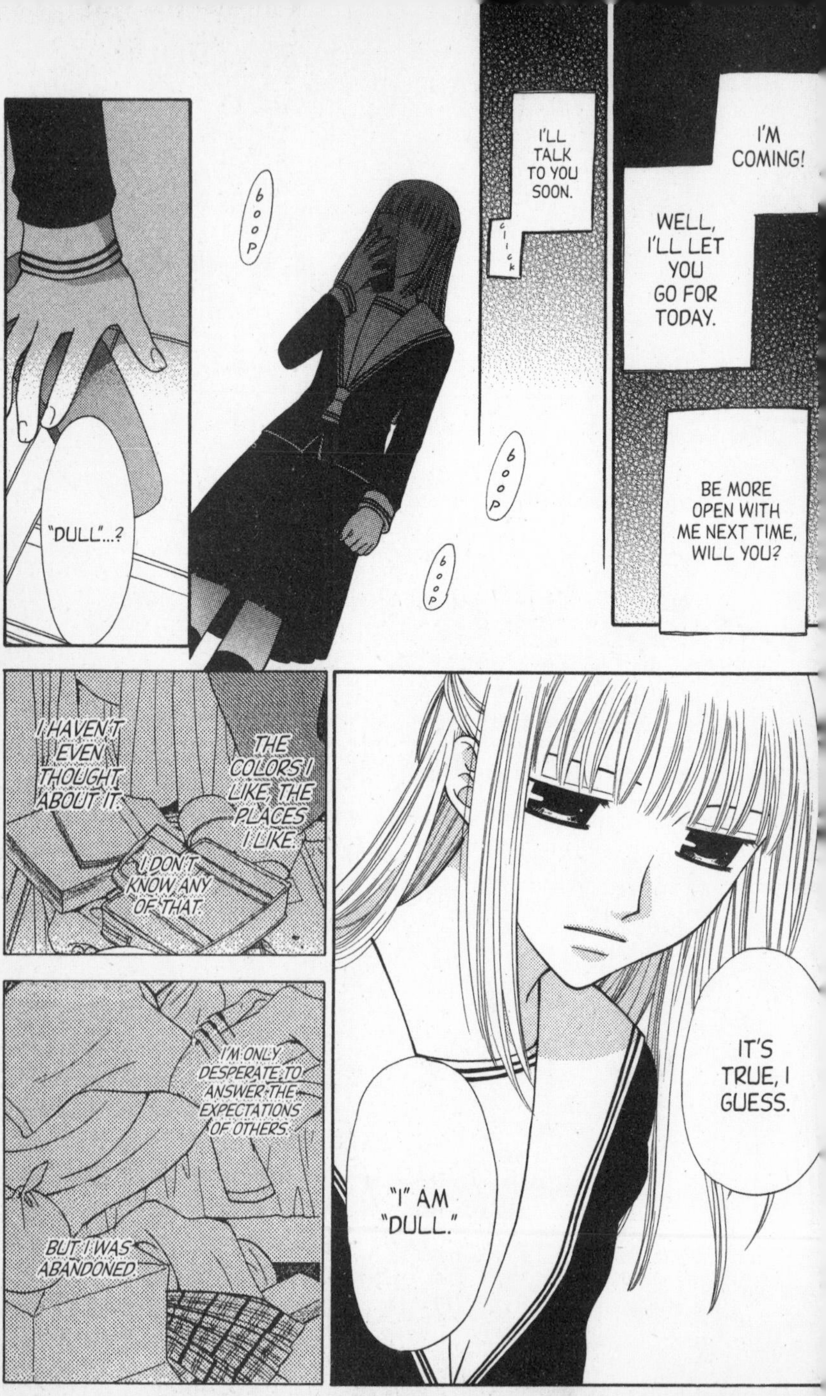
I'M COMING!
WELL, I'LL LET YOU GO FOR TODAY.
BE MORE OPEN WITH ME NEXT TIME, WILL YOU?
I'LL TALK TO YOU SOON.
click
boop
boop
boop
"DULL"...?
IT'S TRUE, I GUESS.
"I" AM "DULL."
THE COLORS I LIKE, THE PLACES I LIKE.
I HAVEN'T EVEN THOUGHT ABOUT IT.
I DON'T KNOW ANY OF THAT.
I'M ONLY DESPERATE TO ANSWER THE EXPECTATIONS OF OTHERS.
BUT I WAS ABANDONED.

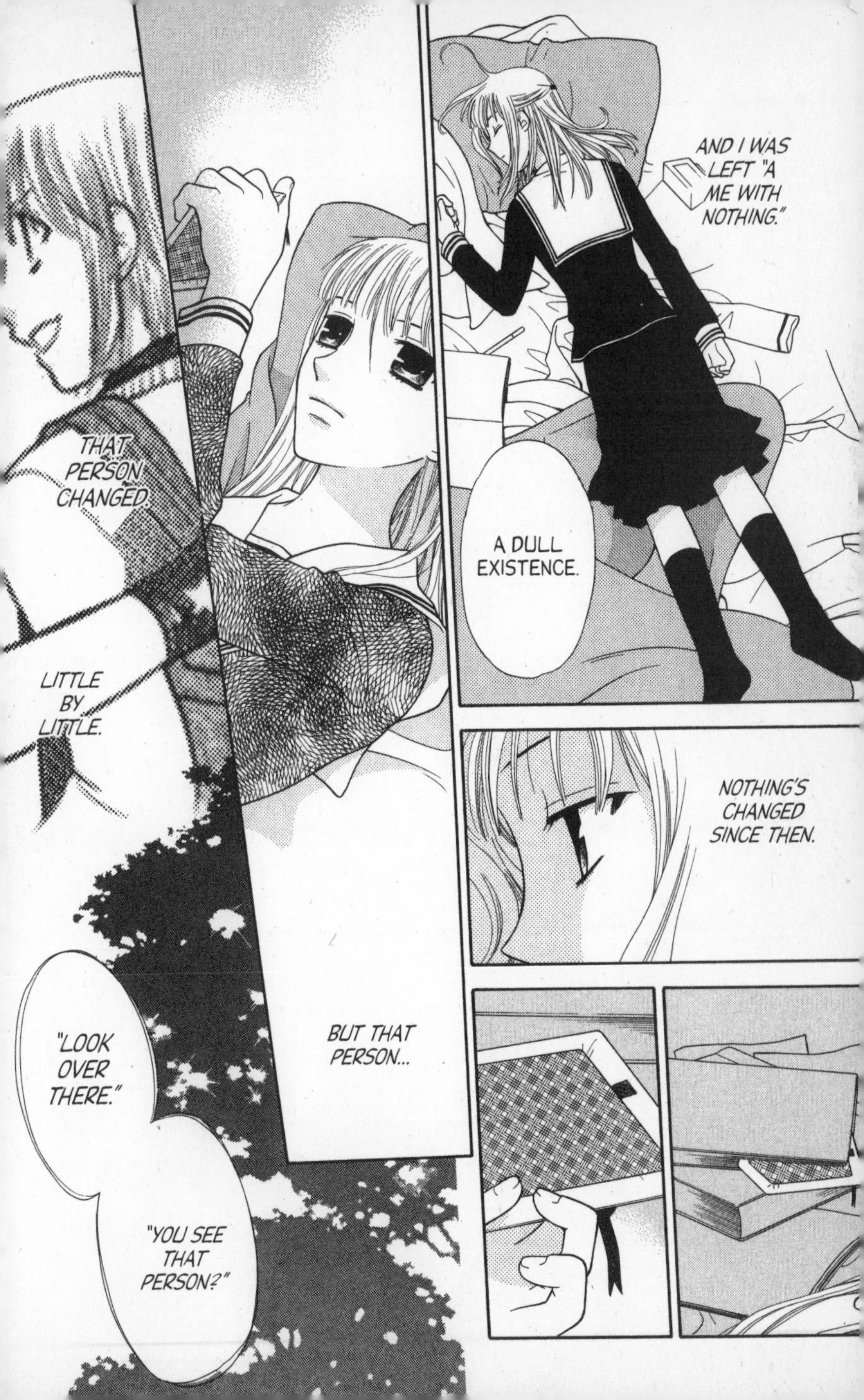
AND I WAS LEFT "A ME WITH NOTHING."
A DULL EXISTENCE.
NOTHING'S CHANGED SINCE THEN.
BUT THAT PERSON...
THAT PERSON CHANGED.
LITTLE BY LITTLE.
"LOOK OVER THERE."
"YOU SEE THAT PERSON?"

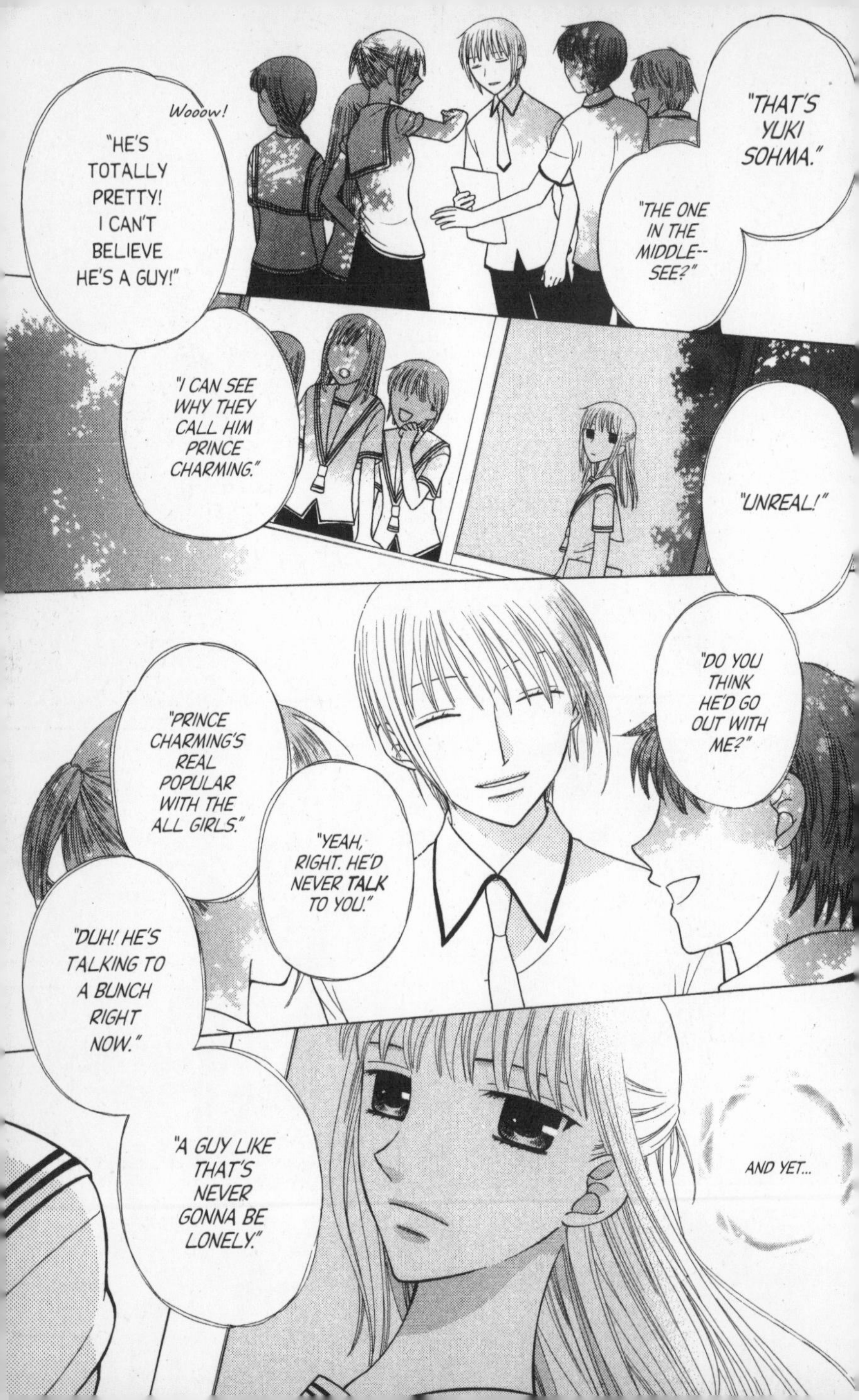
"THAT'S YUKI SOHMA."
"THE ONE IN THE MIDDLE--SEE?"
Wooow!
"HE'S TOTALLY PRETTY! I CAN'T BELIEVE HE'S A GUY!"
"UNREAL!"
"I CAN SEE WHY THEY CALL HIM PRINCE CHARMING."
"DO YOU THINK HE'D GO OUT WITH ME?"
"PRINCE CHARMING'S REAL POPULAR WITH THE ALL GIRLS."
"YEAH, RIGHT. HE'D NEVER TALK TO YOU."
"DUH! HE'S TALKING TO A BUNCH RIGHT NOW."
AND YET...
"A GUY LIKE THAT'S NEVER GONNA BE LONELY."

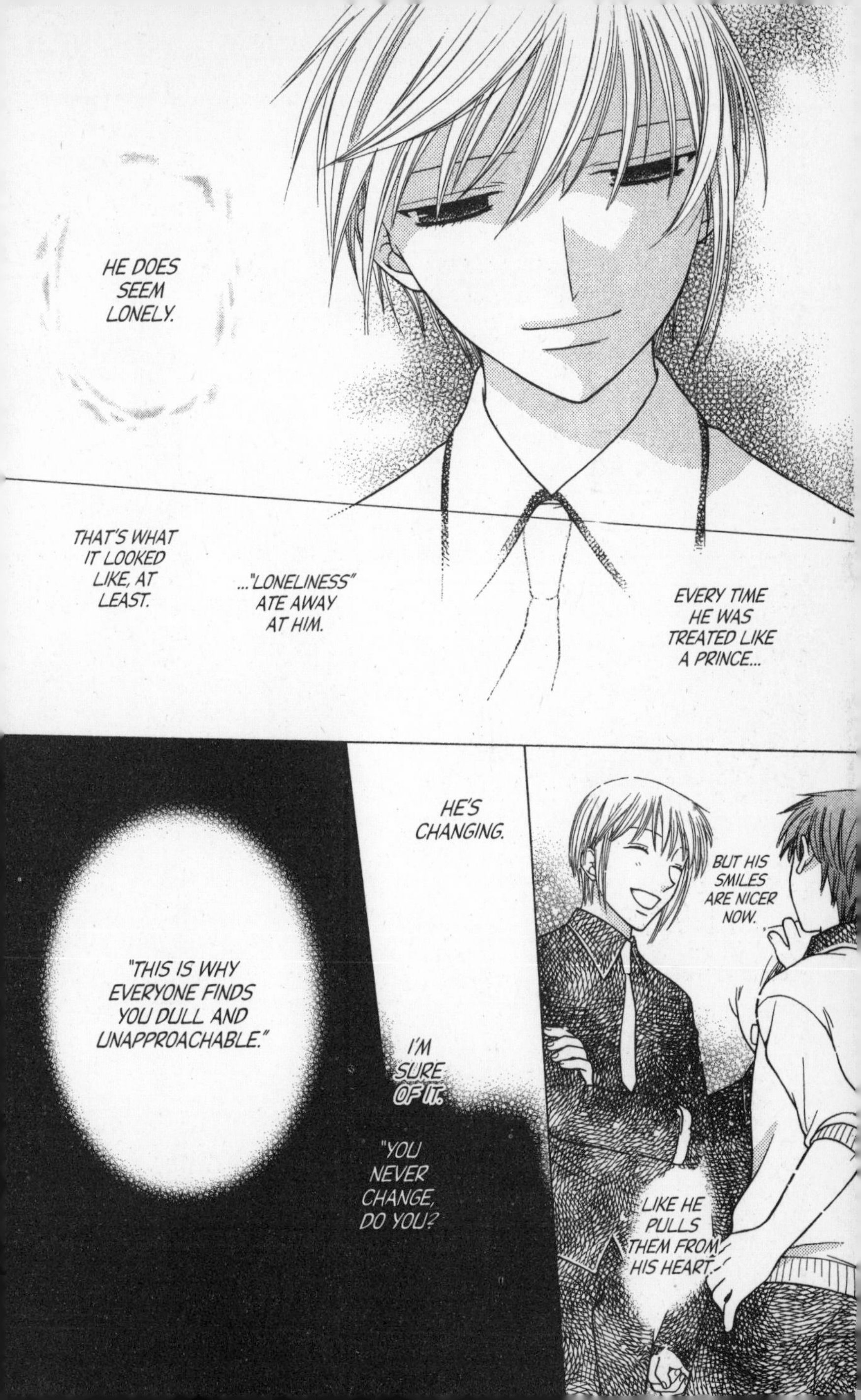
HE DOES SEEM LONELY.
EVERY TIME HE WAS TREATED LIKE A PRINCE...
..."LONELINESS" ATE AWAY AT HIM.
THAT'S WHAT IT LOOKED LIKE, AT LEAST.
BUT HIS SMILES ARE NICER NOW.
LIKE HE PULLS THEM FROM HIS HEART.
HE'S CHANGING.
I'M SURE OF IT.
"YOU NEVER CHANGE, DO YOU?
"THIS IS WHY EVERYONE FINDS YOU DULL AND UNAPPROACHABLE."

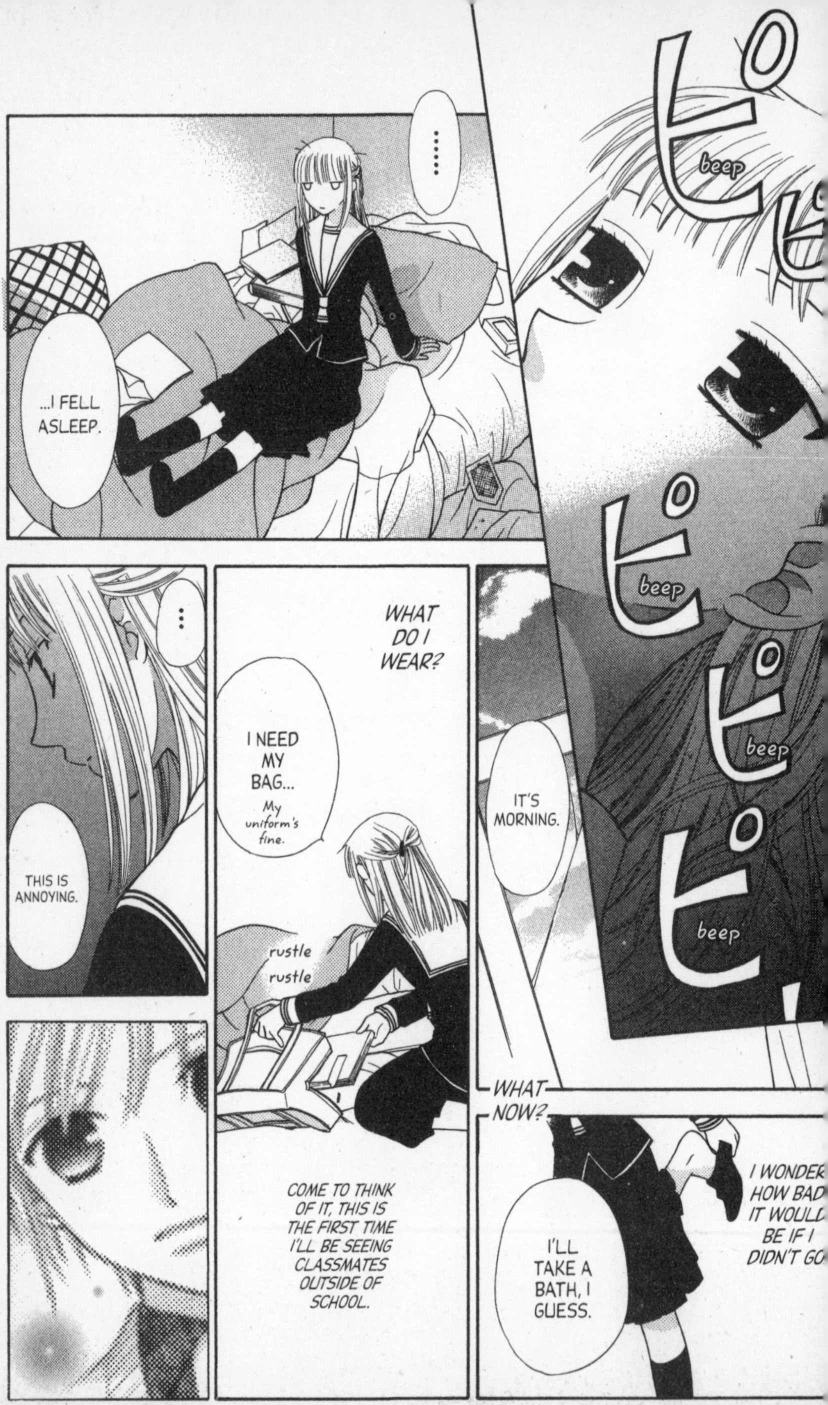
ピ
beep
ピ
beep
ピ
beep
ピ
beep
......
...I FELL ASLEEP.
IT'S MORNING.
WHAT DO I WEAR?
I NEED MY BAG...
My uniform's fine.
rustle rustle
...
THIS IS ANNOYING.
WHAT NOW?
I WONDER HOW BAD IT WOULD BE IF I DIDN'T GO
I'LL TAKE A BATH, I GUESS.
COME TO THINK OF IT, THIS IS THE FIRST TIME I'LL BE SEEING CLASSMATES OUTSIDE OF SCHOOL.

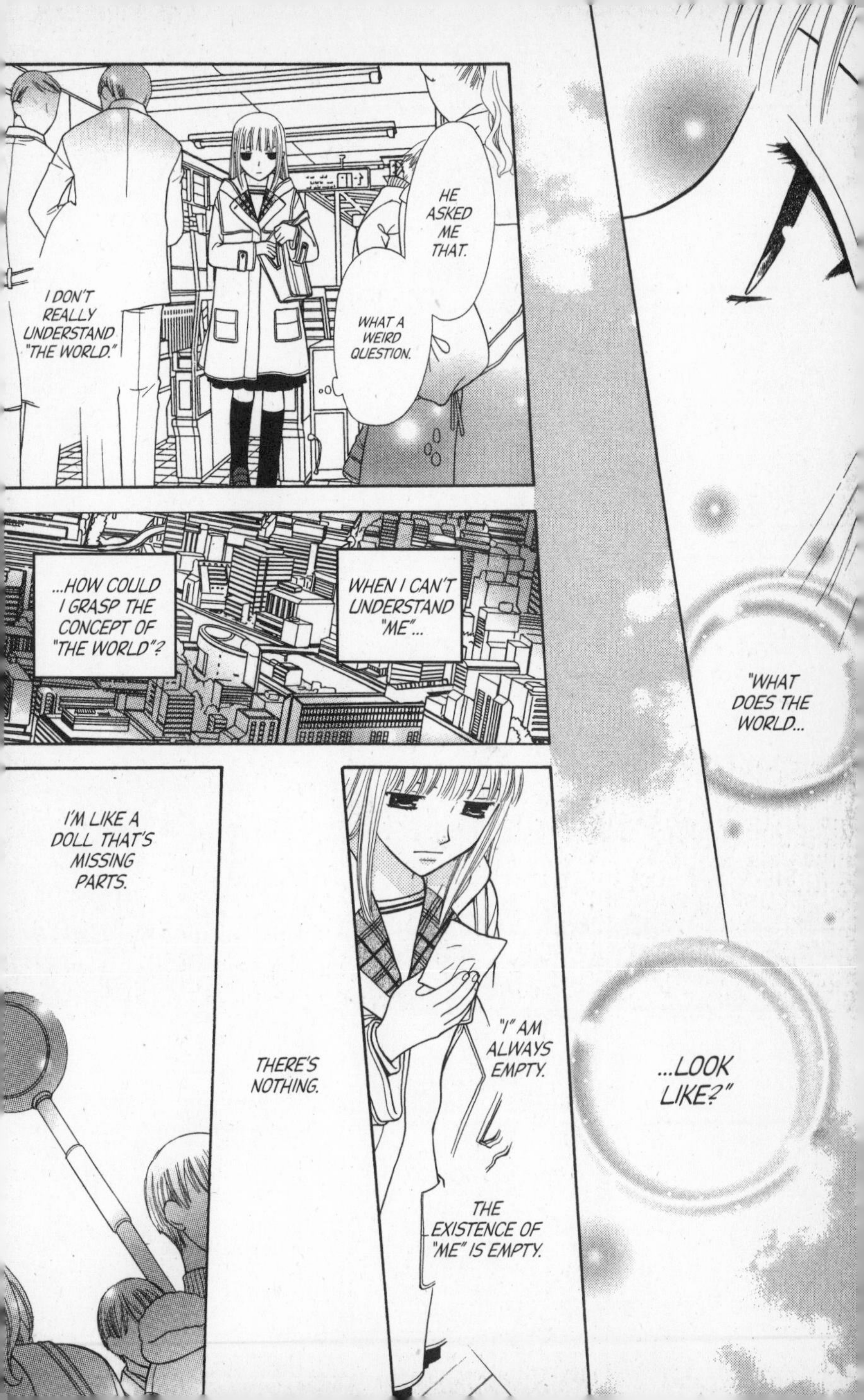
"WHAT DOES THE WORLD...
...LOOK LIKE?"
HE ASKED ME THAT.
WHAT A WEIRD QUESTION.
I DON'T REALLY UNDERSTAND "THE WORLD."
WHEN I CAN'T UNDERSTAND "ME"...
...HOW COULD I GRASP THE CONCEPT OF "THE WORLD"?
"I" AM ALWAYS EMPTY.
THE EXISTENCE OF "ME" IS EMPTY.
I'M LIKE A DOLL THAT'S MISSING PARTS.
THERE'S NOTHING.

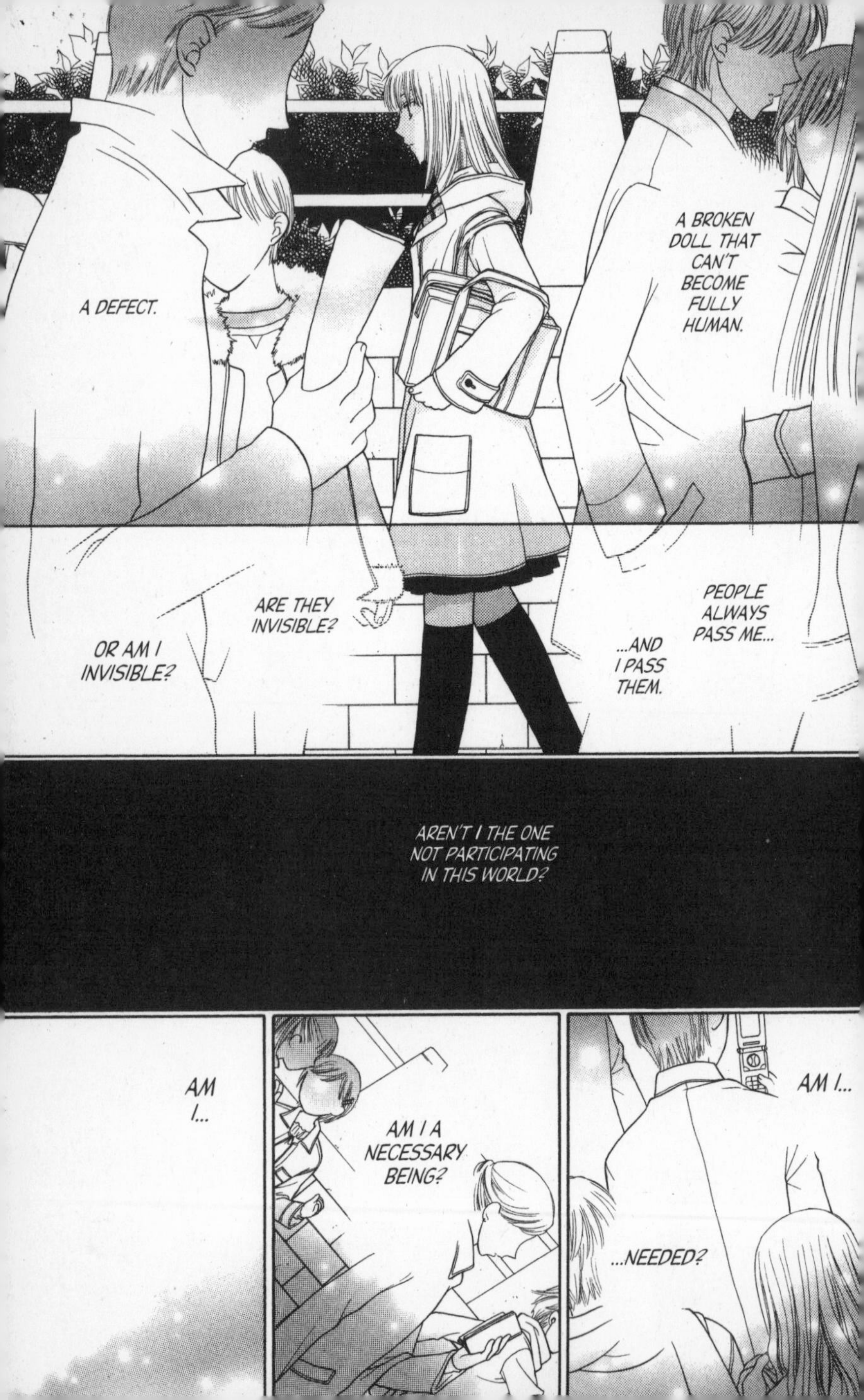
A BROKEN DOLL THAT CAN'T BECOME FULLY HUMAN.
A DEFECT.
PEOPLE ALWAYS PASS ME...
...AND I PASS THEM.
ARE THEY INVISIBLE?
OR AM I INVISIBLE?
AREN'T I THE ONE NOT PARTICIPATING IN THIS WORLD?
AM I...
...NEEDED?
AM I A NECESSARY BEING?
AM I...

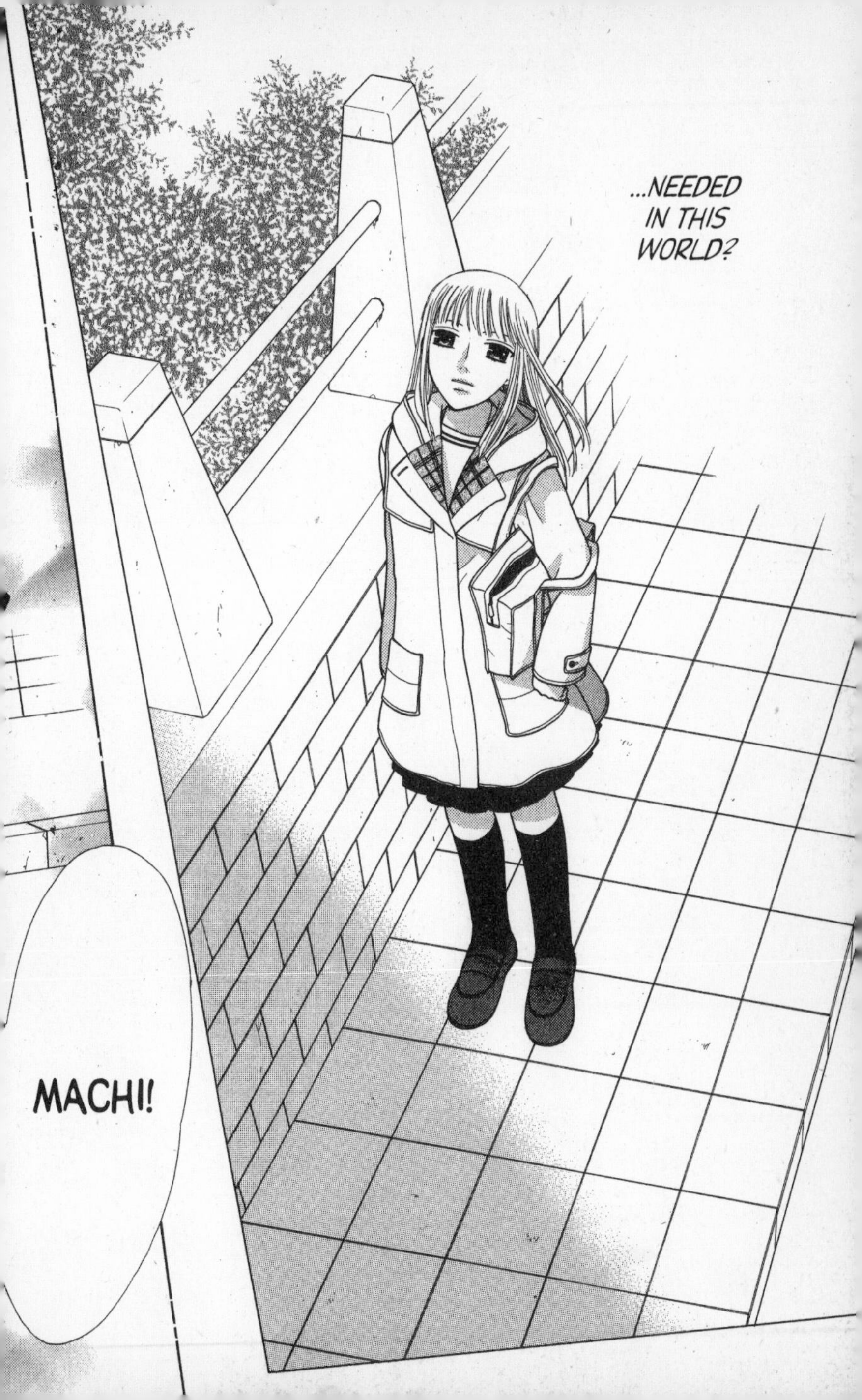
...NEEDED
IN THIS
WORLD?
MACHI!

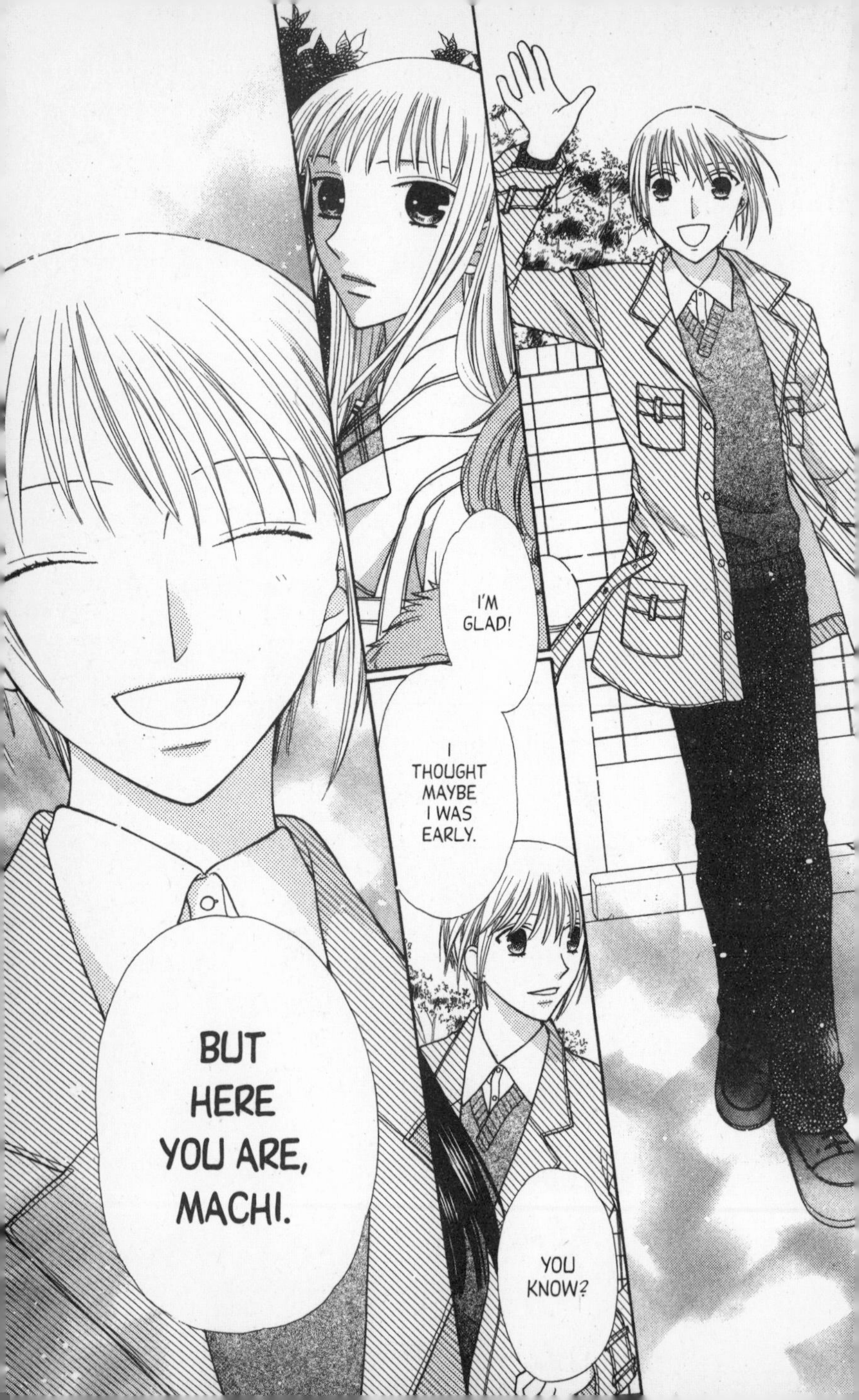
I'M GLAD!
I THOUGHT MAYBE I WAS EARLY.
YOU KNOW?
BUT HERE YOU ARE, MACHI.

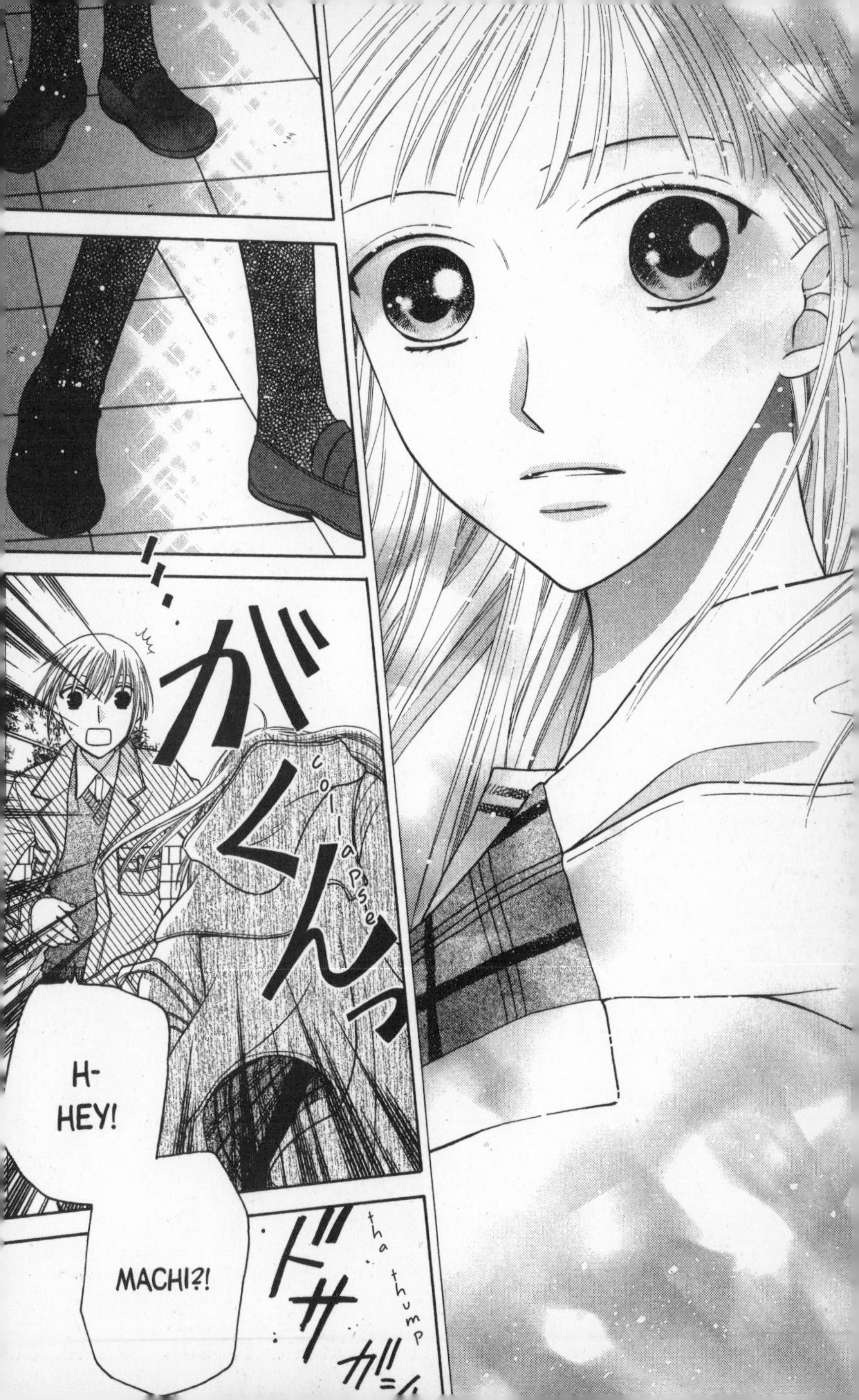
がくんっ
collapse
H-HEY!
MACHI?!
ドサ
tha thump

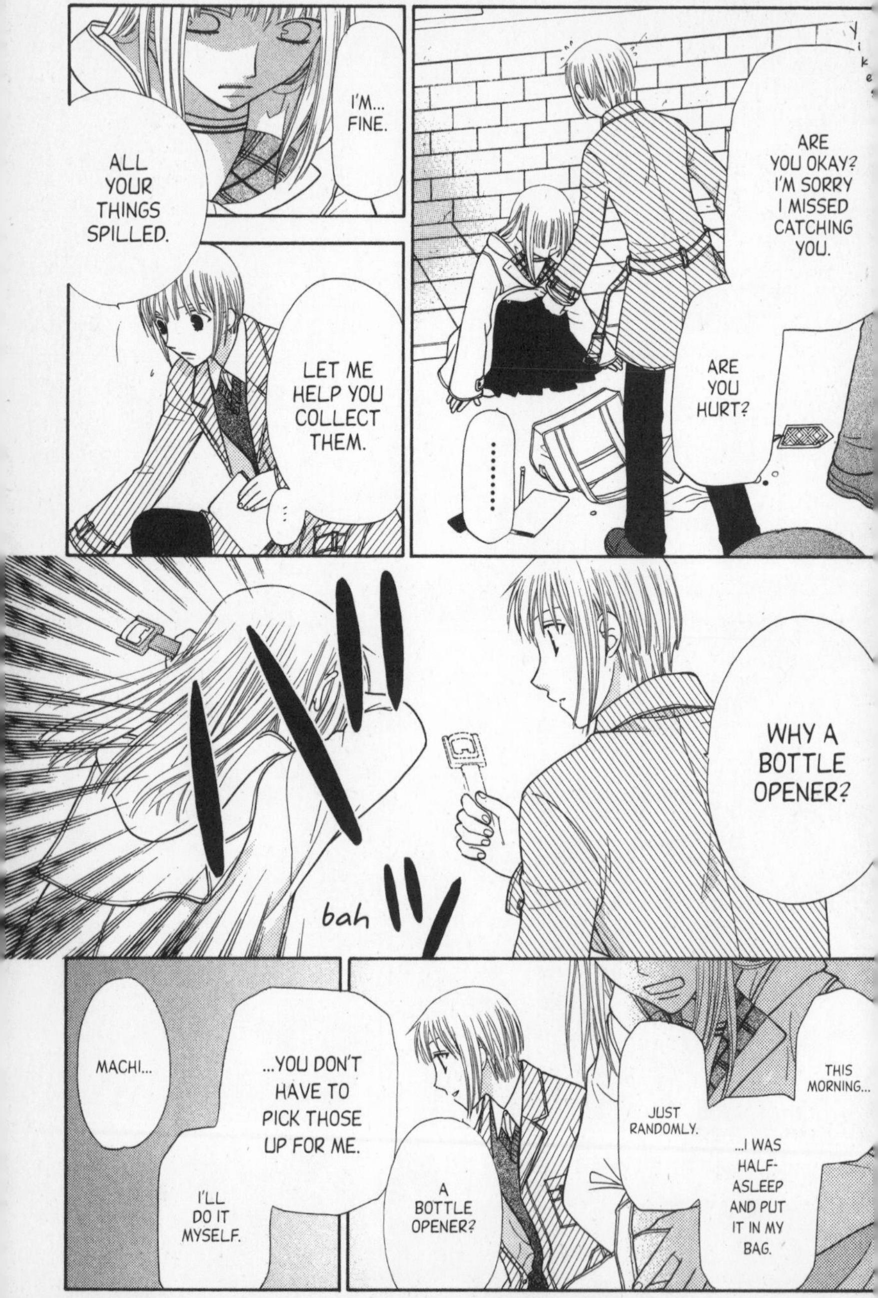
Yike
ARE YOU OKAY? I'M SORRY I MISSED CATCHING YOU.
ARE YOU HURT?
......
I'M... FINE.
ALL YOUR THINGS SPILLED.
LET ME HELP YOU COLLECT THEM.
...
WHY A BOTTLE OPENER?
bah
A BOTTLE OPENER?
THIS MORNING...
...I WAS HALF-ASLEEP AND PUT IT IN MY BAG.
JUST RANDOMLY.
MACHI...
...YOU DON'T HAVE TO PICK THOSE UP FOR ME.
I'LL DO IT MYSELF.

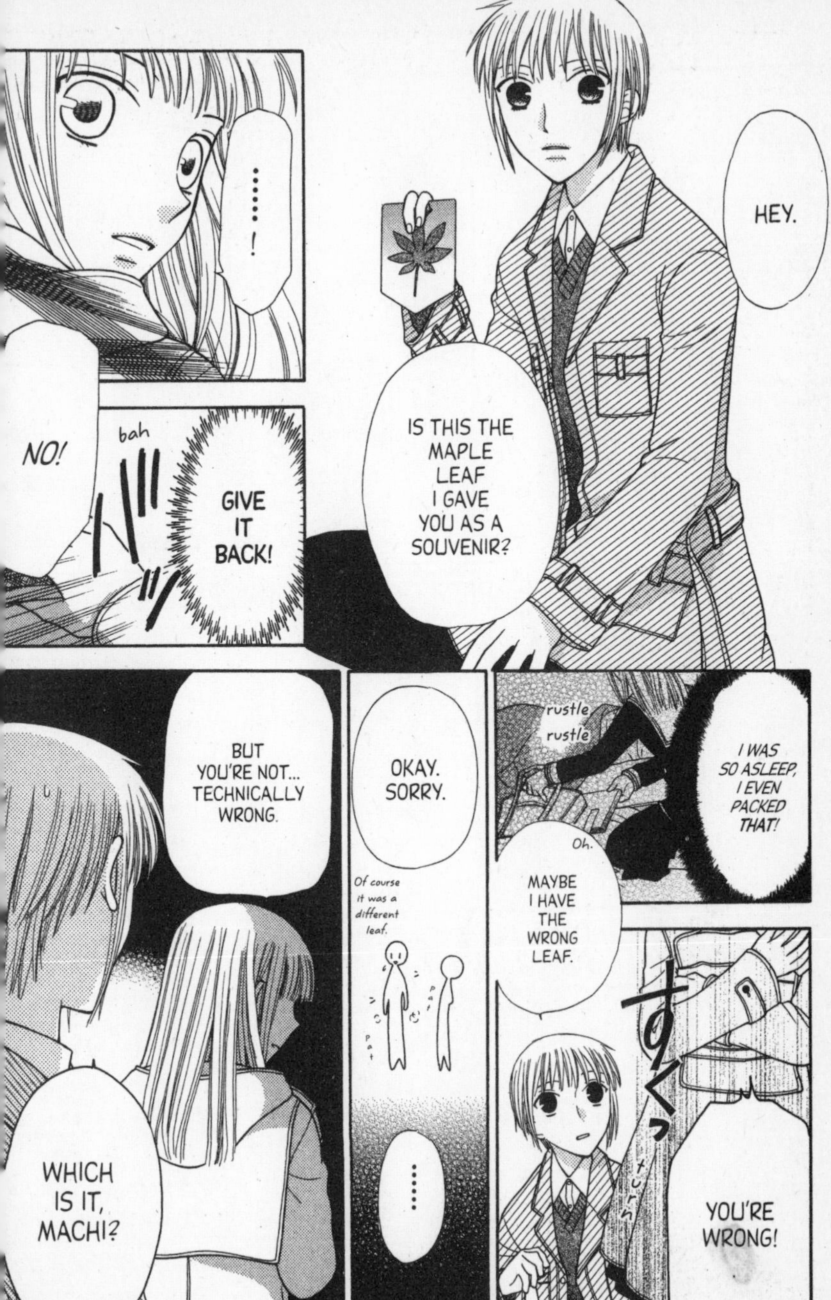
HEY.
IS THIS THE MAPLE LEAF I GAVE YOU AS A SOUVENIR?
......!
GIVE IT BACK!
bah
NO!
rustle
rustle
I WAS SO ASLEEP, I EVEN PACKED THAT!
Oh.
MAYBE I HAVE THE WRONG LEAF.
すくっ
turn
YOU'RE WRONG!
OKAY. SORRY.
Of course it was a different leaf.
pat
pat
......
BUT YOU'RE NOT... TECHNICALLY WRONG.
WHICH IS IT, MACHI?

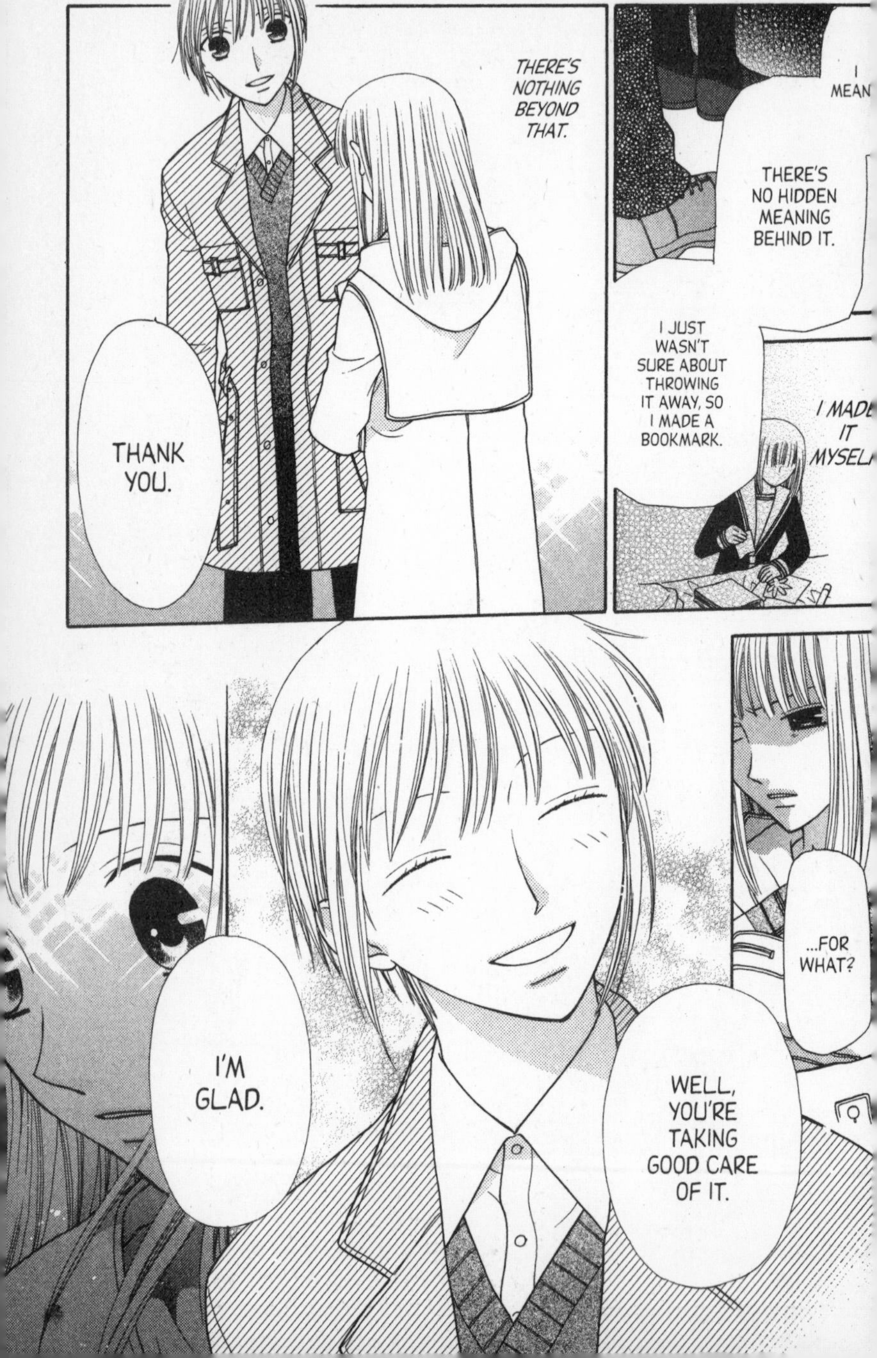
I MEAN
THERE'S NO HIDDEN MEANING BEHIND IT.
I JUST WASN'T SURE ABOUT THROWING IT AWAY, SO I MADE A BOOKMARK.
I MADE IT MYSEL
THERE'S NOTHING BEYOND THAT.
THANK YOU.
...FOR WHAT?
WELL, YOU'RE TAKING GOOD CARE OF IT.
I'M GLAD.

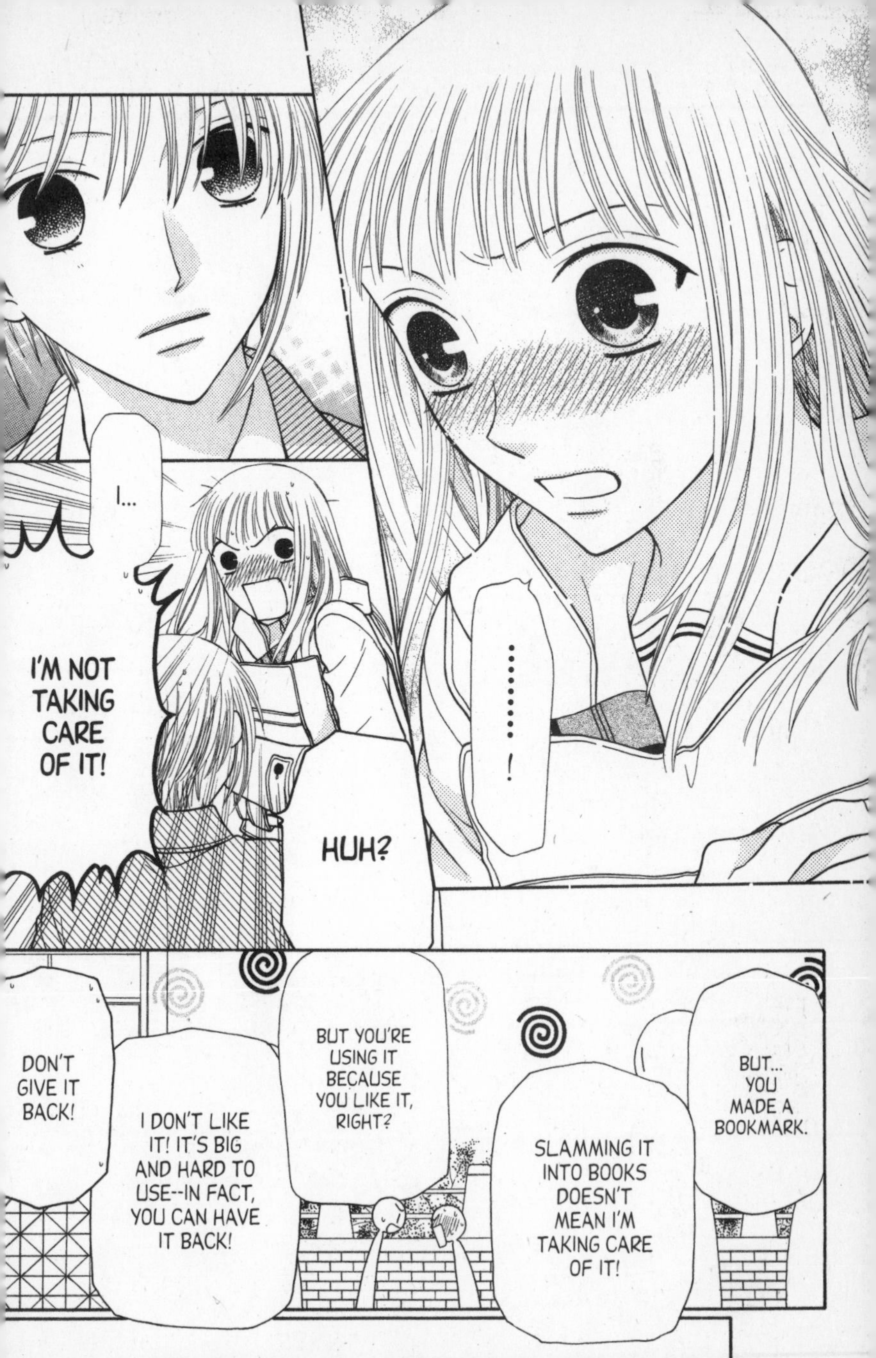
......!
I...
I'M NOT TAKING CARE OF IT!
HUH?
BUT... YOU MADE A BOOKMARK.
SLAMMING IT INTO BOOKS DOESN'T MEAN I'M TAKING CARE OF IT!
BUT YOU'RE USING IT BECAUSE YOU LIKE IT, RIGHT?
I DON'T LIKE IT! IT'S BIG AND HARD TO USE--IN FACT, YOU CAN HAVE IT BACK!
DON'T GIVE IT BACK!

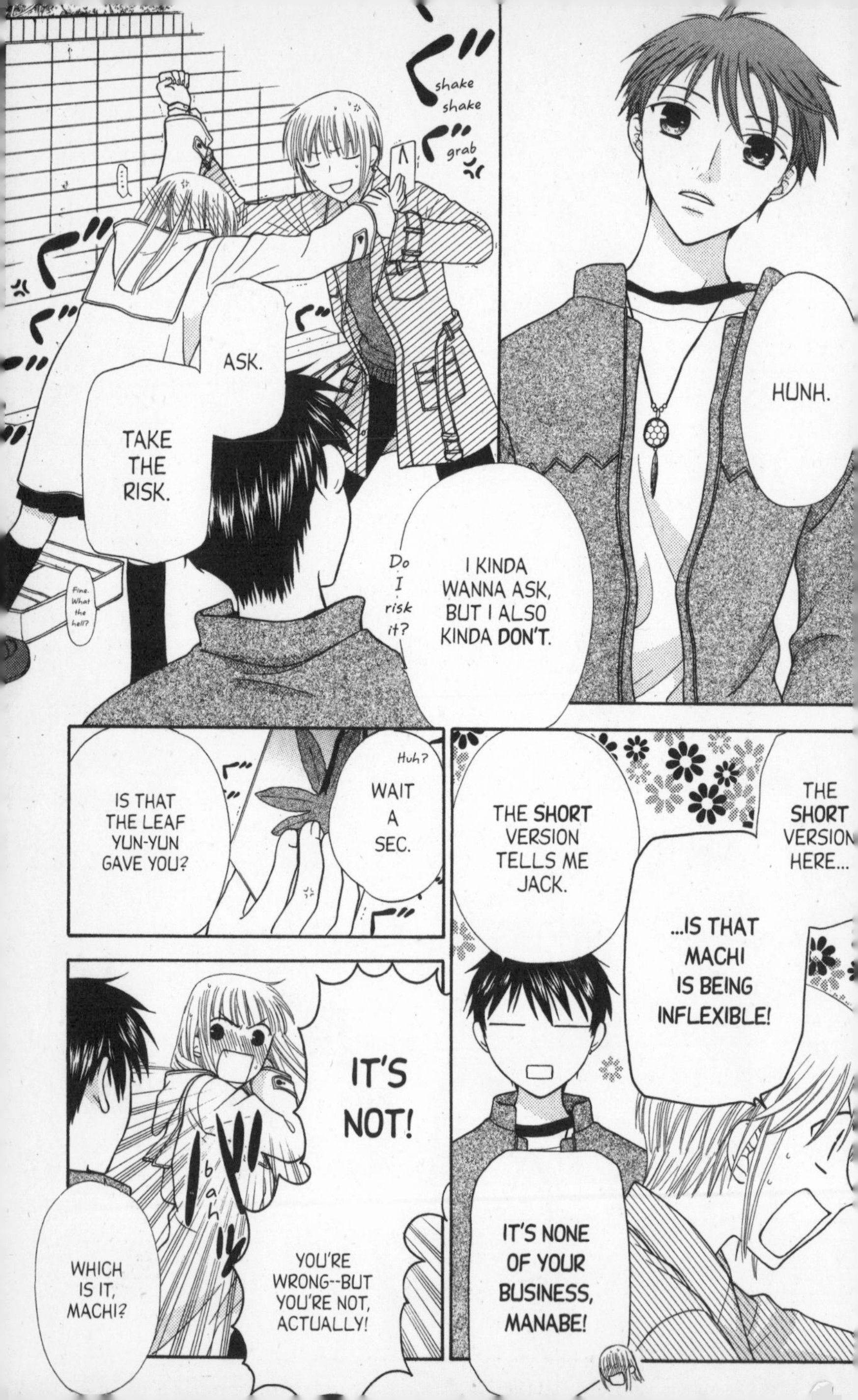
HUNH.
shake
shake
grab
I KINDA WANNA ASK, BUT I ALSO KINDA **DON'T**.
Do I risk it?
ASK.
TAKE THE RISK.
Fine. What the hell?
THE **SHORT** VERSION HERE...
THE **SHORT** VERSION TELLS ME JACK.
...IS THAT MACHI IS BEING INFLEXIBLE!
IT'S NONE OF YOUR BUSINESS, MANABE!
Huh?
WAIT A SEC.
IS THAT THE LEAF YUN-YUN GAVE YOU?
IT'S NOT!
bah
YOU'RE WRONG--BUT YOU'RE NOT, ACTUALLY!
WHICH IS IT, MACHI?

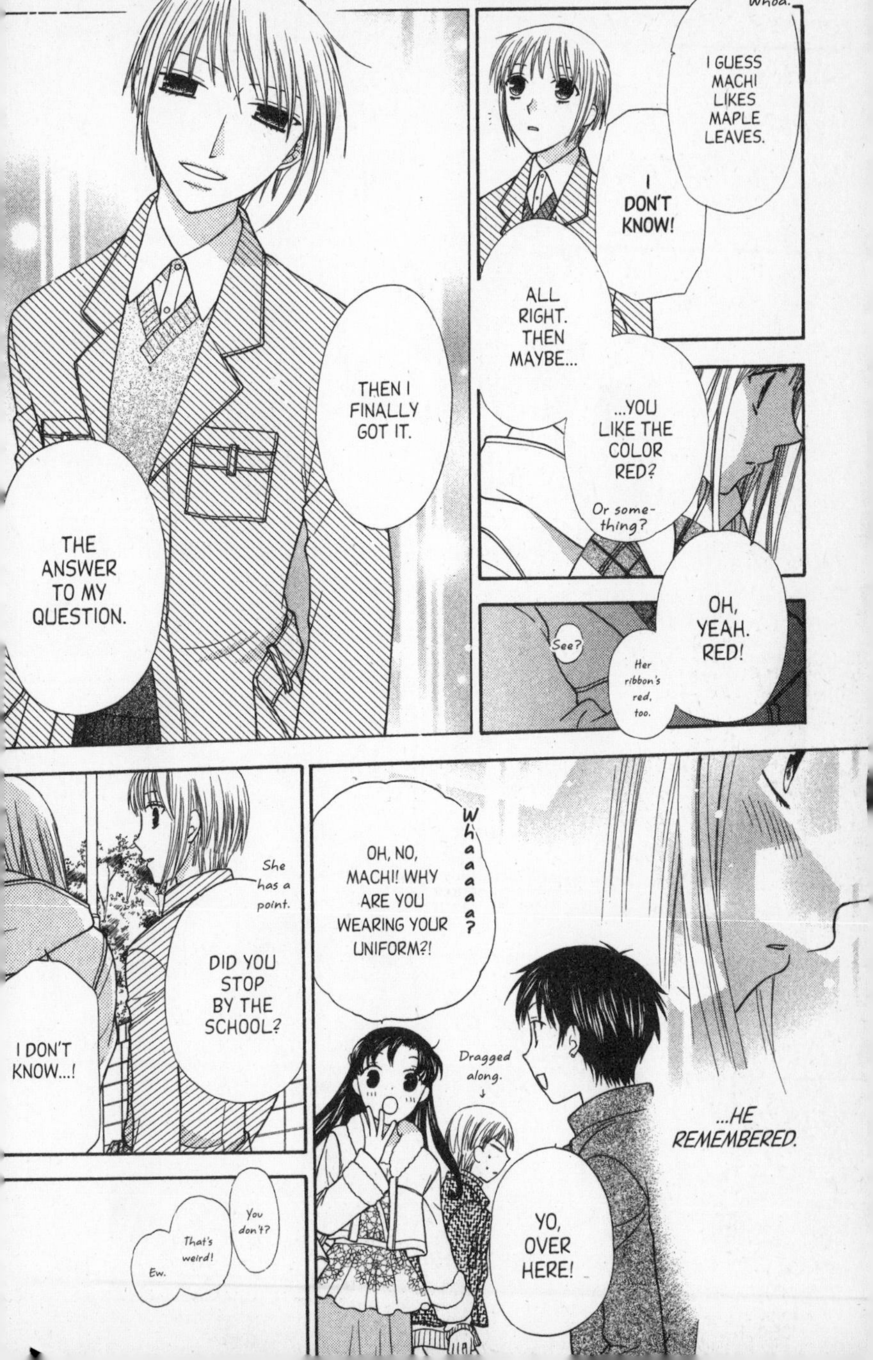
Whoa.
I GUESS MACHI LIKES MAPLE LEAVES.
I DON'T KNOW!
ALL RIGHT. THEN MAYBE...
...YOU LIKE THE COLOR RED?
Or some-thing?
OH, YEAH. RED!
Her ribbon's red, too.
See?
THEN I FINALLY GOT IT.
THE ANSWER TO MY QUESTION.
...HE REMEMBERED.
YO, OVER HERE!
Dragged along.
Whaaaaaa?
OH, NO, MACHI! WHY ARE YOU WEARING YOUR UNIFORM?!
She has a point.
DID YOU STOP BY THE SCHOOL?
I DON'T KNOW...!
You don't?
That's weird!
Ew.

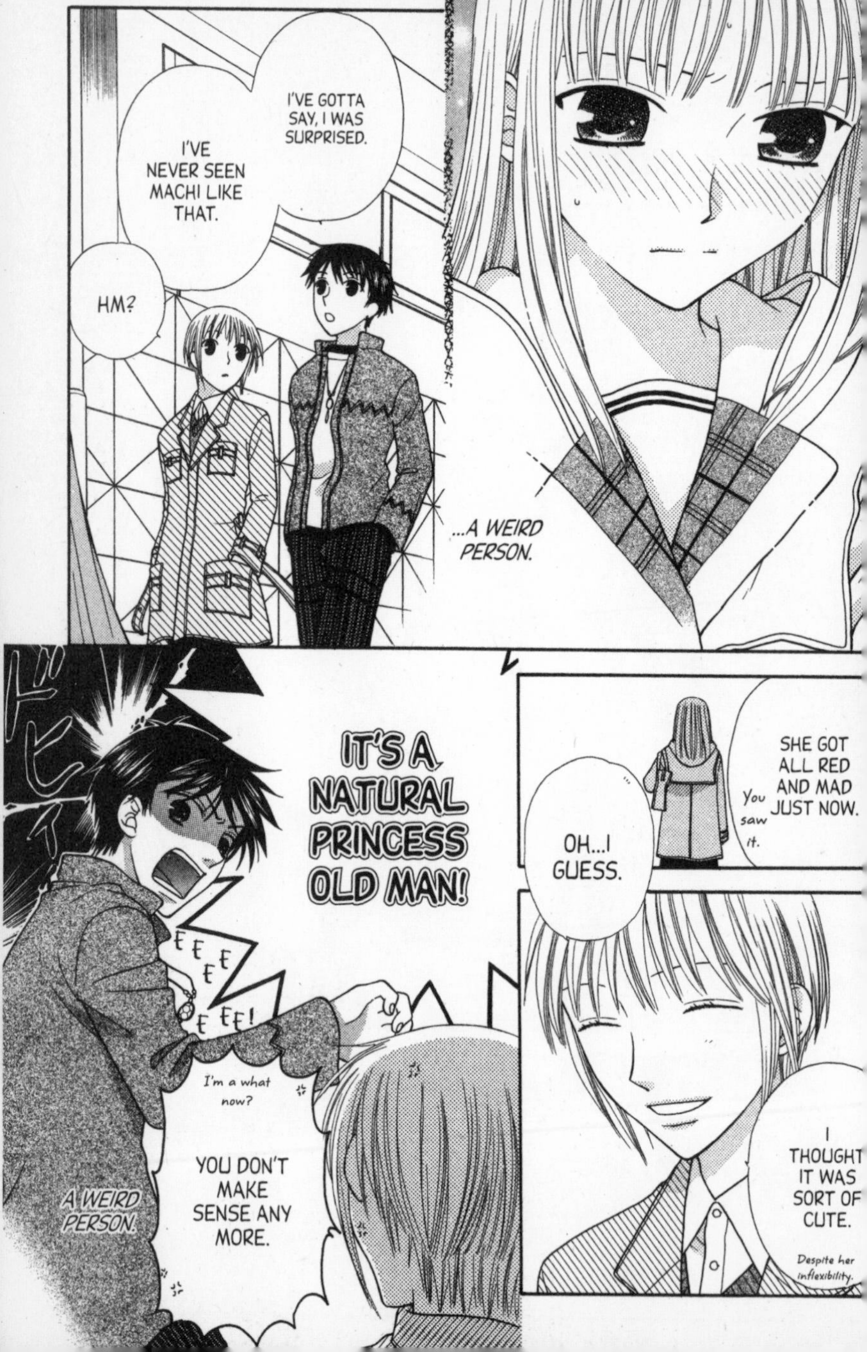
...A WEIRD PERSON.
I'VE GOTTA SAY, I WAS SURPRISED.
I'VE NEVER SEEN MACHI LIKE THAT.
HM?
SHE GOT ALL RED AND MAD JUST NOW.
You saw it.
OH...I GUESS.
I THOUGHT IT WAS SORT OF CUTE.
Despite her inflexibility.
IT'S A NATURAL PRINCESS OLD MAN!
EEEEEEE!
I'm a what now?
YOU DON'T MAKE SENSE ANY MORE.
A WEIRD PERSON.

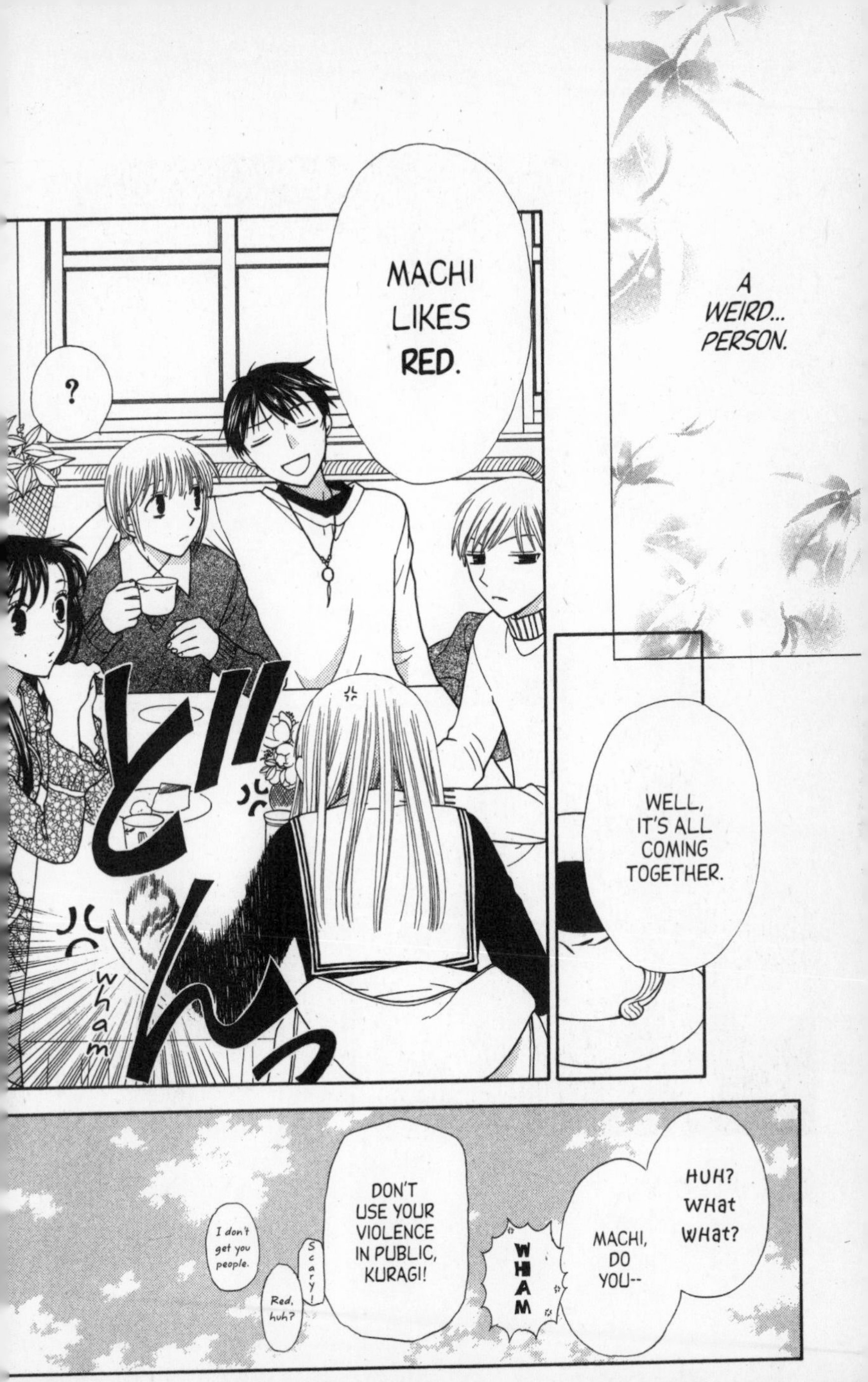
A WEIRD... PERSON.
WELL, IT'S ALL COMING TOGETHER.
MACHI LIKES RED.
?
wham
HUH? WHAT WHAT?
MACHI, DO YOU--
WHAM
DON'T USE YOUR VIOLENCE IN PUBLIC, KURAGI!
Scary!
Red, huh?
I don't get you people.

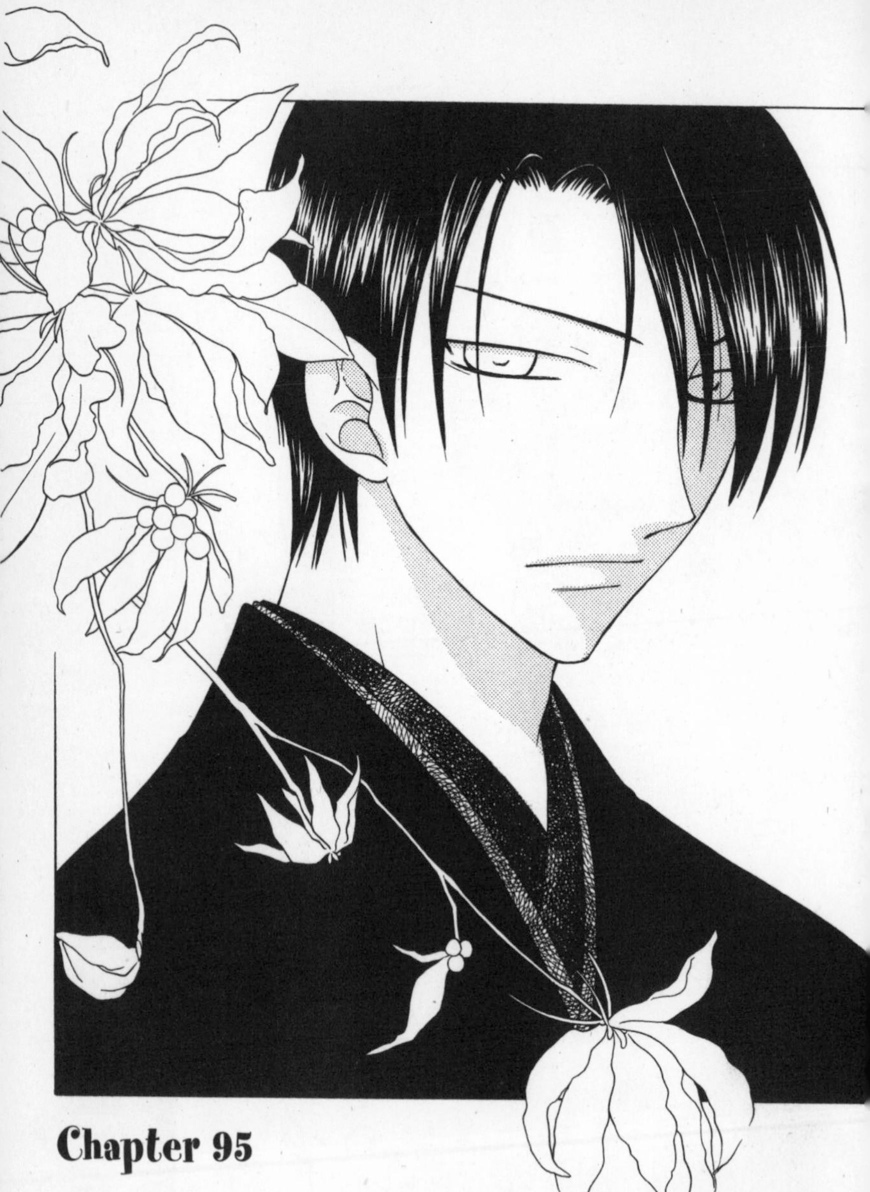

Chapter 95

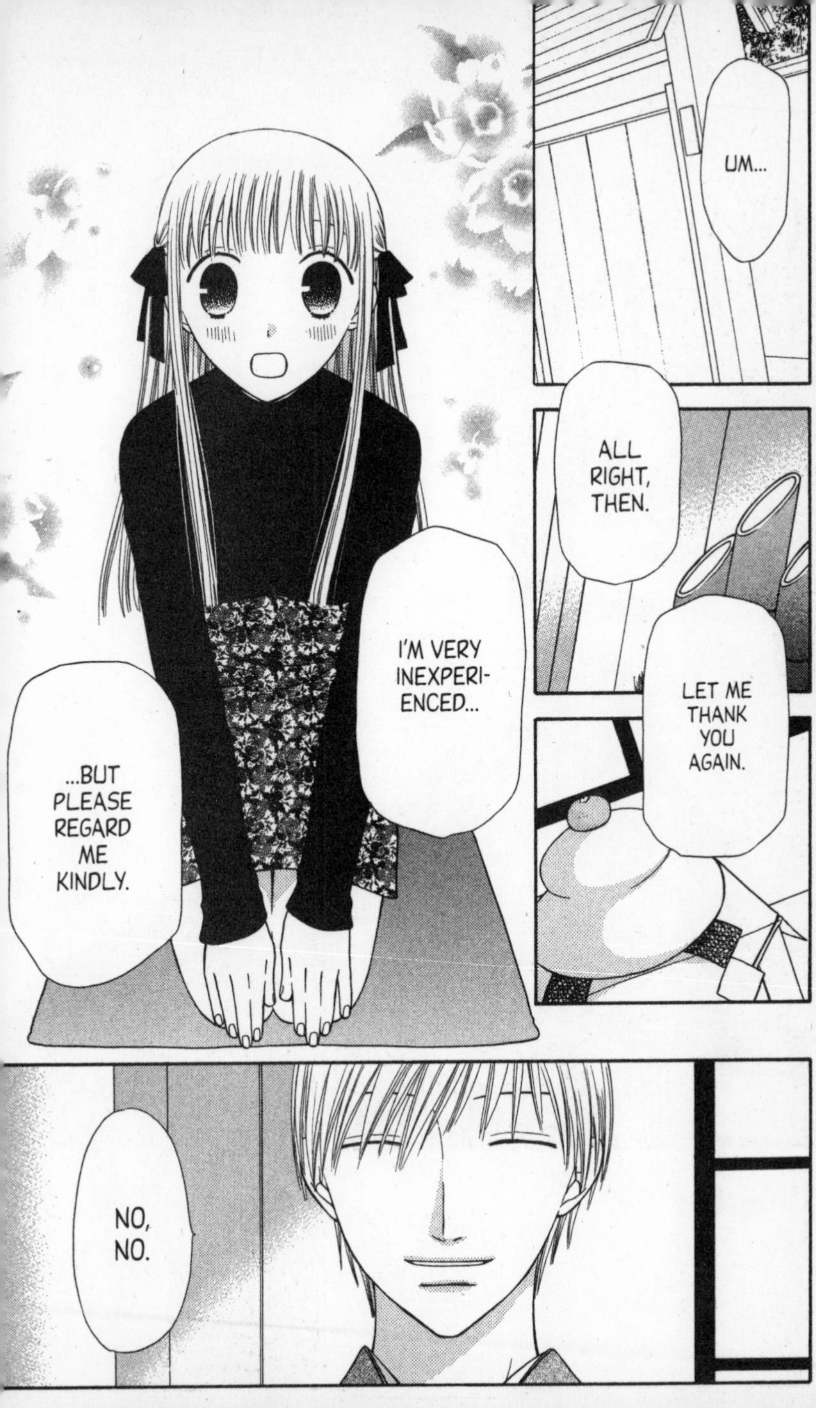
UM...
ALL RIGHT, THEN.
LET ME THANK YOU AGAIN.
I'M VERY INEXPERI-ENCED...
...BUT PLEASE REGARD ME KINDLY.
NO, NO.

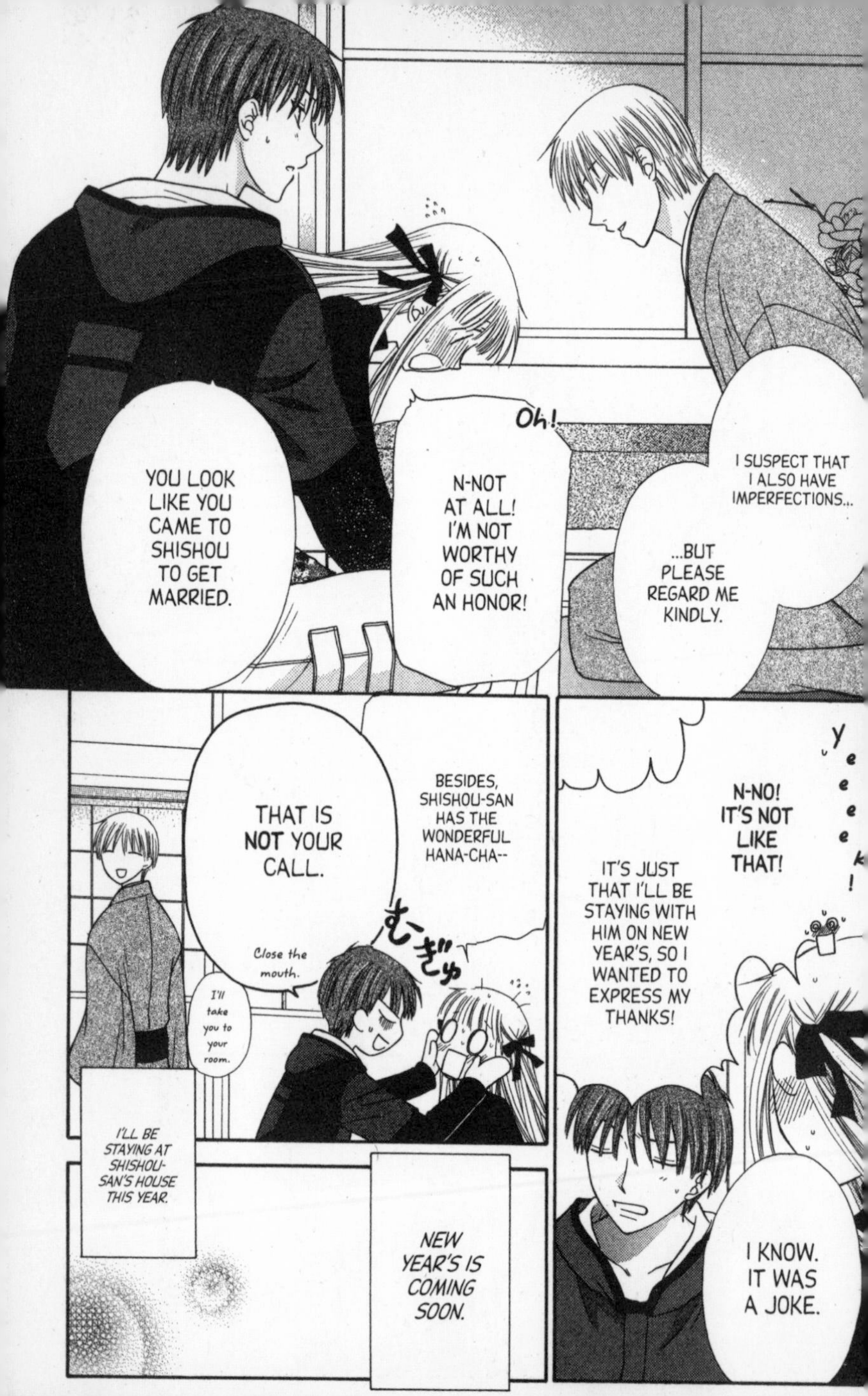
I SUSPECT THAT I ALSO HAVE IMPERFECTIONS...
...BUT PLEASE REGARD ME KINDLY.
Oh!
N-NOT AT ALL! I'M NOT WORTHY OF SUCH AN HONOR!
YOU LOOK LIKE YOU CAME TO SHISHOU TO GET MARRIED.
Yeeeek!
N-NO! IT'S NOT LIKE THAT!
IT'S JUST THAT I'LL BE STAYING WITH HIM ON NEW YEAR'S, SO I WANTED TO EXPRESS MY THANKS!
I KNOW. IT WAS A JOKE.
BESIDES, SHISHOU-SAN HAS THE WONDERFUL HANA-CHA--
THAT IS NOT YOUR CALL.
むぎゅ
Close the mouth.
I'll take you to your room.
I'LL BE STAYING AT SHISHOU-SAN'S HOUSE THIS YEAR.
NEW YEAR'S IS COMING SOON.

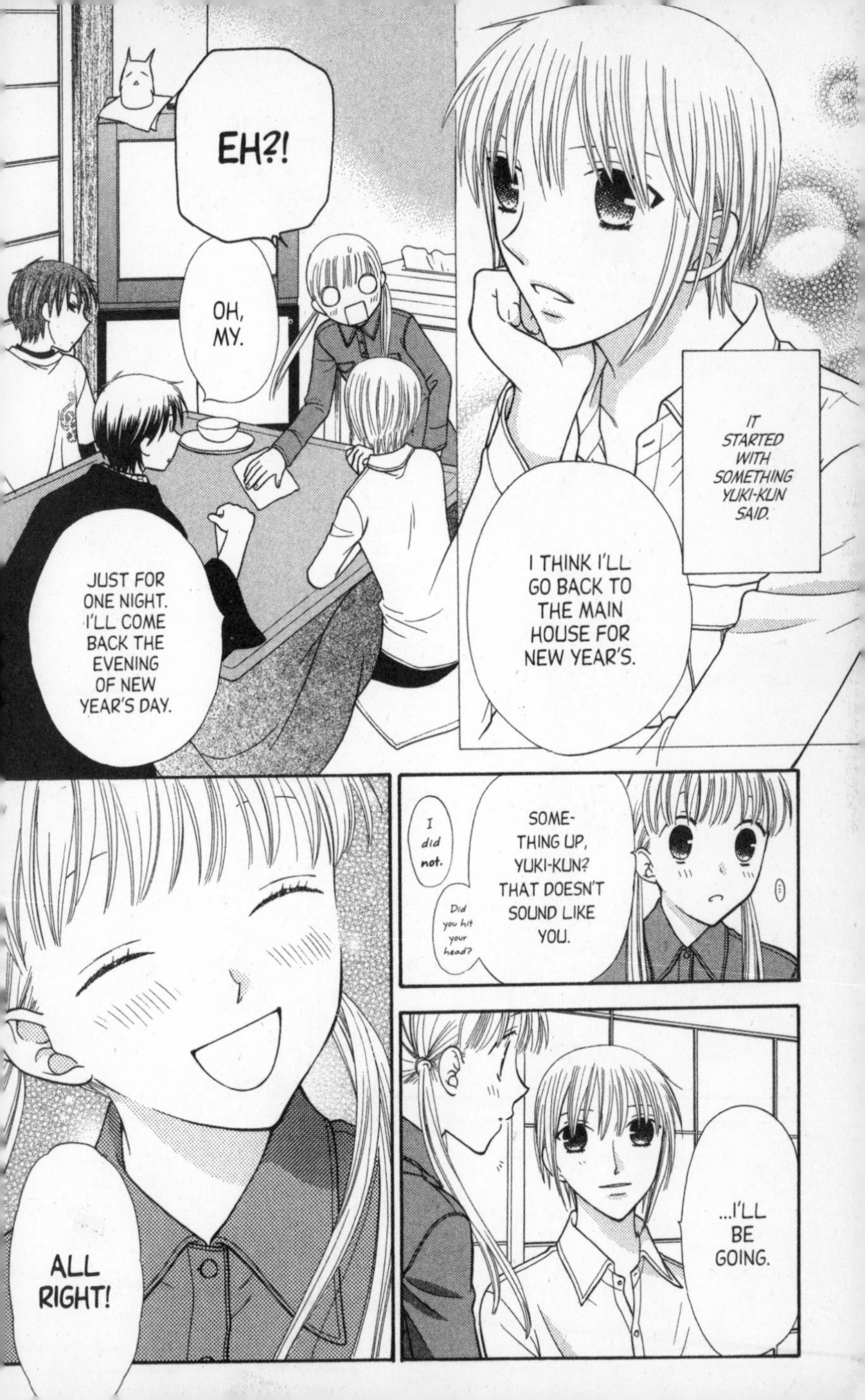
IT STARTED WITH SOMETHING YUKI-KUN SAID.
I THINK I'LL GO BACK TO THE MAIN HOUSE FOR NEW YEAR'S.
EH?!
OH, MY.
JUST FOR ONE NIGHT. I'LL COME BACK THE EVENING OF NEW YEAR'S DAY.
SOME-THING UP, YUKI-KUN? THAT DOESN'T SOUND LIKE YOU.
Did you hit your head?
I did not.
...I'LL BE GOING.
ALL RIGHT!

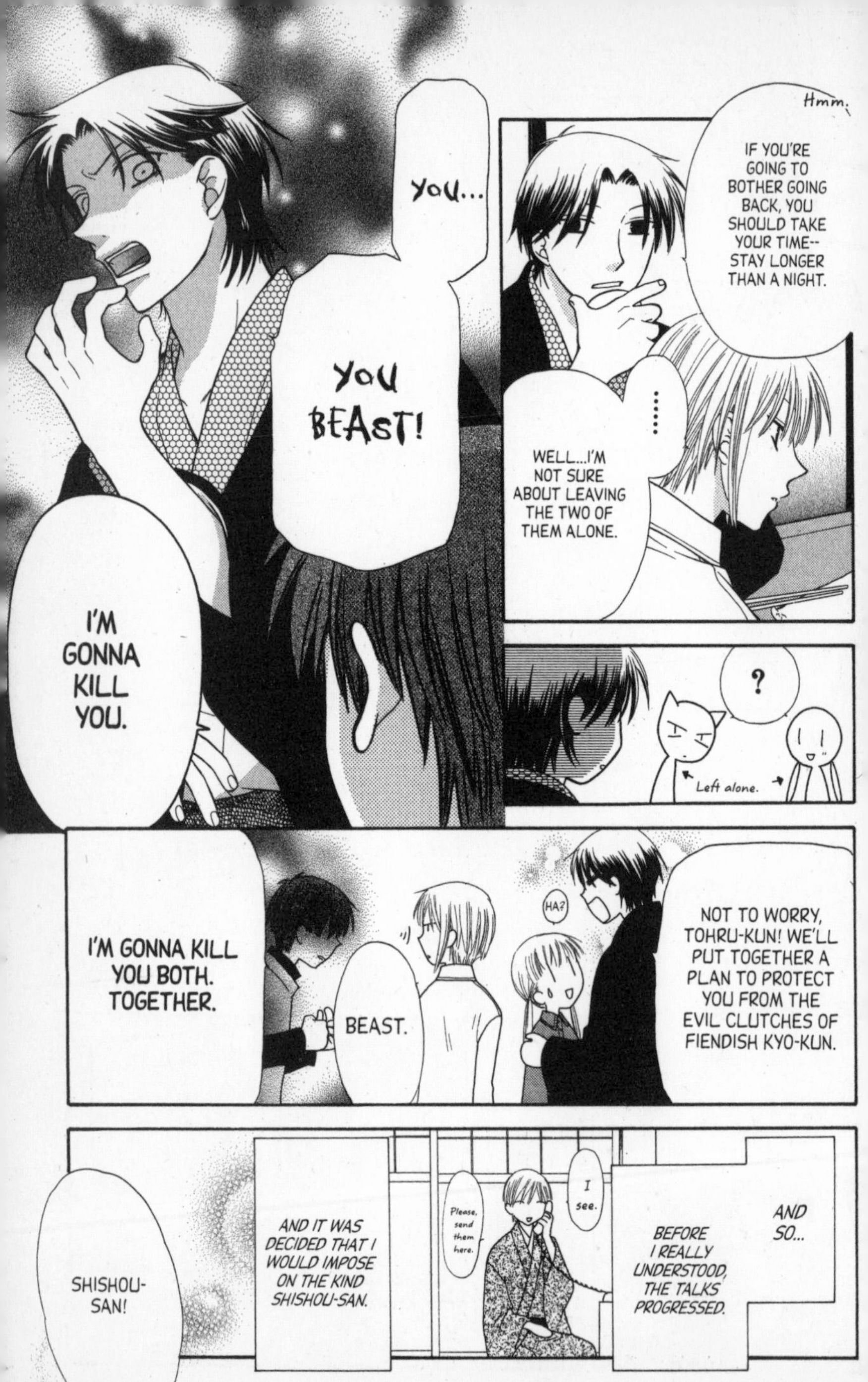
Hmm.
IF YOU'RE GOING TO BOTHER GOING BACK, YOU SHOULD TAKE YOUR TIME-- STAY LONGER THAN A NIGHT.
......
WELL...I'M NOT SURE ABOUT LEAVING THE TWO OF THEM ALONE.
?
Left alone.
YOU...
YOU BEAST!
I'M GONNA KILL YOU.
NOT TO WORRY, TOHRU-KUN! WE'LL PUT TOGETHER A PLAN TO PROTECT YOU FROM THE EVIL CLUTCHES OF FIENDISH KYO-KUN.
HA?
BEAST.
I'M GONNA KILL YOU BOTH. TOGETHER.
AND SO...
BEFORE I REALLY UNDERSTOOD, THE TALKS PROGRESSED.
I see.
Please, send them here.
AND IT WAS DECIDED THAT I WOULD IMPOSE ON THE KIND SHISHOU-SAN.
SHISHOU-SAN!

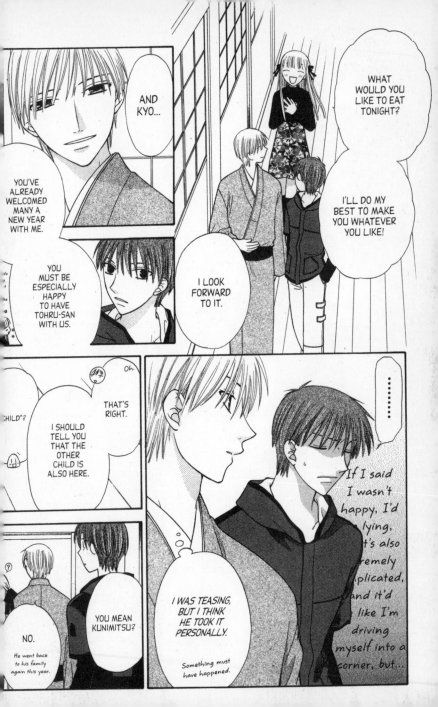

WHAT WOULD YOU LIKE TO EAT TONIGHT?
I'LL DO MY BEST TO MAKE YOU WHATEVER YOU LIKE!
I LOOK FORWARD TO IT.
AND KYO...
YOU'VE ALREADY WELCOMED MANY A NEW YEAR WITH ME.
YOU MUST BE ESPECIALLY HAPPY TO HAVE TOHRU-SAN WITH US.
......
If I said I wasn't happy, I'd
lying,
t's also
remely
plicated,
and it'd
like I'm
driving myself into a
corner, but...
I WAS TEASING, BUT I THINK HE TOOK IT PERSONALLY.
Something must have happened.
Oh.
THAT'S RIGHT.
I SHOULD TELL YOU THAT THE OTHER CHILD IS ALSO HERE.
HILD"?
YOU MEAN KUNIMITSU?
NO.
He went back to his family again this year.

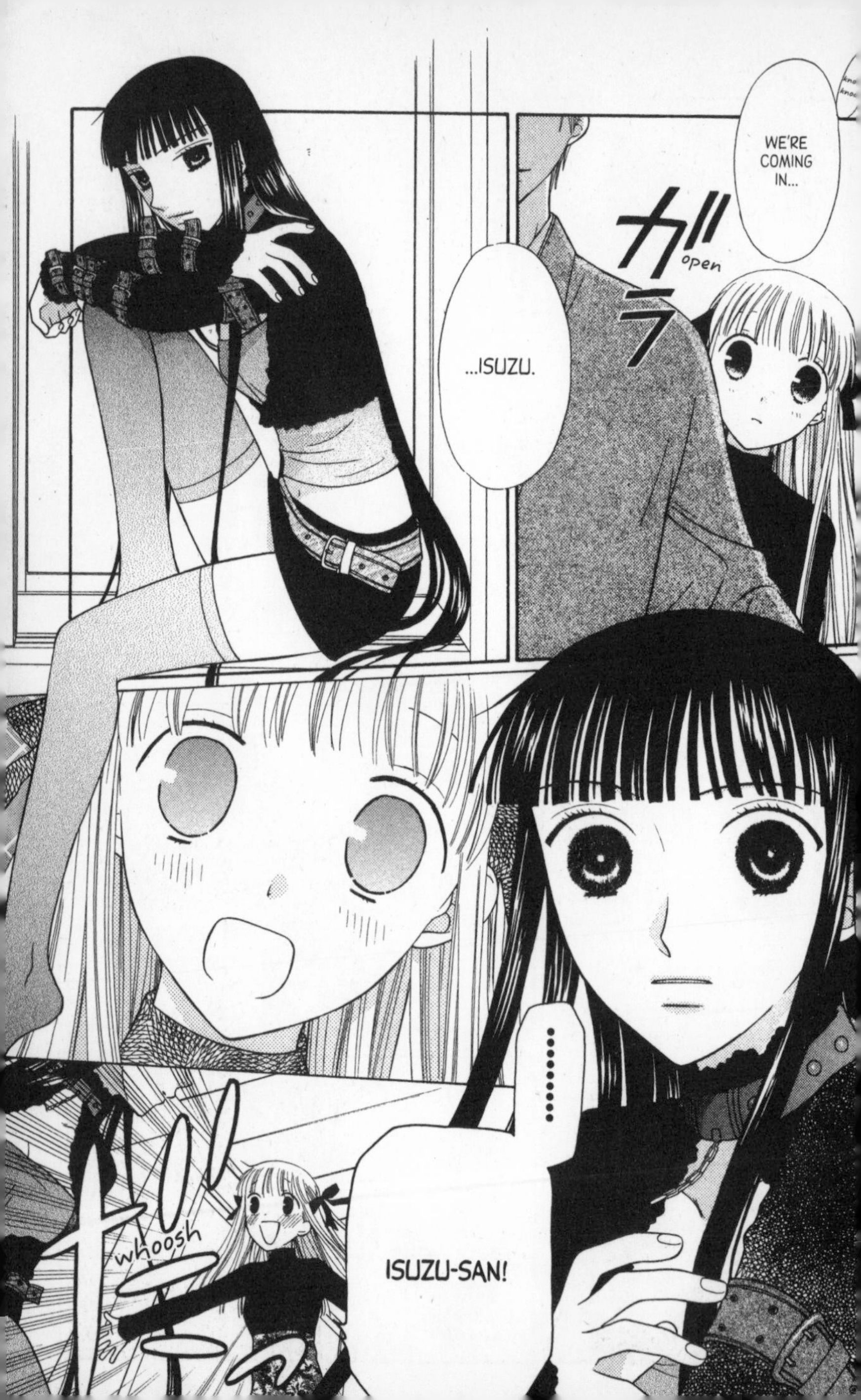
WE'RE COMING IN...
ガラ
open
...ISUZU.
....
ISUZU-SAN!
whoosh

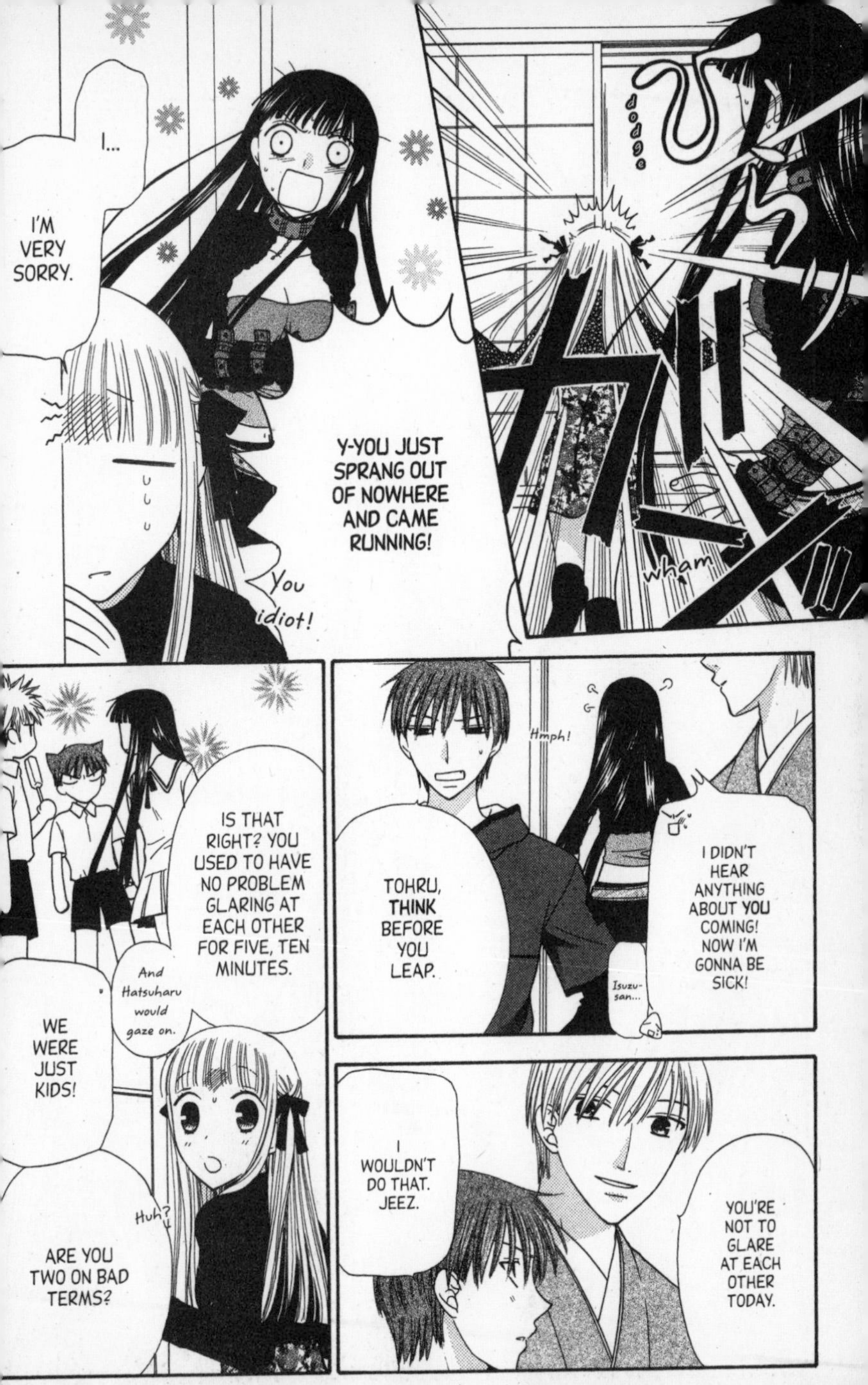
dodge
wham
Y-YOU JUST SPRANG OUT OF NOWHERE AND CAME RUNNING!
You idiot!
I...
I'M VERY SORRY.
Hmph!
I DIDN'T HEAR ANYTHING ABOUT YOU COMING! NOW I'M GONNA BE SICK!
Isuzu-san...
TOHRU, THINK BEFORE YOU LEAP.
YOU'RE NOT TO GLARE AT EACH OTHER TODAY.
I WOULDN'T DO THAT. JEEZ.
IS THAT RIGHT? YOU USED TO HAVE NO PROBLEM GLARING AT EACH OTHER FOR FIVE, TEN MINUTES.
And Hatsuharu would gaze on.
WE WERE JUST KIDS!
Huh?
ARE YOU TWO ON BAD TERMS?

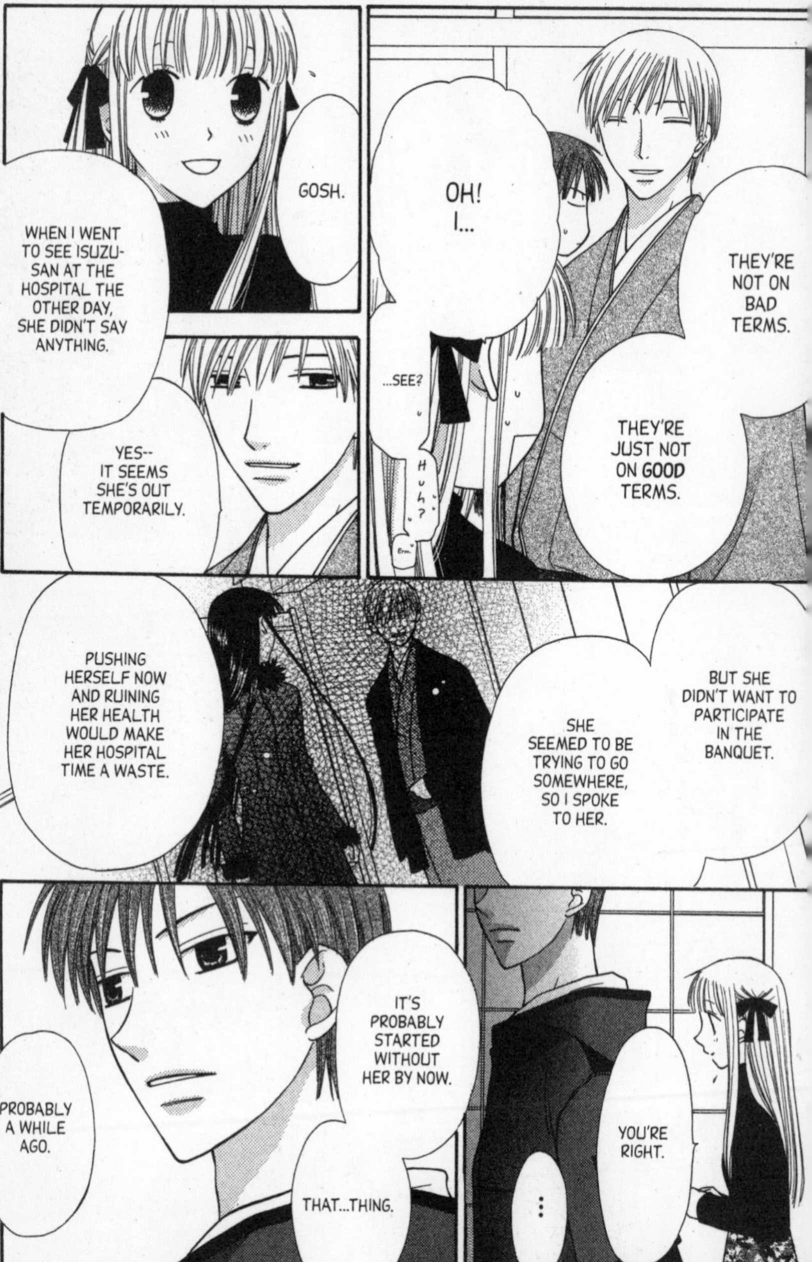
OH! I...
...SEE?
Huh?
Erm.
THEY'RE NOT ON BAD TERMS.
THEY'RE JUST NOT ON **GOOD** TERMS.
GOSH.
WHEN I WENT TO SEE ISUZU-SAN AT THE HOSPITAL THE OTHER DAY, SHE DIDN'T SAY ANYTHING.
YES-- IT SEEMS SHE'S OUT TEMPORARILY.
BUT SHE DIDN'T WANT TO PARTICIPATE IN THE BANQUET.
SHE SEEMED TO BE TRYING TO GO SOMEWHERE, SO I SPOKE TO HER.
PUSHING HERSELF NOW AND RUINING HER HEALTH WOULD MAKE HER HOSPITAL TIME A WASTE.
YOU'RE RIGHT.
...
IT'S PROBABLY STARTED WITHOUT HER BY NOW.
THAT...THING.
PROBABLY A WHILE AGO.

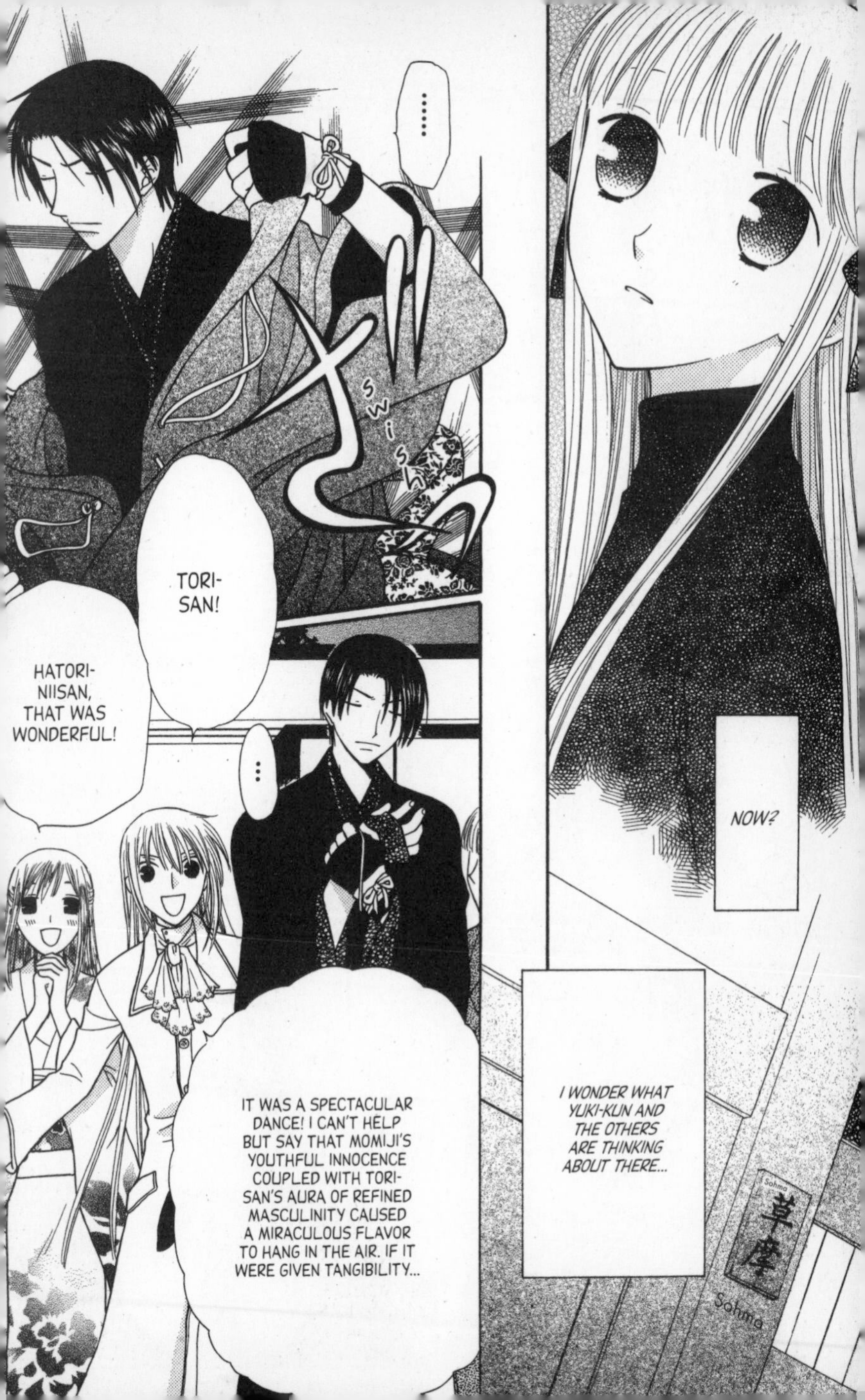

NOW?
I WONDER WHAT YUKI-KUN AND THE OTHERS ARE THINKING ABOUT THERE...
Sohma
草摩
Sohma
......
swish
TORI-SAN!
HATORI-NIISAN, THAT WAS WONDERFUL!
...
IT WAS A SPECTACULAR DANCE! I CAN'T HELP BUT SAY THAT MOMIJI'S YOUTHFUL INNOCENCE COUPLED WITH TORI-SAN'S AURA OF REFINED MASCULINITY CAUSED A MIRACULOUS FLAVOR TO HANG IN THE AIR. IF IT WERE GIVEN TANGIBILITY...

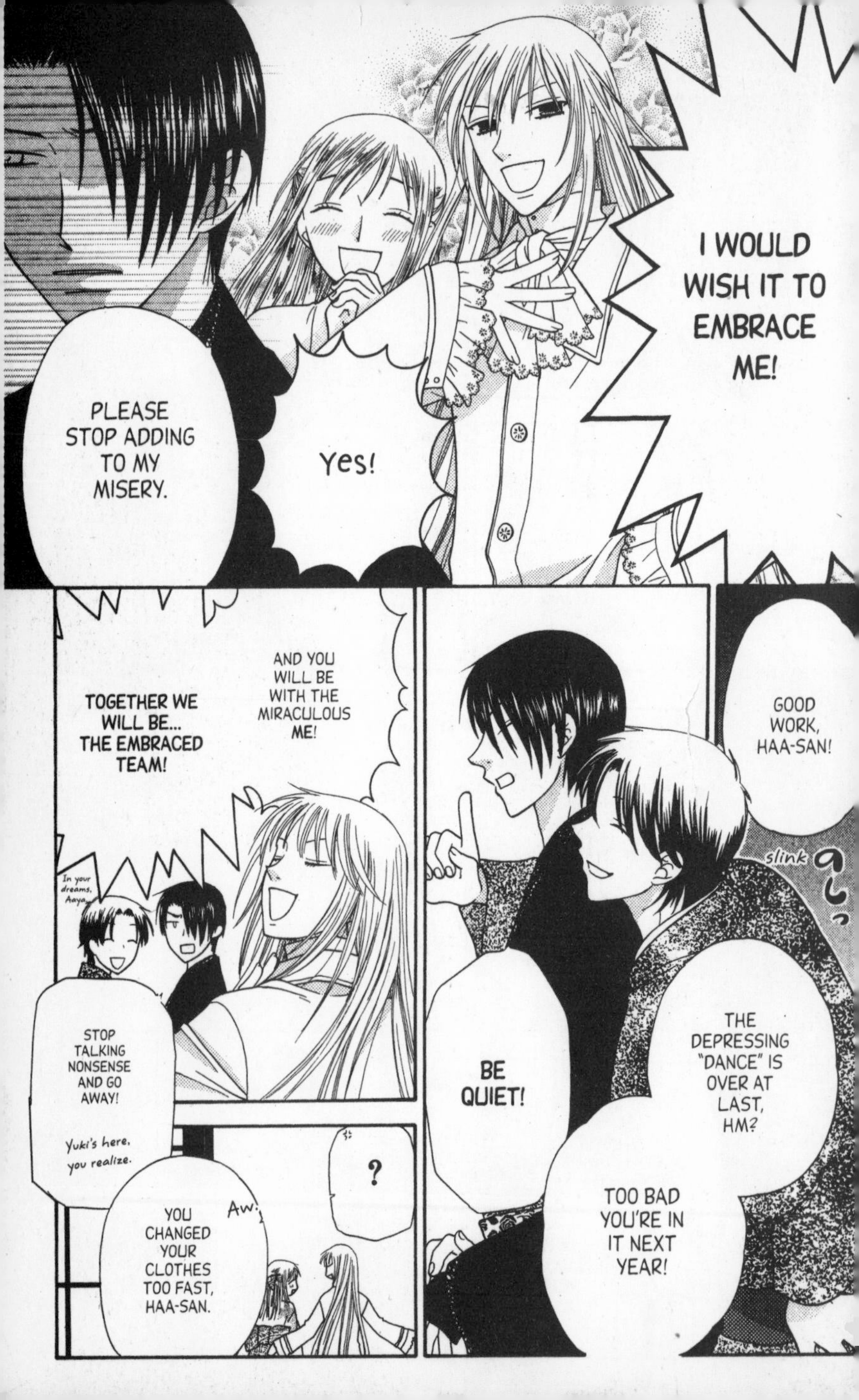
I WOULD WISH IT TO EMBRACE ME!
Yes!
PLEASE STOP ADDING TO MY MISERY.
GOOD WORK, HAA-SAN!
slink
THE DEPRESSING "DANCE" IS OVER AT LAST, HM?
BE QUIET!
TOO BAD YOU'RE IN IT NEXT YEAR!
AND YOU WILL BE WITH THE MIRACULOUS ME!
TOGETHER WE WILL BE... THE EMBRACED TEAM!
In your dreams, Aaya...
STOP TALKING NONSENSE AND GO AWAY!
Yuki's here, you realize.
?
Aw!
YOU CHANGED YOUR CLOTHES TOO FAST, HAA-SAN.

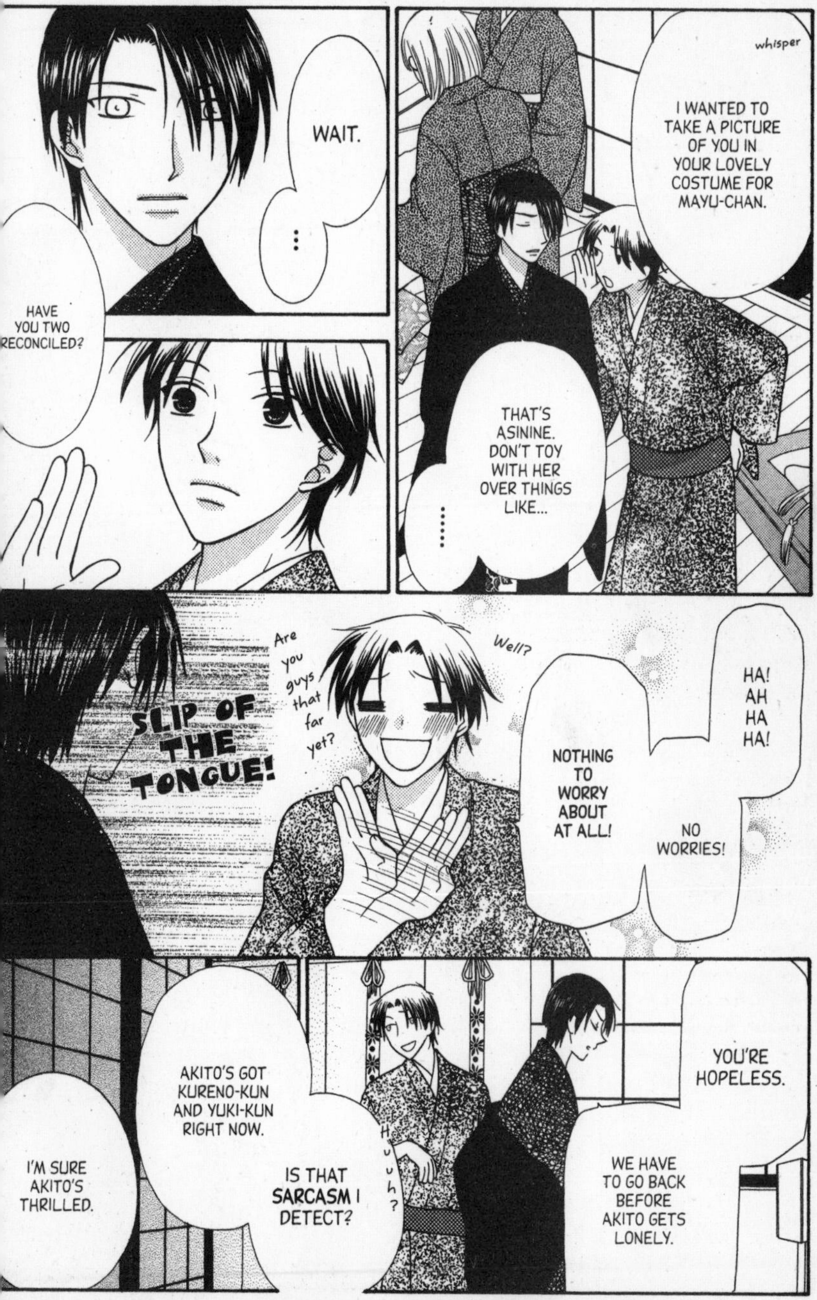
whisper
I WANTED TO TAKE A PICTURE OF YOU IN YOUR LOVELY COSTUME FOR MAYU-CHAN.
THAT'S ASININE. DON'T TOY WITH HER OVER THINGS LIKE...
......
WAIT.
...
HAVE YOU TWO RECONCILED?
HA! AH HA HA!
Well?
NO WORRIES!
NOTHING TO WORRY ABOUT AT ALL!
Are you guys that far yet?
SLIP OF THE TONGUE!
YOU'RE HOPELESS.
WE HAVE TO GO BACK BEFORE AKITO GETS LONELY.
AKITO'S GOT KURENO-KUN AND YUKI-KUN RIGHT NOW.
Huuh?
IS THAT SARCASM I DETECT?
I'M SURE AKITO'S THRILLED.

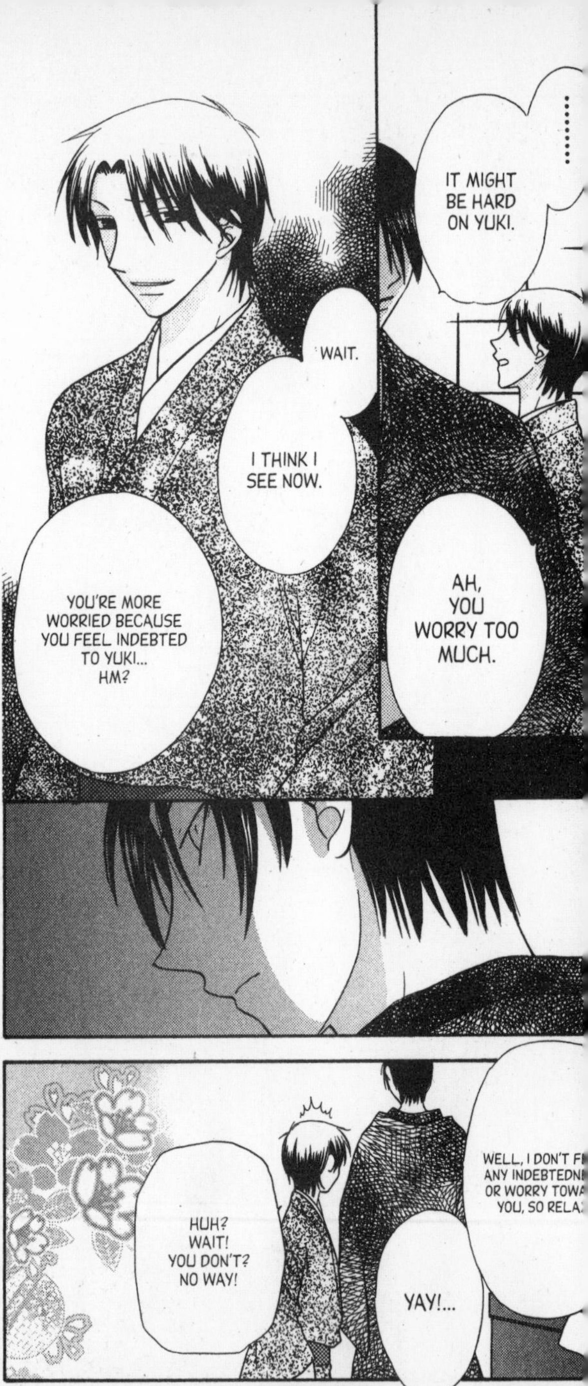
......
IT MIGHT BE HARD ON YUKI.
AH, YOU WORRY TOO MUCH.
WAIT.
I THINK I SEE NOW.
YOU'RE MORE WORRIED BECAUSE YOU FEEL INDEBTED TO YUKI... HM?
WELL, I DON'T F ANY INDEBTEDN OR WORRY TOWA YOU, SO RELA
YAY!...
HUH? WAIT! YOU DON'T? NO WAY!

A Character Contest

...was done by the magazine, so here are the results!

1st place: Kyo
2nd place: Tohru
3rd place: Yuki
4th place: Hatori
5th place: Haru
6th place: Momitchi
7th place: Kakeru
8th place: Aaya
9th place: Kureno-san
10th place: Gure-san
11th place: Rin
12th place: Hana-chan
13th place: Ritchan
14th place: Kisa
15th place: Machi
16th place: Hiro
17th place: Shishou
18th place: Akkii
19th place: Uo-chan
20th place: Kagura

...There you go. I couldn't write them all down, so I had through 20. There are too many characters in Fruits Basket. Anyway, thanks for all the responses!

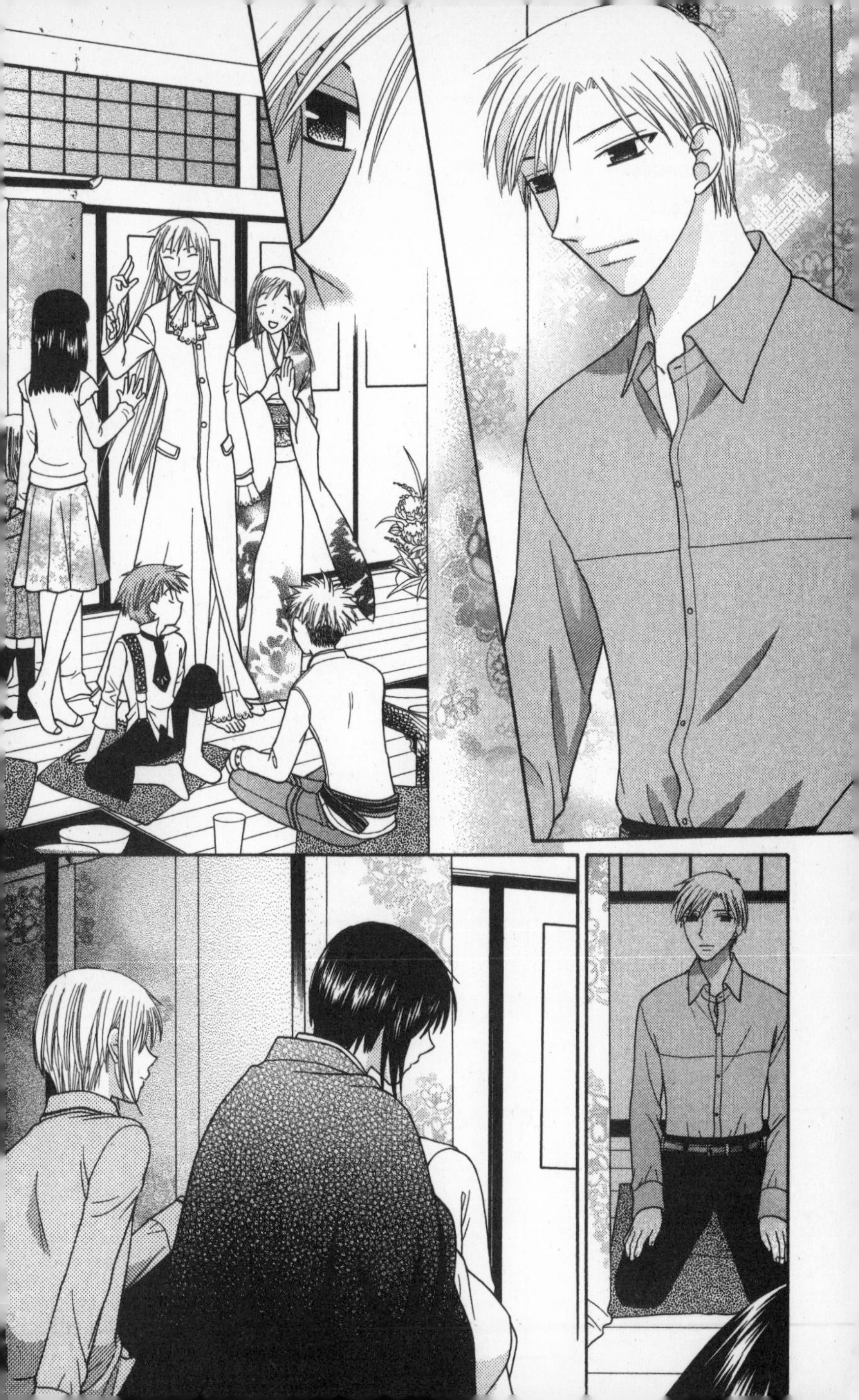

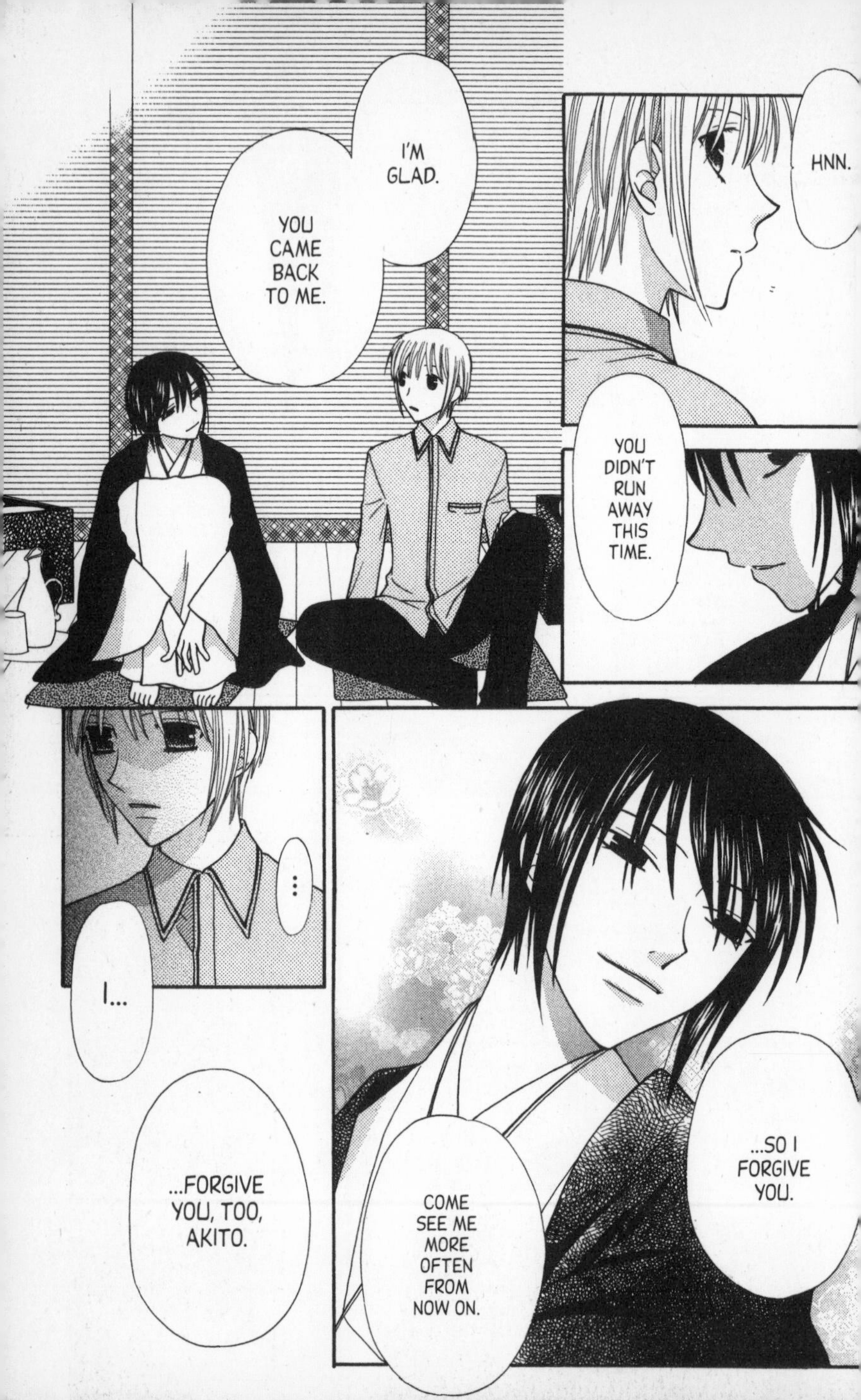
HNN.
YOU DIDN'T RUN AWAY THIS TIME.
I'M GLAD.
YOU CAME BACK TO ME.
...SO I FORGIVE YOU.
COME SEE ME MORE OFTEN FROM NOW ON.
...
I...
...FORGIVE YOU, TOO, AKITO.

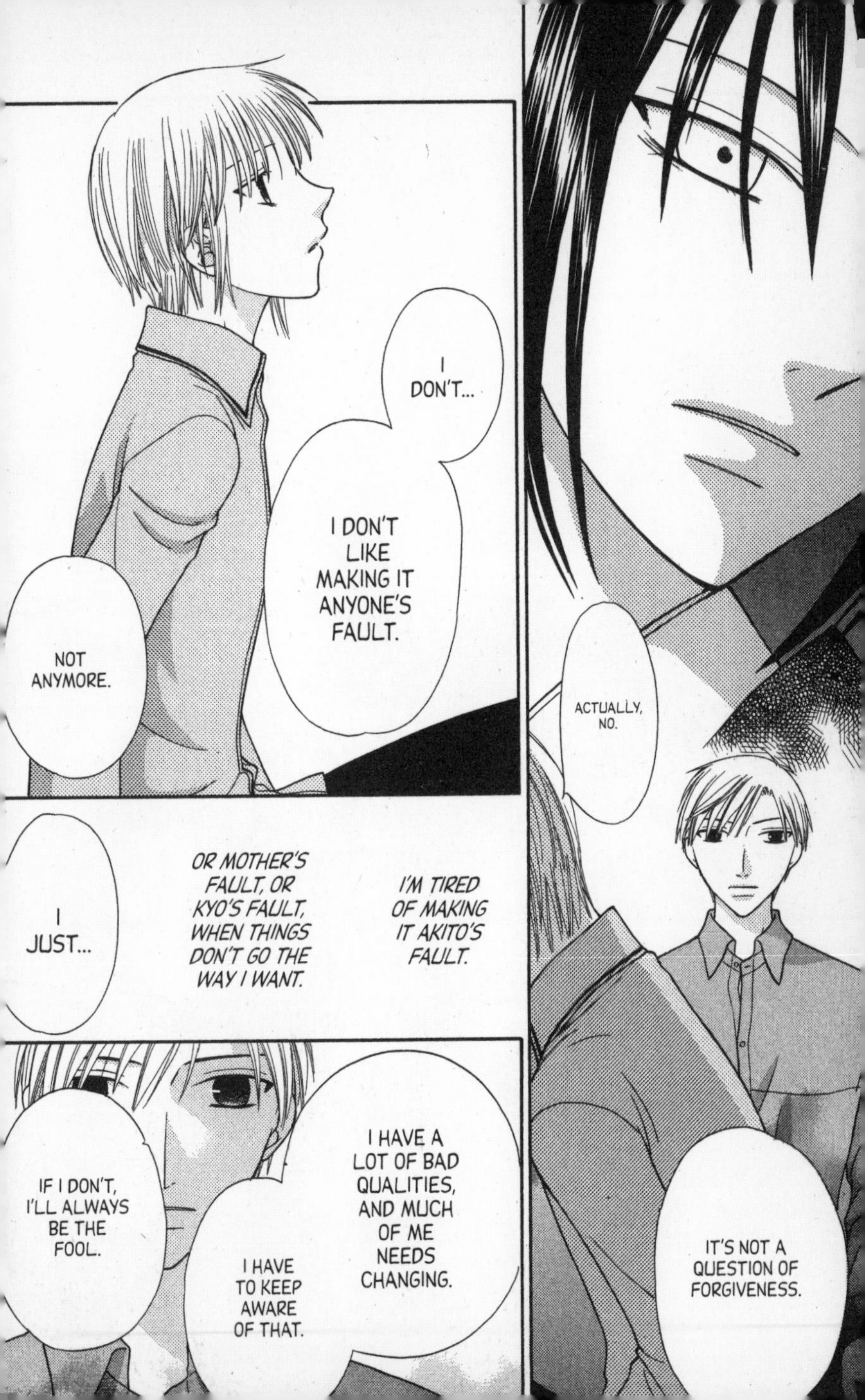
ACTUALLY, NO.
IT'S NOT A QUESTION OF FORGIVENESS.
I DON'T...
I DON'T LIKE MAKING IT ANYONE'S FAULT.
NOT ANYMORE.
I'M TIRED OF MAKING IT AKITO'S FAULT.
OR MOTHER'S FAULT, OR KYO'S FAULT, WHEN THINGS DON'T GO THE WAY I WANT.
I JUST...
I HAVE A LOT OF BAD QUALITIES, AND MUCH OF ME NEEDS CHANGING.
I HAVE TO KEEP AWARE OF THAT.
IF I DON'T, I'LL ALWAYS BE THE FOOL.

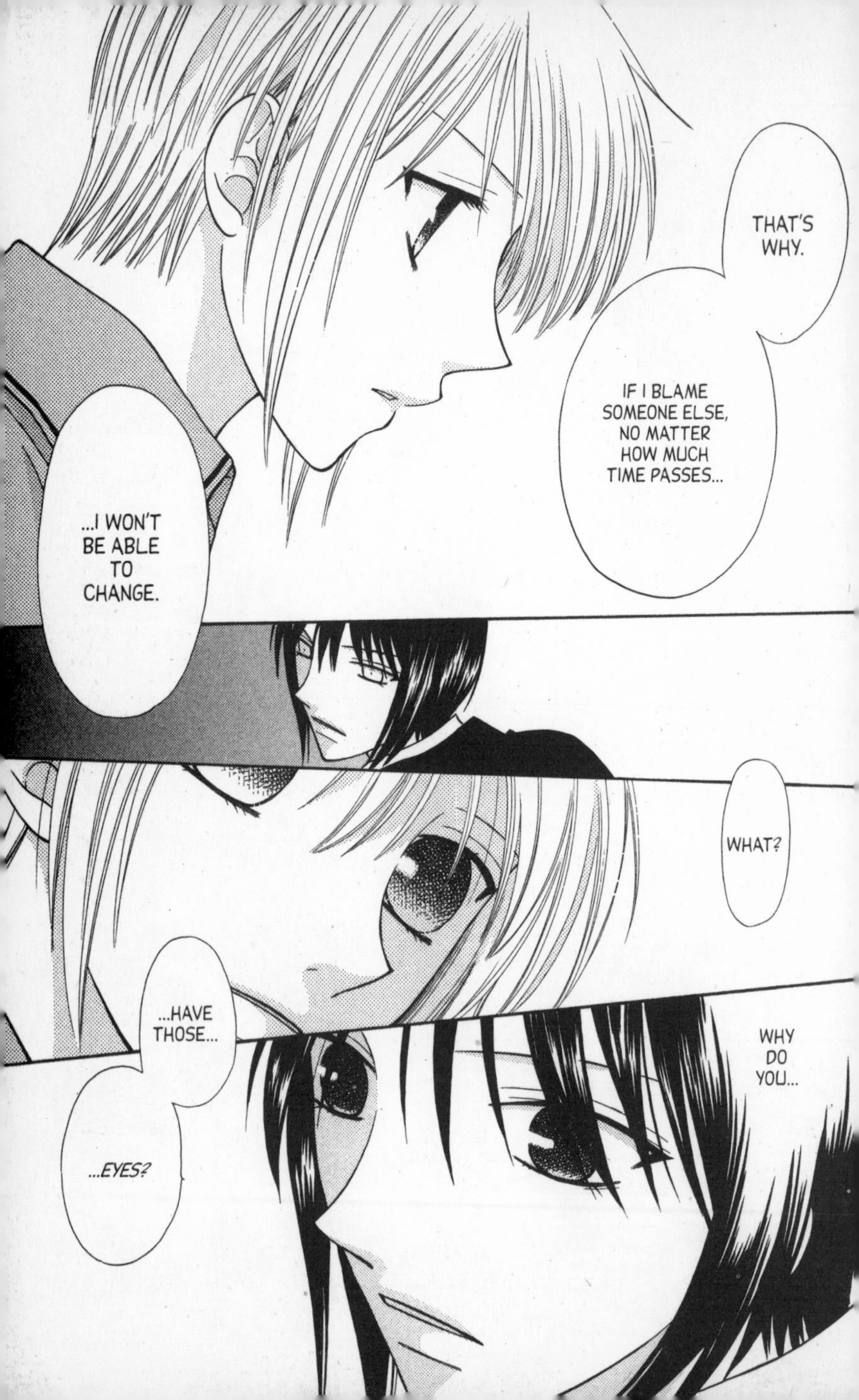
THAT'S WHY.
IF I BLAME SOMEONE ELSE, NO MATTER HOW MUCH TIME PASSES...
...I WON'T BE ABLE TO CHANGE.
WHAT?
WHY DO YOU...
...HAVE THOSE...
...EYES?

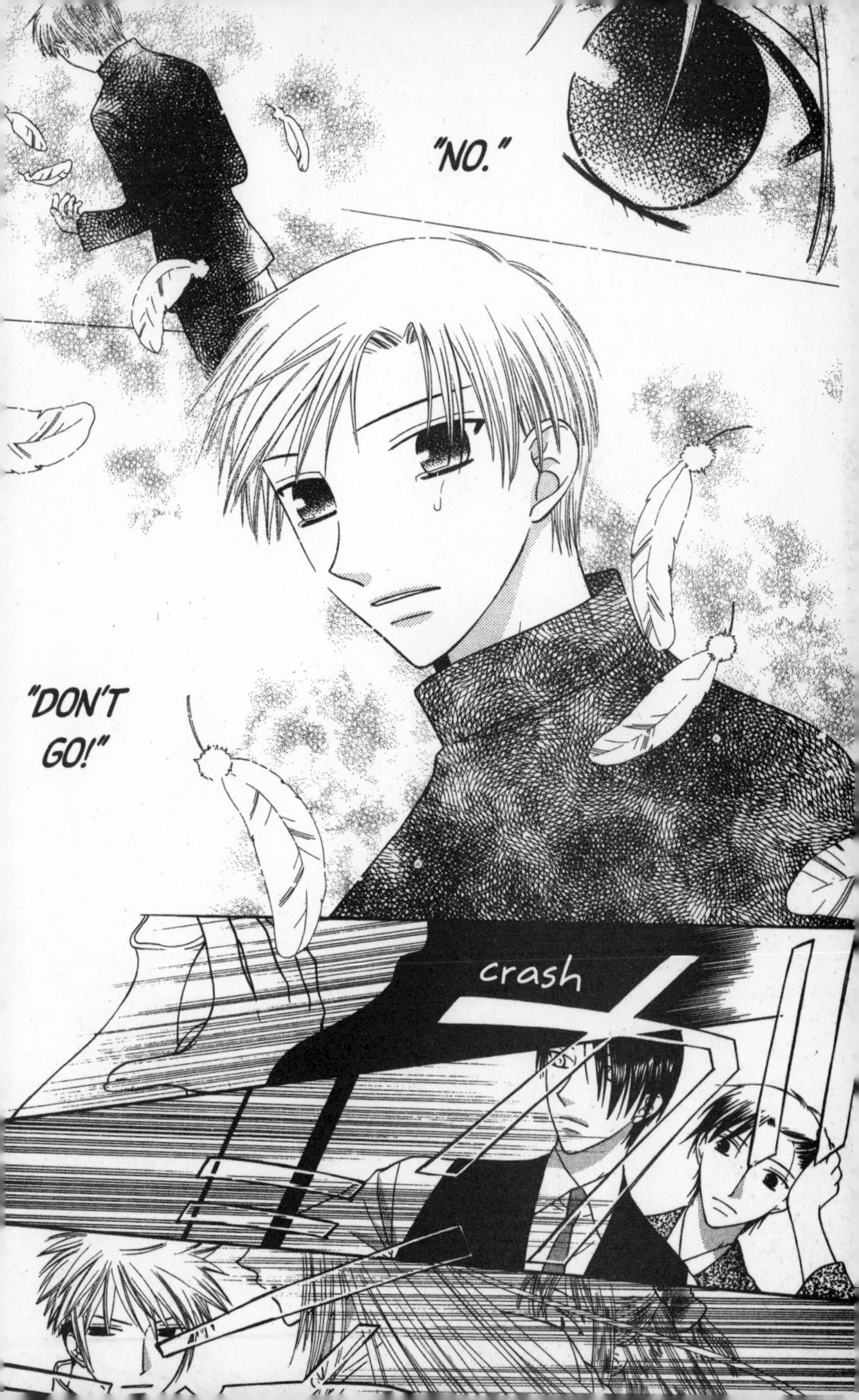
"NO."
"DON'T GO!"
crash

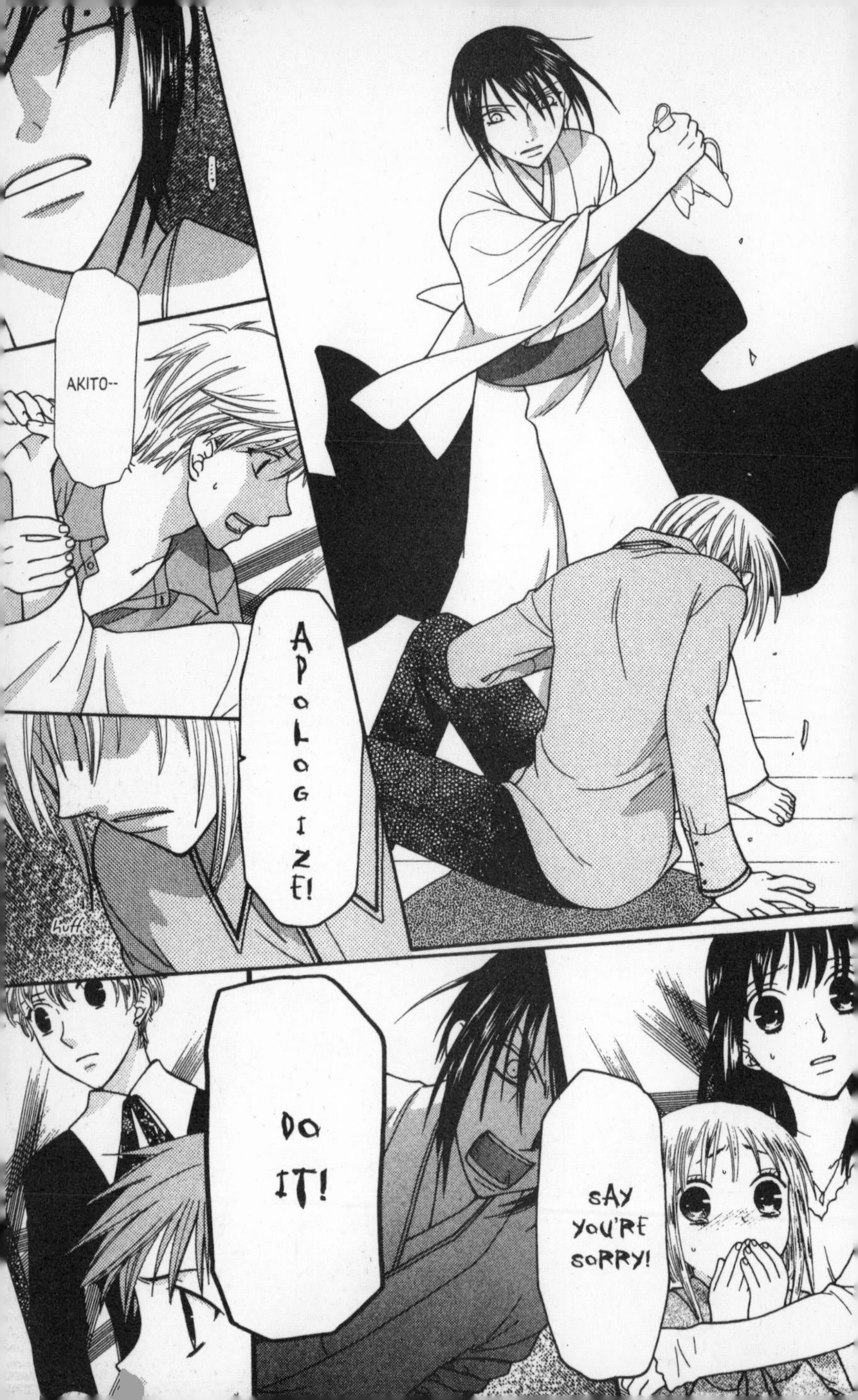
APOLOGIZE!
AKITO--
huff
SAY YOU'RE SORRY!
DO IT!

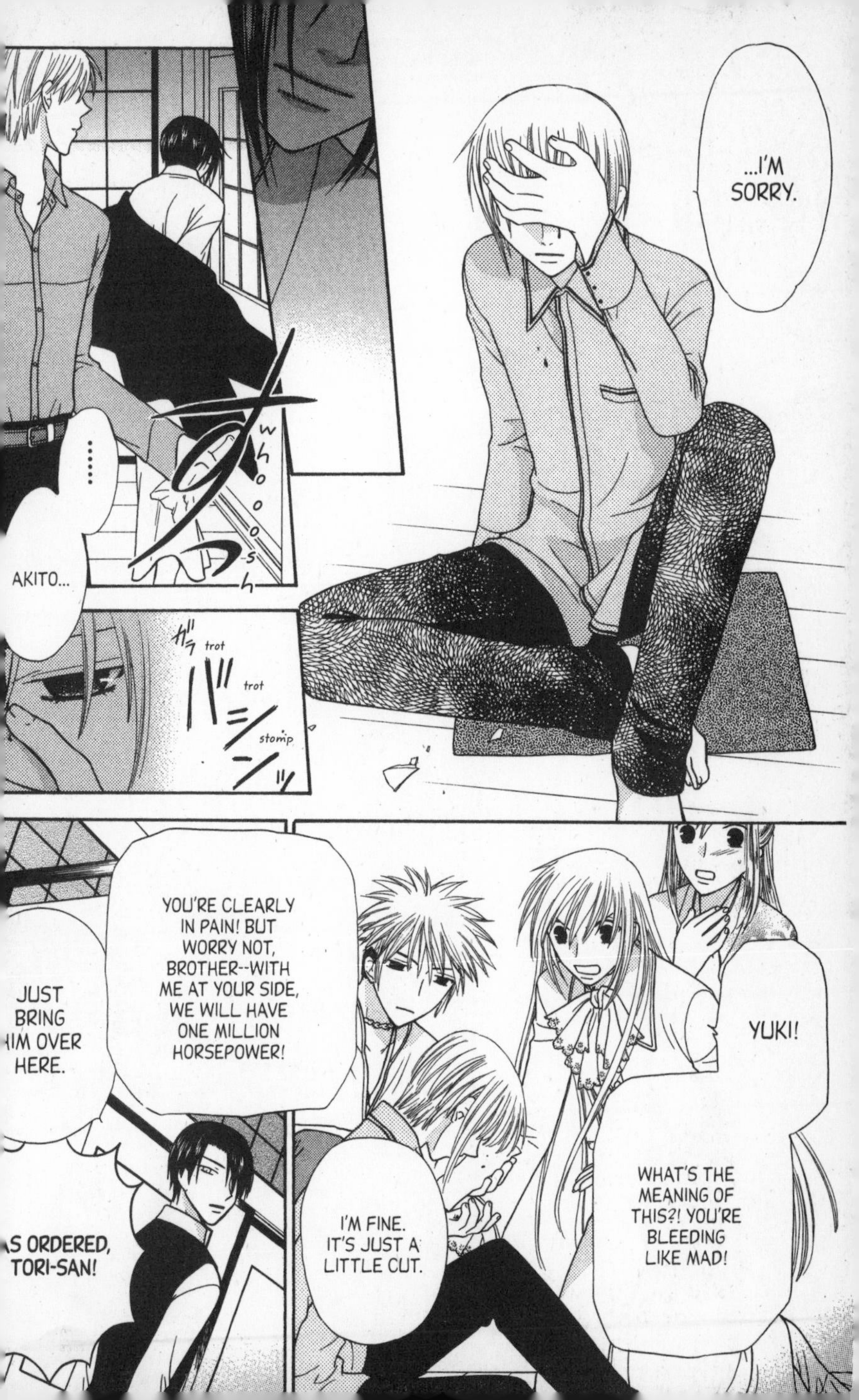
...I'M SORRY.
whoosh
......
AKITO...
trot
trot
stomp
YUKI!
WHAT'S THE MEANING OF THIS?! YOU'RE BLEEDING LIKE MAD!
I'M FINE. IT'S JUST A LITTLE CUT.
YOU'RE CLEARLY IN PAIN! BUT WORRY NOT, BROTHER--WITH ME AT YOUR SIDE, WE WILL HAVE ONE MILLION HORSEPOWER!
JUST BRING IM OVER HERE.
S ORDERED, TORI-SAN!

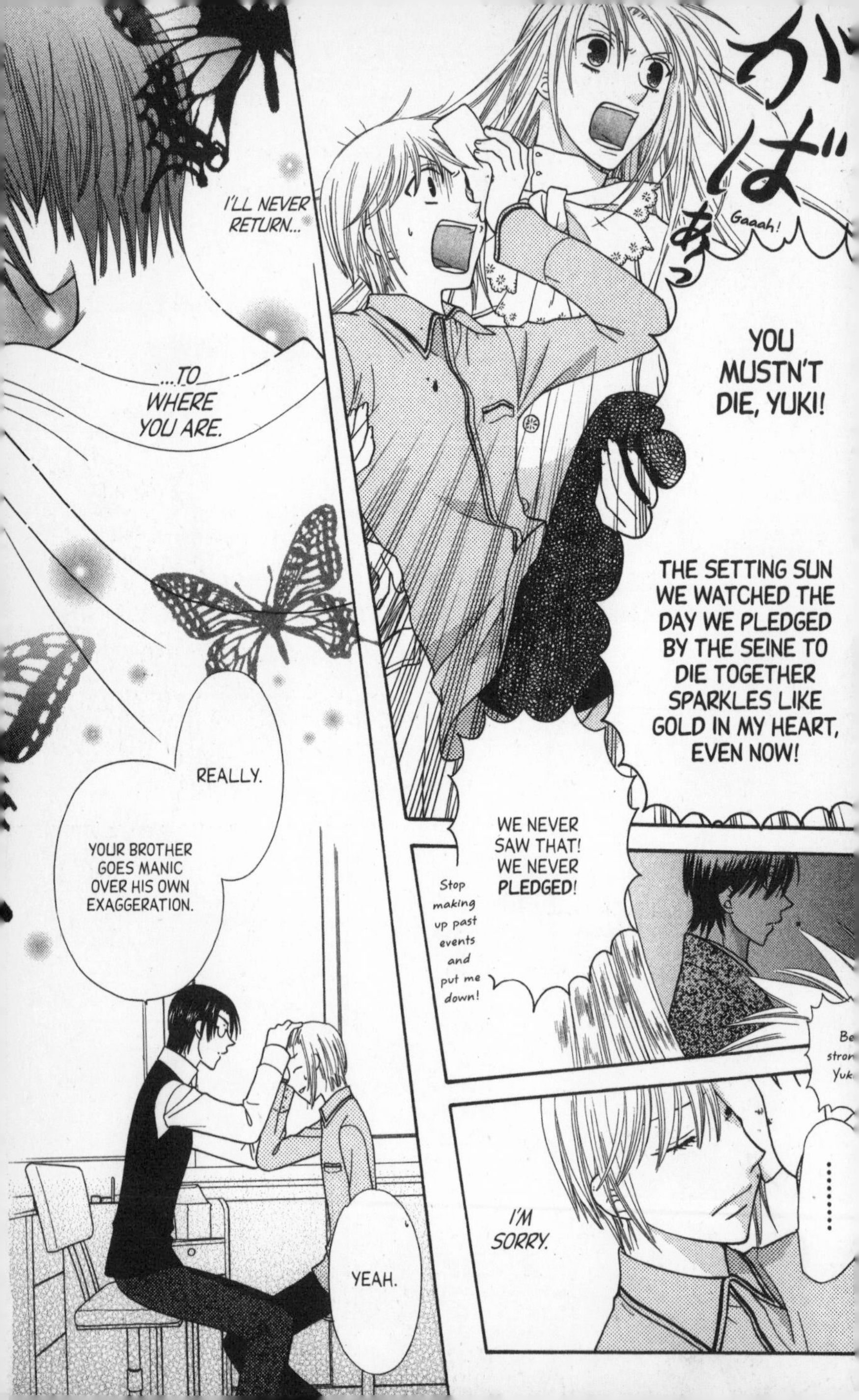

がばあっ
Gaaah!
YOU MUSTN'T DIE, YUKI!
THE SETTING SUN WE WATCHED THE DAY WE PLEDGED BY THE SEINE TO DIE TOGETHER SPARKLES LIKE GOLD IN MY HEART, EVEN NOW!
WE NEVER SAW THAT! WE NEVER PLEDGED!
Stop making up past events and put me down!
....
I'M SORRY.
I'LL NEVER RETURN...
...TO WHERE YOU ARE.
REALLY.
YOUR BROTHER GOES MANIC OVER HIS OWN EXAGGERATION.
YEAH.

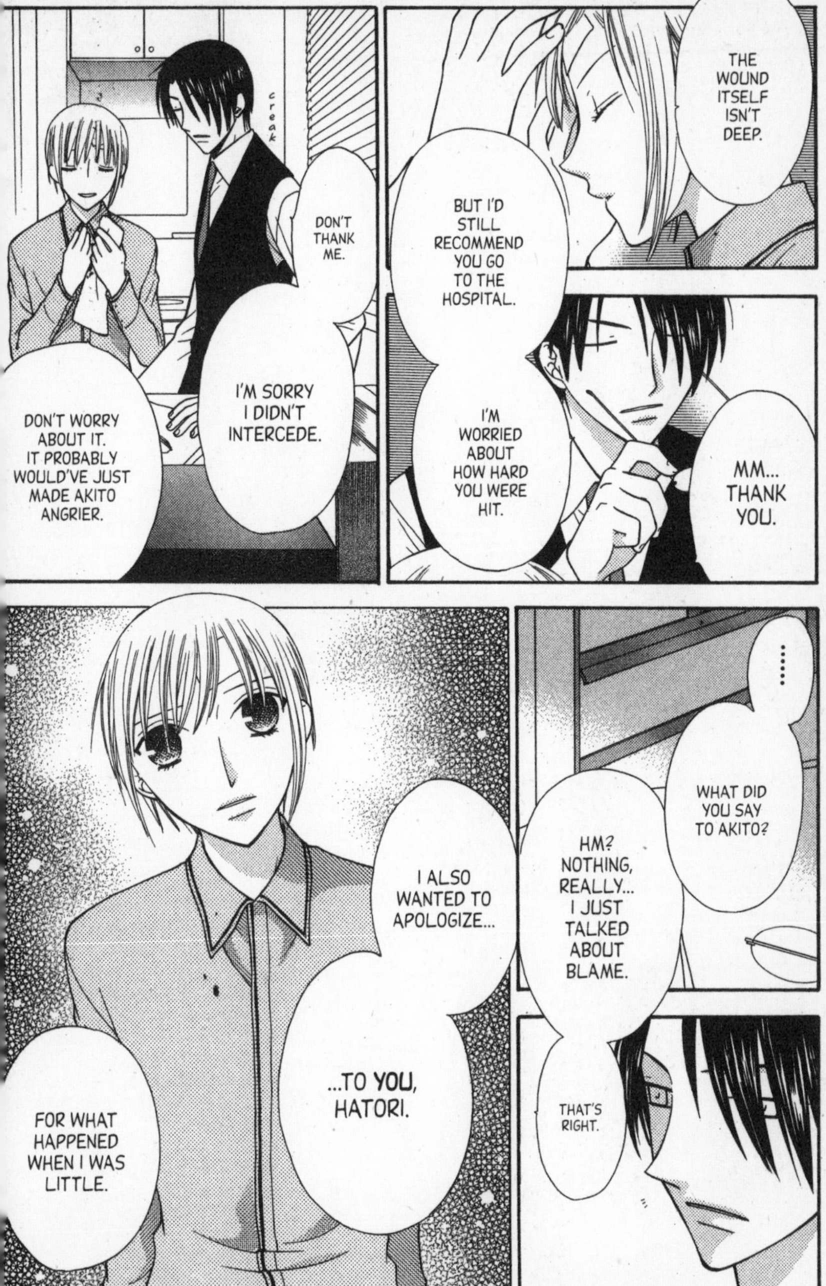
THE WOUND ITSELF ISN'T DEEP.
BUT I'D STILL RECOMMEND YOU GO TO THE HOSPITAL.
I'M WORRIED ABOUT HOW HARD YOU WERE HIT.
MM... THANK YOU.
creak
DON'T THANK ME.
I'M SORRY I DIDN'T INTERCEDE.
DON'T WORRY ABOUT IT. IT PROBABLY WOULD'VE JUST MADE AKITO ANGRIER.
......
WHAT DID YOU SAY TO AKITO?
HM? NOTHING, REALLY... I JUST TALKED ABOUT BLAME.
THAT'S RIGHT.
I ALSO WANTED TO APOLOGIZE...
...TO YOU, HATORI.
FOR WHAT HAPPENED WHEN I WAS LITTLE.

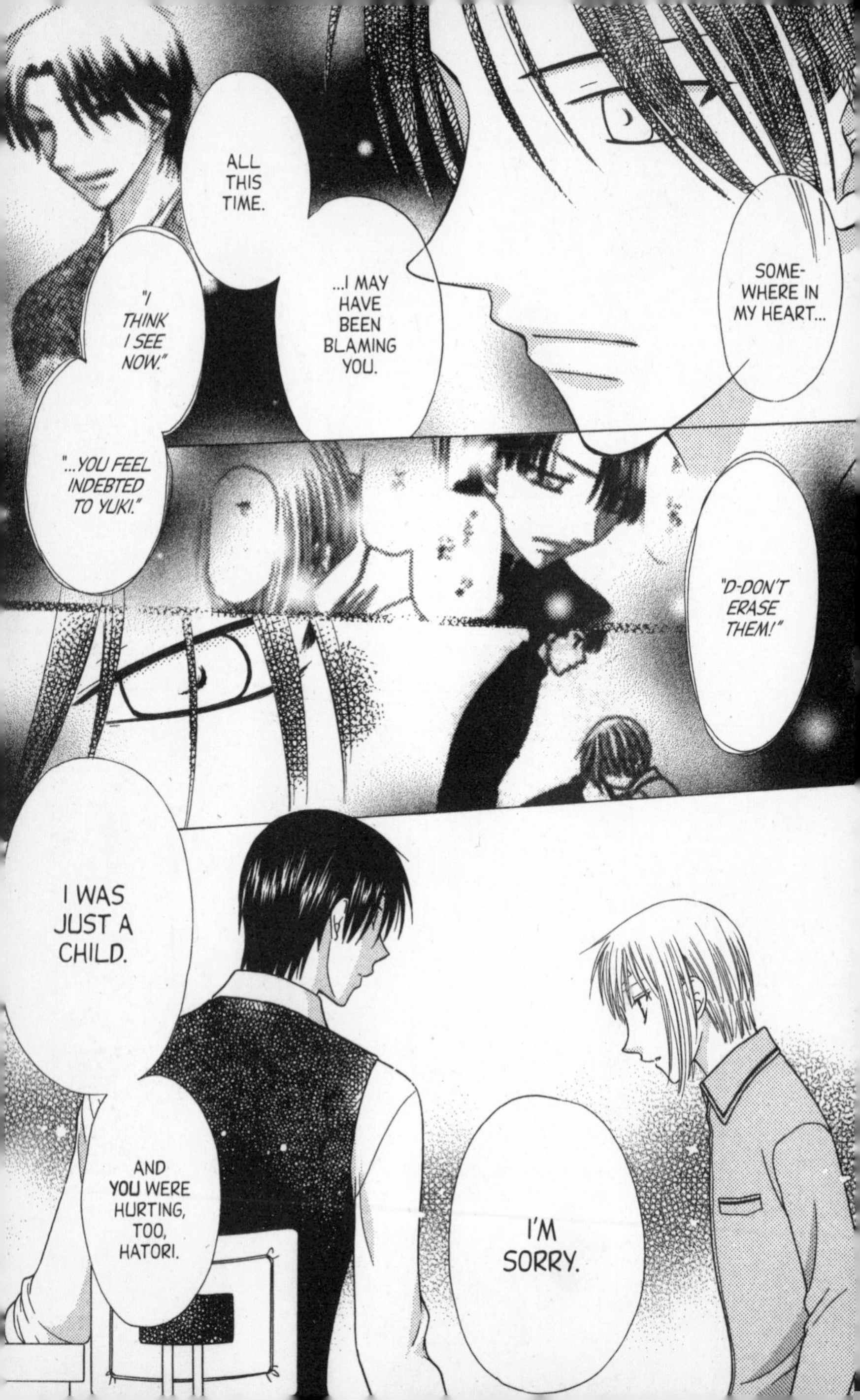
SOME-WHERE IN MY HEART...
...I MAY HAVE BEEN BLAMING YOU.
ALL THIS TIME.
"I THINK I SEE NOW."
"...YOU FEEL INDEBTED TO YUKI."
"D-DON'T ERASE THEM!"
I WAS JUST A CHILD.
AND YOU WERE HURTING, TOO, HATORI.
I'M SORRY.

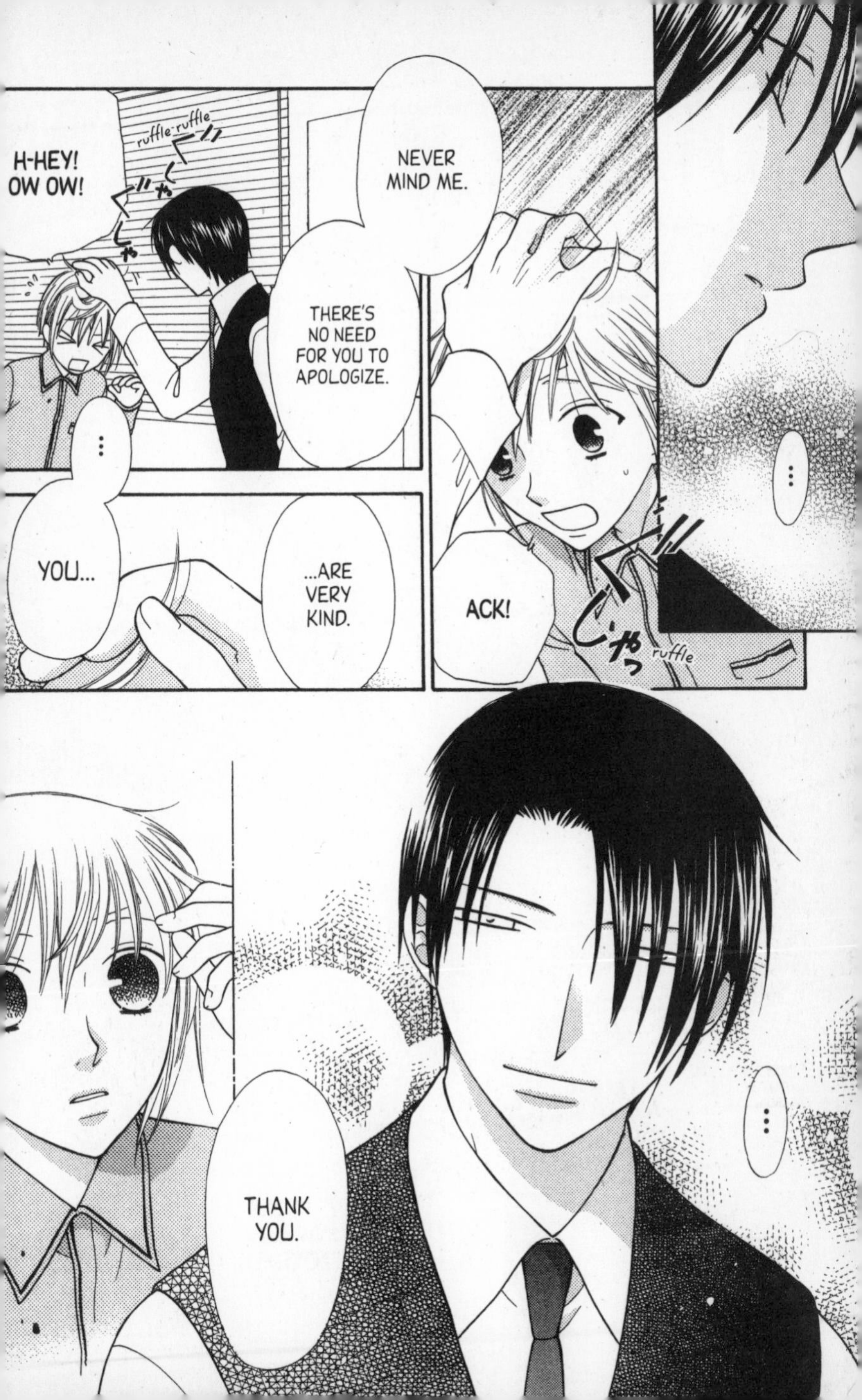
…
ACK!
ruffle
NEVER MIND ME.
THERE'S NO NEED FOR YOU TO APOLOGIZE.
ruffle-ruffle
H-HEY! OW OW!
…
YOU...
...ARE VERY KIND.
…
THANK YOU.

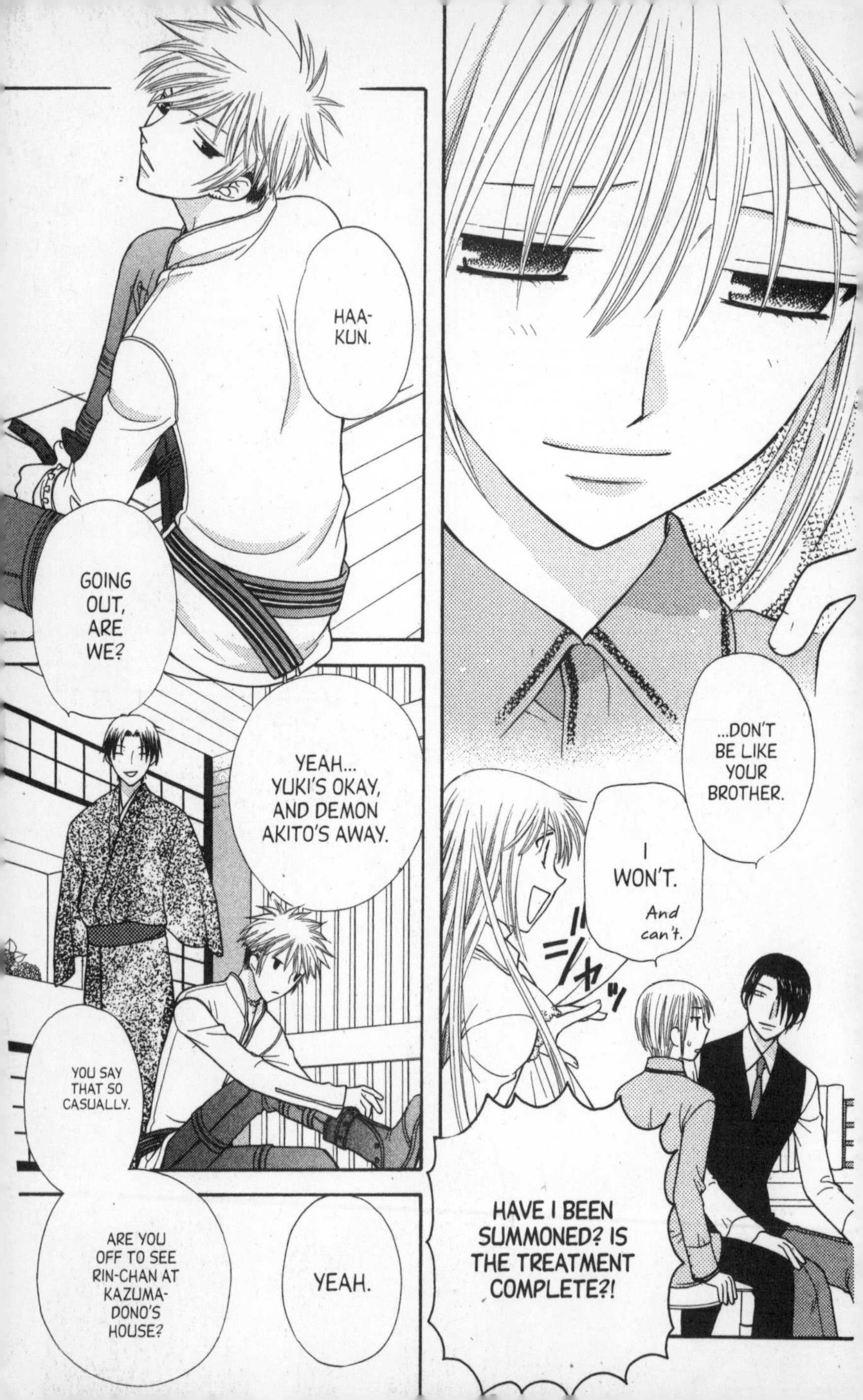
...DON'T BE LIKE YOUR BROTHER.
I WON'T.
And can't.
HAVE I BEEN SUMMONED? IS THE TREATMENT COMPLETE?!
HAA-KUN.
GOING OUT, ARE WE?
YEAH... YUKI'S OKAY, AND DEMON AKITO'S AWAY.
YOU SAY THAT SO CASUALLY.
ARE YOU OFF TO SEE RIN-CHAN AT KAZUMA-DONO'S HOUSE?
YEAH.

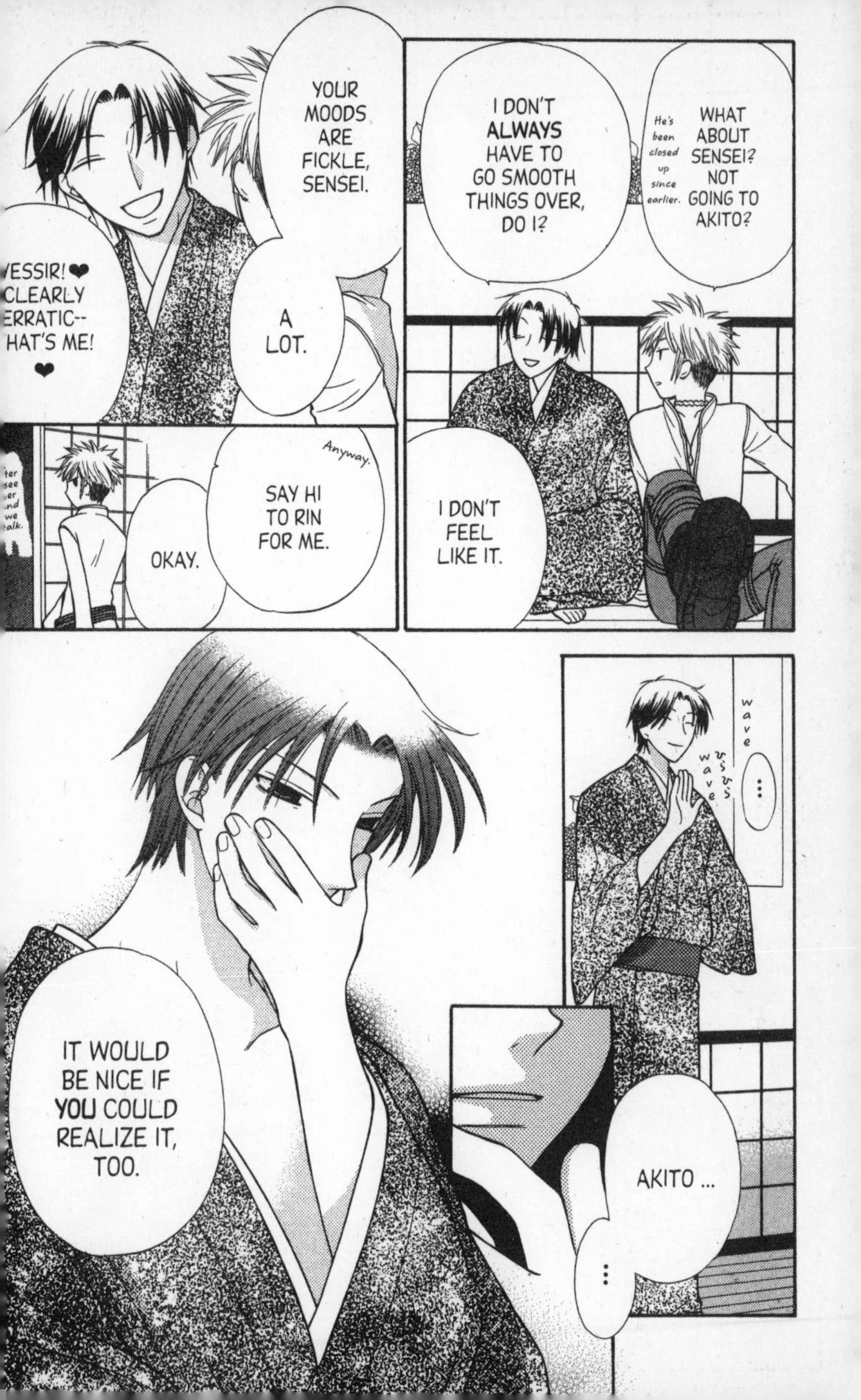
He's been closed up since earlier.
WHAT ABOUT SENSEI? NOT GOING TO AKITO?
I DON'T **ALWAYS** HAVE TO GO SMOOTH THINGS OVER, DO I?
I DON'T FEEL LIKE IT.
YOUR MOODS ARE FICKLE, SENSEI.
A LOT.
ESSIR! ❤ CLEARLY ERRATIC-- HAT'S ME! ❤
Anyway.
SAY HI TO RIN FOR ME.
OKAY.
wave wave
...
AKITO ...
...
IT WOULD BE NICE IF **YOU** COULD REALIZE IT, TOO.

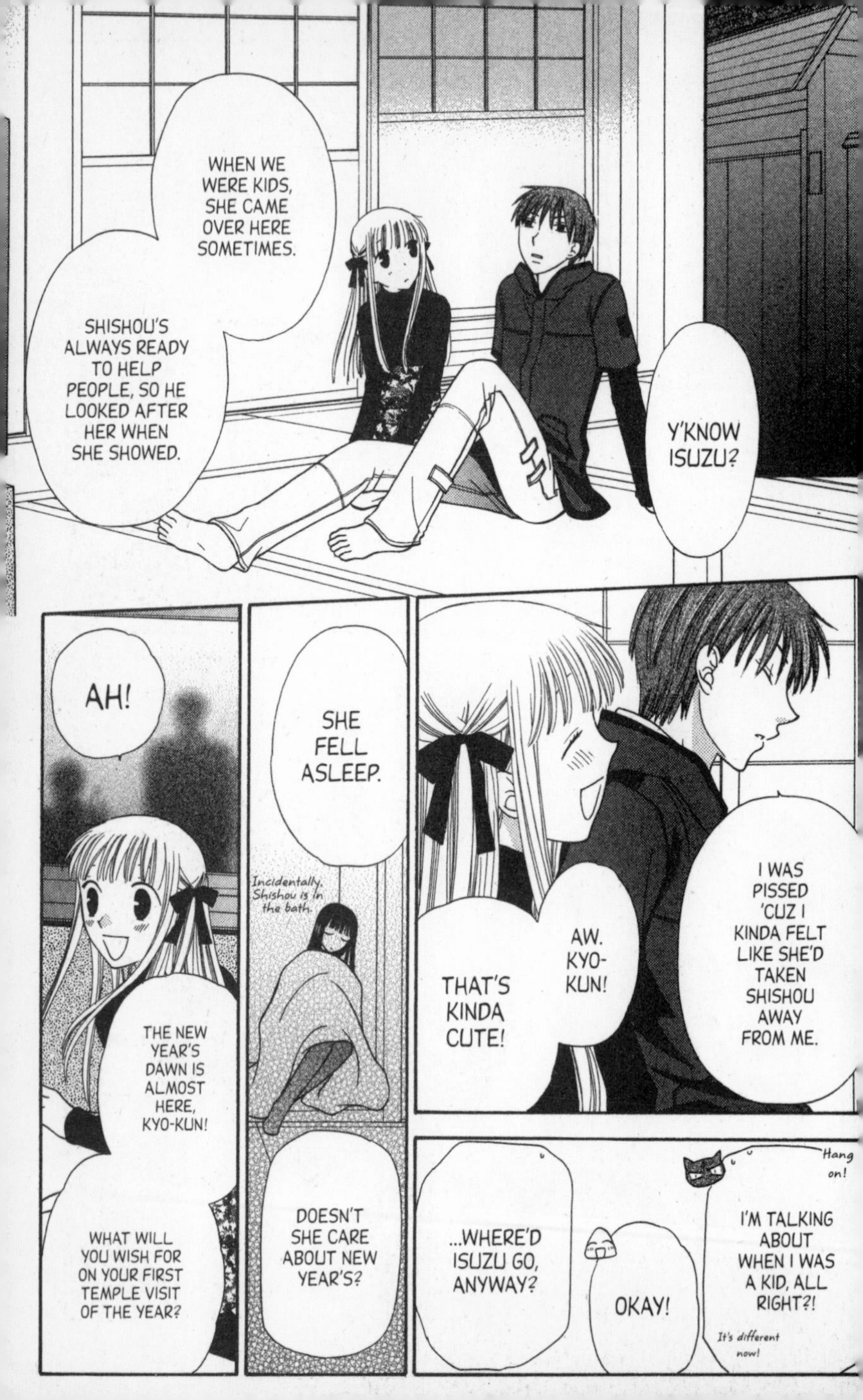
Y'KNOW ISUZU?
WHEN WE WERE KIDS, SHE CAME OVER HERE SOMETIMES.
SHISHOU'S ALWAYS READY TO HELP PEOPLE, SO HE LOOKED AFTER HER WHEN SHE SHOWED.
I WAS PISSED 'CUZ I KINDA FELT LIKE SHE'D TAKEN SHISHOU AWAY FROM ME.
AW. KYO-KUN!
THAT'S KINDA CUTE!
Hang on!
I'M TALKING ABOUT WHEN I WAS A KID, ALL RIGHT?!
It's different now!
OKAY!
...WHERE'D ISUZU GO, ANYWAY?
SHE FELL ASLEEP.
Incidentally, Shishou is in the bath.
DOESN'T SHE CARE ABOUT NEW YEAR'S?
AH!
THE NEW YEAR'S DAWN IS ALMOST HERE, KYO-KUN!
WHAT WILL YOU WISH FOR ON YOUR FIRST TEMPLE VISIT OF THE YEAR?

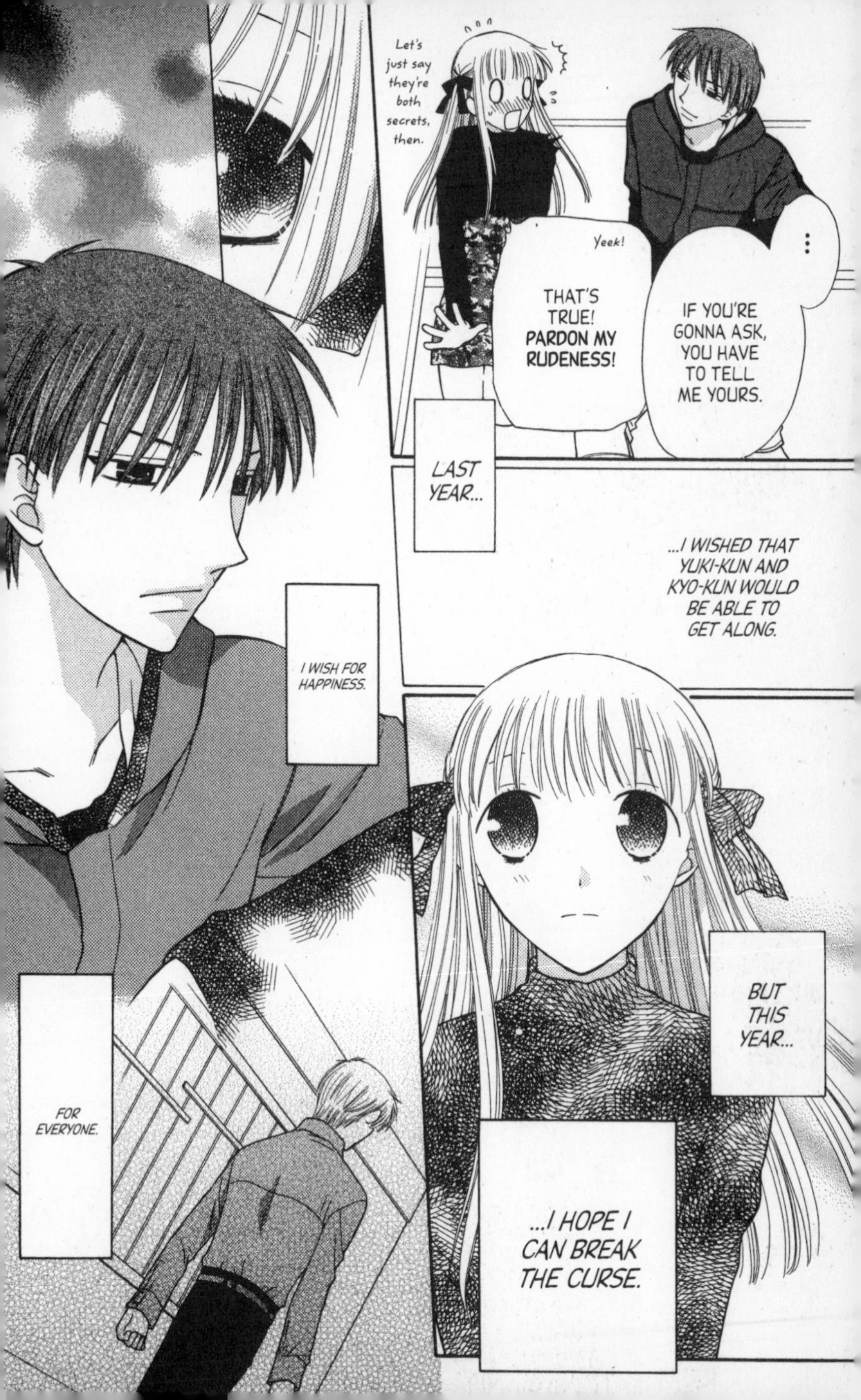

...
IF YOU'RE GONNA ASK, YOU HAVE TO TELL ME YOURS.
Yeek!
THAT'S TRUE! **PARDON MY RUDENESS!**
Let's just say they're both secrets, then.
LAST YEAR...
...I WISHED THAT YUKI-KUN AND KYO-KUN WOULD BE ABLE TO GET ALONG.
BUT THIS YEAR...
...I HOPE I CAN BREAK THE CURSE.
I WISH FOR HAPPINESS.
FOR EVERYONE.

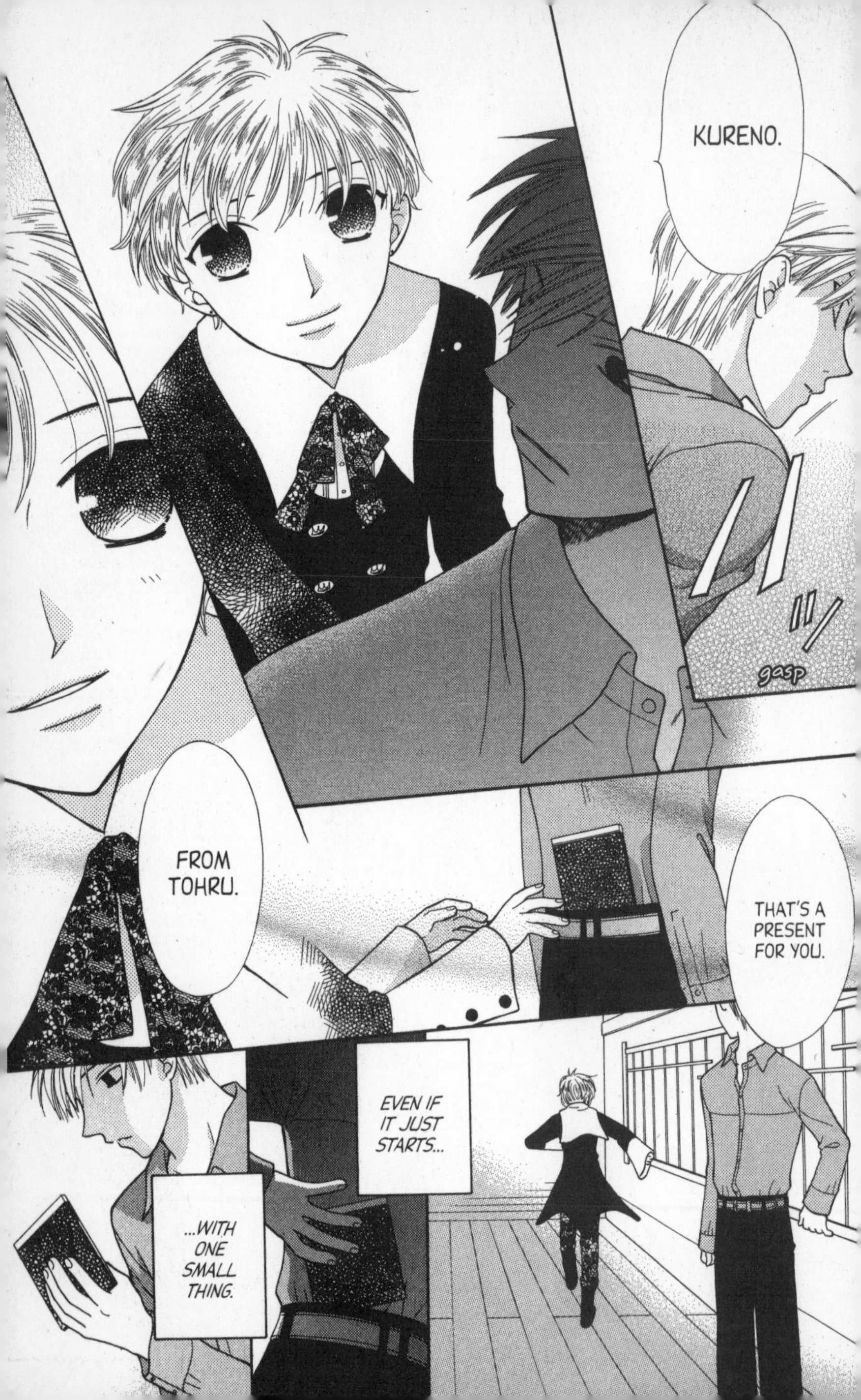
KURENO.
gasp
THAT'S A PRESENT FOR YOU.
FROM TOHRU.
EVEN IF IT JUST STARTS...
...WITH ONE SMALL THING.

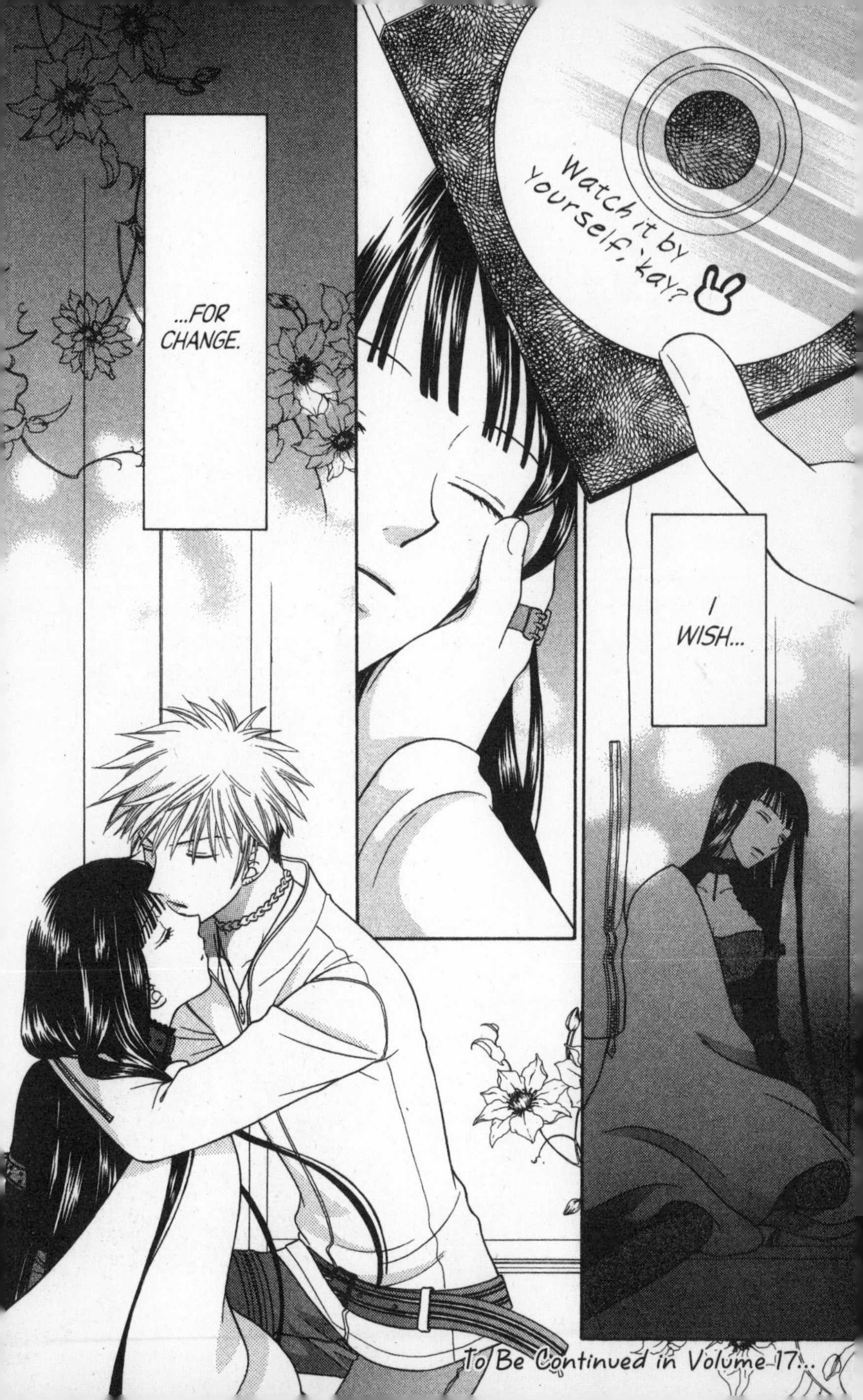
Watch it by yourself, 'kay?
I WISH...
...FOR CHANGE.
To Be Continued in Volume 17...

I feel so grateful!

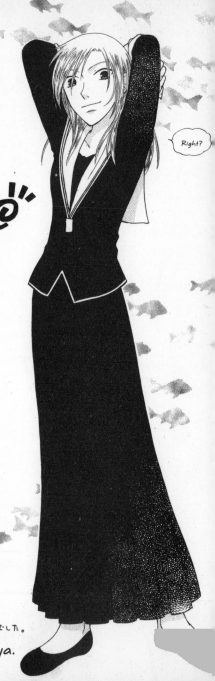

Right?

Harada-sama, Araki-sama,
Mother-sama, Editor-sama

And everyone who reads and
supports this manga.

Please feel the waves...

This has been...

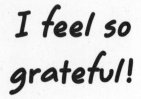

高屋 奈月 でした。

Natsuki Takaya.

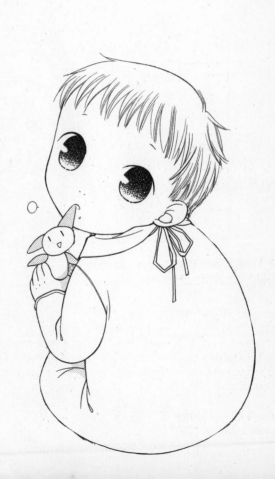

Next time in...

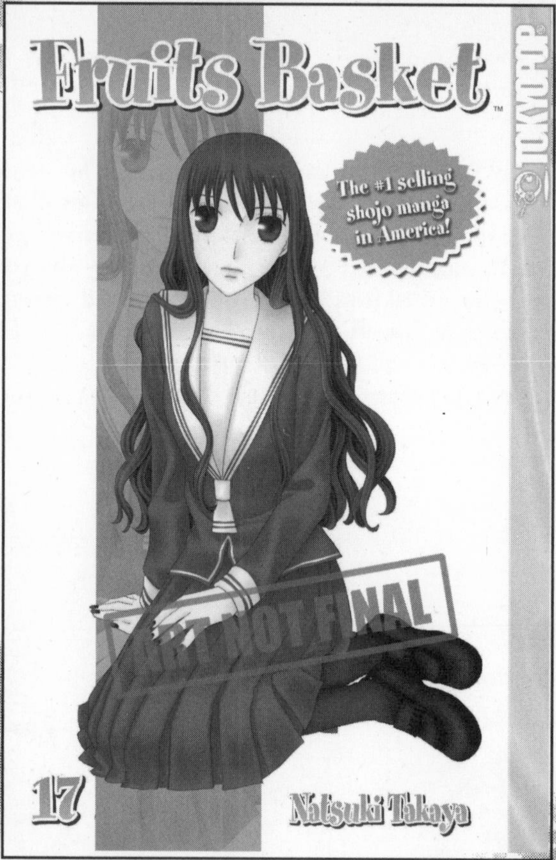
Fruits Basket
TOKYOPOP
The #1 selling shojo manga in America!
17
Natsuki Takaya

All You Wanted to Know About Akito, But Were Afraid to Ask...

Thanks to Momiji, Kureno has a DVD of the class play, in which Arisa breaks character for a second and begs Kureno to see her. And although Kureno loves Arisa, he explains to Tohru that he must remain by Akito's side. During this conversation, Kureno reveals many secrets to a stunned Tohru. And the biggest bombshell of all will forever change the way Tohru views Akito!

Fruits Basket Volume 17
Available August 2007

Fans Basket

Happy New Year, Furuba fans! 2007 is going to be an incredible year for Fruits Basket--you're in for some wonderful surprises in the upcoming volumes! Speaking of surprises, you all continue to amaze me with your intense loyalty and your smile-inducing fan art. It just keeps coming in, and it never stops! And thanks to you all, there are now over 2 million English-edition copies of Fruits Basket in print! Takaya-san is impressed by your dedication, as am I. See you next time.

- Paul Morrissey, Editor

Alyssa Burlage
Age 13
Prairie Du Sac, WI

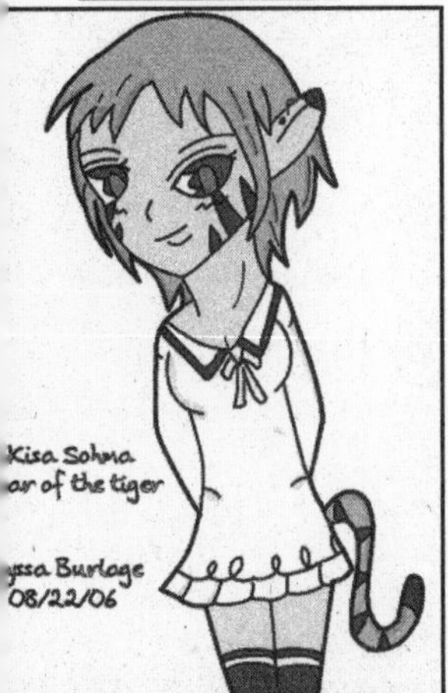
Kisa Sohma
ar of the tiger
yssa Burlage
08/22/06

Wow! Another fan from Wisconsin! Alyssa, Kisa is one of my favorite characters, too! Like you, I grew up in a small town in Wisconsin, and I had a lot of cats when I was a kid. Maybe that's why I like Kisa so much. I thought your sketch was adorable, and you drew it with your own style!

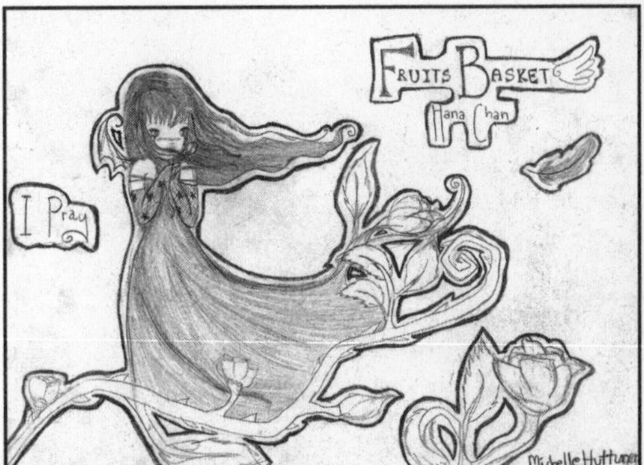
Fruits Basket
Hana Chan
I Pray
Michelle Huttunen

Hello, Michelle! Wisconsin is my home state! I love the fact that Wisconsinites are reading Fruits Basket. If only one of the zodiac animals was a badger... Anywho, I loved your drawing of Hana-Chan. You have a very unique technique.

Michelle S. Huttunen
Age 13
Rhinelander, WI

Seng Ho
Age 22
London, UK

Putting Kyo in a rat suit was a stroke of brilliance! Very funny sketch, Seng Ho!

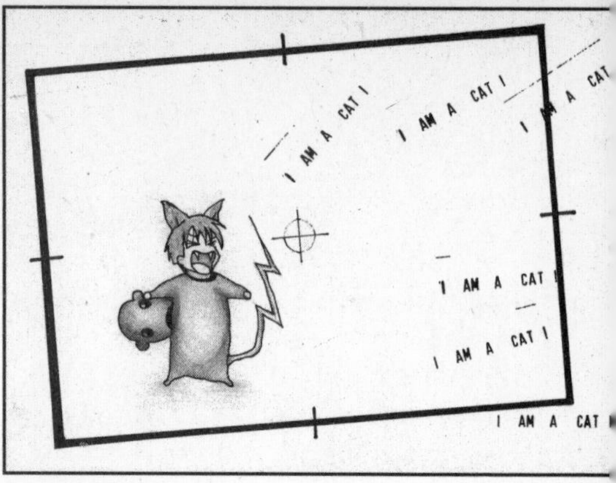
I AM A CAT !
I AM A CAT !
I AM A CAT
I AM A CAT !
I AM A CAT !
I AM A CAT !

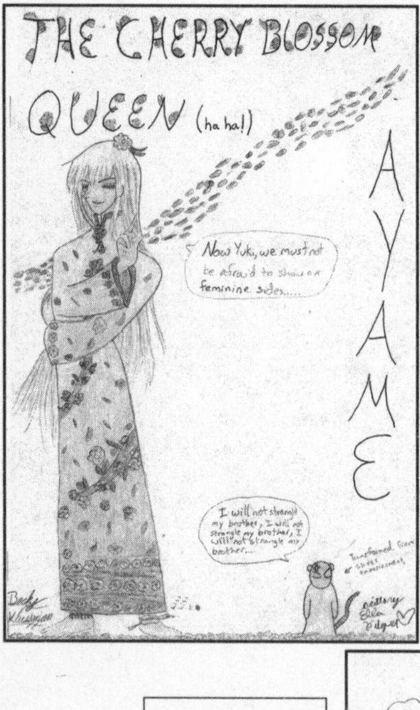
THE CHERRY BLOSSOM QUEEN (ha ha!)
AYAME
Now Yuki, we must not be afraid to show our feminine sides.....
I will not strangle my brother, I will not strangle my brother, I will not strangle my brother...
Becky Klussman
Brittany Ella Hilgert

Rebecca Marie Klussman
Age 14
Manchester, MO

Brittany Ella Hilgert
Age 15
High Ridge, MO

There's nothing like Fruits Basket to bring friends even closer together! Brittany designed the costume for this drawing, and Becky drew Ayame. Awesome teamwork! Your picture of Ayame made me laugh out loud!

Margaret Lamas
Age 17
Orlando, FL

Margaret, your drawing is too precious for words! Kisa with her little litter of "kittens" gives me the warm fuzzies!

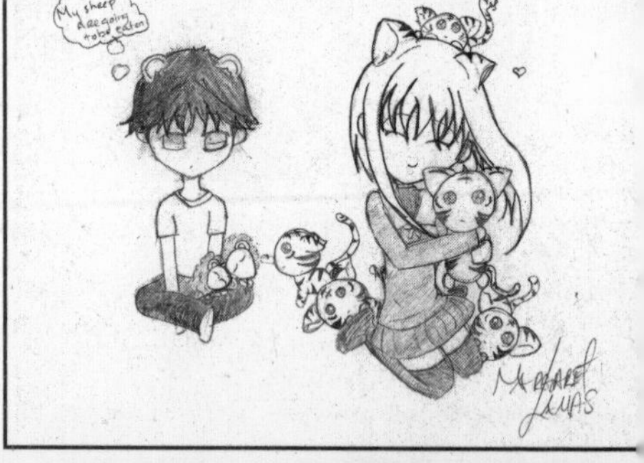
MARGARET LAMAS

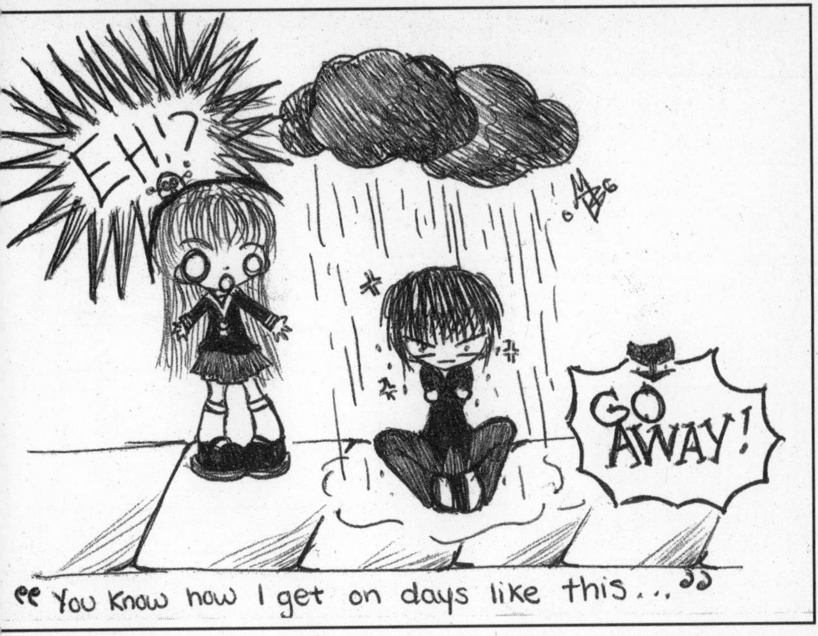
GO AWAY!
EH!?
"You know how I get on days like this..."

Melody Brown
Age 17
Medina, OH

I really liked your ink drawing, Melody! Nicely done! By the way, everyone, Melody mentions that she really likes pandas. And that got me thinking: I wonder what our furuba characters would look like if the Chinese zodiac featured different animals... Okay, everyone, send in your art to show me!

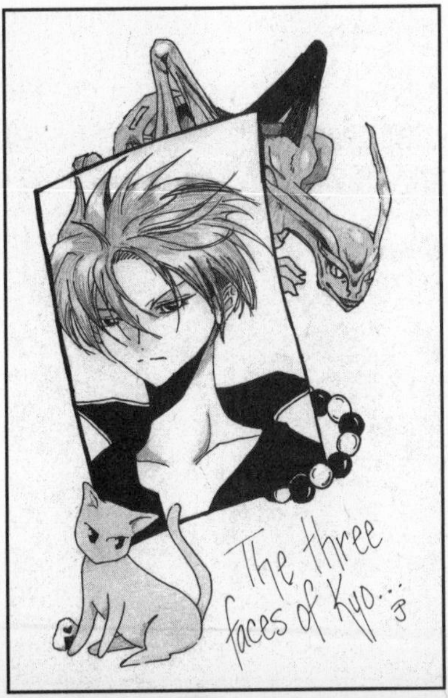
The three faces of Kyo...

Jenn Prickett
Age 32
Glendo, WY

It's really cool to see all three versions of Kyo in one piece of art! Jenn, you might also be the oldest person to have their sketch shown in Fruits Basket! It just goes to show that Furuba has fans of all ages!

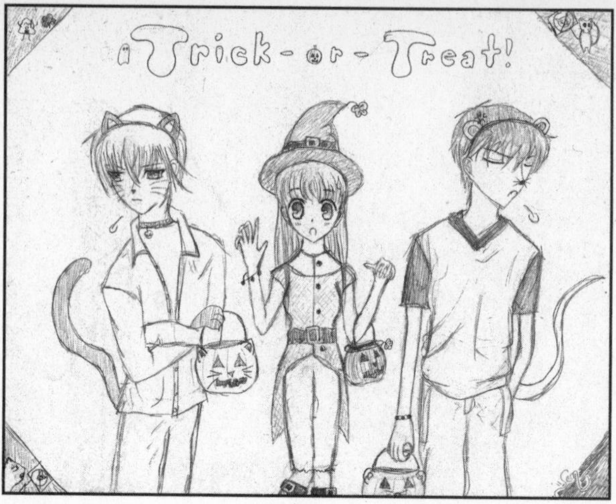
Trick-or-Treat!

Jen Chen
Age 12
Belmont, MA

Kyo and Yuki don't look very happy here--even though they're getting lots of candy! I love Tohru's costume, but she's way too sweet to ever be a witch in real life! This sketch gives me a great idea! If any of you have dressed up as Fruits Basket characters for Halloween, send in a copy of your picture and I might run it in a future installment of Fans Basket!

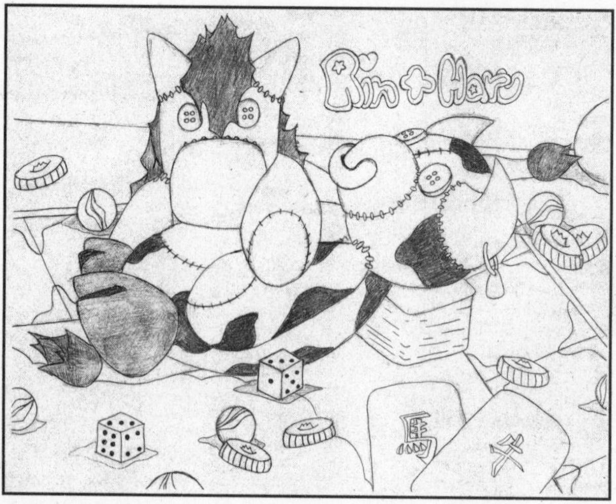
Rin + Haru
馬

Guadalupe Gonzales
Age 15
Dallas, TX

Isn't this amazing? Rin and Haru look sooooo cool as old-fashioned stuffed animals! Guadalupe, it's a shame I can't print all the art you submitted. I was blown away by your sketches!

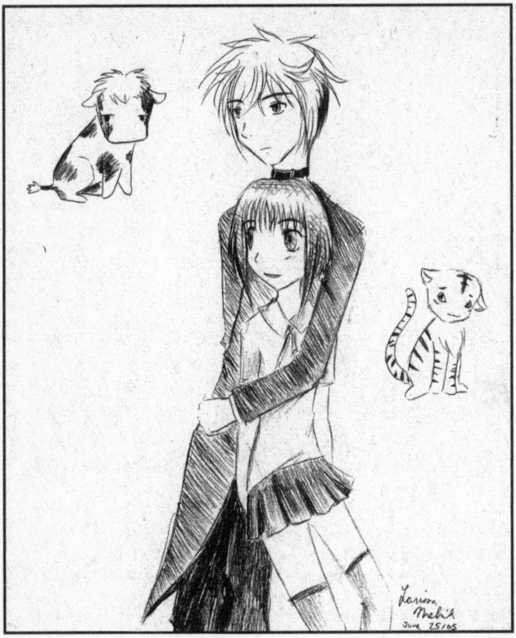

Larissa Melnik
Age 16
Waterloo, Ontario, Canada

Hey, Larissa. I agree: Haru and Kisa do look cute together. I particularly like the way you drew their animal forms! I hope you're still drawing!

Suki
Age 16
Surrey, British Columbia, Canada

Whoa! Suki, your art is very impressive! It's so amazing to see our Fruits Basket characters rendered in this way! I wish I could have printed all your fantastic drawings, but two will have to do!

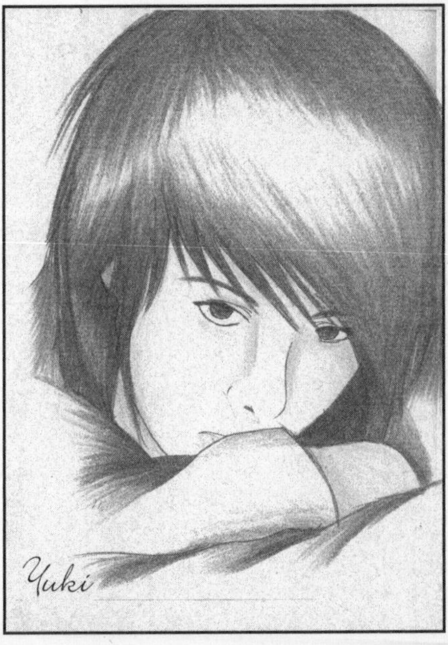
Yuki

Do you want to share your love for *Fruits Basket* with fans around the world? "Fans Basket" is taking submissions of fan art, poetry, cosplay photos, or any other Furuba fun you'd like to share!

How to submit:

1) Send your work via regular mail (NOT e-mail) to:

"Fans Basket"
c/o TOKYOPOP
5900 Wilshire Blvd.
Suite 2000
Los Angeles, CA 90036

2) All work should be in black-and-white and no larger than 8.5" x 11". (And try not to fold it too many times!)

3) Anything you send will not be returned. If you want to keep your original, it's fine to send us a copy.

4) Please include your full name, age, city and state for us to print with your work. If you'd rather us use a pen name, please include that, too.

5) IMPORTANT: If you're under the age of 18, you must have your parent's permission in order for us to print your work. Any submissions without a signed note of parental consent cannot be used.

6) For full details, please check out our website: http://www.tokyopop.com/aboutus/fanart.php

Disclaimer: Anything you send to us becomes the exclusive property of TOKYOPOP Inc. and, as we said before, will not be returned to you. We will have the right to print, reproduce, distribute, or modify the artwork for use in future volumes of *Fruits Basket* or on the web royalty-free.

Suki
Age 16
Surrey, British
Columbia, Canada

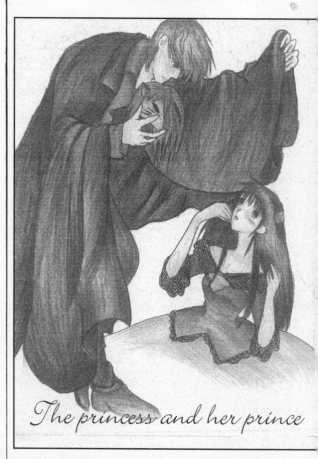

The princess and her prince

If you like **Fruits Basket,** then you will like this!

Sakura is a 14-year-old who's lost her parents and finds out she has four older half brothers who have suddenly appeared to take care of her. Wackiness and angst ensue as they all strive to get along together under the same roof!

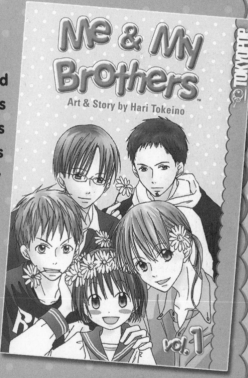

Volume 1 available in July 2007!

ONIICHAN TO ISSHO by Hari Tokeino © 2002 Hari Tokeino
All rights reserved. First published in Japan in 2004 by HAKUSENSHA, INC., Tokyo. English language translation rights in the
United States of America and Canada arranged with HAKUSENSHA, INC., Tokyo through Tuttle-Mori Agency Inc., Tokyo

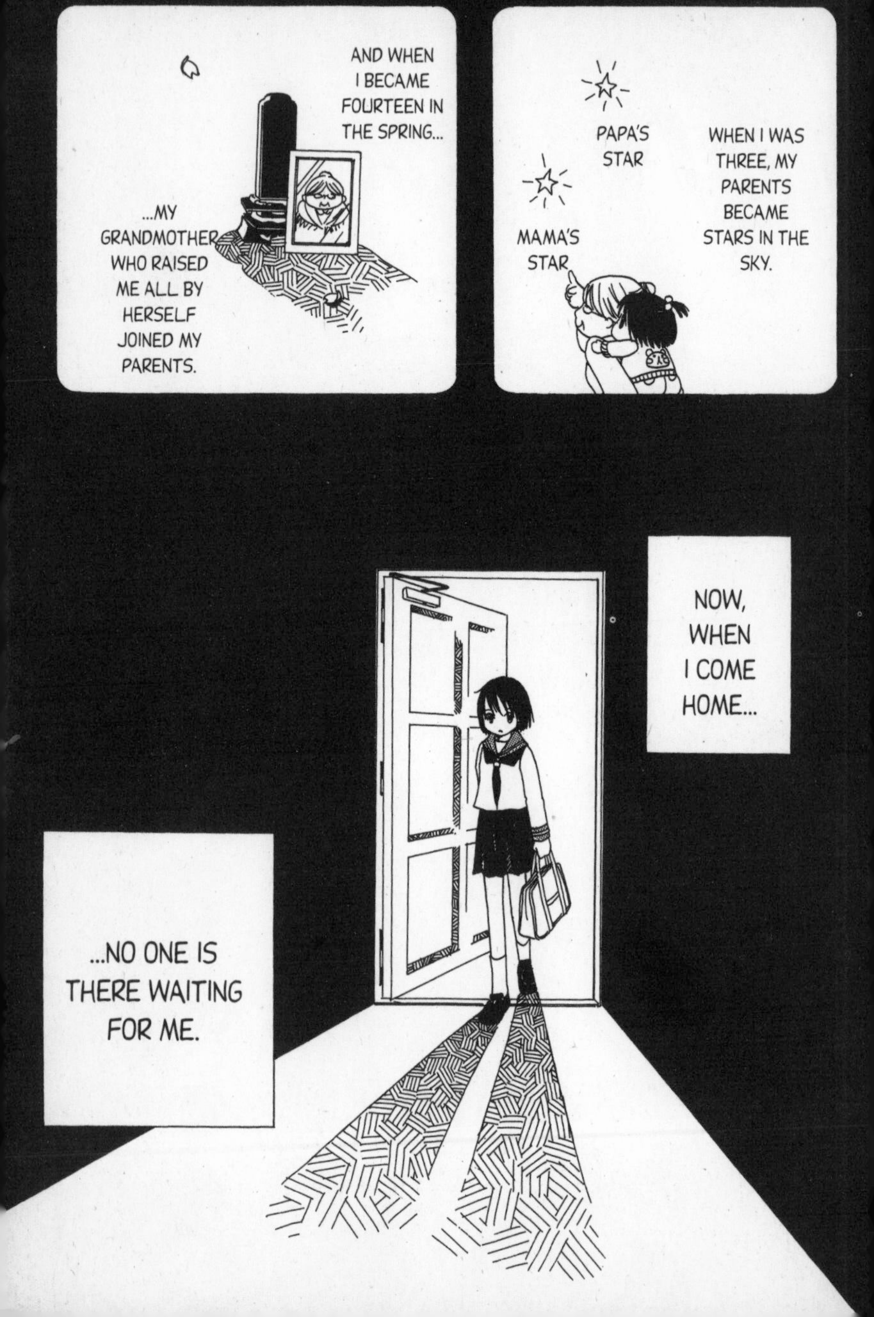
WHEN I WAS THREE, MY PARENTS BECAME STARS IN THE SKY.
PAPA'S STAR
MAMA'S STAR
AND WHEN I BECAME FOURTEEN IN THE SPRING...
...MY GRANDMOTHER WHO RAISED ME ALL BY HERSELF JOINED MY PARENTS.
NOW, WHEN I COME HOME...
...NO ONE IS THERE WAITING FOR ME.

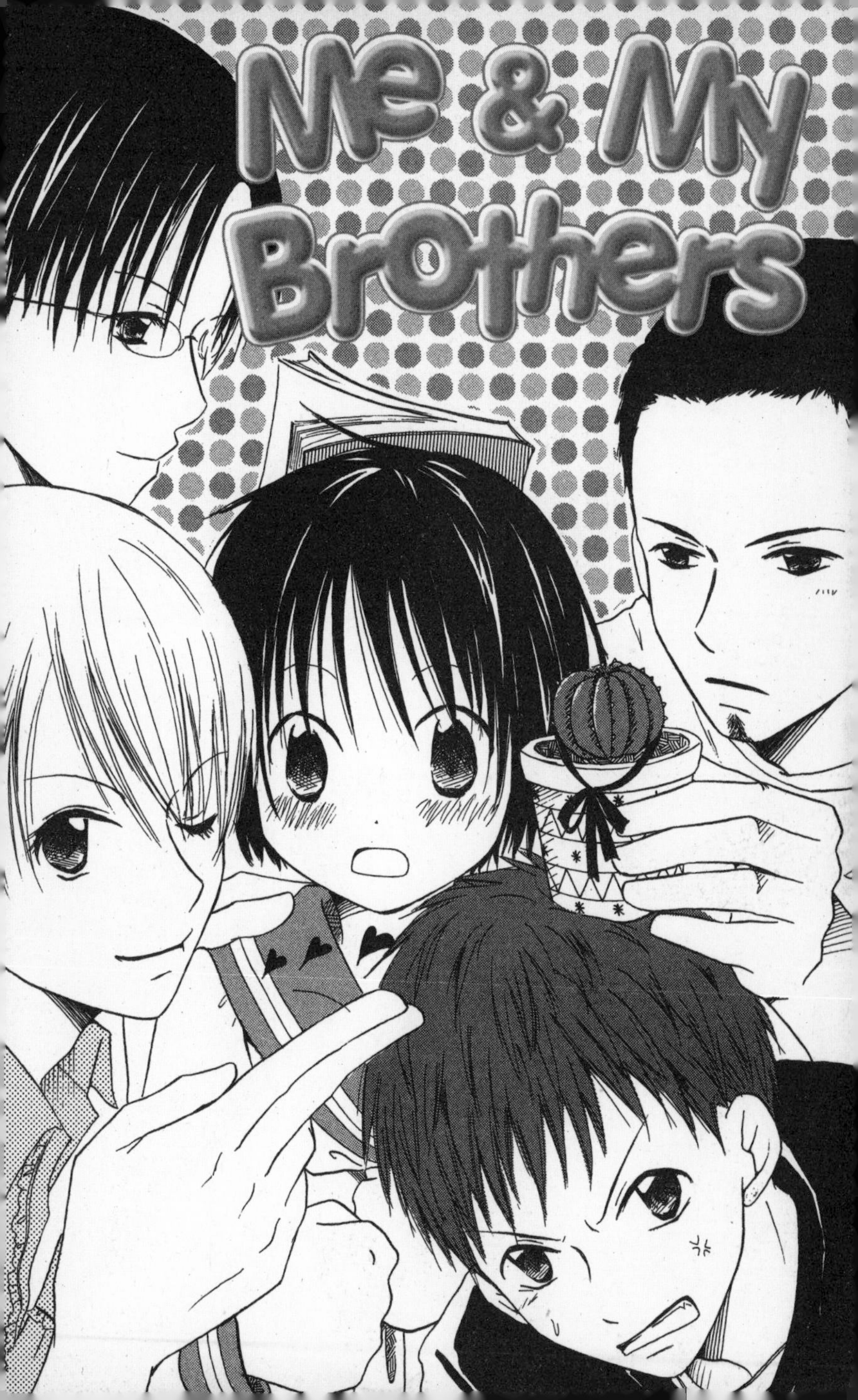
Me & My Brothers

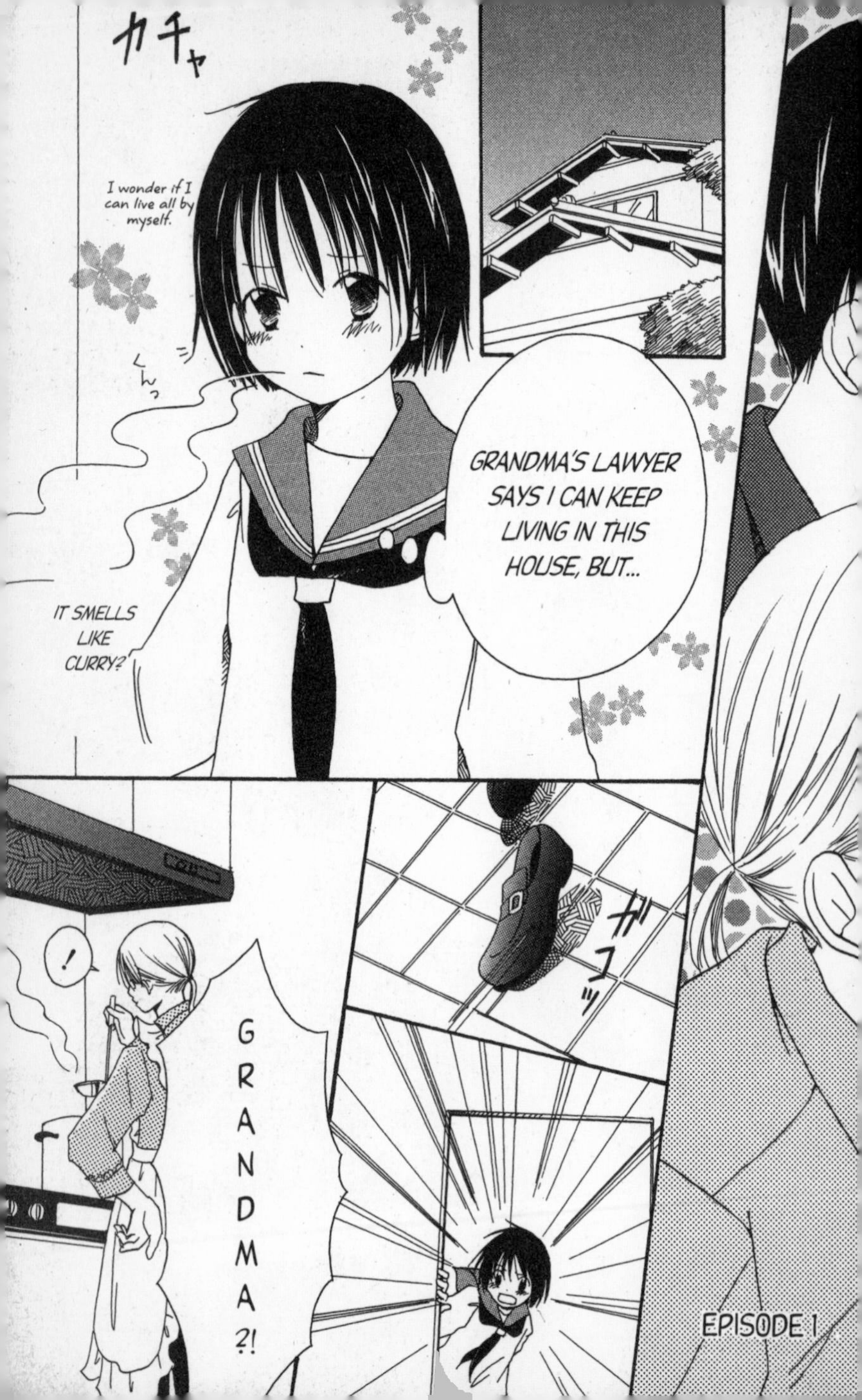
EPISODE 1
カチャ
I wonder if I can live all by myself.
GRANDMA'S LAWYER SAYS I CAN KEEP LIVING IN THIS HOUSE, BUT...
くんっ
IT SMELLS LIKE CURRY?
ガコッ
!
GRANDMA?!

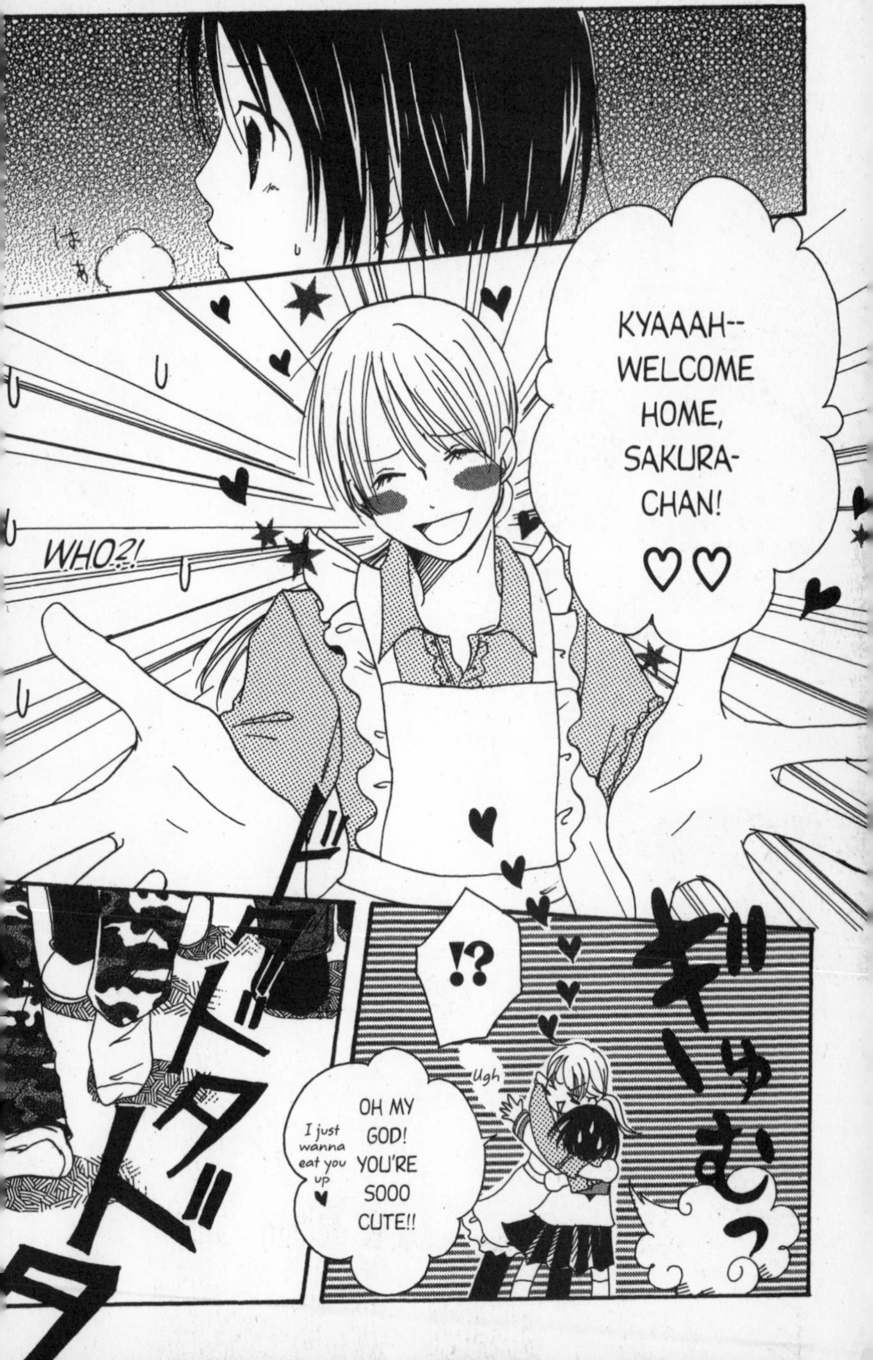
はあ
KYAAAH-- WELCOME HOME, SAKURA-CHAN! ♡♡
WHO?!
!?
ぎゅむっ
OH MY GOD! YOU'RE SOOO CUTE!!
I just wanna eat you up ♥
Ugh

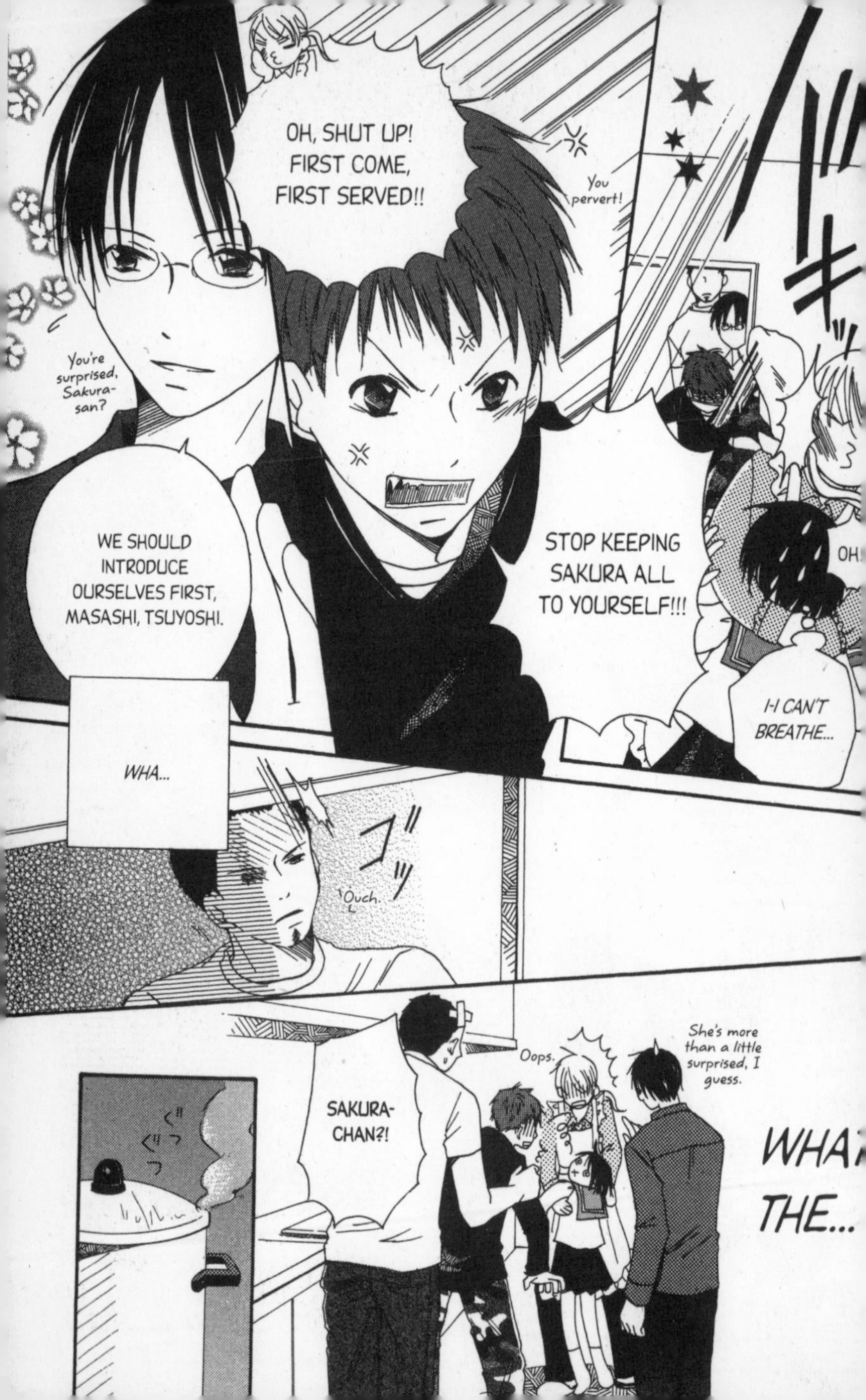
OH!
STOP KEEPING SAKURA ALL TO YOURSELF!!!
I-I CAN'T BREATHE...
OH, SHUT UP! FIRST COME, FIRST SERVED!!
You pervert!
You're surprised, Sakura-san?
WE SHOULD INTRODUCE OURSELVES FIRST, MASASHI, TSUYOSHI.
WHA...
Ouch.
WHA THE...
She's more than a little surprised, I guess.
Oops.
SAKURA-CHAN?!

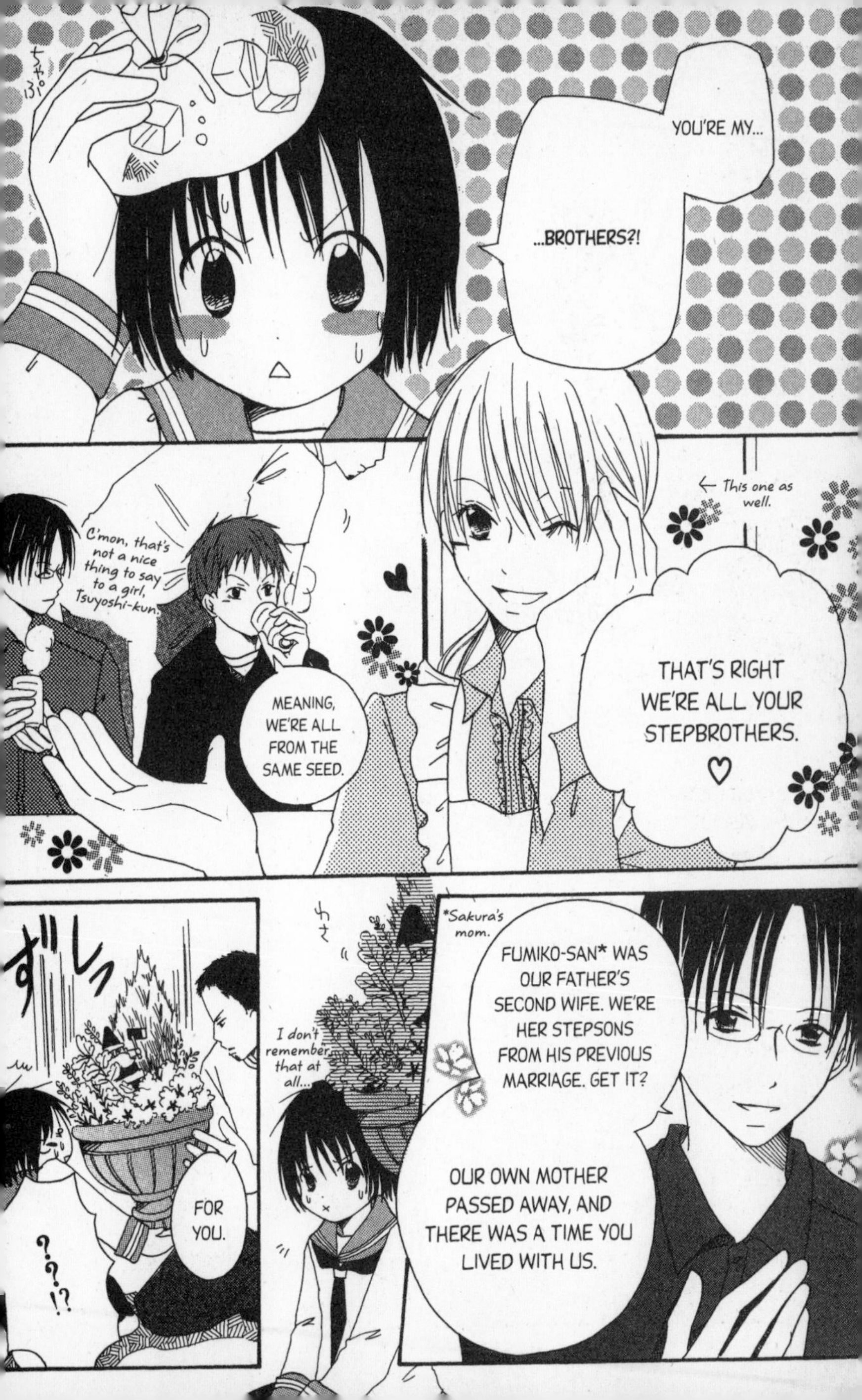
YOU'RE MY...
...BROTHERS?!
← This one as well.
THAT'S RIGHT WE'RE ALL YOUR STEPBROTHERS. ♡
MEANING, WE'RE ALL FROM THE SAME SEED.
C'mon, that's not a nice thing to say to a girl, Tsuyoshi-kun.
*Sakura's mom.
FUMIKO-SAN* WAS OUR FATHER'S SECOND WIFE. WE'RE HER STEPSONS FROM HIS PREVIOUS MARRIAGE. GET IT?
OUR OWN MOTHER PASSED AWAY, AND THERE WAS A TIME YOU LIVED WITH US.
I don't remember that at all...
ずしっ
FOR YOU.
?-?-!?

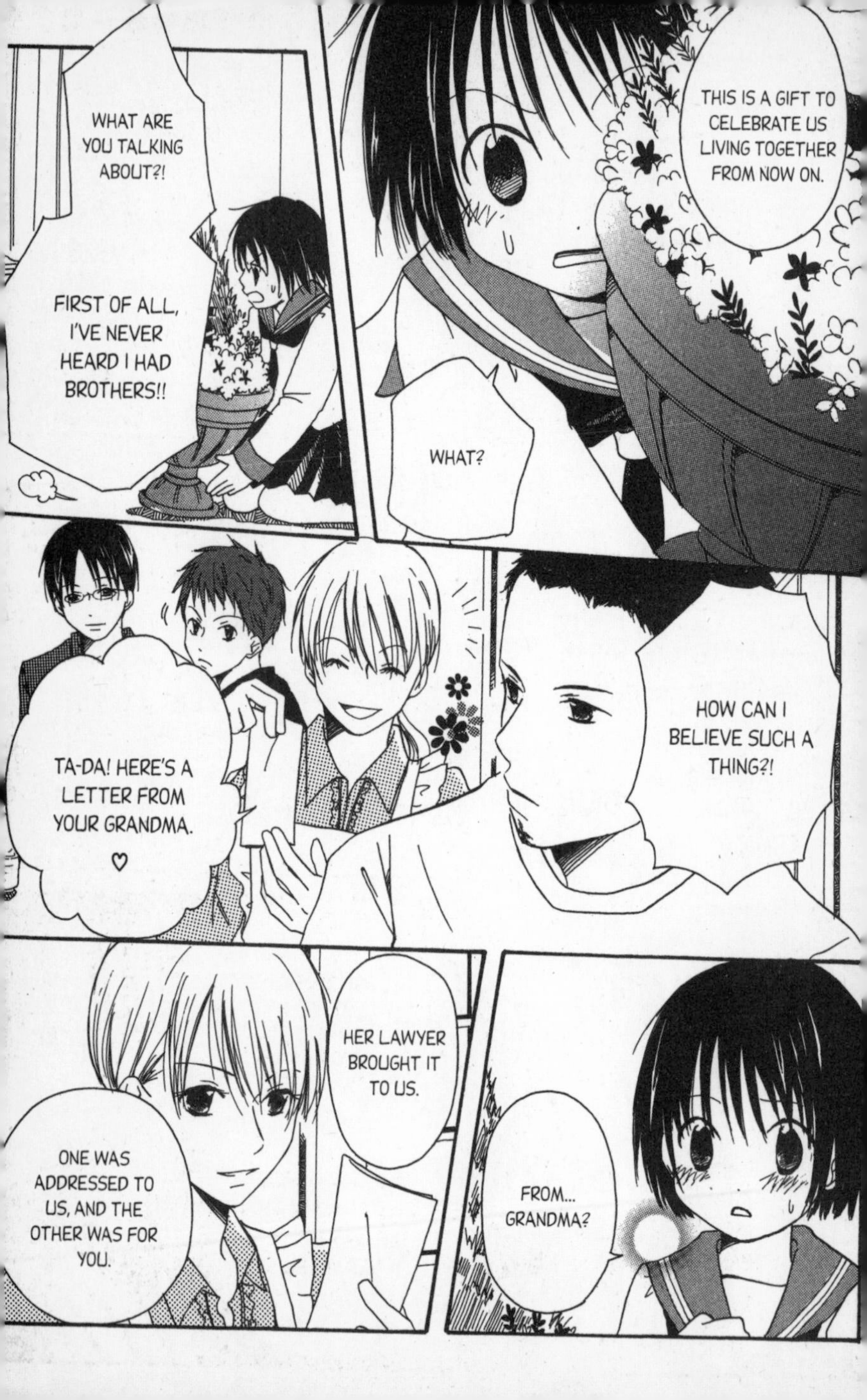
THIS IS A GIFT TO CELEBRATE US LIVING TOGETHER FROM NOW ON.
WHAT?
WHAT ARE YOU TALKING ABOUT?!
FIRST OF ALL, I'VE NEVER HEARD I HAD BROTHERS!!
HOW CAN I BELIEVE SUCH A THING?!
TA-DA! HERE'S A LETTER FROM YOUR GRANDMA. ♡
FROM... GRANDMA?
HER LAWYER BROUGHT IT TO US.
ONE WAS ADDRESSED TO US, AND THE OTHER WAS FOR YOU.

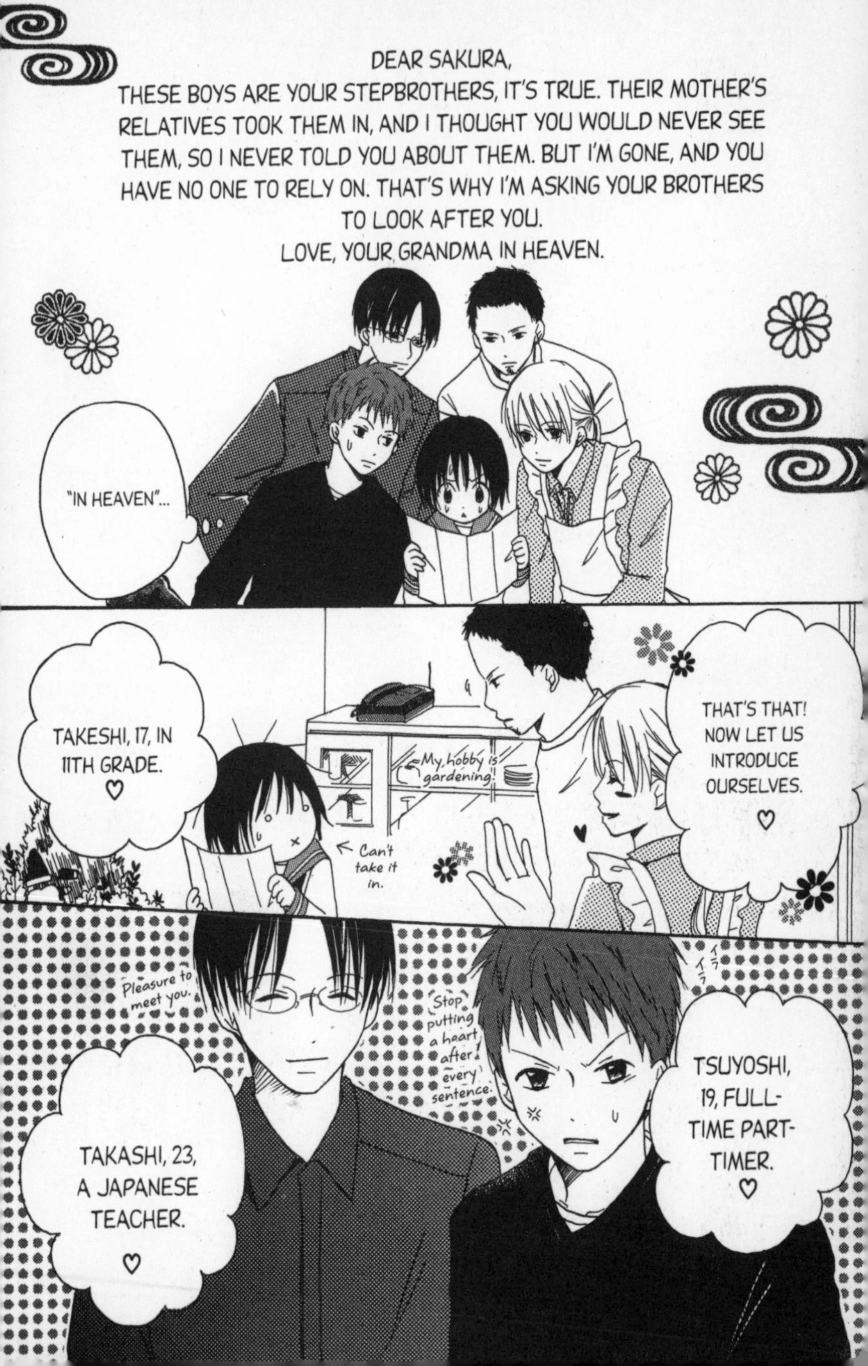
DEAR SAKURA,
THESE BOYS ARE YOUR STEPBROTHERS, IT'S TRUE. THEIR MOTHER'S RELATIVES TOOK THEM IN, AND I THOUGHT YOU WOULD NEVER SEE THEM, SO I NEVER TOLD YOU ABOUT THEM. BUT I'M GONE, AND YOU HAVE NO ONE TO RELY ON. THAT'S WHY I'M ASKING YOUR BROTHERS TO LOOK AFTER YOU.
LOVE, YOUR GRANDMA IN HEAVEN.
"IN HEAVEN"...
THAT'S THAT! NOW LET US INTRODUCE OURSELVES. ♡
My hobby is gardening!
Can't take it in.
TAKESHI, 17, IN 11TH GRADE. ♡
イラ イラ
TSUYOSHI, 19, FULL-TIME PART-TIMER. ♡
Stop putting a heart after every sentence.
Pleasure to meet you.
TAKASHI, 23, A JAPANESE TEACHER. ♡

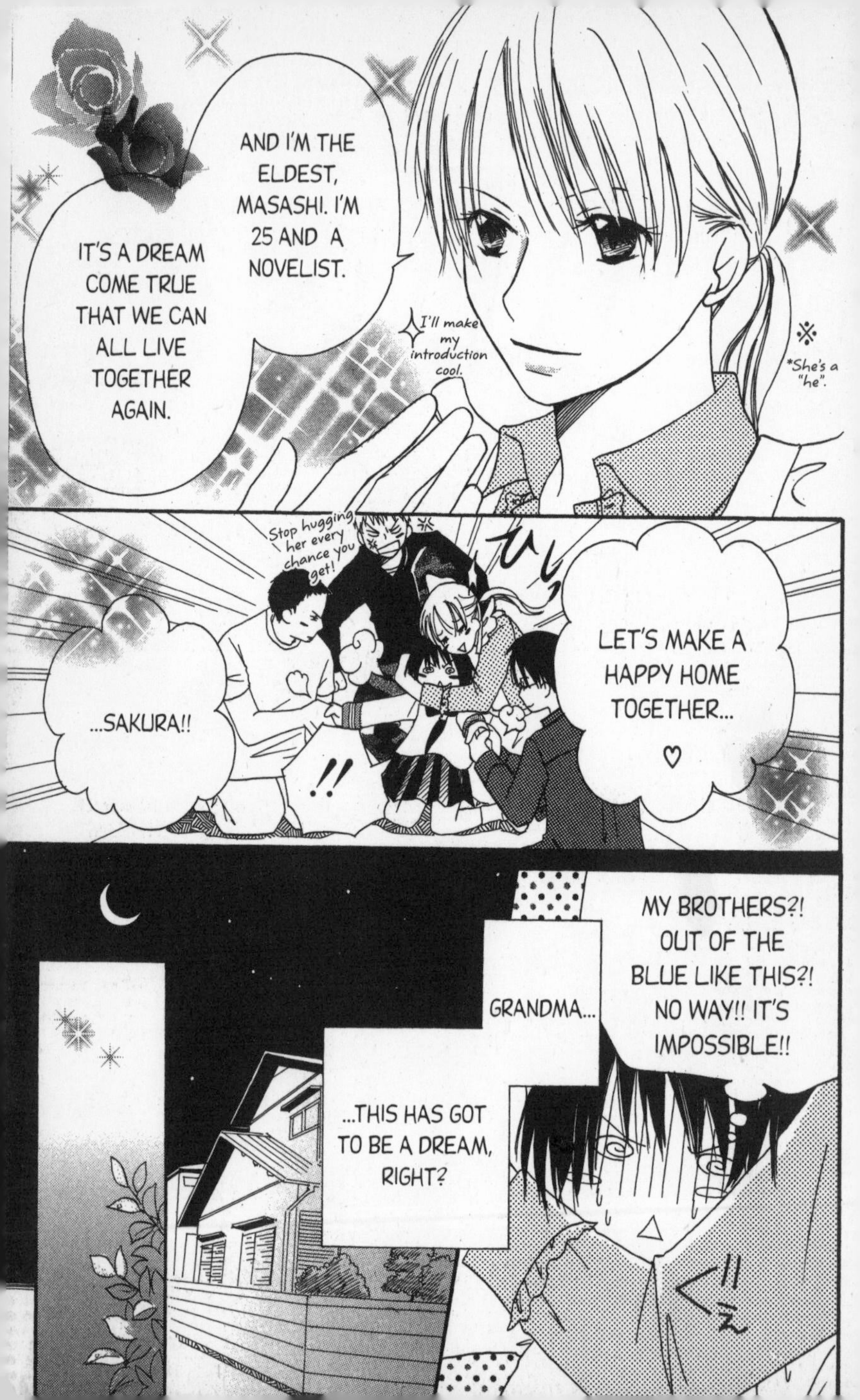
AND I'M THE ELDEST, MASASHI. I'M 25 AND A NOVELIST.
I'll make my introduction cool.
*She's a "he".
IT'S A DREAM COME TRUE THAT WE CAN ALL LIVE TOGETHER AGAIN.
LET'S MAKE A HAPPY HOME TOGETHER... ♡
Stop hugging her every chance you get!
...SAKURA!!
!!
MY BROTHERS?! OUT OF THE BLUE LIKE THIS?! NO WAY!! IT'S IMPOSSIBLE!!
GRANDMA...
...THIS HAS GOT TO BE A DREAM, RIGHT?

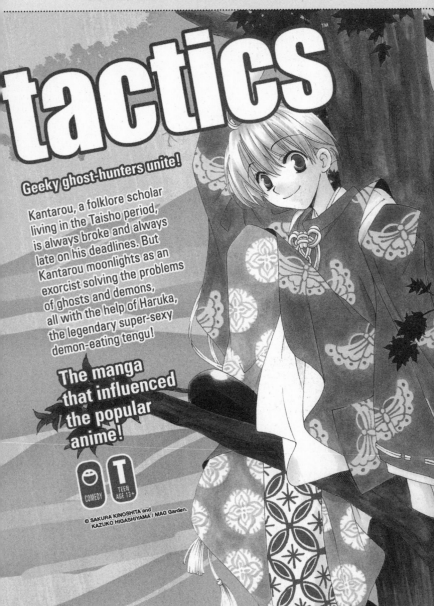

TOKYOPOP MANGA SUPPLEMENT

tactics

Geeky ghost-hunters unite!

Kantarou, a folklore scholar living in the Taisho period, is always broke and always late on his deadlines. But Kantarou moonlights as an exorcist solving the problems of ghosts and demons, all with the help of Haruka, the legendary super-sexy demon-eating tengu!

The manga that influenced the popular anime!

COMEDY

T TEEN AGE 13+

© SAKURA KINOSHITA and KAZUKO HIGASHIYAMA / MAG Garden.

FOR MORE INFORMATION VISIT: WWW.TOKYOPOP.COM

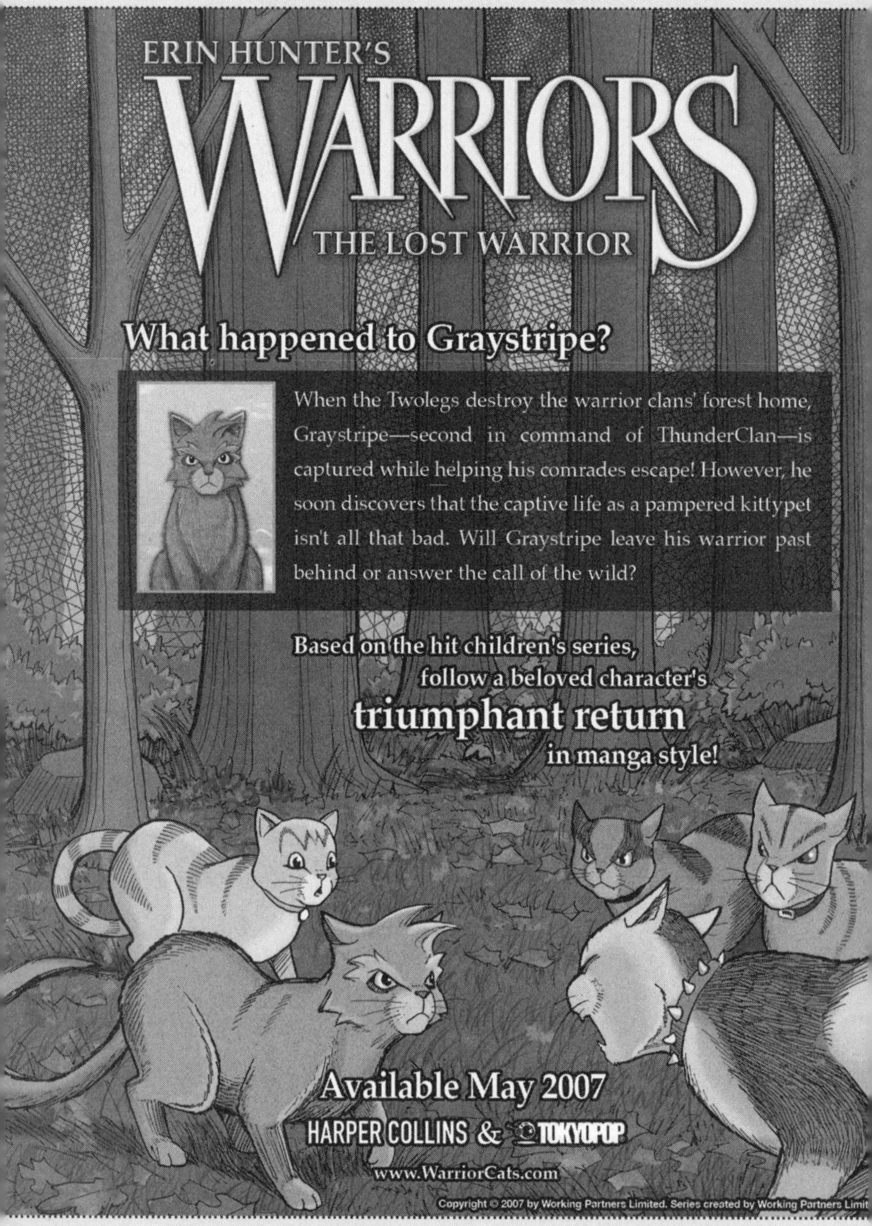
ERIN HUNTER'S
WARRIORS
THE LOST WARRIOR
What happened to Graystripe?
When the Twolegs destroy the warrior clans' forest home, Graystripe—second in command of ThunderClan—is captured while helping his comrades escape! However, he soon discovers that the captive life as a pampered kittypet isn't all that bad. Will Graystripe leave his warrior past behind or answer the call of the wild?
Based on the hit children's series, follow a beloved character's triumphant return in manga style!
Available May 2007
HARPER COLLINS & TOKYOPOP
www.WarriorCats.com
Copyright © 2007 by Working Partners Limited. Series created by Working Partners Limit

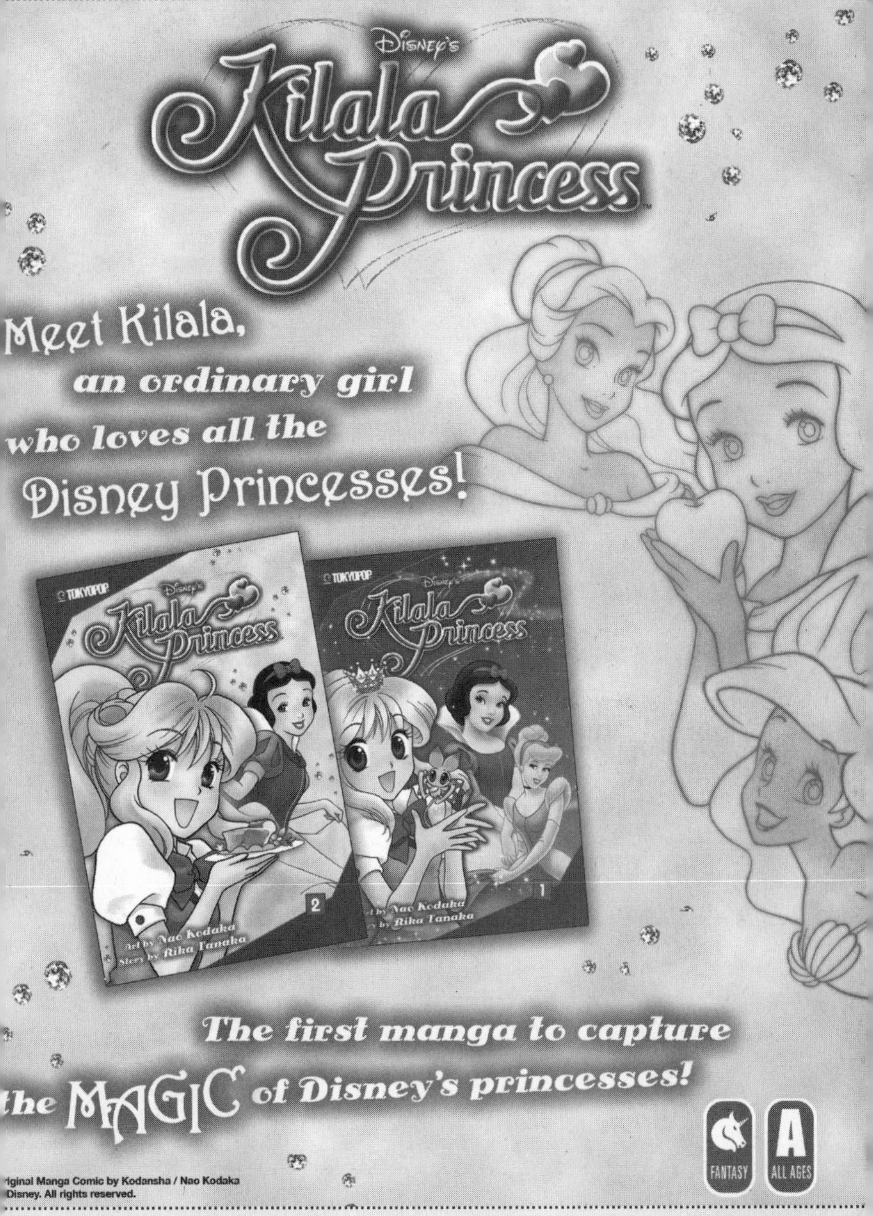
Disney's
Kilala Princess™
Meet Kilala,
an ordinary girl
who loves all the
Disney Princesses!
TOKYOPOP
Disney's
Kilala Princess
2
Art by Nao Kodaka
Story by Rika Tanaka
TOKYOPOP
Disney's
Kilala Princess
1
The first manga to capture
the MAGIC of Disney's princesses!
FANTASY
A
ALL AGES

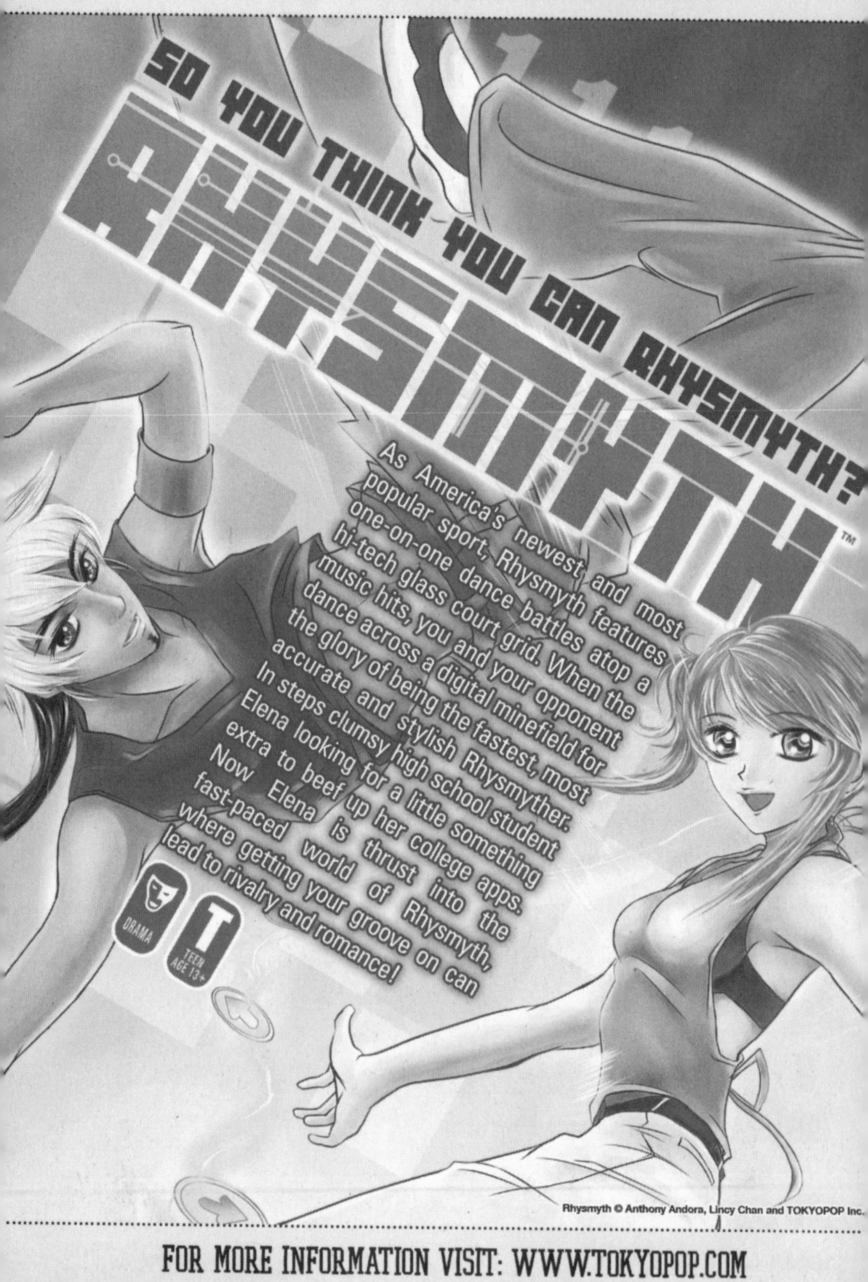
SO YOU THINK YOU CAN RHYSMYTH?
RHYSMYTH™
As America's newest and most popular sport, Rhysmyth features one-on-one dance battles atop a hi-tech glass court grid. When the music hits, you and your opponent dance across a digital minefield for the glory of being the fastest, most accurate and stylish Rhysmyther. In steps clumsy high school student Elena looking for a little something extra to beef up her college apps. Now Elena is thrust into the fast-paced world of Rhysmyth, where getting your groove on can lead to rivalry and romance!
DRAMA
T
TEEN AGE 13+
Rhysmyth © Anthony Andora, Lincy Chan and TOKYOPOP Inc.

STOP!

This is the back of the book.
You wouldn't want to spoil a great ending!

This book is printed "manga-style," in the authentic Japanese right-to-left format. Since none of the artwork has been flipped or altered, readers get to experience the story just as the creator intended. You've been asking for it, so TOKYOPOP® delivered: authentic, hot-off-the-press, and far more fun!

DIRECTIONS

If this is your first time reading manga-style, here's a quick guide to help you understand how it works.

It's easy... just start in the top right panel and follow the numbers. Have fun, and look for more 100% authentic manga from TOKYOPOP®!

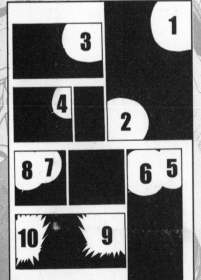

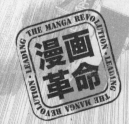